SUNDAY

SUNDAY

*The History of the Day of Rest
and Worship
in the Earliest Centuries
of the Christian Church*

by Willy Rordorf

The Westminster Press • Philadelphia

© SCM PRESS LTD 1968

Translated by A. A. K. Graham from the German
DER SONNTAG: *Geschichte der Ruhe- und Gottesdiensttages*
im ältesten Christentum
(Abhandlungen zur Theologie des Alten und Neuen Testaments 43)
Zwingli Verlag, Zürich, 1962

LIBRARY OF CONGRESS CATALOG CARD No. 68-15920

Published by The Westminster Press ®
Philadelphia, Pennsylvania

PRINTED IN GREAT BRITAIN

Dedicated with gratitude
to
DR OSCAR CULLMANN
a revered teacher
by one of his former assistants
who had the privilege of accompanying him
on his journeys to both England and America

CONTENTS

PREFACE

THE German text of this study appeared in 1962 and it had a favourable reception in specialist circles. This is not the place for the discussion of detailed points; broadly speaking, however, the reviewers of this work are agreed in finding here the fullest possible collection of material on all questions bearing on the early history of the Christian Sunday. They have also recognized that this book is objective in its approach, and for this reason the conclusions reached in it have proved generally acceptable.

Some questions, of course, have still not been settled: two related problems which come in this category are the question whether Sunday really was kept by Christians as early as I have supposed and whether the observance of the sabbath did not have a stronger influence in the earliest period of the Church's history than I am inclined to assume. Despite careful and prolonged consideration of the arguments on either side, I abide by my original opinion on both problems and for this reason I have seen no cause to make any substantial alterations to the text of this edition. In the evaluation of these disputed points almost everything seems to depend on the underlying bias of the particular scholar's mind, and strict proof is impossible. I must, therefore, leave it to every reader to make his own judgement. I should add that I have, of course, removed some errors which appeared in the German edition and that I have referred to more recent literature in all passages where this seemed necessary. It is possible that there have been some omissions in this respect, but I hope I may be pardoned these, for nowadays it is almost impossible to work through all newly published or reprinted literature.

I am also very much concerned that this work should receive sympathetic attention beyond the bounds of specialist circles, for its subject is of considerable importance today (as I indicate in my opening and concluding chapters). Many discussions with clergy and lay people of different Christian confessions and also with Seventh Day Adventists and Jews have served to confirm me in this opinion. Far and wide one comes across a lively interest in all questions concerning the 'sanctification' of a particular day of the week, whether it be Saturday or Sunday; but equally widespread is the lack of knowledge concerning the historical and theological bases from which both theoretical considerations and practical efforts would have to proceed. I dare to suggest that this work may be of some assistance in clarifying the principles which underlie this problem.

There is yet another reason which leads me to wish that this book may be widely known in English-speaking countries. The 'New Morality' has raised heavy seas on both sides of the Atlantic, and one has the impression that the real storm is yet to come. Moreover, it seems as if this reform of traditional teaching has brought with it not only a feeling of liberation, but also the accompanying danger of a lack of direction, to an extent hitherto unknown. The problem of Sunday is, of course, not central to the questions with which the New Morality is principally concerned. Nevertheless closer inspection will show that the transition from Jewish sabbath to Christian Sunday which the Christian Church (not without a struggle) effected nearly 2,000 years ago provides an excellent example of that combination of freedom and restriction which should characterize the Christian, and this example could be instructive in other areas. In contrast with Christians of later generations who have often been dull of hearing on this point, the earliest Christians understood that, thanks to Christ their Lord, they were no longer bound to the law of the old covenant, including the sabbath commandment in the decalogue. Furthermore, these earliest Christians also understood that, again thanks to Christ their Lord, they were under an obligation to assemble on every Sunday for communal worship. Just as on the one hand they recognized that they were free and behaved accordingly, so on the other hand they adhered strictly and unconditionally to the new ordering of their life. Perhaps we could learn something from them in this respect.

I have to thank the SCM Press of London and the West-minster Press of Philadelphia for their decision (on the recommendation of the Bishop of Woolwich, the Right Rev. J. A. T. Robinson) to publish this edition simultaneously in England and in the United States of America. My warm thanks are also due to the Rev. A. A. K. Graham, Fellow and Chaplain of Worcester College, Oxford, for the care which he has taken with the translation.

Neuchâtel   WILLY RORDORF
27 January 1967

TRANSLATOR'S NOTE

THE Revised Standard Version has generally been used for quotations from the Bible. Quotations from patristic and classical authors have, in most cases, been taken from the standard series of translations, e.g. Ancient Christian Writers, Loeb Classical Library, Ante-Nicene Christian Library, Nicene and Post-Nicene Fathers. In a few instances where a separate translation of a particular work is readily available use has been made of this edition.

I am much indebted to Mr P. V. Fisher for his help with the transliteration of words in Hebrew.

A. A. K. G.

ABBREVIATIONS

AGL	Abhandlungen der Sächsischen Gesellschaft der Wissenschaften, Leipzig
ANET	Ancient Near Eastern Texts relating to the Old Testament, Princeton, 1950
AThANT	Abhandlungen zur Theologie des Alten und Neuen Testaments, ed. W. Eichrodt and O. Cullmann, Zürich, 1942ff.
AuC	Antike und Christentum, Münster
BJRL	Bulletin of the John Rylands Library, Manchester
Bonnet	M. Bonnet, Acta Apostolorum Apocrypha II, Leipzig, 1903, reprinted 1959
Botte	B. Botte, La Tradition Apostolique de Saint Hippolyte (Liturgiewissenschaftliche Quellen und Forschungen 39), Münster, 1963
BZ	Biblische Zeitschrift, Freiburg
BZAW	Beiheft zur Zeitschrift für die alttestamentliche Wissenschaft, Berlin
BZNW	Beiheft zur Zeitschrift für die neutestamentliche Wissenschaft, Berlin
CCSL	Corpus Christianorum, Series Latina, Turnhout, 1953ff.
Connolly	R. H. Connolly, Didascalia Apostolorum, the Syriac Version translated, Oxford, 1929
CSEL	Corpus Scriptorum Ecclesiasticorum Latinorum, Vienna, 1866ff.
DACL	F. Cabrol and H. Leclercq, Dictionnaire d'archéologie chrétienne et de liturgie, Paris, 1907ff.
Enc. Bibl.	T. K. Cheyne and J. S. Black, Encyclopaedia Biblica, London, 1899ff.
ERE	J. Hastings, Encyclopaedia of Religion and Ethics, Edinburgh, 1908ff.

ET	English translation
EvTh	*Evangelische Theologie*, Munich
ExpT	*Expository Times*, Edinburgh
FRLANT	Forschungen zur Religion und Literatur des Alten und Neuen Testaments, Göttingen, 1903ff.
Funk	F. X. Funk, *Didascalia et Constitutiones Apostolorum* I, Paderborn, 1905
GCS	Die griechischen christlichen Schriftsteller der ersten Jahrhunderte, Berlin, 1887ff.
Goodspeed	E. J. Goodspeed, *Die ältesten Apologeten*, Göttingen, 1914
HE	*Historia ecclesiastica*
Hefele	C. J. Hefele, *Conciliengeschichte*, 2nd ed., Freiburg-im-Breisgau, 1873ff.
HNT	Handbuch zum Neuen Testament, founded by H. Lietzmann, ed. G. Bornkamm, Tübingen, 1923ff.
JBL	*Journal of Biblical Literature*, Philadelphia
JTS	*Journal of Theological Studies*, Oxford
Lidzbarski	M. Lidzbarski, *Mandäische Liturgien* (Abhandlungen der königlichen Gesellschaft der Wissenschaften zu Göttingen, phil.-hist. Klasse, NF 17.1), Berlin, 1920
	M. Lidzbarski, *Ginza: der Schatz oder das grosse Buch der Mandäer*, Göttingen and Leipzig, 1925
Lipsius	R. A. Lipsius, *Acta Apostolorum Apocrypha* I, Leipzig, 1891, reprinted 1959
LQF	*Liturgiegeschichtliche Quellen und Forschungen*, Münster
Mansi	J. D. Mansi, *Sacrorum Conciliorum nova et amplissima collectio*, Florence, 1759ff.
Meyer	Kritisch-exegetischer Kommentar über das neue Testament, founded by H. A. W. Meyer, Göttingen, 1832ff.
NF	Neue Folge
NS	New series
NT Apoc.	E. Hennecke and W. Schneemelcher, *New Testament Apocrypha*, ET ed. R. McL. Wilson, London, 1963–5

NTD	Das Neue Testament Deutsch, ed. P. Althaus and J. Behm, Göttingen, 1952ff.
NTS	*New Testament Studies*, Cambridge
Pauly-Wissowa	A. Pauly and G. Wissowa, *Real-Encyclopädie der klassischen Altertumswissenschaften*, 1894ff.
PG	J. P. Migne, *Patrologiae cursus completus*, series Graeca, Paris, 1857ff.
PL	J. P. Migne, *Patrologiae cursus completus*, series Latina, Paris, 1844ff.
RAC	T. Klauser, *Reallexikon für Antike und Christentum*, Stuttgart, 1941ff.
Rahmani	I. E. Rahmani, *Testamentum Domini Nostri Jesu Christi*, Mainz, 1899
RE[3]	*Realencyklopädie für protestantische Theologie und Kirche*, 3rd ed., Leipzig, 1896ff.
RGG[3]	*Die Religion in Geschichte und Gegenwart*, 3rd ed., Tübingen, 1957ff.
RHR	*Revue de l'histoire des religions*, Paris
SB	(H. L. Strack and) P. Billerbeck, *Kommentar zum Neuen Testament aus Talmud und Midrasch*, Munich, 1922ff.
SBT	Studies in Biblical Theology, London, 1950ff.
SC	Sources chrétiennes, ed. H. Lubac and J. Daniélou, Paris, 1943ff.
TLZ	*Theologische Literaturzeitung*, Leipzig
TQS	*Theologische Quartalschrift*, Tübingen
TR	*Theologische Rundschau*, Tübingen
TS	Theologische Studien, Zollikon, Zürich, 1938ff.
TU	Texte und Untersuchungen zur Geschichte der altchristlichen Literatur, founded by O. von Gebhardt and A. Harnack, Leipzig, 1882ff.
TWNT	*Theologisches Wörterbuch zum Neuen Testament*, begun by G. Kittel, ed. G. Friedrich, Stuttgart, 1933ff.
TZ	*Theologische Zeitschrift*, Basel
VT	*Vetus Testamentum*, Leiden
ZAW	*Zeitschrift für die altestamentliche Wissenschaft*, Berlin

ZDWF	*Zeitschrift für deutsche Wortforschung*, Strassburg
ZKT	*Zeitschrift für katholische Theologie*, Innsbruck
ZNW	*Zeitschrift für die neutestamentliche Wissenschaft*, Berlin
ZTK	*Zeitschrift für Theologie und Kirche*, Freiburg

THE PROBLEM

THE time has come for the Christian Church to re-examine the basis of its observance of Sunday.

Until now the seven-day week with its rhythm of six working days and one day for rest and worship has held what might almost be called absolute sway throughout the world. There has, of course, been the difference that for Christians the weekly day of rest and worship has been Sunday, for Jews Saturday and for Moslems Friday. Isolated breaches, such as those brought about in the West by the French and Russian revolutions, have been made in this long-established pattern, but these breaches have been only temporary. The seven-day week and with it the weekly day of rest have always reasserted themselves. This is certainly not solely due to the statement in the Bible that God in the beginning made heaven and earth in six days and rested on the seventh day, but simply because the seven-day week answering in every respect to mankind's accustomed rhythm of work and life has been observed through the centuries.

Both the industrialization and the technological transformation of the whole economy have, however, now made such progress that they have led to a demand for a re-examination of the traditional pattern of work and leisure. Nowadays people are not afraid to call in question once again and more radically than ever before the seven-day week and its day of rest and worship. To the modern industrial concern this pattern, which may have had real sense in societies predominantly composed of farmers and craftsmen, appears more and more as a hindrance, as an outmoded, irrational legacy of earlier ages. Why should the ordering of work and leisure depend on days and weeks? Can it not be much more suitably arranged merely by counting hours? Various attempts in this direction have been made in the past: nowadays they are the order of the day. One realizes this as soon as one thinks of shift-work in factories, of the working week reckoned by hours in the welfare state and, in the recent past, of the gradual staggering of the working week. In the majority of countries, however, the day of rest and worship recurring after every six days is still protected by law, but in the foreseeable future this may well no longer be the case.

Christians, Jews and Moslems are the first to be affected by these present-day questions, for it is they who have long been the protagonists of the seven-day week and, with it, of the weekly day of rest and worship. It is, therefore, for them to decide whether they wish to preserve intact this pattern of living in the technological age when life is being entirely transformed. It is for them to decide whether they have to preserve it or whether they can adapt themselves in this matter to the demands of recent technological development. In other words, they are faced with the need to question the grounds on which they have hitherto clung to the seven-day week and to the weekly day of rest and worship. Have they done so merely out of habit, or can they with reasons derived from their faith explain why they cannot agree with any other pattern for times of rest and worship than the one which has hitherto been observed?

Naturally this problem is posed in different terms for each of the three religions which we have mentioned. The Christian Church in particular will have to reconsider the nature and significance of its Sunday. Only then will it be able to adopt a reasoned attitude with regard to the questions of the day to which we have alluded. For most Christians it will indeed be axiomatic that Sunday is in no circumstances to be abandoned as a day of rest and worship—not even in the changed economic conditions of the present day. But the reasons for this attitude must be carefully thought out, for there is also an opposing point of view which one might hold—that Christianity is not committed to the religious observance of any particular day, not even of Sunday, that it therefore has a free hand to give its consent to a new pattern of times for rest and worship.

If we are concerned to make up our minds objectively about this problem, we must first of all be clear about the origins of the observance of Sunday. In particular, the relationship of Sunday to the Jewish sabbath needs to be more precisely determined, for there are Christians who totally reject Sunday, saying that the Bible enjoins only the observance of the sabbath, that neither Jesus nor the apostles replaced it by Sunday observance and that the Church in introducing this practice has departed from divinely given precept. This is the opinion held by the Seventh Day Adventists, who rest and worship on the same day as the Jews, that is to say on Saturday. In the history of the Church many before them have adopted the same position, and the attitude of these Christians does, in fact, raise some questions which deserve to be raised. How did the Church come to abandon the sabbath and to elevate in its place Sunday as the day of rest and worship? Can the change from the sabbath to Sunday be justified on really valid grounds? The resurrection of Jesus Christ which is said to have taken place on a Sunday may certainly have given a special importance to Sunday in the eyes of Christians, but was that a sufficient reason for abandoning the sabbath and replacing it by Sunday as the day of rest and worship? It has become customary for us to regard Sunday simply as the Christian heir of the sabbath. In teaching the catechism, for example, we expound the commandment about keeping holy the sabbath day as if it were applicable to our Sunday, although it plainly commands the observance not of Sunday but of the sabbath.

It will be an important part of our task in this study to shed as much light as possible on these questions. We believe that we can best do this if we attack the whole problem of Sunday from the *historical* angle. In this investigation we are concerned to make a careful assessment of the history of the Christian day of rest and worship from its earliest beginnings down to the time of the Emperor Constantine the Great. By means of this historical investigation we hope to be able to make some positive contribution to the present-day debate concerning Sunday. The earliest period in the long history of the Christian Sunday is, in fact, particularly illuminating and can show us the Christian day of rest and worship in a perspective which we have largely forgotten.

It is well known that the evidence for the early history of the Christian Sunday is scanty. Therefore we cannot help taking refuge in conjectures and *ex post facto* judgements. Many question marks must remain for the time being, until further evidence becomes available. This state of affairs will impose on us a certain amount of reserve in making critical judgements. Equally, we shall make no secret of it whenever, here and there, we venture into the field of pure hypothesis. Nevertheless it is our conviction that from the evidence which is at present available a fairly consistent picture can be derived which may be said to correspond by and large with the historical facts; moreover, and this is most important of all, it is clear that the main outlines of this picture are firmly established.

In the course of our investigation it will be apparent that Sunday did not become a day of rest and of worship at one and the same time. At first it was only the day on which Christians worshipped; it was only later that it came to be a day of rest. It is therefore advisable for the purposes of this study to treat separately the two aspects of Sunday, first the day of rest and then the day of worship, and to study the historical development of each by itself.

The first section deals with the day of rest in earliest Christian history, and here the question of the sabbath will occupy much space. The day of rest in Palestine in the time of Jesus and in the time of the apostolic Church was the Jewish sabbath. We shall have to examine the attitude of Jesus and of the apostolic Church towards the sabbath. When and why did the Christian Church come to abandon the observance of the Jewish sabbath? How did it finally manage to be rid of the commandment to keep holy the sabbath day? It stood in the Old Testament, and the Christian Church had taken over the Old Testament as holy scripture! Further, we shall have to turn our attention to the question how the Christian Sunday became a day of rest.

The second section is devoted to the Christian Church's day of worship. The problem of the origins of the Christian observance of Sunday has never been satisfactorily solved, and this will have to be investigated. It has been surmised that the Christian observance of Sunday was originally due to the Church's wish to have its own day of worship both beside and in opposition to the Jewish sabbath. Parallels from other religions have often been adduced to prove that the celebration of Sunday existed in pre-Christian times, either in Jewish or in pagan circles. Recently there has come to light a type of calendar which was known in Qumran and in which Sunday already plays a special role. We shall have to examine whether the precursor of the Christian Sunday has, in fact, been discovered here.

Moreover, there arise all sorts of questions about the original form of Christian Sunday observance. At what time of day or night did the members of Christian communities meet for worship? What was the content and character of these gatherings? It is important for us today to know about these matters, for our Sunday worship is almost universally recognized to be in need of reform, and the investigation of the history of its origins may give us valuable hints for its revision.

Finally we shall try to determine the origin of the different names for Sunday which were current in the primitive Christian Church: they will in their brief compass shed some light for us on the significance of Sunday in this early period.

In 'Retrospect and Prospect' we shall then draw the conclusions for the present day which have resulted from this study of the history of Sunday in the early Church. Right at the outset, however, we have to say that these comments may not be taken by themselves: they are part of the warp and woof of the complete work and can be understood only in their context if one is to take them as they are meant to be taken—that is as epitomizing the conclusions of a work of historical and theological research into the origins of the Christian observance of Sunday. We are also aware that the drawing up of terms of reference does not lead to any definitive conclusions, for the same questions appear in practice in a very different light from that in which they appear in theoretical discussion: patience, wisdom and experience are needed for the establishment of a common basis on which theory and practice can meet. Nevertheless, we are of the opinion that the historical and theological insights derived from our study should in some way be capable of practical application.

INTRODUCTION

I

THE SEVEN-DAY WEEK

THE seven-day week as we know it today has a complicated history behind it. It will be as well if we call to mind its most important points. As we do so, we shall be able to form a clearer picture of the week's basic structure without which our Sunday as a weekly day of rest and worship would not be possible.

In its essentials, the history of the seven-day week, as we know it, is as follows:

First, in order of time, comes the Jewish week. We shall have to inquire whether this in turn has not developed from yet earlier antecedents. Conjectures about this are, however, so uncertain that we prefer to confine ourselves to the statement that clear evidence for a seven-day week is first found in Israel.

Right at the beginning of our era we meet another seven-day week, the so-called planetary week. This was closely connected with astrological beliefs widely held at that time. Each day of the week was associated with one of the seven planets known in antiquity. The planetary week was soon known all over the Mediterranean area. It was not a rival to the Jewish week; it existed side by side with it and remarkably it was even super-imposed on it. If we study its origins, we shall not be able to rid ourselves of the suspicion that the planetary week originated after the Jewish week and that it has impregnated the Jewish week with astrological ideas. The truth of this suspicion still remains to be established.

The Christian Church has therefore entered on the inherit-ance of both the Jewish and the planetary week. Having emerged from Judaism, it took over the Jewish week, but it also soon pressed into service the planetary week by using some of its names for the days of the week. Today the seven-day week is still to be seen as the fusion of the Jewish week with the planetary week which took place in the area covered by the Christian

Church. In our linguistic area the only difference is that instead of using the names of the planetary deities of antiquity we use those of the corresponding Nordic deities.

As we survey the history of the seven-day week, we must speak of a veritable triumphal procession on the part of the Jewish week. It has indeed been modified in important respects by Christendom and later by Islam, but in all its variations it has preserved its basic seven-day structure. We have, moreover, to bear in mind that *in the whole of the ancient world there was known no firm division into weeks independent of the lunar month except for this seven-day week*: this fact naturally made the general introduction of the seven-day week very much easier. Only in Italy had a regular eight-day market week long been observed, but it had to yield to the seven-day week.[1]

I. THE JEWISH WEEK

It does not need to be emphasized that the Jewish week has derived its significance principally from the sabbath, its last day.[2] The individual weekdays do not have any special designations, but are simply numbered consecutively first day (=Sunday), second day (=Monday), third day (=Tuesday), etc. Only Friday, the day before the sabbath, has a special name: it is called in Greek παρασκευή (day of preparation) or προσάββατον (day before the sabbath) and in Hebrew ʿereb šabbāt or maʿᵃlēy (eve of the sabbath) because it played a special

---

[1] The Roman market week was called *nundinae*. The *nundinae* were an old institution; cf. W. Kroll, '*Nundinae*', in Pauly-Wissowa, 17.2, col. 1467–72. By the time of Augustus we see the conflict of the seven-day week with the eight-day week well under way: in an extant fragment of a calendar both are placed continuously parallel with one another (in the so-called '*fasti Sabini*', *Corp. Inscr. Lat.*, I, 1863, p. 302, and IX, 1885, p. 453). The seven-day week which is here taking its place alongside the eight-day week is probably the Jewish week. (Otherwise E. Schürer, 'Die siebentägige Woche im Gebrauch der christlichen Kirche der ersten Jahrhunderte', *ZAW* 6, 1905, pp. 26f., who holds it to be the planetary week; but the horoscopes added for each day do not at all correspond with those of the planetary week and they tell against this assumption.) The complete supersession of the eight-day week by the seven-day week was, in fact, delayed until well into the fourth century; the chronographer of AD 354 (*Chronica minora*: Monumenta Germaniae Hist., auctores antiquissimi, IX, 1892) has included in his compilation a calendar which for the whole year takes into account the days both of the eight-day week and of the seven-day week.

[2] Hebrew šabbāt, Greek σάββατον or σάββατα; ἑβδομάς also occurs.

role as a day of preparation for the sabbath.[1] So even the names for Friday point to the predominant position of the sabbath within the Jewish week.

The seven-day week and its day of rest naturally have their own history within the Jewish religion. There is a great distance to cover from their origins right through to the sabbath casuistry of the Pharisees and rabbis. In this introductory chapter we shall be concerned only with the *original* form of the seven-day week and of the sabbath in Israel. We shall deal with its later development when we come on to describe the significance of the sabbath for Jesus and for the earliest Christians.

The sabbath commandment which contains within itself the institution of the seven-day week is to be found in all strata of the Pentateuch.[2] This indicates its extreme antiquity. Even our oldest written sources do not, however, take us back to the time before the establishment of the Kingdom of Israel. In the last analysis we can, therefore, say no more than that the seven-day week and the sabbath were known at the beginning of the mon-archical period in Israel.

In order to understand what follows we shall find it necessary to consider the individual passages in the Pentateuch and the critical problems associated with them. The most important passage in which we find the sabbath commandment is the so-called Yahwistic decalogue (Ex. 34.21). The composition and age of this collection of legal material are still much discussed, but this material will, in the main, go back to J.[3] In the Book of the Covenant, which according to general opinion belongs to the Elohistic tradition, we find the sabbath commandment (Ex. 23.12) formulated in the same way as in Ex. 34.21. The origin of this commandment may well, therefore, lie at a time before the composition of E. *We are certainly justified in regarding Ex. 23.12 and 34.21 as our earliest versions of the sabbath command-ment.* They give the impression of being older than the versions of the sabbath commandment which we find in the E (Ex. 20.9, 10a) and D

---

[1] Since on the sabbath no meals may be prepared, the meals for the fol-lowing day are cooked, the lamps lighted, etc., on Friday. The meaning of the Latin name used by the Church fathers for Friday is disputed: *cena pura* (also Matt. 27.62 D). Cf. E. Schürer (see p. 10, n. 1), pp. 7f.

[2] See the list of W. W. Cannon, 'The Weekly Sabbath', *ZAW* 49, 1931, pp. 325–7.

[3] Cf. H. H. Rowley, 'Moses and the Decalogue', *BJRL* 34, 1951, p. 93, reprinted in *Men of God*, 1963, pp. 26ff. For a contrary opinion see A. Alt, 'The Origins of Israelite Law', *Essays on Old Testament History and Religion*, ET 1966, pp. 117f., n. 95.

(Deut. 5.13–14a) decalogues.[1] The passage in the Holiness Code (Lev. 23.1–3) should be considered with the decalogues in Ex. 20 and Deut. 5 (cf. also Ex. 31.15a). We shall not consider here the passages which are to be assigned to P,[2] because we can draw from them no conclusions about the earliest period.

In the Book of the Covenant the basic commandment is, 'Six days you shall do your work, but on the seventh day you shall rest (from work)' (Ex. 23.12, almost word for word as in the J decalogue Ex. 34.21).[3] There follows the characteristic reason, 'that your ox and your ass may have rest, and the son of your bondmaid, and the alien, may be refreshed'.[4] In the oldest stratum of the Pentateuch the sabbath is, therefore, to be understood as a *social institution*. After every six days of work a day of rest is inserted for the sake of the cattle and of the slaves and employees. The conclusion of the sabbath commandment in J's decalogue points in exactly the same direction, '(also) in time of ploughing (or sowing) and in harvest you shall rest (from work on the seventh day)'.[5] The day of rest had to be observed even during the rigorous time of sowing and harvest when the Israelite employer was most dependent on his assistants, on cattle and slaves and day labourers. The observance of the sabbath does, therefore, point us to the period after the occupation of Canaan. It makes sense only if we suppose that the Israelites were already settled in cultivated land, possessed slaves and employed day labourers in their service. From extant sources we cannot be more precise about our dating of the introduction of the sabbath.[6]

[1] See the following discussion.
[2] See pp. 45ff. below; despite A. Alt (p. 11, n. 3), p. 112, Ex. 31.14b–15b also belongs to P.
[3] The only difference is that in Ex. 23.12 it reads *ma'aseykā ta'aseh*, in Ex. 34.21 *ta'abōd*. The decalogues in Ex. 20 and Deut. 5 combine both expressions.
[4] The Samaritan Pentateuch is dependent upon the formulation in the Elohistic and Deuteronomic decalogues.
[5] J. Meinhold, *Sabbat und Woche im Alten Testament* (FRLANT 5), 1905, wanted to conclude from this passage that the seven-day week was at first observed *only* during the time of sowing and harvest. But this exegesis does violence to the text, especially when the parallel passage Ex. 23.12 is taken into consideration. Also it would be inexplicable how the uninterrupted observance of the seven-day week throughout the year could have developed from a periodic observance of seven days. Cf. also pp. 22ff. below.
[6] We must not think in this connection of the later monarchical period (Jehu's revolution), as does A. Menes, *Die vorexilischen Gesetze Israels* (BZAW

Naturally the view that the sabbath was originally adopted in Israel for social reasons after the occupation of Canaan is rejected by all scholars who maintain the Mosaic origin of the sabbath or who at least wish to trace the institution of the sabbath back to the time in the desert.

In this case the social motivation for the sabbath commandment provided by the Book of the Covenant is regarded as a secularization of the sabbath.[1] In connection with this view it may be said that legal provision for the protection of cattle, slaves and day labourers may very well be closely linked with the law of Yahweh, even if it is not to be found expressed in these precise terms.[2] If this is so, the sabbath commandment in the Book of the Covenant does not belong to casuistic law (probably taken over from the Canaanites), but it has developed from the language of apodeictic law with its characteristic address in the second person singular. It does in fact carry this stamp which is unmistakably Israelite and is associated with the covenant with Yahweh.[3]

What view should we hold, then, about the origin of the sabbath in Mosaic or in pre-settlement times? the mere fact that the decalogue is taken back to Moses by biblical tradition and once again by recent Old Testament scholarship[4] does not mean that the sabbath commandment contained in it also goes back to the desert period.[5] Secondly, the investigations of the form critics lead us to suppose that the ten commandments were used at covenant renewal festivals either every year or

---

50), 1928, pp. 37ff. The sabbath interpreted as a day of rest for slaves and cattle presupposes only land under cultivation and does not necessarily point to social abuses.

[1] So E. Jenni, *Die theologische Begründung des Sabbatgebotes im Alten Testament* (TS 46), 1956, p. 16.

[2] This is demonstrated by the deuteronomic reason for the sabbath commandment (see pp. 15f. below) which follows exactly that of the book of the covenant.

[3] For the distinction between case-law and apodeictic law see A. Alt (p. 11, n. 3), pp. 79–132.

[4] See the investigation by J. J. Stamm and M. E. Andrew, *The Ten Commandments in Recent Research*, ET (SBT NS 2), 1967.

[5] Thus, for example, H. Schmidt, 'Mose und der Dekalog', in *Eucharisterion*, Festschrift für H. Gunkel (FRLANT 36.1), 1923, pp. 78–119, assumes that the decalogue as a whole derives from Moses, but not, however, the sabbath commandment. In fact, the motives which might have caused Moses to command the people at Sinai to keep holy the sabbath day are not at all clear, unless one supposes that he introduced a pre-Israelite sabbath into the religion of Yahweh, and this is extremely improbable; see pp. 18ff. below.

every seventh year and that they were in any case a very brief and even arbitrary selection from the stock of apodeictic law. If the form critics are correct in this insistence, we are in all probability forced to abandon any precise dating so far as the traditional material contained in the decalogue is concerned, for we have to reckon with a complicated history of the tradition for the decalogue as a result of its long cultic use, and we must regard the form in which the ten commandments have been preserved as the product of a relatively late stage in the tradition.[1] Evidence for this is provided by the variety of forms in which the sabbath commandment has been handed down in the different versions of the decalogue. The two motivations (deuteronomic and priestly) for the sabbath commandment which are contained in the decalogue have long been recognized as secondary additions.[2] Similarly it has always been noticed that the sabbath commandment is phrased positively ('You shall keep holy the sabbath day') and not negatively like the other commandments in the decalogue.[3] But we can take a third step. In both the Elohist and also the deuteronomic decalogue we find (Ex. 20.9–10a; Deut. 5.13–14a) the same basic commandment as we found in the Book of the Covenant and in the J decalogue, 'Six days you shall labour, and do all your work; the seventh day is a sabbath to the Lord your God.' The only alteration is that the seventh day is now called sabbath[4] and has a clear association with Yahweh. Furthermore, there

---

[1] Cf. S. Mowinckel, *Le décalogue*, 1927, pp. 75ff.; A. Alt (p. 11, n. 3), pp. 117ff.; M. Noth, *The History of Israel*, ET 1960[2], pp. 103ff. G. von Rad, *Old Testament Theology* I, 1962, p. 18, n. 9, leaves the question undecided.

[2] On this point see the work of E. Jenni (p. 13, n. 1), which presupposes that this conclusion is fact. K. Budde, *Die biblische Urgeschichte*, 1883, pp. 492ff., had indeed assigned Ex. 20.11 to a stage in the tradition before P; cf. G. Schrenk, *Judaica* 2, 1946, p. 176, and now A. R. Hulst, 'Bemerkungen zum Sabbatgebot', *Studia Biblica et Semitica* (Festschrift for T. C. Vriezen), 1966, pp. 152–64. It will hardly be possible to agree with this opinion.

[3] The commandment, 'Honour thy father and thy mother', is another exception. For this reason it has been conjectured that the sabbath commandment and the commandment to honour father and mother were also originally formulated in negative terms; see perhaps the reconstruction of K. Rabast, *Das apodiktische Recht im Deuteronomium und im Heiligkeitsgesetz*, 1949, pp. 35ff.: Thou shalt not do any work on the sabbath. Thou shalt not curse thy father and thy mother.

[4] For this reason it is to be doubted whether the verb form *šbt* really is derived from *šabbāt*, as is frequently assumed; cf. R. North, 'The Derivation of *Sabbat*', *Biblica* 36, 1955, pp. 182–201.

is now added to the positive basic commandment the negative minatory formula which does no more than repeat the basic commandment, 'You shall not do any work, you, or your son, or your daughter, your manservant, or your maidservant (Deut.: or your ox, or your ass; cf. Ex. 23.12), or your cattle, or the sojourner who is within your gates' (Ex. 20.10b; Deut. 5.14b). Is not this an indication that the sabbath commandment of the various versions of the decalogue, even in the form in which we find it in the oldest stratum of the Pentateuch, has been inherited and also revised in the course of its long process of transmission?

Important support for the contention that the sabbath was originally a social institution is to be found in the deuteronomic tradition. Here we find fully preserved the connection with the oldest tradition about the sabbath as it appears in the Book of the Covenant and in the J decalogue. We find clear evidence for this in the motivation which Deuteronomy provides for the sabbath commandment. First it repeats almost word for word the motive which is to be found in the Book of the Covenant, '(Observe the sabbath,) that your manservant and your maidservant may rest as well as you' (Deut. 5.14c). Then it adds, 'You shall remember that you were a servant in the land of Egypt, and the Lord your God brought you out thence, with a mighty hand and an outstretched arm' (Deut. 5.15a). Here it is plain that social and ethical requirements are intimately associated with the Yahwistic covenant, with the character of the covenant God as protector of all the afflicted and oppressed. Now that the Israelites are masters in their own land and employ slaves, they should remember that they themselves were once slaves in Egypt and that God had mercy on them when they cried to him. This means that if the slaves of the Israelites have cause to cry to God he will vindicate them also against their masters. We may also compare other deuteronomic passages which display the same unconditional demand for consideration towards the underprivileged: in this respect, too, these passages agree only with the Book of the Covenant.[1]

---

[1] Deuteronomy again and again champions the cause of slaves and strangers, widows and orphans: Deut. 10.19; 16.11f.; 24.10ff., etc.; cf. Lev. 23.38, 42. In so doing Deuteronomy is only picking up the tradition of the Book of the Covenant: Ex. 22.21f.; 23.9.

The sabbath year is also relevant here.[1] It naturally originated by analogy with the seven-day week and its day of rest.[2] The *social* aim of this institution is again unmistakable: 1. The poor of the land, slaves and animals (!) should be able to support themselves free of charge from the produce of the land (Ex. 23.11; Lev. 25.6f.; similarly Deut. 24.19–22; Lev. 19.9–10). 2. The sabbath year is at the same time a year of remission of all debts owed by fellow citizens (Deut. 15.1ff.). 3. Hebrew slaves[3] are released if they so desire (Ex. 21.2–6; Deut. 15.12–18).[4] The fiftieth year which came after every seven sabbath years[5] was regarded as an intensified sabbath year when the release of all citizens and the restitution of their patrimony were required (Lev. 25.8ff.). While this so-called jubilee year (it had to be proclaimed with a loud trumpet = *yobel*: hence the name jubilee) was never put into operation, we have evidence that the sabbath year was in fact observed.[6]

If we link the deuteronomic motivation for the sabbath with the demand for a day of rest which may bring to the slaves relaxation from work, we shall see that, according to Deuteronomy, the sabbath had only one purpose: that the Israelite may reflect that he himself was a slave, that he may reflect what it is like to be a slave. The reference to Egypt and to God's vengeance on the oppressors of Israel (as in the passages in the Book of the Covenant, Ex. 22.21ff.; 23.9) is solely intended to emphasize the seriousness of the injunction that the Israelite should not oppress his slaves.[7]

[1] Cf. H. Wildberger, 'Israel und sein Land', *EvTh* 16, 1956, pp. 402–22; E. Lohse, 'σάββατον', *TWNT* VII, pp. 6, 18f.

[2] According to A. Alt (p. 11, n. 3), p. 128, n. 118, this happened very early.

[3] These are not citizens: cf. A. Alt (p. 11, n. 3), pp. 93ff.

[4] One might suppose that this 'general amnesty' was connected with the covenant renewal festival which, according to Deut. 31.10f., took place every seventh year.

[5] By analogy with the fifty days until Pentecost; this was seen as early as J. Wellhausen, *Prolegomena to the History of Israel*, 1885, pp. 116ff.

[6] Cf. Jer. 34.8ff.; Lev. 26.43; II Chron. 36.21. Further information from post-exilic and New Testament times in E. Schürer, *A History of the Jewish People in the Time of Jesus Christ*, ET 1885ff., I.i, pp. 40–45 (§ 3A 3), 224 (§ 5, n. 13), 274 (§ 8). E. Lohse (n. 1 above), pp. 18f. J. Jeremias, 'Sabbatjahr und neutestamentliche Chronologie', *ZNW* 27, 1928, pp. 98ff., holds that the collection arranged by Paul was levied to alleviate a famine caused by a sabbatical year.

[7] It is in this sense that v. 15b, 'Therefore the Lord your God commanded you to keep the sabbath day', is also to be understood, and not in the sense that the sabbath was founded to commemorate the exodus from Egypt. We should not give too much weight to the element of salvation history in

In the motivation of the sabbath commandment to be found as early as in the decalogues of Ex. 20 and Deut. 5 we hear a new note. This takes us beyond the original character of the sabbath as a day of rest which was introduced on grounds of social ethics. Now the sabbath is held to be a day holy to Yahweh, the God of Israel, a day which is therefore to be kept holy by the Israelites in an appropriate manner (Deut. 5.12; Ex. 20.8). As a result the sabbath was given prominence above the other days no longer merely for the sake of slaves and cattle, but for God's sake. The day of rest had indeed been repeatedly commanded by the covenant God, and as a result it had come to occupy so central a place in the religion of Yahweh that its social and ethical orientation seemed to be forced into the background and to yield ground to a purely theological evaluation of the day. The decisive factor in this development may have been the admission of the sabbath commandment into the

---

the deuteronomic motivation of the sabbath commandment, as if the sabbath were for the Jews of that time a day on which they remembered the liberation from Egypt in the joyous celebration in which the slaves also shared. Equally, in this connection, we should not think that the sabbath had become a token of the future blessing of peace which God had already symbolically procured for Israel by leading them into the promised land, as is supposed by E. Jenni (p. 13, n. 1), pp. 17ff. In Deuteronomy the thought of the blessing of peace is not connected with the sabbath, although the idea of peace is very important for the deuteronomic writers, but in a more this-worldly sense associated with the possession of property. The connection of sabbath and future peace was effected as a result of the *Priestly* motivation of the sabbath commandment which, in this respect as well, went further than the deuteronomic motivation; cf. on this whole subject G. von Rad, 'There Remains still a Rest for the People of God', *The Problem of the Hexateuch and Other Essays*, ET 1966, pp. 94–102, esp. 97ff.; and see pp. 48ff. below. The reference to slavery in Egypt, as it is to be found in the deuteronomic motivation for the sabbath commandment, is best understood if it is taken closely with the command to treat slaves with consideration. By means of a conclusive example from their own history, the Israelites should be vividly reminded how important in the eyes of God is considerate treatment of social dependants. It was only in rabbinic times that the sabbath became, in addition, a weekly memorial of the exodus from Egypt and so became an observance comparable with the annual passover festival: the passover still remained the festival at which *par excellence* the exodus was commemorated. (Here we meet with a development similar to that which is to be found in the Christian observance of Sunday; the Christian Sunday also became a weekly memorial of the resurrection of Jesus and so became comparable with the annual Easter festival, which was *par excellence* the festival commemorating the resurrection.)

select number of Israelite laws which formed the decalogue.[1]
It is also probable that the command to *keep holy* the sabbath day
is connected with the fact that the distinctive character of the
sabbath was becoming marked by cultic activities. Already in
the time of the prophets we hear of festal gatherings on the
sabbath.[2] The emphasis on the holiness of the sabbath found
its peak and at the same time its final form in the motivation of
the sabbath commandment which is to be found in the priestly
writers. They left a distinctive and definitive mark on the
theology and the observance of the sabbath in the post-exilic
period. But of that more later.[3]

We have tried to understand the sabbath and also the seven-
day week as an Israelite institution explicable in terms of social
ethics. We are of the opinion that it originated after the occupation of Canaan and that the evidence is to be found in
documents which date from the early monarchical period. The
subsequent history of the sabbath is its development as a day of
Yahweh which was marked by cultic observances. Nevertheless
one fascinating problem still remains unsolved: why did the
Jews come to distinguish every *seventh* day as a day of rest in the
manner already described? In Gen. 1–2 we are told that God
created the world in six days and rested on the seventh day, but
this motivation was added after the institution of a day of rest
recurring after every six days had already been in existence for
a long time.[4]

The fact that the Israelites in the early monarchical period
already knew the seven-day week is all the more astonishing, as
this institution runs contrary to every natural arrangement of
time. Neither in the natural processes on earth, nor in the
revolutions of the stars is a periodicity of seven days to be
found; moreover, the seven-day week rolls on throughout time

---

[1] This development was helped by the fact that from the time when the
Jews were no longer in their own country they no longer had any slaves,
and so they scarcely knew what to make of the motivation of sabbath observance on the grounds of social ethics.

[2] Isa. 1.13. A passage like Lev. 23.3 is also important in this context;
already the holiness code knew the *miqrā'-qōdeš*, the 'holy convocation', on
the sabbath. Slaves obviously took part in it; cf. Deut. 16.11ff.

[3] See pp. 45ff. below.

[4] See p. 14, n. 2, above and pp. 46ff. below.

without regard to seasons or to sun and moon.[1] Credit for such an 'invention' has not been given to the Israelites; research has repeatedly been made into the pre-Israelite origins of the sabbath and of the seven-day week. In the next few pages we shall give an outline of the various possibilities which have been proposed, but we do not consider that any of them can claim a high degree of probability. We shall divide them into four categories.[2]

(i) It has often been surmised that the seven-day week does, after all, depend on a *division into four of the original lunar month*.[3] In support of this opinion is the fact that nearly all the peoples of the ancient world (including those of Indo-Germanic stock) for the most part calculated time by means of the moon.[4] We find periods of time of five, seven, eight, nine, ten and fifteen days, all of which are clearly related to the lunar month.[5] It is characteristic of these periods of time that they have never parted company with the lunar month. We cannot, therefore, refer to them as weeks in our sense which recur in a regular cycle. This is also true of the most famous example of an early stage in the development of the seven-day week, the Assyro-Babylonian seven days.[6] Among the numerous days which the

---

[1] Neither the lunar year (354 days, 8 hours, 48 minutes, 38 seconds) nor the solar year (365 days, 5 hours, 48 minutes, 48 seconds) can be exactly subdivided into smaller units of time.

[2] On the question of the pre-Israelite origin of the seven-day week and of the sabbath see the informative studies by E. G. Kraeling, 'The present Status of the Sabbath Question', *American Journal of Semitic Languages and Literatures* 49, 1932–3, pp. 218–28; G. J. Botterweck, 'Der Sabbath im Alten Testament', *TQS* 134, 1954, pp. 134–47, 448–57; also R. North, 'The Derivation of the Sabbath', *Biblica* 36, 1955, pp. 182–201.

[3] See above all W. H. Roscher, *Die enneadischen und hebdomadischen Fristen und Wochen der ältesten Griechen* (AGL, phil.-histor. Kl. XXI.4), 1903, pp. 4 and 68ff.; *Die Sieben- und Neunzahl im Kultus und Mythus der Griechen* (AGL XXIV.1), 1904, p. 68; D. Nielsen, *Die altarabische Mondreligion und die mosaische Überlieferung*, 1904, p. 169; J. Hehn, *Siebenzahl und Sabbat bei den Babyloniern und im Alten Testament* (Leipziger Semitistische Studien 2/5), 1907, pp. 57ff.; H. Webster, *Rest Days: a Sociological Study* (University Studies of the University of Nebraska 11), 1911, p. 100; and also J. Wellhausen, *Prolegomena to the History of Israel*, ET 1885, reprinted 1962, pp. 112ff.

[4] See perhaps the list in W. Kornfeld, 'Der Sabbat im Altem Testament' in *Der Tag des Herrn*, ed. H. Peichl, 1958, pp. 11ff.

[5] W. Roscher (n. 3), and H. Webster (n. 3), have gathered voluminous material on this subject; cf. F. K. Ginzel, *Handbuch der mathematischen und technischen Chronologie*, 3 vols, 1911ff.

[6] The cuneiform material in E. Schrader, *Die Keilinschriften und das Alte*

former inhabitants of Mesopotamia distinguished by means of taboos and special regulations, the seventh, fourteenth, twenty-first and twenty-eighth days of each month gained more and more importance from the time of Assurbanipal onwards: these days were closely connected with the phases of the moon.[1] Even here, however, precisely because of the association with the moon's phases, we cannot suppose that there was any continuous reckoning by weeks. The Babylonian seven days lead us, therefore, to give up any attempt to derive the Jewish seven-day week from the phases of the moon.[2] The Israelite week is at least as old as this parallel phenomenon, and it was from the very beginning completely independent of the lunar cycle; the sabbath also never had the character of a lunar day.[3]

(ii) We may be tempted to consider the seven-day week in connection with the great importance which the number seven possessed among nearly all ancient peoples.[4] We must, however, first ask how the number seven came to occupy a position of such importance. Is it not largely to be attributed to the existence of seven-day periods and of the seven-day week?[5] Nature at all events, as we have already remarked, gives no recognizable preference to the number seven. There are, it is true, seven stars in the Pleiades, in Orion and in the Great Bear, but most of the other instances of groups of seven in the natural order (e.g. the seven winds)[6] have been discovered or invented after the number seven had already acquired its

---

Testament (3rd edition compiled by H. Zimmern and H. Winckler, 1903), pp. 592–4; B. Landsberger, *Der Kultische Kalender der Babylonier und Assyrer*, 1915; S. Langdon, *Babylonian Menologies and the Semitic Calendars*, 1935.

[1] Cf. the Creation Epic (Enuma Elish), V 15ff. (*ANET*, p. 68).

[2] The interpretation of the nineteenth day of the month which was at this time provided with special regulations as a forty-ninth day (taking into account the thirty days of the preceding month) whereby it could count as another seventh day is very uncertain.

[3] On the *šapattu* question see p. 23 below.

[4] Once again W. Roscher (p. 19, n. 3) should be mentioned; also J. Hehn (p. 19, n. 3), pp. 6ff.; J. Meinhold (p. 12, n. 5), pp. 14ff.; P. Jensen, 'Die siebentägige Woche in Babylon und Niniveh', *ZDWF* 1, 1901, pp. 151ff.; Zoeckler, 'Siebenzahl', *RE*³ 18, pp. 310–17.

[5] The supporters of the view that the seven-day week developed from a division into four of the lunar week are understandably of this opinion.

[6] J. and H. Lewy, 'The Origin of the Week and the Oldest West-Asiatic Calendar', *Hebrew Union College Annual* 17, 1942–3, pp. 1ff., have tried to derive the seven-day week from the seven winds.

peculiar importance. The seven planets of the ancient world seem to have been an exception: here the sun and moon were included together with the five planets which were then known. Besides, as we shall see, there was, in fact, a seven-day week linked with the seven planets.[1] Have we not, therefore, conclusive proof that the seven-day week may be traced back to the veneration of the planets?[2] This conclusion may well be overhasty, and the greatest possible caution is necessary. The reckoning of the two great luminaries, sun and moon, together with the five planets, which are in part so difficult to observe, to make the number seven is a very late development in Babylonian astronomical science. Moreover, as we shall see, it is almost impossible to know how we shall ever manage to establish whether the knowledge of the seven planets really did lead to the formation of a seven-day week.[3] Even if this were the case, it would be extremely difficult to explain why one of the seven days has become a day of *rest*.[4] For this reason the hypothesis that the sabbath may have developed from an earlier Saturn day observed by Kenite smiths in the desert fails to convince, even though it has supporters right up to recent times.[5] It is constructed on the basis of two passages, Ex. 35.3 (prohibition of lighting a fire on the sabbath; cf. Num. 15.32f.) and Amos 5.26 (where a reference to Saturn worship is generally understood).[6] But this is too slender a basis on which to justify a conclusion from the Old Testament about a Kenite Saturn day. It is, moreover, quite impossible that there was already among the Kenites any belief about the good or harmful effects

[1] See pp. 24ff. below.
[2] So perhaps Th. Nöldeke, 'Die Namen der Wochentage bei den Semiten', *ZDWF* 1, 1901, p. 161.
[3] See pp. 25ff. below. Also J. Hehn, 'Zur Bedeutung der Siebenzahl' in *Festschrift für K. Marti* (BZAW 41), 1925, p. 129, expresses the same doubt.
[4] It can, of course, be said that Saturn was regarded as an unlucky star and therefore its day was thought to be a black day; but the same would then have to be true of Mars' day, as Mars also counted as an unlucky star.
[5] Saturn worship among the Israelites was assumed as early as Kuenen, *Der Godsdienst van Israel I*, 1869, p. 260. The hypothesis about a weekly taboo day among the Kenites was first fully set out by B. D. Eerdmans, 'Der Sabbat' in *Festschrift für K. Marti* (BZAW 41), 1925, pp. 79ff.; he was followed by K. Budde, 'The Sabbath and the Week', *JTS* 30, 1929, pp. 1–15; L. Köhler, 'Der Dekalog', *TR*, NF 1, 1929, p. 181. Finally H. H. Rowley (p. 11, n. 3), pp. 99ff.; he even wanted to trace the decalogue back to the Kenites.
[6] Cf. on this subject the controversy between J. Meinhold and K. Budde: *ZAW* 48, 1930, pp. 134ff., 144f.

of planets. Furthermore, the weekly recurrence of this Saturn day would presuppose the existence of the planetary week, but not even in Babylon, where we should most expect a system of time based on belief in planets, do we ever find the planetary week.[1]

(iii) Other scholars make no attempt to explain the origin of the number seven and are content to indicate the economic value of a seven-day week. They think that an original *market week* has developed into a sabbath week.[2] Regular markets are, of course, a necessity of life where settled townships exist depending on the barter of foodstuffs and other necessaries with the countryside. Market weeks are certainly to be found among many peoples.[3] In Palestine, however, we have no evidence of market weeks, much less of seven-day market weeks. Moreover, from the standpoint of Old Testament tradition it does, on the whole, seem quite improbable that the sabbath was originally a market day. In Amos 8.5, for instance, it says that many people could hardly wait until new moon and sabbath were over, because it was only when they were past that they were allowed to sell their grain and corn. In this case how could the sabbath have originally been a market day? It must, of course, be granted that days of rest and festivity normally have a tendency subsequently to become market days as well,[4] and the sabbath was no exception, as we see in Neh. 13.15–22 (cf. 10.31 and Jer. 17.19ff.). But so far as its origins are concerned, the sabbath had no connection with a market day.

(iv) There are still two theories to be mentioned which seek to associate the sabbath with days and periods which do not recur after every six days week by week: in this very fact lies their principal weakness.

---

[1] See p. 27, n. 1, below.

[2] First of all M. P. Nilsson, *Primitive Time-Reckoning*, 1920, pp. 324ff.; then M. Weber, *Aufsätze zur Religionssoziologie* III, 1921, pp. 159f.; Ed. Meyer, *Geschichte des Altertums* II.2, 1931[2], pp. 318f.; E. G. Kraeling (p. 19, n. 2), pp. 227f. Also E. Jenni (p. 13, n. 1), pp. 12f., inclines to this point of view.

[3] Cf. M. P. Nilsson (previous note). We have already mentioned the Roman *nundinae* week. See above p. 10, n. 1.

[4] Constantine the Great, for example, permitted markets to be held on Sundays in Pannonia, *Corp. Inscr. Latin.* III.4121. In this connection it is interesting to note the shift in the word 'Messe': divine service—fair—industrial exhibition. Even today in many rural areas a market is regularly held on Sunday.

(a) The day of the full moon is called *šapattu* in Babylonian sources.[1] The relationship of the Hebrew word sabbath with *šappatu* seems obvious. H. Zimmern[2] did, therefore, surmise that the sabbath was originally the day of the full moon. J. Meinhold[3] then tried with extreme ingenuity to prove this theory. He could appeal to the fact that in the Old Testament the sabbath is often mentioned in close association with the new moon (II Kings 4.23; Amos 8.4–5; Hos. 2.11; Isa. 1.13–14, etc.; cf. also Col. 2.16). From this he concluded that the sabbath originally stood exactly parallel to the new moon and that it means 'day of the full moon' corresponding to the Babylonian *šappatu*.[4] Meinhold is also of the opinion that, quite independently of this, the Israelites even before the exile had begun to introduce a seven-day week in the time of ploughing and of harvest (Ex. 34.21). Under Ezekiel and Nehemiah the name sabbath, originally the name of the day of the full moon, was transferred to the seven-day week which had in the meantime become a permanent institution. The theory is untenable in this form. Not only is the Hebrew for the day of the full moon *keṣe'* (Ps. 81.4) and not sabbath, but it is also impossible to give a plausible explanation how the name sabbath came to be transferred to a weekly day of rest observed alongside the day of the full moon. The similarity of the names sabbath and *šappatu* remains striking, but there needs to be closer investigation into the etymology of the two words.[5]

(b) Equally unsatisfactory is the suggestion of J. and H. Lewy[6], who in connection with their studies on the *ḫamuštu* periods of the Cappadocian cuneiform tablets[7] would like to understand the original sabbath as the

[1] E.g. the Creation Epic (Enuma Elish) V. 18 (*ANET*, p. 68).

[2] 'Sabbath', *Zeitschrift der deutschen Morgenländischen Gesellschaft* 58, 1904, pp. 199–202, and a postscript, pp. 458–60.

[3] (P. 12, n. 5), 'Sabbat und Sonntag', *Wissenschaft und Bildung* 45, 1909; 'Die Entstehung des Sabbats', *ZAW* 29, 1909, pp. 81–112; 'Zur Sabbatfrage', *ZAW* 36, 1916, pp. 108–10. He was followed by G. Hölscher, *Geschichte der israelitisch-jüdischen Religion*, 1922, p. 142; W. Nowack, 'Einleitung zum Traktat "Sabbat"' in the *Giessener Mischnaausgabe*, 1924, pp. 8ff.

[4] N. H. Snaith, *The Jewish New Year Festival*, 1947, pp. 103ff., is of the opposite opinion and holds that the sabbath was originally the day of the new moon.

[5] *šapattu* is now understood by R. North (p. 14, n. 4), p. 194, following B. Lansberger, *ZAW* 48, 1930, p. 134, as an alternative form of 'seven' with a feminine ending, *šab'āntu*.

[6] (P. 20, n. 6), pp. 78ff., 105f.; they are followed by J. Morgenstern, 'The Calendar of the Book of Jubilees, its Origin and its Character', *VT* 5, 1955, p. 41, and passim. In his book *Some Significant Antecedents of Christianity* (Studia Post-Biblica 10), 1966, pp. 16ff., Morgenstern develops from this far-reaching consequences for the Christian theology of Easter. See p. 24, n. 1, below.

[7] They interpret it as a fifty-day period and from it they reconstruct an ancient Semitic calendar of the seasons; on this see p. 187 below. N. H. Tur-Sinai (Torczyner), 'Sabbat und Woche', *Bibliotheca Orientalis* 8, 1951, pp. 16ff., is sharply critical of this attempt, but unjustly so.

7 or 8 *intercalary days* at the end of each half year. However interesting this theory is in itself, it is quite unsuitable for explaining how the weekly sabbath can have developed from these yearly intercalary periods.[1]

The background of the seven-day week does, therefore, still remain a mystery. It is nothing more than mere conjecture to assert that it goes back to the phases of the moon, or that it has developed from the numinousness of the number seven, or that it is connected with the economic necessity of holding markets, let alone that it may be traced back to one of the non-weekly models which we have mentioned last of all. No certain proof can be adduced for any of these conjectures: in fact, all they do is to complicate our understanding of the Israelite week. The Old Testament sources themselves give us clear information about the original *meaning* of the seven-day week and of the weekly day of rest in Israel, but they do nothing to explain the *provenance* of the seven-day structure of this week. Perhaps one day more light will be shed for us on this question by the discovery of fresh material.[2]

2. THE PLANETARY WEEK OF THE GREEKS AND ROMANS

The other seven-day week in the Mediterranean basin at the beginning of our era was the planetary week. What do we mean by this?

Seven planets were known in antiquity. All seven were thought of as satellites revolving round the earth which was then supposed to be the hub of the universe. The planets were closely connected with divine elemental powers; they were called by the names of gods and were reverenced accordingly.

---

[1] In her answer to J. Morgenstern, A. Jaubert, *VT* 7, 1957, p. 47, suggests that the seven-day week may have formed the basis of the calendar of the *ḥamuštu* periods. But this is open to question, since the number fifty is not exactly divisible by seven and since Morgenstern emphasizes that the calendar of the fifty-day periods was adapted to suit the seasons of the year and so was capable of modification: its co-ordination with a rigid time-pattern like the seven-day week would, therefore, have only given rise to confusion. Besides, it is hardly to be accepted that the seven-day week is of *such* great antiquity. If it were, what has become of the intermediate stages down to the Israelite sabbath?

[2] H.-J. Kraus, *Worship in Israel*, 1966, pp. 85–87, draws attention to the significance of the Ugaritic 'prototype', but this thesis still remains very hypothetical.

In Babylonian astrology they played a considerable role,[1] but it was the Greeks who first established a scientific relationship between the planets. They arranged their order in accordance with the distance of each one of them from the earth.[2] This order went as follows: Saturn (the planet at the greatest distance from the earth)—Jupiter—Mars—Sun—Venus—Mercury—Moon, or *vice versa*.[3] This order gradually replaced earlier arrangements of the planets.[4]

The planetary week originated in the association of the seven planets with seven consecutive days in such a way that each planet was allotted the control over a particular day and that day was then named after it. It is, however, remarkable that we here encounter an entirely different arrangement of the planets. The sequence runs thus: Saturn—Sun—Moon—Mars—Mercury—Jupiter—Venus.[5] It is difficult to account for the origin of this order.

[1] The Babylonian sequence of planets was generally as follows: Moon—Sun—Jupiter—Venus—Saturn—Mercury—Mars; cf. E. Schrader, *Die Keilinschriften und das Alte Testament* (3rd edition compiled by H. Zimmern and H. Winckler, 1903), p. 622. On the individual planetary gods see W. H. Roscher, 'Planeten', *Allgemeines Lexikon der griech. und röm. Mythologie* III.2, 1902–9, col. 2525f., 2529.

[2] This planetary sequence is traced back to Pythagoras: Pliny, *Hist. nat.* 2.22; Censorinus, *De die natali* 13. F. Boll, 'Hebdomas', Pauly-Wissowa VII.2, col. 2561ff., gives detailed proof that it could not derive from either Babylon or Egypt. He is of the opinion that it more probably originated in the second century BC, and so could not come from Pythagoras.

[3] This order is, in fact, still valid today if the moon is left out and the earth is inserted in place of the sun. But more planets have since been discovered: Uranus, Neptune and Pluto.

[4] F. Boll (n. 2), col. 2588, advances the view that the place of eminence accorded to the sun within the planetary sequence (it is to be found in the middle) helped this particular order to be more widely accepted. But can we speak here in terms of a position of eminence? The Greek planetary sequence probably became established thanks to its evident scientific basis. The Greek sequence of planets has, in fact, led to the idea of *seven* heavens. The seven heavens correspond to the seven spheres which lie on top of one another and in which the planets revolve; cf. the idea of the harmony of the spheres derived from the heptachord, W. Roscher (n. 1), col. 2531. Even in the second century AD we have evidence of the so-called septizones (or septizodes), buildings which somehow or other represented the seven heavens, cf. E. Schürer, 'Die siebentägige Woche im Gebrauch der christlichen Kirche der ersten Jahrhunderte', *ZNW* 6, 1905, pp. 29ff., 63ff. The seven heavens have, of course, been extremely important in the realm of religious ideas; on this see p. 30, n. 2 below.

[5] The sequence with its Greek names runs: Kronos—Helios—Selene—Ares—Hermes—Zeus—Aphrodite. Other names were used before the time of Plato; see W. H. Roscher (n. 1), col. 2518–2525.

At the beginning of the third century AD, Dio Cassius gives two explanations[1] in his *Roman History* (37.18–19).

First, if we take from the scientific planetary sequence of the Greeks (Saturn
—Jupiter—Mars—Sun—Venus—Mercury—Moon) every third planet and
omit the two in between, we then have the order of the planetary week
(*Saturn*—Jupiter—Mars—*Sun*—Venus—Mercury—*Moon*—Saturn—Jupiter
—*Mars*—Sun etc.; this procedure works on the principle of a musical fourth).

Secondly, we get the same result if we distribute the 168 hours of a week
to each of the planets in the scientific order: then the planets of the first hour
of each day give us the sequence of the planetary week. The first hour of the
first day stands under *Saturn*, the second under Jupiter, etc; the 8th, 15th and
22nd hours of the first day consequently fall to Saturn: as we continue to
count, the 23rd hour will be under Jupiter and the 24th under Mars. The
first hour of the second day, therefore, falls to the *Sun*, the first hour of the
third day to the *Moon*, the first hour of the fourth day to *Mars*, etc.

This second explanation is particularly interesting. If it did in fact happen
in this way, it would mean that the planetary week developed from a belief
in the control exercised by the planets not over *days*, but over the individual
hours of the days of the week.[2] This sort of explanation has, however, a very
artificial appearance. It is hard to believe that such a sophisticated scientific
process (for there is no room here for naïve astrological beliefs) can have
produced the sequence of planets which we find in the planetary week,
especially as this sequence was most probably known first in the lower strata
of society.[3] Yet for the present no better explanation can be suggested.[4]

We can be more precise in our assertions about the origin of
the planetary week itself. This question closely affects our
subject, since the opinion has several times been expressed that
the Christian observance of Sunday is intimately connected
with the planetary week. We shall see in what sense this is so.[5]

When and where did the planetary week first appear? We
can, of course, talk of a planetary week only in the cases where

[1] Cf. also Vettius Valens I.10, *Catalogus codicum astrol. graec.* II.

[2] We find the same theory in the chronographer of the year AD 354 (see
p. 10, n. 1); cf. *Catalogus codicum astrol. graec.* VII, 1908, pp. 88ff.; VIII, 1911,
pp. 144ff. This theory based on hours can be found among the Ssabians, a
Mohammedan sect of star-worshippers and baptists on the lower Euphrates
in the ninth century. See D. Chwolson, *Die Ssabier und der Ssabismus* I, 1856,
738. He connects them with the Elkasaites (*op cit.*, pp. 100ff.).

[3] Convincingly F. H. Colson, *The Week*, 1926, pp. 33, 38.

[4] In any case see p. 33, n. 2, below. Unfortunately we no longer
possess that part of Plutarch's table-talk which was entitled, 'Why do we
count the days of the week which are named after planets not in their
(usual) order but in a rearranged order?' Perhaps we should have come
across much informative material here.

[5] See pp. 37ff. below.

all (or at least some) of the individual days of a seven-day week appear with the names of planets. A general reverence for the seven planets does not mean that a seven-day week was also associated with them.[1] We cannot assemble here a complete list of all the extant evidence for the existence of the planetary week, especially as reference may be made to the works of other scholars.[2] Above all, however, Dio Cassius must once again be quoted. In his *Roman History* (37.18) he makes three points: (1) The planetary week originated in Egypt. (2) It was of relatively recent date. (The ancient Greeks did not know it.) (3) It had by his time spread everywhere. Even without Dio Cassius, we know from many other sources that the planetary week had been in general use since the beginning of the third century AD.[3] Much more important, however, is the statement of Dio Cassius that it had come into use not so very long before. This is confirmed by the literary and pictorial evidence which is at our disposal. We cannot prove that the planetary week existed before the first century AD, however,[4] and we are unable to check whether

[1] This necessary distinction prevents us from seeking the origin of the planetary week among, for instance, the Babylonians, although it is surmised that it first emerged there, on account of their developed astrology. There is, however, no trace among them either of the sequence of planets in the planetary week (cf. F. Boll [p. 25, n. 2], col. 2556) or of the existence of a seven-day week (see pp. 19f. above). E. Schürer (p. 25, n. 4), p. 15; F. H. Colson (p. 26, n. 3), p. 57; W. Lotz, 'Woche', *RE*³ 21, p. 412, all come to the same conclusion. In particular the assertion that the tower of the temple in Borsippa bore the colours of the planets in the sequence of the planetary week cannot be maintained; cf. P. Jensen (p. 20, n. 4), pp. 157f.; F. Boll (p. 25, n. 2), col. 2562. The lack of discrimination on this point and on other points impairs the usefulness of the work of R. L. Odom, *Sunday in Roman Paganism*, 1944.

[2] In addition to the works mentioned above (n. 1), see also F. J. Dölger, 'Die Planetenwoche der griechisch-römischen Antike und der christliche Sonntag', *AuC* 6, 1941, pp. 202–38; A. Thumb, 'Die Namen der Wochentage im Griechischen', *ZDWF* 1, 1901, pp. 163–73; G. Gundermann, 'Die Namen der Wochentage bei den Römern', *ZDWF* 1, 1901, pp. 175–86.

[3] Cf. E. Schürer (p. 25, n. 4), pp. 31ff.; R. L. Odom (n. 1), pp. 99ff. The final stage in the spread of the planetary week may perhaps be traced to the predilection of the Emperor Septimius Severus (193–211) for astrology.

[4] The date of the evidence from Pompeii is indisputable (destruction of Pompeii AD 79). Two mural inscriptions and a mural painting refer to the gods of the various days of the week; see E. Schürer (p. 25, n. 4), pp. 27f.; R. L. Odom (n. 1), pp. 88ff. The 'fasti Sabini' should not be considered in this connection although they date back to the time of Augustus; see p. 10, n. 1, above.

it did, in fact, originate in Egypt, as Dio Cassius suggests.[1]

We have, of course, the evidence from Tibullus which belongs to the first century BC and also several hints from Dio Cassius which bear on this century, but in both Tibullus and Dio Cassius reference is made not to the planetary week as such but only to Saturn's day or to the Kronos day. The planetary week seems, therefore, to have had a preliminary stage consisting in the regular observance, in pagan circles, merely of a day of Saturn. This day of Saturn did, however, stand in a peculiar relationship to the Jewish sabbath. Tibullus (*ob.* 19 BC) says in an elegy (I.3.17f.) that the day of Saturn prevented him from leaving Rome. There is certainly no mention here of the sabbath, but the prohibition of travelling is associated with the Jewish sabbath.[2] Dio Cassius (*Hist. Rom.* 37.16; 49.22; 66.7) maintains that all three conquests of Jerusalem (under Pompey, Sosius and Titus) took place on the Kronos day, by which he meant the Jewish sabbath.[3] In 49.22 he explicitly states that the sabbath was already called Kronos day by that time (37 BC, the date of the conquest by Sosius).

In fact, we can establish that from the very beginning the two

[1] Clement of Alexandria, *Stromateis* VII.12.75, presupposes its existence when he says of the fourth day that it was named after Mercury and of the sixth day that it was named after Venus. He is interpreting the names with reference to the Christian fast-days: the true gnostic abstains from covetousness(=Mercury) and sensuality (=Venus). This passage, however, says nothing on the subject of the origin of the planetary week in Egypt, since it was, of course, already in general use by the time of Clement. Cf. p. 34, n. 4. F. H. Colson (p. 26, n. 3), pp. 52ff., hazards the conjecture (he bases it on Vettius Valens I.10) that the planetary week, together with the solar calendar, was introduced on Sunday, 31 August 30 BC. But this suggestion is unacceptable, because the planetary week always began with Saturday and never with Sunday: see pp. 33ff. below.

[2] In another source reference is expressly made to the connection with the sabbath: Ovid, *Remedia amoris* 219f.

[3] Cf. Frontinus, *Strategem.* II.1.17, where the same statement is made; this is confirmed by Josephus, *Bell. jud.* II.16.4.392. This information is certainly in some degree historically trustworthy, since the Jews were not allowed to wage war on the sabbath and it was, therefore, particularly advantageous to attack them on the sabbath. Cases are, in fact, known when the Jews, on account of their strict observance of the sabbath, let themselves be massacred on the sabbath without resistance: Josephus, *Ant.* XII.1.1.4; 6.2.274f.; I Macc. 2.32–38. There is also an echo of this in Plutarch, *De superstitione* 8. In the case of self-defence it was normally permitted to engage in military activity on the sabbath: I Macc. 2.39–41; 9.43f.; Josephus, *Ant.* XII.6.2. 276.; cf. *Bell. jud.* II.19.2.517; even by Shammai, b. Shabbath 19a. Cf. also Lohse (p. 16, n.1), p. 9.

days were closely parallel with one another. The Saturn day of the planetary week always coincided with the sabbath of the Jewish week. In addition, the Greeks and Romans kept their Saturn day in a manner remarkably similar to the sabbath observance of the Jews.[1] This coincidence is so striking that it cannot escape our attention: moreover, it should not be assumed that it arose entirely by chance. Even in those days it provided food for thought. Tacitus[2] informs us that many people in his time asserted that the Jewish sabbath was associated with the Jews' veneration for Saturn. This is completely out of the question, for the Jewish week is certainly older than the planetary week and has nothing to do with star worship.[3] The reverse process might, however, very well have taken place: the Jews' custom of doing no work on the sabbath may have led the people among whom they lived to have superstitious ideas about the Jewish sabbath. If the Jews were not allowed to work on a particular day, they obviously regarded it as a 'dies ater', a day of misfortune. We know that Saturn was generally reckoned in the ancient world to be a maleficent planet.[4] Would it not be a natural step for the Jewish observance of the sabbath to be associated with the astrological belief in the evil influences of the planet Saturn? It is even possible that the Jews, for reasons of their own self-interest, may have encouraged the superstitious fear which as a result of their sabbath observance had begun to be associated with the sabbath day.[5] For what other

[1] Reference has already been made to the prohibition of travelling (p. 28, n.2); we shall quote other examples; see pp. 32f. below.

[2] *Hist.* V.4: 'Others say that this [the choice of the seventh day by the Jews] is done in honour of Saturn, whether it be that the primitive elements of their religion were given by the Idaeans, who, according to tradition, were expelled with Saturn and became the founders of the Jewish race, or is due to the fact that, of the seven planets that rule the fortunes of mankind, Saturn moves in the highest orbit and has the greatest potency.' The Idaeans were a tribe on Crete and were confused with the Jews (*Hist.* V.2).

[3] See pp. 20f. above. Star-worship occurs in Judaism only occasionally and peripherally (Deut. 4.19; 17.3; II Kings 21.3; 23.5, 11; Jer. 8.2; 19.12; Ezek. 8.16; Zeph. 1.5). Cf. W. Baudissin, *RE*[3] 18, pp. 516ff.; H. Gressmann, *RGG*[2]I, col. 588ff.; G. Hölscher (p. 23, n. 3), pp. 205ff.

[4] Cf. E. Schürer (p. 25, n. 4), pp. 17, 55ff.; Bouché-Leclercq, *L'astrologie grecque*, 1899, pp. 93ff. Mars as well as Saturn was supposed to be harmful in its influence: Jupiter and Venus were beneficent: the other three, Sun, Moon and Mercury, were neutral.

[5] F. J. Dölger (p. 27, n. 2), pp. 221f., 'The Jews were very numerous in the centres of international trade . . . and they also knew how to turn the

reason would they have called the planet Saturn by the name of *šabᵉtay*[1] of all names? This was a name which by reason of its similarity with the word sabbath was bound to lead to confusion.[2]

There is much to be said for the theory associating the Jewish sabbath with the origins of Saturn's day. According to the evidence in our possession (and that must be emphasized), this was the first day to be called after a planet long before there was any proper planetary week.[3] Moreover, this theory becomes more likely if we bear in mind that at the beginning of our era the Jews and the Jewish sabbath played a role of considerable importance in the Roman empire.

---

religious observance of the sabbath day to their own advantage in business; this they managed not least by adroit assimilation to the astral beliefs of the time and by an appropriate assessment of the significance of the planet Saturn and of its day.'

[1] In Greek σαβήθ, according to Epiphanius, *Haer.* 16.2.3.

[2] We have further evidence which suggests that the Jews were then beginning to incorporate a belief in planets into their religion: they certainly did not do this because these ideas were an integral part of their religion, but as a conscious act of assimilation. Thus the seven-branched candlestick was linked with the seven planets, Josephus, *Ant.* III.6.7.146; cf. *Bell. jud.* V.5.5.217 and the other interpretations of the temple fittings which are given there; Philo, *Vita Mosis* II.102f. The seven archangels were mentioned in connection with the seven planets, Philo, *De opif. mundi* 50.144; Clement Alex., *Strom.* VI.16.143; cf. W. H. Roscher (p. 25, n.1), col. 2531. Above all, the idea of the seven heavens (in connection with the seven heavenly spheres; see p. 25, n. 4, above) acquired considerable importance among both Jewish and Christian gnostics, particularly in teaching about the descent of the redeemer and the ascent of the soul; cf. W. Bousset, 'Die Himmelsreise der Seele', *Archiv für Religionswissenschaft* 4, 1901, pp. 136–69, 229–73; J. Daniélou, *The Theology of Jewish Christianity*, ET 1964, pp. 207ff. See also pp. 95ff below for a selection of passages in which the seven heavens are to be found: Test. Levi 2–3; the (Christian) Ascens. Isaiah 7–9; Clement Alex., *Strom.* IV. 25.159.2; Origen, *c. Celsum* VI.21; Epiphanius, *Haer.* 31.4.1–2; 40.2.3. Cf. also II Cor. 12.2. In a Jewish source (b. Shabbath 156a) we even find the belief that the star under which a person is born materially affects the course of his life. On the whole question see H. Gressmann, *Die hellenistische Gestirnsreligion*, 1925. It must remain an open question whether the seven ages of the world are to be traced back to planetary beliefs (see p. 48 below). Christian polemic later denounced Jewish astral beliefs and angel worship; see pp. 133f. below.

[3] F. H. Colson (p. 26, n. 3), pp. 39ff. (cf. pp. 54, 80), has already suggested this; we shall only develop this theory. The objection made by Colson himself (p. 42) that the planetary week would have had to end with the Saturn day just as the Jewish week did with the sabbath, is not valid. The very fact that the planetary week began on Saturn's day is an indication that there was possibly some connection with the sabbath. See p. 35 below.

There were Jews almost everywhere in the Mediterranean basin in ancient times.[1] Even in the period of the Diadochi the Jewish migration from Palestine had begun.[2] About the middle of the second century BC the Sibyl sings the praises of the Jewish people that 'every country and every sea is full of them'. (Sib. Or. III.271; cf. I Macc. 15.16–24; Josephus, *Bell. jud.* VII.3.3.43.) From the time of Sulla (about 85 BC) Strabo reports, 'The Jews have already come into every town, and it is hard to find any place in the world which would not give shelter to this people or come under its influence' (quoted in Josephus, *Ant.* XIV.7.2.115). In the letter of Agrippa (Philo, *Legat. ad Gaium* 281f.) we find a list of Jewish colonies: in Egypt, Phoenicia, Syria, Coelesyria, Pamphylia, Cilicia, in most parts of Asia up to Bithynia,[3] in the most remote areas of Pontus; in Europe, Thessaly, Boeotia, Macedonia, Aetolia, Attica, Argos, Corinth, in most parts and certainly in the most beautiful parts of the Peloponnese, on the most prominent islands like Euboea, Cyprus, Crete, etc.[4]

The Jews' distinctive faith and their distinctive manner of life could not remain hidden from their pagan neighbours. The Jews developed extensive propaganda activity by skilful emphasis on the universalist trend in their religion.[5] The Old Testament was translated into Greek, the Jews themselves spoke Greek;[6] the synagogues were open to everyone, and the venerable philosophy which was taught in them attracted educated people in particular.[7] Contemporary Jewish literature provides striking documentary evidence for the spirit of the open-minded Hellenistic Judaism of that time.[8] It is a fact that the Jews enjoyed a great prestige in the ancient world, particularly after the time of the Maccabees and after Herod.[9] Many proselytes and godfearers[10] joined them;[11] pilgrims came from all directions

[1] On their numerical strength see J. Juster, *Les Juifs dans l'Empire romain* I, 1914, pp. 209ff.

[2] E. Schürer (p. 16, n. 6), II.ii, p. 221 (§ 31).

[3] Cf. G. Kittel, 'Das kleinasiatische Judentum in der hellenistisch-römischen Zeit', *TLZ* 69, 1944, col. 9–20.

[4] Cf. Acts 2.9–11. Paul also was to find a Jewish community and its synagogue in almost every town.

[5] Moreover, not only in the Diaspora; cf. Matt. 23.15; Slav. Enoch 48.6–9; 33.8f.; 36.1; W. Bousset and H. Gressmann, *Die Religion des Judentums im späthellenistischen Zeitalter*, 1926, pp. 81ff.

[6] But not always: b. Sota 49a; b. Menahoth 99b.

[7] E.g. Justin, *Dial* 7–8; Tatian, *Orat. ad Graecos* 29.

[8] Cf. E. Schürer (p. 16, n. 6), §§ 31–34, ET, Vol. II.ii–iii.

[9] W. Bousset and H. Gressmann (n. 5), p. 65. Nowadays we also see more clearly the strength of the Jewish influence on both pagan and Christian gnosis. (See, for instance, the *Corpus Hermeticum* and the manuscripts discovered at Nag-hammadi.)

[10] Gentiles who observed the sabbath and the food laws, but were not circumcised: Acts 10.2, 22, 35; 13.16, 26, 43, 50; 17.4; 18.7.

[11] Especially many women—even influential ones: Josephus, *Ant.* XX. 8.11.195; *Bell. jud.* II.20.2.560. Cf. Acts 16.14; 17.4, 34.

to sacrifice at Jerusalem (Josephus, *Bell. jud.* V. 1.3.15ff.). Outwardly also the Jews enjoyed numerous privileges (right of assembly on the sabbath, exemption from military service, etc; cf. Josephus, *Ant.* XIV.10, where the edicts issued by the Roman authorities are collected). At the same time anti-Semitism had, of course, been a factor from the beginning of the second century BC.[1] Juvenal (*Sat.* XIV. 96–106) for example made fun at the Jews' expense. We have already quoted part of the passage from Tacitus (*Hist.* V. 2ff.).

We find the same situation with regard to Jewish customs and, in particular, Jewish sabbath observance.[2] On the one hand they were ridiculed by pagans (Ovid, *Ars amatoria* I. 75.415; *Remedia amoris* 219f.; Horace, *Sat.* I. 9.116ff.), while on the other hand they undeniably had a great influence on the Gentile population and were widely imitated. Seneca (quoted by Augustine, *Civ. dei* 6.11), laments: 'Meanwhile, the customs of this accursed nation have gained such influence that they are now received throughout all the world. The vanquished have given laws to their victors. . . . [The Jews] are aware of the origin and meaning of their rites; the greater part of the [non-Jewish] people go through a ritual not knowing why they do so.'

Strabo reports, 'And it has come about that Cyrene, which had the same rulers as Egypt, has imitated it in many respects, particularly in notably encouraging and aiding the expansion of the organized groups of Jews, which observe the national Jewish laws' (quoted in Josephus, *Ant.* XIV. 7.2.116).[3] Even Tertullian gives a similar report about pagans who imitate the sabbath, 'You have selected one day in preference to other days as the day on which you do not take a bath or you postpone it until the evening and on which you devote yourself to leisure and abstain from revelry. In so doing you are turning from your own religion to a foreign religion, for the sabbath and *cena pura* are Jewish ceremonial observances . . .' (*Nat.* I.13); and again, 'We (Christians) are only second to those who set apart Saturn's day for idleness and feasting, and who themselves deviate from the Jewish custom which they misunderstand' (*Apol.* 16.11). All this shows that the observance of Jewish sabbath customs was very widespread— to such a degree that some pagans who practised them did not know the

---

[1] W. Bousset and H. Gressmann (p. 31, n.5), pp. 75f.; E. Schürer (p. 16 n. 6), II.ii, pp. 291ff. (§ 31.v).

[2] Cf. M. Wolff, 'Het oordeel der Heleensen-Romeinsche schrijvers over den Oorsprong, nam en viering van den Sabbath', *Theol. Tijd.* 44, 1910, pp. 162–72. Wolff emphasizes (p. 171) that the sabbath was regarded by foreigners as a fast-day. The Emperor Augustus did, in fact, once write to Tiberius that he had kept his fast on the sabbath more strictly than a Jew (Suetonius, *Divus Augustus* 76.2).

[3] Mention may be made of Diogenes of Rhodes, who was accustomed to dispute only on the sabbath and, also, was willing to receive Tiberius only on that day (Suetonius, *Tiberius* 32).

origin of these customs. Josephus is hardly exaggerating when he writes, '. . . for a long time there has been a keen desire to adopt our religious observance; and there is not one Greek or barbarian nor a single nation to which our custom of abstaining from work on the seventh day (ἑβδομάς) has not spread, and where the fasts and the lighting of lamps and many of our prohibitions in the matter of food are (not) observed' (C. Apionem II. 39f.282).[1]

Considering the spread of Jewish sabbath customs in the Roman empire at that time, is it at all surprising that with the passage of time and with the spread of astrological beliefs some superstitious ideas came to be associated with the observance of Jewish sabbath customs, especially as not everyone who adopted these customs had been aware of their Jewish origin? We may perhaps have found a plausible explanation for a fact which is by no means self-explanatory: that the veneration of a planet came to be concentrated on a particular day, that this day was the sabbath day, which is also the first day known to us under a planetary name.

After the last few pages it is but a short step to suggesting not only that Saturn's day originated by association with the Jewish sabbath but also that the planetary week as a whole developed in association with the Jewish week. Of course, it still remains a puzzle how to explain the sequence of planets in the planetary week and why it differs from the scientific planetary sequence.[2] This suggestion does, nevertheless, make it possible for us to understand how the planetary week came to begin with Saturn's day as its first day. If it had developed quite independently of the Jewish week, it could have begun with any weekday (e.g. Sunday!). Since the order of the planets in the planetary week does not in any case depend on the distance of each planet from the earth, the argument from the fact that Saturn is the planet most distant from the earth is seen to be

---

[1] A similar passage is to be found in Philo, Vita Mosis II.20ff.

[2] We probably have to believe the theory of Dio Cassius after all (see p. 26 above). We could, in fact, also suppose that the sun and moon, which are popularly thought of as the most important planets, quite naturally came to occupy the next places in the list after Saturn, the planet which had already come to reoccupy the first place. P. Jensen (p. 20, n. 4), p. 157, takes a different line; he holds that the sequence of the planets in the planetary week came about because the planets were arranged according to the colour of the metal allotted to them. W. H. Roscher (p. 25, n.1), col. 2537ff., provides a table of metals and colours.

untenable. The beginning of the planetary week with Saturn's day (=sabbath) is, therefore, a further strong argument for an original connection between the sabbath and the day of Saturn.[1] As soon as Saturn's day was firmly established as the first day of the week, the other six planets divided among themselves the control over the remaining six days of the Jewish week.

Another trait peculiar to the planetary week points quite decisively to its Jewish origin: its days were reckoned from evening to evening and not from midnight to midnight, as was the custom in the official Roman calendar. This can be seen in the tables of the chronographer of the year 354 AD,[2] which show that the night hours were then reckoned to be under the control of the same star as were the hours of the following day. This phenomenon cannot easily be explained by any other way than by admitting the presence of Jewish influence, for since the Julian reform of the calendar in 30 BC days were reckoned in the Roman empire from midnight to midnight.

Even if in the last analysis no certain conclusion is possible on this point, the view that the Jewish week did, in fact, influence the early development of the planetary week is easier to hold than the opposing view that the planetary week developed independently of the Jewish week and as a result of nothing but belief in the seven planets.[3] It is indisputable that astrology was very widespread in the Roman empire.[4] If, however, astral worship alone had given rise to an institution like the seven-day week which was so basic and formative in the structure of social and economic life, we should at least have to be surprised that we do not ever find a seven-day planetary week among the Babylonians. J. Wellhausen's judgement still stands: 'It was not until after people had got their seven days that they began to call them after the seven planets; the number seven is the only bond of connection between them.'[5] But since we know only

---

[1] Against F. H. Colson (p. 26, n. 3), p. 42. See p. 30, n. 3 above.
[2] See p. 10, n. 1, above.
[3] E. Schürer (p. 25, n. 4), pp. 18f., strongly advocates this point of view.
[4] F. H. Colson (p. 26, n. 3), pp. 65ff.; Bouché-Leclercq (p. 29, n. 4). Cf. also Acts 19.19. It is not certain whether 'Chaldaean science' penetrated into the West principally via Asia Minor, as is held by J. Bidez and F. Cumont, Les mages hellénisés (2 vols), 1938. P. Cotton, From Sabbath to Sunday, 1933, pp. 136ff. rightly quotes Matt. 2 in this connection. E. Schürer (p. 25, n. 4), p. 46, holds that Egypt played the part of the middleman.
[5] Prolegomena to the History of Israel, ET 1885, p. 113.

one seven-day week (the Jewish) in existence before the planetary week, the planetary week may have evolved out of the Jewish week, and in the course of its evolution its seven days received planetary names. The bridge for this development was provided by the sabbath, which became Saturn's day.

The second day of the planetary week was Sunday, Helios day or *dies solis*. We must now discuss this day, for it is repeatedly asserted that from the very beginning it played a special part in the planetary week. It must, however, be emphasized straight away that in the planetary week Sunday always occupied only the second place in the sequence of days: to outward appearances, therefore, it had nothing to distinguish it from the other days.[1] Furthermore, in astrology the sun was never regarded as a benign planet.[2] There is, however, another possibility which we have to take into account, that the Sunday of the planetary week acquired a special significance by association with the sun cult. This seems to have been the case particularly in the Mithras cult which, originating in the East, gained a firm foothold in the western part of the Roman empire at the beginning of our era.[3]

Mithras is, strictly speaking, a Persian god of light who came to assume more and more of the characteristics of the *sol invictus*.[4] The service of Mithras developed into a mystery religion pure and simple, a kind of secret society with initiation rites, various degrees of membership, sacral offerings,

[1] Christian influence is to be detected when Sunday becomes the first day of the planetary week; see pp. 40f. below. In this respect the views of F. J. Dölger (p. 27, n. 2), pp. 206ff., and of E. Schürer (p. 25, n. 4), pp. 38f., are to be accepted: they have come to this conclusion after a thorough study of the sources. F. J. Dölger strongly opposes the opinion of A. Dieterich, 'Die Religion des Mithras', *Bonner Jahrbuch des Vereins von Altertumsfreunden im Rheinlande* 108/9, 1902, p. 36 (cf. F. Boll [p. 25, n. 2], col. 2577, and G. Gundermann [p. 27, n. 2], pp. 180f.) that in Mithraism the week began with Sunday.

[2] See p. 29, n. 4 above.

[3] According to Plutarch, *Vita Pomp.* 24, Cilician pirates who had been taken captive by Pompey in 67 BC had brought the Mithras cult to Rome. It seems, however, that this information is not historically reliable. Probably it was later, about the beginning of our era, that the Mithras cult found its way to Italy; cf. F. Cumont, *The Mysteries of Mithra*, ET 1910², pp. 36f. Nero may have been initiated into the cult by Tiridates I (Pliny, *Hist. nat.* 30.6).

[4] F. Cumont, *Textes et monuments figurés relatifs aux mystères de Mithra* II, 1899, p. 532.

etc. In many places are still to be seen remains of the so-called Mithraea, the meeting places of the Mithras worshippers.[1] The pictorial representations of Mithras are well known. They show him with a Phrygian cap, in the act of killing a bull whose blood is being licked up by a puppy; this is the symbol of Mithraic deliverance.[2] The Mithras cult was primarily a soldier's religion: it was a strong influence (but by no means the only influence) in the spread of sun worship in the Roman empire. Christianity spread at about the same time as the Mithras cult, and at the end of the second century AD both religions had many adherents throughout the empire, especially among the lower strata of society.[3] For a long time, however, the two religions did not come into contact with one another, because they did not take root in the same areas. (The Mithras cult was widespread particularly in the West, in Rome and Africa, and Christianity more in the East, in Asia Minor, Greece, Egypt and Palestine.) Nevertheless Christian authors in Rome and North Africa were soon lamenting 'the diabolical mimicry' of Christian customs in the religion of Mithras (Justin, I *Apol.* 66.4; Tertullian, *Cor. mil.* 15; *Bapt.* 5).

There can be no question of the Mithras cult having created the planetary week, even though veneration of the planets does seem to have played a not unimportant part in this cult.[4] It was to the sun and to the day of the sun that particular veneration was paid in the Mithras cult. We can infer this from the evidence extant in the area of the Mithras cult. Here we find the sequence of planets in the planetary week appearing in reverse order, so that the sun occupies the last place: the sequence runs as follows: Saturn—Venus—Jupiter—Mercury—Mars—Moon —Sun.[5] On this sequence depended a symbolism about which we learn from Origen. According to this system souls had to ascend to heaven by a ladder which led through seven metal

---

[1] They were called 'caves'; cf. Justin, *Dial.* 70.1; 78.6.
[2] For further information see the two volumes by F. Cumont (p. 35, n. 4), I (1896), II (1899); also F. Cumont, *Religions orientales dans le paganisme romain*, 1929²; also R. L. Odom (p. 27, n. 1); and more recently M. J. Vermaseren, *Corpus inscriptionum et monumentorum religionis Mithraicae*, 1956, and *Mithra, ce dieu mystérieux*, 1960.
[3] F. Cumont (p. 35, n. 3), pp. 188ff.
[4] F. Cumont (p. 35, n. 4), I, 1896, pp. 112–20.
[5] This evidence has been used in support of the assertion that in the area of the Mithras cult the planetary week began with Sunday; see p. 35, n. 1. The following sequence is also found on one occasion: Moon—Mars—Mercury—Jupiter—Venus—Saturn—Sun (F. Cumont [p. 35, n. 4], pp. 261, 99). The intention here is exactly the same as in the normal sequence—to place the sun at the top.

gates. Each one of these gates was dedicated to a planet: at the bottom was Saturn, and at the top Sol with a golden gate.[1] We have no direct information whether the day consecrated to the sun was marked by any sort of cultic observance in the Mithras cult.[2] It is, however, certain that a Mithraic observance of Sunday is *only thinkable if the planetary week had already been introduced*. Since the earliest evidence for the existence of the planetary week is to be dated towards the end of the first century AD, a Mithraic observance of Sunday before that time is quite out of the question. So if the question is raised whether the origins of the Christian observance of Sunday are in any way connected with the Sunday observance of the Mithras cult, it must be answered with a definite No. At the end of the first century the Christian observance of Sunday was, as we shall see,[3] a practice of long standing.[4] It is, therefore, a lamentable error to assert that for his churches in Asia Minor[5] or in Corinth[6] Paul adopted and gave a Christian interpretation[7] to the Mithraic observance of Sunday which had been habitually kept by Gentile Christians before their conversion. This mistake can be made only by those who uncritically conclude that every

---

[1] *C. Celsum* VI.22; cf. F. Cumont (p, 35, n. 4) I, pp. 261, 106, 99. Behind this symbolism there stood the idea of the seven heavens; this notion thrived in the religious syncretism of that time: see n. 24 above and pp. 95ff. below.

[2] F. Cumont (p. 35, n. 4), I, pp. 189, 325, 339, is of the opinion that it was; cf. F. Cumont, *Les mystères de Mithra*, 1913³, p. 173. We should also bear in mind that in his *First Apology* Justin speaks of the Mithraic cultic meals as a diabolical mimicry of Christian rites (ch. 66), but in ch. 67 where he deals with Sunday he makes no complaint about any Mithraic aping of the Christian observance of Sunday. Why does he not mention the Mithraic Sunday observance, if there was one? He would have been *obliged* to point out to the Emperor that Christians did not observe Sunday as a special day for the same reasons as did the Mithras worshippers. Of even greater consequence is the passage in Tertullian, *Nat.* I.13, 'It is you who have taken the sun also into the seven-day calendar and out of the seven days have chosen the day preceding the day of the sun as that on which you omit to have a bath or postpone it until the evening. . . .' The reference here is to the observance of Saturn's day. If a pagan Sunday observance had existed, Tertullian would definitely have alluded to it, since he is anxious to discover among non-Christians observances similar to that of Sunday, and, in fact, he is able to point only to Saturn's day.

[3] See pp. 193ff., 215ff. below.

[4] So even F. Cumont (p. 35, n. 4), I, p. 339, n. 5; cf. W. Baudissin, 'Sonne, bei den Hebräern', *RE*³ 18, p. 520.

[5] S. V. McCasland, 'The Origin of the Lord's Day', *JBL* 49, 1930, p. 80.

[6] F. H. Colson (p. 26, n. 3), p. 107.

[7] Cf. also Schneider, *Geistesgeschichte des antiken Christentums* II, 1954, p. 218.

mention of the sun-god Mithras proves the existence not only of the Mithras cult but also at the same time of the Mithraic observance of Sunday.[1]

As soon as the Christian liturgical observance came to be on the day consecrated to the sun,[2] the Church naturally took advantage of its opportunity. It was at pains to point out the inner affinity of its worship on Sunday with the sun's day, and it did this by means of a rich symbolism which had the effect of contrasting Christ, the true sun, with other solar deities.[3] This effort on the part of the Church did, however, have the reverse effect in that it helped to make it possible for Christians to be mistaken for sun worshippers.[4]

3. THE CHRISTIAN WEEK

The seven-day week in use today is a mixture of the Jewish week and of the planetary week; this mixture has developed in the area of the Christian Church.

(a) It is obvious that our week has borrowed from the planetary week. Today the individual days of the week still

[1] S. V. McCasland (p. 37, n. 5), pp. 76ff. We shall have to devote further discussion (see p. 41f., n. 8, below) to the principal reason for the assumption of F. H. Colson (p. 26, n. 3), pp. 105ff., that the sun-cult influenced Christianity. He holds that in predominantly Gentile-Christian congregations the Jewish seven-day week would not have held its own if the planetary week had not come to its help.

[2] We might even be tempted to believe that the position of Sunday as the second day in the planetary week (like the coincidence of the sabbath and Saturn's day) was not a matter of chance, but was connected with the Christian worship which took place on Sunday. This conclusion can hardly be correct, since Christian worship on Sunday had even less similarity with sun-worship than had Jewish sabbath observance with Saturn worship. Research should, however, some time be undertaken into the question whether the Mithraic observance of Sunday (in so far as there was any) was influenced by the Christian observance of Sunday.

[3] See pp. 285ff. below.

[4] Tertullian, *Nat.* I.13, says, 'Others . . . think that the sun is the Christian god, because it is well known that we pray towards the rising sun, or because we give ourselves over to rejoicing on the day of the sun.' Cf. *Apol.* 16.9–11 and pp. 289f. below. The situation was, therefore, in some sense parallel to that which characterized the relationship between the sabbath and Saturn's day. Like the Jews, Christians used to their own advantage pagan ideas which seemed to lend support to their practices and views, but this resulted in people outside the Church mistaking the symbol for the reality, and for this reason they came to believe that Christian practices and beliefs were pagan in origin.

bear the names of the seven planetary deities or of their Nordic equivalents.

The original *dies solis* became Sunday (German *Sonntag*);[1] *dies lunae* (Italian *lunedi*; French *lundi*) became Monday (German *Mon(d)tag*); *dies Martis* (Italian *martedi*; French *mardi*) received its name from the god Thingus or Tyr/Ziu, and from this came Tuesday (German *Dienstag*); *dies Mercurii* (Italian *mercoledi*; French *mercredi*) was put under the protection of Wotan—cf. Wednesday (the German *Mittwoch* is a new formation); similarly Thursday (German *Donnerstag*) is derived from the god Donar or Thor, a translation of the Latin *dies Jovis* (Italian *giovedi*; French *jeudi*); and Friday (German *Freitag*) is the day of the goddess Fr(e)ia, the nordic Venus (*dies Veneris* gives us Italian *venerdi* and French *vendredi*). *Dies Saturni* became Saturday in English.[2]

(*b*) In the names for Saturn's day to be found in the German and romance languages, however, we find *Jewish* influence at work. The Italian *sabato* has clearly adopted the word sabbath, and the French *samedi* and German *Samstag* (from the late Greek *sam(n)baton?*)[3] have probably done so. In general the basic structure of the Christian week corresponds to that of the Jewish week. The assimilation to the planetary week was a secondary development. This fact is substantiated by historical investigation. (1) The early Christian Church first of all called the days of the week and the week as a whole by exactly the same names as was customary in contemporary Judaism. The last day of the week was called sabbath,[4] Friday was the day of preparation or eve of the sabbath, and the other weekdays were simply numbered first, second, third day, etc.[5] This cannot surprise us if we reflect that Christianity emerged from Judaism and that the planetary week did not, in fact, exist at

---

[1] See p. 213 below for further discussion about the names for Sunday in the romance languages.

[2] On this whole subject see J. Grimm, *Deutsche Mythologie* I, 1875⁴, pp. 101ff.; F. H. Colson (p. 26, n. 3), pp. 108ff.

[3] Also see p. 136, n. 5, below.

[4] This is true not only in discussions concerning the Jewish sabbath, but also in purely Christian linguistic usage; cf., perhaps, Acts of Peter 15f., 18. The designation of Saturday as 'sabbath' on the part of Christians does not imply that the Christians observed the sabbath, as is concluded by C. W. Dugmore, *The Influence of the Synagogue upon the Divine Office*, 1944, pp. 30f.

[5] E.g. *Did.* 8.1. Copious material in Schürer (p. 25, n. 4), pp. 8ff. For the situation with regard to Mohammedans, and to Christians in Abyssinia and Iran, see T. Nöldeke, 'Die Namen der Wochentage bei den Semiten', *ZDWF* I, 1901, p. 162.

that time. (2) Like the Jewish week, the Christian week began on Sunday and ended on the sabbath.[1] This order was preserved by the Church with great tenacity even when the Jewish names for the days of the week were in process of being replaced by the new pagan planetary names.[2]

About 150 AD Justin Martyr in his *First Apology* to the Emperor Antoninus Pius is the first Christian author to speak of the Kronos day and of the Helios day, by which he means Saturday and Sunday.[3] In the Latin linguistic area the names *dies solis* and *dies Saturni* for Sunday and Saturday respectively are first used by Tertullian in the passages in his *Apology*[4] and *Ad Nationes*[5] which we have already mentioned.[6] It is precisely here that the adherence

---

[1] This is true even today. The week does not begin with Monday: it is often assumed that it does, presumably on the supposition that Sunday is the Christian sabbath and so the seventh day of the week. J. A. Jungmann, 'Beginnt die christliche Woche mit Sonntag?' *ZKT* 55, 1931, pp. 605–21, has indeed argued (but not convincingly) for Monday as the beginning of the Christian week. In particular, the designation of Sunday as the 'eighth day' in the early Church, which Jungmann adduces in support of his contention that the week ends with Sunday, presupposes that Sunday nevertheless remains the first day of the week (see p. 278, n. 1, below): there is, indeed, no proper 'eighth day' in a week of seven days. We can see this with regard to the octave, to which Jungmann also refers. The Sunday of the Easter octave, for instance, is indeed the concluding day of Easter week, but at the same time the opening day of a new week.

[2] Since the beginning of the fourth century (i.e. since the time of the widest spread of the sun cult in the Roman empire and, equally, the time of mass conversions of pagans to Christianity) the planetary names also came into general use in everyday Christian speech, although the Church has always officially retained the Jewish designations; cf. E. Schürer (p. 25, n. 4), p. 53. It almost seems as if to an increasing extent astrology had been imported into the Christian Church together with the planetary week. The proof that astrology turned out to be a powerful influence in the Christian Church is to be found in the numerous anti-astrological treatises written at that time by Church fathers who were largely directing their attack on a superstition which was spreading among *Christians*; cf. E. Schürer (p. 25, n. 4), pp. 49f.; W. Gundel, 'Astrologie', *RAC* I, pp. 817ff.

[3] I *Apol.* 67.3, 7.

[4] *Apol.* 16.9–11.

[5] *Nat.* I.13.

[6] It must be evident that the planetary names first appear in Christian literature in apologies directed to pagan readers. This shows that Christians were not accustomed to calling the days of the week by these names, but only did so in order to be better understood by pagans. Justin, at all events, seems to have been only moderately familiar with the designation 'Kronos day'; he refers to Sunday as the 'so-called' Helios day (ἡ τοῦ ἡλίου λεγομένη ἡμέρα); possibly he did not know the planetary name for Friday, for he calls it merely 'the day before the Kronos day'. The fact that the Kronos day was clearly the planetary name in widest use agrees very well with our remarks on pp. 28ff. about the origin of the planetary week.

of the Christian Church to the Jewish week becomes particularly noticeable, for in Christian sources the week obviously began with Sunday,[1] while the planetary week always began with Saturn's day.[2] So whenever in our sources we come across a week with its days named after the planets, but *beginning* on the Sunday, this is a clear indication of Christian influence at work.[3] The Christian Church quite naturally continued to count the weekdays in Jewish fashion even when it named the individual days after the planets.

We have still to discuss a question touched on by E. Schürer in his study which we have already mentioned several times, 'Die siebentägige Woche im Gebrauch der christlichen Kirche der ersten Jahrhunderte'.[4] It is not at all strange, according to Schürer, that the Jewish week was retained by the Christian Church in Palestine and in all other areas where Jewish influence was preponderant. But what is strange, Schürer maintains, is the fact that the Jewish week was used from the outset in the Gentile Christian churches of Asia Minor and Greece.[5] This leads Schürer to conclude that Paul *introduced* the seven-day week among Gentile Christians.[6] On the other hand we come across passages in Paul's letters which display a marked hostility towards the Jewish sabbath on the part of the apostle.[7] Is this not a contradiction?, asks Schürer. The sabbath was the veritable backbone of the Jewish week: if Paul let the sabbath go, what interest could he have in maintaining the Jewish week? Schürer refrains from suggesting any solution to the problem.[8] In discussing this question it will perhaps help us to notice that

---

[1] This becomes apparent in a later passage in ch. 67 of Justin's *First Apology*.

[2] See pp. 33f. above.

[3] Some references in E. Schürer (p. 25, n. 4), pp. 23, 25, 32.

[4] *ZNW* 6, 1905, pp. 41ff.

[5] He cites I Cor. 16.2 and Acts 20.7; these passages receive detailed discussion on pp. 193ff. below.

[6] This is an overstatement. Schürer himself admits that the first Gentile-Christian churches were partly composed of former Jews, Jewish proselytes and 'God-fearers', who naturally needed no 'introduction' to the Jewish week. All that happened was that those Christians who were, properly speaking, Gentiles adopted the Jewish week because they themselves had not previously been acquainted with any division of the week. (The planetary week was at this time not yet generally observed; see also n. 8 below.)

[7] Gal. 4.9–11; Col. 2.16f. See also pp. 130ff., 135f. below.

[8] F. H. Colson (p. 26, n. 3), p. 107, suggests a solution (cf. p. 38, n. 1). He holds that the planetary week had already been adopted and had taken the place of the Jewish week. We must, however, put to him another question:

in the earliest passages where the use of the Jewish week in Gentile Christian circles is attested, the Christian Sunday is called 'the first day of the week'.[1] Had Sunday perhaps so soon become the backbone of the *Christian* week that the regular rotation of seven days managed to continue or even had to continue without the sabbath? Sunday was, in fact, the only day of the week which was given its own name within the Christian Church: very early it was known as 'the Lord's day'.[2]

But we are anticipating matters. We shall first of all have to concern ourselves with the problem how the Gentile Christian Church came to give up the Jewish sabbath at the very same time as it was so tenaciously observing the Jewish week. With this problem we come to the first major part of our study.

Why, then, does Paul in I Cor. 16.2 speak not of the 'Sunday' of the planetary week, but of the 'first day' of the Jewish week, even though in this passage he certainly wishes to be understood not only by Jewish Christians but also by Gentile Christians?

[1] Apart from I Cor. 16.2 and Acts 20.7 the Easter narratives belong here: Mark 16.2; Matt. 28.1; Luke 24.1; John 20.1, 19; the gospels—at any rate Mark, Luke and John—were also (at least principally) intended for Gentile Christian readers.

[2] Rev. 1.10. See pp. 205ff. below.

PART ONE

THE DAY OF REST

The first major part of this study is principally concerned with the sabbath, the day of rest, which the
early Church found already in existence and with
which it had to come to terms. The sabbath question
did in fact have its own history in primitive Christianity, and we shall have enough material to fill several
chapters. No less important will be the investigation
of the question how Sunday, the newly created
Christian day of worship, became the day of rest.

If in the following pages we treat the sabbath
problem as a whole without distinguishing between
the two functions of the sabbath (day of rest and day
of worship), it is only because we do not wish to
divide up the material even further: clarity of presentation would suffer as a result. It will also be
apparent that for the first Christians the sabbath
problem was essentially whether or not they still felt
themselves bound by the Old Testament commandment to mark the sabbath by *rest*. We shall see in the
second major part that Sunday had very early taken
over the function of the day of worship.

II

THE SABBATH PROBLEM

I. THE SABBATH IN JUDAISM

IN post-exilic Judaism the sabbath and with it the seven-day week had acquired unique importance far exceeding the importance of the pre-exilic day of rest. Not only was rest from work very strictly enforced on this day[1] (whereas earlier practice in this respect had been fairly flexible),[2] but the observance of the sabbath was established on a quite different and much broader foundation. In pre-exilic times the sabbath had been primarily important as a social institution, the observance of which was indeed required by the covenant God, the advocate of all the underprivileged and of social outcasts. Now the sabbath became an article of faith, the direct concern of theology, integrally associated with the election of Israel. The new motivation for the sabbath and for the commandment about its observance was principally the work of the priestly leaders who after the fall of the Israelite royal house assumed the leadership of Judaism in this formative period.

It must of course be admitted that there are some lines of development which lead from pre-exilic to post-exilic times and that the priestly motivation for the sabbath is not an entirely new creation. We should, however, misunderstand the character of the priestly work if we were to deny that there are present in it essentially new points of view which had not been present in this form within the framework of the pre-exilic theology. On the other hand, we should be equally wide of the mark if we were to look for the origins of the fresh features merely in the Babylonian environment or if we were to see in the increased strictness of post-exilic sabbath observance the direct or indirect influence of the superstitious scrupulosity with which

---

[1] See pp. 51ff. below.
[2] For example, a journey was undertaken on a sabbath to a man of God (II Kings 4.23). Also the tyrant Athaliah was overthrown and murdered on a sabbath (II Kings 11).

Babylonian taboo days were observed:[1] there is no trace of such influence. Yet if it is asserted that the sabbath acquired such great importance in exilic and post-exilic Judaism merely because the Jews knew themselves to be taken out of their own environment, this explanation does not reach the heart of the matter. The priestly view of the sabbath provides different and deeper reasons for this development (see the following pages). Furthermore, the observance of the sabbath was much stricter in Palestine than in the Diaspora, and this fact is not easily reconciled with this point of view.

In the following pages we shall briefly discuss the priestly motivation for the sabbath commandment which had such deep influence on the whole post-exilic sabbath theology and sabbath observance. It is, however, most important to notice that this motivation has two elements which stand in a peculiar tension to one another, but which nevertheless also influence one another. In the first place we can talk of a universalist element and, secondly, of a particularist element in the priestly motivation of the sabbath commandment.

(i) *The sabbath as a commemoration of creation and salvation*

We are well acquainted with the reference to Gen. 1–2 in the version of the decalogue in Ex. 20.11.[2] Here the observance of the sabbath is enjoined because God instituted the sabbath in connection with his work of creation. This point of view is not to be found in pre-exilic theology, and it opened up a vast new perspective. The Jewish sabbath and the seven-day week were now no fortuitous arrangements found only in Israel, but they had their origin in the work of creation itself; the universe as a whole was established on this rhythm. The seven-day week and its day of rest were, therefore, inviolable ordinances valid for all time and all people so long as the world should last.[3]

The universalist tendency which is to be seen here has been turned to good effect by Judaism in the Dispersion, as we should expect.[4] The sabbath

---

[1] Cf. A. Clamer, *Lévitique*, 1946, p. 131; N. H. Tur-Sinai (Torczyner), 'Sabbat und Woche', *Bibliotheca Orientalis* 8, 1951, p. 15; R. North, 'The Derivation of the Sabbath', *Biblica* 36, 1955, p. 192.

[2] Also in Ex. 31.17b, which may be the primary source; cf. E. Jenni, *Die theologische Begründung des Sabbatgebotes im Alten Testament* (TS 46), 1956, p. 20.

[3] According to Isa. 66.23, the sabbath would remain in force even after the creation of the new heaven and the new earth.

[4] On the following see also E. Lohse, *TWNT* VII, pp. 10f., and A.-M. Dubarle, 'La signification religieuse du sabbat dans la Bible', *Le dimanche: Lex orandi* 39, 1965, pp. 43–60.

depended on a pattern of creation dominated by the number seven; this number was also extolled by Greek mathematicians and poets as a motherless, unbegotten[1] number, the very image of the Logos (Aristobulus in Eusebius, *Praep. evang.* XIII. 12.9–16; Philo, *Opif. mundi* 89–127; *Leg. spec.* II. 56–59; *Leg. alleg.* I. 9–15; *Decal.* 102–105;[2] also Clement Alex., *Strom.* V. 14.107, whose evidence from the poets is partly unreliable,[3] as is that of Aristobulus).

Moses now appeared as 'the lover of virtue who inscribed the beauty (of the number seven) on the most holy tables of the Law, and impressed it on the minds of all who were set under him, by bidding them at intervals of six days to keep a seventh day holy . . .' (Philo, *Opif. mundi* 128). The sabbath was thought of as the 'festival . . . of the universe, and it alone strictly deserves to be called "public", as belonging to all people and the birthday of the world' (Philo, *ib.* 89).[4]

It is also interesting to note how the idea of the sabbath rest was transformed and spiritualized in the Jewish Diaspora, even though the Diaspora adhered to the literal observance of the sabbath commandment quite as strictly as did Palestinian Judaism.[5] The true sabbath rest was thought of as the 'effortless activity' of the philosophical spirit (Philo, *Cherub.* 87) which God perfectly enjoys. Only in this way can Philo interpret the anthropomorphic expression in Gen. 2. 2–3, that God rested, since God never ceases to be active (*Leg. alleg.* I. 5f.).[6] We shall see that Christianity has taken over this spiritualizing interpretation of the sabbath rest, and on the basis of this interpretation it has criticized the literal observance of the sabbath commandment.[7] In view of this new understanding of the proper meaning of the sabbath rest it is not accidental that in Diaspora Judaism

---

[1] Inasmuch as it resembles the number one; cf. Philo, *Quod deus sit immut.* 3.10ff.; *Poster. Caini* 18.64f. See also L. Troje, 'Sanbat', in R. Reitzenstein, *Die Vorgeschichte der christlichen Taufe*, 1929, pp. 328–77.

[2] Cf. K. Staehle, *Die Zahlenmystik bei Philon von Alexandreia*, 1931.

[3] W. Bousset and H. Gressmann, *Die Religion des Judentums im späthellenistischen Zeitalter*, 1926, p. 28, n. 1.

[4] We have, moreover, seen (p. 25, n. 4) that in Hellenism, under the influence of astronomy, the notion of the seven heavens also developed, and this was not without its influence on Alexandrian Judaism.

[5] See p. 53 below.

[6] Cf. C. K. Barrett, *The New Testament Background*, 1956, pp. 173ff. By contrast, there are also statements like Jubilees 2.18, where even God keeps the sabbath.

[7] On John 5.17 see pp. 83f. below. Judaism never went so far as this fundamental criticism, but it sought to reconcile the idea of God's uninterrupted activity with the obligation of men to observe the sabbath rest: Aristobulus (in Eusebius, *Praep. evang.* XIII.12.11; Clement Alex., *Strom.* VI.16.141.7–142.1). A favourite solution of the problem was to distinguish God's activity as creator from his activity as judge; cf. C. H. Dodd, *The Interpretation of the Fourth Gospel*, 1953, pp. 322f.

we first find the day on which no work was permitted being occupied with the study of the Torah and philosophy.[1]

Closely associated with the priestly writers' idea of the seven-day week of creation is the notion that the whole time process corresponds to a 'world week' of six epochs of 1,000 years each, after which there would come the 'world which is entirely sabbath'.[2] This notion is certainly not scriptural; it first appears in late Jewish apocalyptic, where it seems, moreover, to have supplanted older speculations about the generations of the universe.[3] Since Iranian religion knew several ages in the history of the world, we may assume that late Jewish teaching about a succession of generations received its stimulus from that direction.[4] In Jewish thought such notions were easily combined with the story of creation recounted in Gen. 1–2. When, for instance, we read in Ps. 90.4 that in the sight of God a thousand years are like a single day,[5] we can see in the account of creation in seven days an image of the whole temporal process of the universe: as God has created the world in seven days, so he will bring the history of the universe to fulfilment in exactly the same number of millennia. Thus as a consequence of the teaching of the priestly tradition which saw the prototype of the sabbath in the work of creation, the sabbath came to be the object of eschatological expectation.[6] It is difficult, however,

[1] See p. 54, n. 2.

[2] Cf. SB III.687; IV.2, pp. 839f. The same idea is to be found in Samaritan eschatology: P. Volz, *Die Eschatologie der jüdischen Gemeinde*, 1934[2], p. 62.

[3] There were speculations about the successive generations of the universe which were constructed on the number 70 (Dan. 9.24ff.; Enoch 89.59ff.), on the number 12 (IV Ezra 14.11), on the number 10 (Enoch 93.91) or on the number 4 (Syriac Baruch 39; Dan. 2). Cf. H. Gressmann, *Der Ursprung der israelitisch-jüdischen Eschatologie* (FRLANT 5), 1905, pp. 165f.

[4] Cf. M. Cumont, 'La fin du monde chez les mages occidentaux', *RHR* 103, 1931, pp. 46ff.; H. Wikenhauser, 'Weltwoche und 1000-jähriges Reich', *Tübinger Theologische Quartalsschrift* 127, 1907, pp. 399ff.; J. Daniélou, 'La typologie millénariste de la semaine dans le christianisme primitif', *Vigiliae christianae* 2, 1948, pp. 1–16; H. Bietenhard, *Das tausendjährige Reich*, 1955, pp. 48ff.

[5] Ps. 90.4 was first used in Jubilees 4.30; in Christian literature in II Peter 3.8.

[6] The Alexandrian interpretation of the statement in Gen. 2 that God already rests could well favour the eschatological interpretation. H. Riesenfeld, *Jesus transfiguré*, 1947, pp. 206ff., assumes that the idea of the eschatological rest is to be derived from the rest in booths at the autumnal festival, but this can hardly have been the original source of the idea: later it was

to be precise about the content of this expectation, for the evidence is partly contradictory.

1. In the overwhelming majority of passages the sabbath of the end time was thought to be paradise restored; it would consist in a superabundance of all earthly goods, in deliverance from disease, death and injustice, and it would never pass away. The circumstances of this ideal state of affairs were so depicted that Israel naturally occupied a pre-eminent position among the nations.[1] In the description of paradise certain stereotyped traits also repeatedly recur, e.g. the brightness of the stars which were supposed to become many times their normal brightness,[2] long expectation of life, boundless fertility of the land, peaceableness on the part of man and beast, etc.[3]

2. According to other views, however, the sabbath of the end time would be an empty time which would follow the days of the Messiah and precede the new age; it would resemble the deep silence of the universe's origin when the earth lay void and waste.[4]

This diversity of expectation can be traced back to the course of Jewish eschatology. In the first view the effect of earlier prophetic teaching can be discerned; this world order is viewed optimistically, and the Messiah will once and for all eliminate from the human race and the natural order all the ravages caused by sin. The second view is influenced by apocalyptic teaching with emphasis on the other world; this world order is viewed with despair, and an entirely new order is expected. Two different eschatological conceptions stand here side by side: one sees the consummation in the earthly days of the Messiah, while the other sees in them only a preliminary stage which belongs to the present aeon and which is to be sharply contrasted with the new creation.

---

certainly a contributory factor; cf. J. Daniélou, 'La fête des Tabernacles', *Studia Patristica* I (TU 63), 1957, pp. 262–79.

[1] Cf. as early as Isa. 2.2–5; 25.6ff.; 60–61 and *passim*; Assumption of Moses 10.1; Test. Dan. 5; Enoch 107.1; Syriac Baruch 73f.; Sib. Or. III. 367–80, 652–60, 767–95; V.281–3. See also SB IV.2, pp. 799–976; esp. pp. 88off.

[2] Isa. 30.26: 'the light of the sun will be sevenfold.' See also p. 291 below.

[3] Descriptions of the golden age have their origin in such ideas, which do, however, more pessimistically place the golden age at the beginning: Hesiod, *Works and Days* 109–23; Horace, *Epode* 16; Vergil, *Eclogue* 4 (moreover, the Mithraic planetary sequence seems to lie behind his progression). Cf. Lactantius, *Div. inst.* VII.14f., 24 (CSEL 19.1. 629ff., 658ff.), who quotes the Greek and Roman authors. On the whole subject see A. Kurfess, 'Aetas aurea', *RAC* I, col. 144–50.

[4] IV Ezra 7.27–31; b. Sanh. 97a divides the 6,000 years of this age (i.e. before the sabbath of the world) into 2,000 years of time without the Torah, 2,000 years of Torah-time and 2,000 years of messianic time; SB III.826; IV.2.989ff.

3. There are, of course, also hybrid forms in which the interim period of the Messiah without losing its essential character of an interim period does, nevertheless, already bear the marks of an anticipation of the eternal consummation.[1] In this case we can speak of chiliastic expectations, although the duration of the interim kingdom does not always need to be more precisely determined.[2]

To help with easier understanding of the material we shall provide a table with the three variants of the eschatological time scheme:

Present World		Future World
1. First to Sixth Millennia		Sabbath = Paradise Days of the Messiah
2. First to Sixth Millennia Days of the Messiah	Sabbath = Primeval Silence	New Aeon
3. First to Sixth Millennia	Sabbath = Chiliasm Days of the Messiah	New Aeon

We shall see[3] that this scheme was adopted by Christian eschatology and reinterpreted in the light of Christ. The first and third elements were especially important for Christians.[4] Chiliasm in particular enjoyed great popularity: in the chiliastic framework Sunday, the eighth day, the day following the sabbath could not help appearing as a symbol of the coming aeon and of the consummation at the end, whereas the sabbath

[1] On IV Ezra 7.28, H. Gunkel, in E. Kautsch, *Die Apokryphen und Pseudepigraphen des Alten Testaments*, 1900, II, p. 370, n. h, writes, 'The dogma of chiliasm is a compromise between the old this-wordly hope of the prophet and the transcendental hope of more recent Judaism, and the emphasis falls on the latter.' See Syr. Bar. 29f.; Sib. Or. III, 652–731. Cf. SB IV.2. 808f.

[2] The rabbis developed yet another doctrine: the 'rest' signifies the place of departed souls; SB IV.2.819ff.; cf. the idea of Sheol: SB IV.2.1016ff.; also in the NT, Rev. 14.13.

[3] See pp. 88ff. below.

[4] The second variant is possibly represented by the Fourth Gospel in an idiosyncratic foreshortening; see pp. 98f. below.

by contrast foreshadowed only the stage before the consummation, namely the thousand-year kingdom.[1] Naturally the inner
tensions between these eschatological views could not remain
hidden. The Church in general decided against chiliasm either
on the lines of the first variant (the sabbath was a symbol of the
eternal world of the future) or in such a way that the promised
sabbath was held to have already dawned in the era of the
Church.[2]

(ii) The sabbath as a characteristic of Israel

Hitherto we have discussed only one half of the priestly
tradition about the sabbath and we have noticed the over-
arching sweep of this sabbath theology which embraced both
creation and the end of the ages. The seven-day week and its
linchpin, the sabbath, encompassed and permeated both the
cosmic realm and the divine plan of salvation as their common
principle of order. But over against this universalist view was a
particularist outlook: to Israel alone among the nations was
given a sabbath to be observed week by week. God had bestowed
on Israel a mark of unique distinction in giving to the Jews the
sabbath and the seven-day week which had supreme importance
as the principle of order in the cosmic realm and in the divine
plan of salvation. For this reason Israel could think of the
sabbath in no other terms than as God's most precious gift: the
sabbath became for Israel, in fact, the sign of God's covenant
loyalty.[3] This great gift did, however, bring with it a great
responsibility. Israel had to be on the alert to ensure that the
treasure committed to her charge was not dishonoured and that

---

[1] See pp. 282ff. below. The idea of the 'eighth day' played scarcely any
part in Judaism at that time. Slavonic Enoch 33.1f. seems to be a Christian
interpolation (cf. J. Daniélou [p. 48, n. 4], p. 3, and p. 94 below). It was,
therefore, in the Christian sphere that this idea was first fully developed. We
shall also see (see pp. 275ff. below) that Sunday was already called the 'eighth
day' before the eschatological time-table was associated with this title.

[2] Thus Tyconius/Augustine and, following them, Roman Catholic
exegesis. This view has its roots in the very earliest years of the Christian
Church. See pp. 108ff. below.

[3] Ex. 31.13, 17a; Ezek. 20.12, 20; Jubilees 2.17ff. C. A. Keller, Das Wort
Oth als Offenbarungszeichen Gottes, 1946, p. 145, is right in saying that the
word oth is almost synonymous here with 'sacrament'. The sabbath could,
in fact, be described as the 'bride of Israel' and as 'queen': b. Shab. 119a;
cf. F. M. Nielen, Das Zeichen des Herrn, 1940, p. 24.

every Jew strictly observed his sabbath obligation. It is from this background that we can explain both the relentless severity with which the death penalty was threatened on the sabbath-breaker[1] and also the magnitude of the reward which was promised to the loyal sabbath-keeper.[2]

The priestly legislation with its strict command derived from its sabbath theology, 'You shall keep my sabbaths, for they are a perpetual obligation',[3] was an indirect cause of all the later sabbath casuistry, and Judaism never found her way out of its labyrinthine complications.[4] It cannot be denied that there was among devout observers of the law much goodwill and genuine enthusiasm to keep the sabbath strictly.[5] On the other hand, however, the distinction bestowed on Israel by the sabbath commandment was very great and the practical directions for its fulfilment to be found in the biblical tradition were also very meagre:[6] this meant that the sabbath commandment necessarily became a burden for the Jews and drove them to interpret the law in a way which could be fulfilled or, if need be, evaded by means of fresh definitions.

---

[1] Ex. 31.14f.; 35.2; Ezek. 20.11f.; Num. 15.32–36; Jubilees 2.25, 27; 50.8, 13. The Damascus Document (XII.3–6) did indeed forbid the slaying of the violator of the sabbath, and the rabbis merely said, 'May God punish him'; SB II.195. This illustrates the whole development of the interpretation of the law: especially with the Pharisees, it came to assume a markedly milder form.

[2] Isa. 56.1–8; 58.13f.; Jer. 17.24–26; Jubilees 2.28. Loyalty in the fulfilment of the sabbath commandment would bring deliverance from eschatological tribulations and would procure for Israel the country, the coming new age, the kingdom of David, the priestly and the levitical orders; Mekhilta Ex. 16.25ff. If Israel could really keep two sabbaths, the day of deliverance would dawn; b. Shab. 118b.

[3] Ex. 31.13, 16; Lev. 19.3, 30; 26.2; Ezek. 44.24 and passim.

[4] E. Lohse, TWNT VII, pp. 8–15, has collected the various regulations and considered their development, together with the relevant literature.

[5] Evidence of this is provided by the Jews, who in time of war let themselves be massacred on the sabbath. See p. 28, n. 3, above.

[6] In the law and the prophets there were to be found very few precise regulations concerning the right observance of the sabbath: Ex. 16.23–30 (prohibition of boiling and baking and of going outside); Num. 15.32–36 (prohibition of gathering wood); Ex. 35.1–3 (prohibition of lighting a fire); Ex. 34.21 (prohibition of ploughing and harvesting); Jer. 17.21f. (prohibition of carrying burdens). Almost the whole of the Jews' sabbath practice was based and is still based on the Mishnah tractate Shabbat and on its interpretation: this tractate in its turn is derived from the halakah, the oral tradition of the law.

Sabbath practice was very rigorous[1] both in the case of the Essene sects (including Qumran), whose members regarded themselves as the remnant of Israel, and also among the Sadducees, who reacted against the lenience of the Pharisees' casuistry. The literal observance of the sabbath commandment was, of course, never questioned in the very slightest degree among the Jews of the Diaspora (cf. Philo, *Vita Mosis* II. 21f.). Nevertheless the question has to be asked whether the whole population really did take part in the rigorous observance of the sabbath. Was it not observed principally by people zealous for the law who had separated themselves from the general run of the population, Essenes, Sadducees, Pharisees[2], i.e. people who wished to appear as the true Israel of God? In Palestine, however, there were the '*am-ha'arez* who were less particular about the observance of the law.[3] The 'righteous' kept themselves vehemently apart from these people who were so ignorant of the law. It is interesting to note where Jesus stood in this controversy: clearly on the side of those ignorant of the law. He was rejected among devout law-keepers, but he was heard gladly by the simple people, the sinners.[4] This sheds a sidelight on the attitude of Jesus to the law which we shall approach from the angle of 'Jesus and the sabbath'.

At the end of this chapter it must be added that since the exile (and partly even beforehand)[5] *worship* had formed an essential part of the image of the sabbath. Particularly rich

[1] Cf. E. Lohse (p. 52, n. 4), pp. 9f.; H. Braun, *Spätjüdisch-häretischer und frühchristlicher Radikalismus* (Beiträge zur hist. Theol. 24.1), 1957, pp. 117–20; H. Bietenhard, 'Die Sabbatvorschriften von Qumran im Lichte des rabbinischen Rechts und der Evangelien', in *Qumran-Probleme*, ed. by H. Bardtke, 1963, pp. 53–74. This led E. Stauffer, *Die Botschaft Jesu damals und heute*, 1959, p. 14, to conclude that Jesus, for this reason, could not have had anything to do with Qumran.

[2] The Hebrew name *perūšim* meant the 'separated ones'. According to T. W. Manson, 'Sadducee and Pharisee: The Origin and Significance of the Names', *BJRL* 22, 1938, pp. 3–18, the Aramaic root of the word means 'the Persians'.

[3] The differences were much less considerable in the Diaspora, where every single Jew stood in an exposed situation.

[4] Nevertheless there is no point in reconsidering the theories which used to be advanced that Jesus came from that group of Galilaeans which sat fairly loosely to the law (W. Bauer, 'Jesus der Galiläer', *Jülicher-Festschrift*, 1927, pp. 16–34; against this view see A. Alt, 'Galiläische Probleme', *Palästina-Jahrbuch*, 1939) or had originated from the group of the Anawim (W. Sattler, 'Die Anawim im Zeitalter Jesu Christi', *Jülicher-Festschrift*, 1927, pp. 1–15): these theories are to be completely abandoned. See the criticism of E. Goppelt, *Christentum und Judentum im ersten und zweiten Jahrhundert*, 1954, pp. 32ff., who holds that Jesus did not belong to any particular trend in Judaism.

[5] See p. 18, n. 2, above.

sacrifices were offered in the temple (Num. 28.3f.; Ezek. 46.4f.) and the shewbread was freshly laid up (Lev. 24.5–9). At home the head of the family said special graces and blessings at the beginning of the sabbath on the Friday evening (*kiddush*) and at the end of the sabbath on the Saturday evening (*habdalah*).[1] Of decisive importance was the synagogue worship on the sabbath (morning and afternoon); this practice may well have originated in the Jewish Diaspora.[2] In these 'houses of instruction and prayer' the *shema* and *tephillah* were recited by the congregation, and there were also readings from the law and the prophets and (possibly) an exposition of the readings.[3] The joyous character which the sabbath had and still has for the Jews can be traced back to the distinctive mark of worship rather than to the meticulous observance of the commandment to rest.[4] In our second major section we shall have to inquire whether Christian worship on Sunday is to be considered the liturgical heir of worship on the sabbath day.

2. THE ATTITUDE OF JESUS TO THE SABBATH

Nowadays we can once again venture to talk of the historical Jesus without being decried as unscientific. This is a recent development and it is evidence of the considerable revolution which has taken place within the world of German Protestant research into the New Testament.[5] Until recently it was taken

---

[1] On the prayers in detail see J. Elbogen, *Der jüdische Gottesdienst in seiner geschichtlichen Entwicklung*, 1924², pp. 107ff., 120ff., 236f.; H. Lietzmann, *Mass and Lord's Supper*, ET, 1954ff., pp. 165f.; E. Lohse (p. 52, n. 4), p. 16. It is repeatedly claimed that the prayers of the *kiddush* and *habdalah* are prefigurations of Christian eucharistic prayers. But one can, in fact, say no more than that the Jewish custom of saying a prayer of thanksgiving at meals was taken over by Jesus and the disciples, but not necessarily in the particular forms of the *kiddush* and *habdalah*. See pp. 241f. below.

[2] M. Friedländer, *Synagoge und Kirche in ihren Anfängen*, 1908, pp. 54–56. Josephus, *C. Apion.* II.17.175, traces the establishment of the synagogue back to Moses; this shows that people were convinced of its great antiquity. According to J. Wellhausen, *Israelitische und jüdische Geschichte*, 1901⁴, pp. 196f., and E. Schürer, *A History of the Jewish People in the Time of Jesus Christ* ET 1885 ff., II.ii, pp. 52ff. (§ 27.2), it derives from the Babylonian exile.

[3] Cf. SB IV.1.153–88; E. Lohse (p. 52, n. 4), pp. 15f.

[4] The Jews' custom of eating well on the sabbath (SB I.611ff.) has certainly also contributed to the intensification of the festal joy.

[5] The dawn of the new era was marked by the essay of E. Käsemann, 'The Problem of the Historical Jesus' reprinted in *Essays on New Testament*

for granted that our Gospel tradition was principally the construction of the early Church and was moulded by the post-resurrection faith of the early Christians. The earthly Jesus was certainly assumed to be behind this tradition: it seemed, however, a hopeless task to try to recover the true picture of the human Jesus and of his life and teaching from the message of the primitive Church, for this message was itself so deeply influenced by the early kerygma and testified to belief in the risen Lord.

Naturally we should not abandon the insight of form criticism that our Gospels are not biographies, but proclamation. This insight marked a great step forward by comparison with the 'quest of the Jesus of history' which was characteristic of the past century. That quest had indulged in historicism and spurious psychology and so it had failed to do justice to the message of Jesus. A reaction has, however, now set in against the altogether disproportionate emphasis which since the twenties has been placed on the kerygma of the primitive Church in its various developments and versions. The part which belonged to the historical Jesus (or did not belong to him) in the formation of this kerygma has been completely disregarded.[1] Now the attempt is being made to get back behind the division or break, which the first Easter has hitherto been held to mark,[2] and to show the threads connecting the earthly Jesus with the primitive Church. This attempt is being made because scholars have rightly become aware that there was a danger of treating Jesus docetically and of replacing him by a mere cipher.

This new view assumes that the words and deeds of Jesus

Themes ET, (SBT 41), 1964, pp. 15–47. It must, in any case, be emphasized that even within the New Testament scholarship of German-speaking Protestants—to make no mention of French, Anglo-Saxon and, especially, Catholic exegesis—not all scholars have been encased in the particular strait-jacket to which we shall refer in the following pages: we have only to remember the names of O. Cullmann, J. Jeremias, L. Goppelt, W. G. Kümmel and B. Reicke.

[1] Cf., for example, the much-quoted first sentence of R. Bultmann's *Theology of the New Testament* I, ET 1952, that 'the message of Jesus is a presupposition for the theology of the New Testament, rather than a part of that theology itself'. Nevertheless Bultmann has himself written a book entitled *Jesus*, 1926, 1951[2] (ET, *Jesus and the Word*, 1935).

[2] The 'shift of the aeons' is now placed at the time of the coming of John the Baptist; cf. the discussion of Matt. 11.11–14 in J. M. Robinson, *A New Quest of the Historical Jesus* (SBT 25), 1959, pp. 116ff.

already imply an 'indirect Christology',[1] inasmuch as Jesus with his divine authority placed the people who met him in the presence of God and in a sense called them to make a decision. This transferred them into the eschatological 'Now', placed them under judgement and at the same time spoke to them of grace. The primitive Church looking back after the resurrection and after the unveiling of the secret of the Son of Man proceeded to transform this message of Jesus into one which had a 'direct Christology' and which plainly proclaimed the master to be Lord over all things and all people. Nevertheless the primitive Church continued to have a living awareness that as they proclaimed the glorified one, they were proclaiming no one else but Jesus of Nazareth who had called the disciples and had lived together with them. Clear evidence for this is to be seen in the fact that they did not abandon all recollection of the life and particularly of the teaching of Jesus. They were, on the contrary, convinced that only by using the life and teaching of Jesus were they able to proclaim their kerygma in a manner which did him justice. The Gospels are the most eloquent evidence for this.[2]

From this starting-point there has begun a new quest for the historical Jesus.[3] Just at present, as one might well expect at a preliminary stage, methodological problems are being discussed and exegetical rules drawn up by means of which the authentic

[1] This formulation comes from H. Conzelmann, 'Zur Methode der Leben-Jesu-Forschung', *ZTK* 56, Beiheft 1, 1959, p. 12; and in *RGG*³ III, 1959, col. 650. H. Conzelmann here follows R. Bultmann, *Theology of the New Testament* I, p. 43; 'Jesus' call to decision implies a christology.'

[2] Even the author of the Fourth Gospel, who wishes to proclaim in the plainest possible terms the glory of the risen Lord, uses the figure of the earthly Jesus for this purpose. This is not the place to examine the motives which led to the collection of oral traditions about Jesus and to their preservation in writing. It was probably not only the practical needs of the life of the community, but equally those of the Christian mission which were responsible for this process. This is emphasized by C. F. D. Moule, 'The Intention of the Evangelists', *New Testament Essays, Studies in Memory of T. W. Manson*, ed. A. J. B. Higgins, 1959, pp. 165–77, reprinted in *The Phenomenon of the New Testament* (SBT, NS 1), 1967, pp. 100–14.

[3] See the study by J. M. Robinson, *A New Quest of the Historical Jesus*, 1959 (p. 55, n. 2); also the volume of essays, *Der historische Jesus und der kerygmatische Christus*, ed. H. Ristow and K. Matthiae, Berlin, 1960; also W. G. Kümmel, 'Diakritik zwischen Jesus von Nazareth und dem Christusbild der Urkirche', *Zum dankbaren Gedächtnis an D. Joh. Bauer*, 1960, pp. 54–67. Space does not permit the addition of literature which has subsequently appeared on this subject.

tradition about Jesus may be discovered.[1] There is a desire at all costs to avoid falling back into the old mistakes made by the Jesus of history school and by source criticism. If in the Gospel tradition a distinctive 'faith' and a distinctive 'attitude' are attributed to Jesus[2] and these bear witness to his unique consciousness of his mission, this can, however, in future no longer be used as a criterion for denying particular actions or words to Jesus when the sole reason for this denial is that they are similar to the Church's kerygma. Instead we should almost expect that genuine tradition about Jesus will bear marks of his messianic consciousness, where a direct claim, hidden indeed, but audible for those who have ears to hear, is making itself heard. It is, therefore, to be expected that the amount of material which can be regarded as genuine tradition of Jesus' deeds and words will come to be larger than has been admitted hitherto: up till now this material has been restricted to parables, sayings about the kingdom of God, etc.

Using these new questions as our starting-point, we shall attempt to shed some light on Jesus' attitude to the sabbath. In his book which has now become a classic, *The History of the Synoptic Tradition*,[3] R. Bultmann sets out from form-critical presuppositions to analyse the Gospels. He endorses the view which had recently come into vogue that the Gospels were manifestoes of the faith of the primitive Church. He is, however, completely uninterested in the question whether Jesus' sabbath conflicts reported in the Gospels or even this or that detail in them are historically reliable. For him they were all without exception typical accounts, ideal scenes: they had been developed in the course of oral tradition in the primitive community, constructed on the pattern of question and counter-question

---

[1] Cf. the points made in O. Cullmann, 'Out of Season Remarks on the Historical Jesus of the Bultmann School', *Union Seminary Quarterly Review*, January 1961, pp. 131ff.; F. Mussner, 'Der historische Jesus und der Christus des Glaubens', *BZ*, NF 1, 1957, pp. 227-30. E. Käsemann (p. 54, n. 5) also lays down a rule which we shall have to discuss, because it affects Mark 2.27f.; see p. 65 below.

[2] The first expression comes from G. Ebeling, the second from E. Fuchs; see their contributions in *Sonderheft 1 zur ZTK*, 1959.

[3] ET 1963, of *Die Geschichte der synoptischen Tradition* (FRLANT, NF 12), 1921, 1931², 1957³. Even before Bultmann's work there had appeared K. L. Schmidt, *Der Rahmen der Geschichte Jesu*, 1919, and M. Dibelius, *From Tradition to Gospel*, ET 1934.

like the rabbinic dialogues and provided with a narrative framework which was partly invented to match the conclusion. Their *Sitz im Leben* was, according to Bultmann, the debates on the sabbath question which took place in the primitive Church. By contrast, the most recent examinations of the sabbath stories in the Gospels (those by E. Lohse)[1] display a definite interest in the words of Jesus about the sabbath. In these words Lohse uses Bultmann as his starting-point, but he takes up the question neglected by Bultmann concerning the genuine kernel of particular apophthegmata. He comes to the conclusion that a whole series of sayings about the sabbath probably derives from Jesus and that in the account of one sabbath healing even the original historical framework may perhaps have been preserved.[2] The investigations of Lohse prepare the ground for finding our way back to the historical Jesus in this particular question. The following discussion is an attempt to make some additional points which may perhaps serve to bring out more clearly than has been done by Lohse the distinctive position of Jesus with regard to the sabbath, even in comparison with that of the primitive Church. In this discussion there will be no detailed treatment of Bultmann's *History of the Synoptic Tradition*. At the very end we shall have to ask whether we can endorse Bultmann's opinion that the conflict stories are the deposit of debates which were carried on in the primitive Church.

We have already stated that Lohse is prepared to accept only one narrative framework as possibly historical, that of the healing of the man with the withered hand.[3] The chronological setting of at least three sabbath conflicts is, in fact, less credible. In the Fourth Gospel the stories of the healing of the man at the pool of Bethesda (John 5.1ff.) and of the man born blind (John 9.1ff.) may have been intentionally transferred to a sabbath day, for in both cases the point is subsequently made, 'Now that day was a sabbath' (John 5.9b; 9.14), and the conflict only developed

---

[1] (*a*) ʻσάββατον', *TWNT* VII, pp. 20–31; also (*b*) ʻJesu Worte über den Sabbat', *Judentum—Urchristentum—Kirche, Festschrift für J. Jeremias* (BZNW 26), 1960, pp. 79–89.
[2] The words of Jesus are Mark 2.27; 3.4 par.; Matt. 12.11f.; Luke 14.5. The controversy is reported in Mark 3.1ff. par., and its historical setting may possibly be accurate.
[3] But he insists (n. 1b), p. 84, that the details of the event may no longer be capable of reconstruction.

when the scribes, who were not present in person, receive information about the healing done by Jesus on the sabbath.[1] The narrative framework of the story of the man with the dropsy (Luke 14.1ff.) also does not seem to be original. The passage may well be a doublet of Luke 6.6–10 to which there has been added a piece of tradition peculiar to Luke (v. 5; cf. Matt. 12.11f.). What about the account of the plucking of the ears of corn by the disciples (Mark 2.23ff. par.)? Both Bultmann and Lohse see here a composite story: the primitive Church is thought to have inserted into Jesus' mouth the justification of its own (post-resurrection) sabbath practice.[2] Jesus is, in fact, made responsible for an action of the disciples in which he clearly played no part.[3] But is this a compelling argument for asserting that this story is composite? Even during Jesus' lifetime the disciples may very well have caused offence to other people by following the example or even the precept of their master. We shall rather have to inquire whether members of the primitive Church would have later dared to provoke their neighbours in the way presupposed by the story in Mark 2.23ff. par.[4] Moreover, there is a further consideration: it concerns the unity of the 'composite' passage. If the episode of the plucking of the ears of corn does not rest on an historical tradition from the life of Jesus but is to be regarded as a composition by the primitive Church, we might expect it to appear more or less as a unity. We should expect it either to have been developed from a thought present in the subsequent debate or at least that from the very beginning it should have been closely associated with a thought in this debate: neither is, in fact, the case. But, examining the first assumption, we find that the account of the plucking of the ears of corn by the disciples is immediately followed by the story of David (Mark 2.25f. par.), who, fleeing from Saul, had, with his companions, eaten of the shewbread in the sanctuary

---

[1] Even the healings themselves seem to have been stylized for the sake of a symbolic message; cf. H. Strathmann, *Das Evangelium nach Johannes* (NTD 4), 1961, pp. 102ff.

[2] R. Bultmann (p. 57, n. 3), p. 16; E. Lohse (p. 58, n. 1a), p. 20 and n. 172; E. Lohse (p. 58, n. 1b), p. 82. Similarly E. Lohmeyer, *Das Evangelium nach Markus* (Meyer), 1957, p. 65.

[3] Analogous instances in Mark 2.18 par.; 7.5 par.

[4] See pp. 72f. below.

(I Sam. 21.1–7). This part of the subsequent conversation is intended to justify the disciples' behaviour, and so far as its content is concerned, it is the part which is most closely connected with the story of the plucking of the ears of corn by the disciples.[1] Nevertheless this association is clearly very loose, for the quotation from I Sam. 21.1–7 is employed in the Gospels only to shew that in their necessity David and his companions had eaten the shewbread and so had done something which was forbidden, just as the disciples had done something which was forbidden by plucking ears of corn on the sabbath. I Sam. 21.1–7 cannot yield any more, and it cannot possibly be used to justify a violation of the sabbath by plucking ears of corn.[2] If, therefore, the narrative of the plucking of the ears of corn by the disciples had been invented in order to provide a setting for the quotation from I Sam. 21.1–7, we should have to admit to some surprise that a more suitable setting had not been selected. On the other hand, the view that the incident and the scriptural quotation had belonged to one another from the very beginning seems to come to grief, since in the (original) Marcan version there is no mention of the disciples having plucked ears of corn because they were *hungry*. It is only the Matthaean version (Luke is less explicit) which adds this feature to the narrative. Is not this addition to be explained as an attempt to assimilate the story of the plucking of the ears of corn to the quotation from scripture, I Sam. 21.1–7?[3] The scriptural quotation and

---

[1] At any rate, if like Bultmann (p. 57, n. 3), p. 16, one defines the point of the apophthegm as the justification of sabbath-breaking on grounds of hunger. We do not regard this as the original meaning of the pericope; see the following discussion.

[2] There is, of course, a rabbinic tradition that David assuaged his hunger with shewbread on a *sabbath day*: cf. SB I, pp. 618f.; B. Murmelstein, 'Jesu Gang durch die Saatfelder', *Angelos* 3, 1930, pp. 112ff. This does not, however, make any difference to the situation. Even if it were the case, David's trespass would still have consisted not in a breach of the sabbath, but in the eating of the shewbread. Furthermore, in the Synoptic Gospels no reference whatsoever is made to this rabbinic tradition. D. Daube, *The New Testament and Rabbinic Judaism*, 1956, pp. 77ff., rightly draws attention to the fact that in Mark 2.25f. par. conclusions valid for a *halakah* cannot safely be drawn from the province of *haggadah*. (For this reason Matt. 12.5 provides a further halakic proof from scripture.)

[3] This view is, however, more plausible than the opposite view that the motive of hunger has been intentionally eliminated from the tradition underlying the Marcan text; E. Schlatter, *Der Evangelist Matthäus*, 1929, p. 392, is of this opinion, and he also holds the priority of Matt. *vis-à-vis* Mark.

the narrative illustration in Mark 2.23–26 par. are clearly inappropriate to the account of the sabbath breach and its justification. This lack of unity in the 'composite' passage does, therefore, confirm our impression that in the account of the plucking of the ears of corn by the disciples on the sabbath we have in front of us the recollection of an historical event from the life of Jesus.

The real reason for the infringement of the sabbath by the disciples cannot indeed be precisely determined. The text of Mark tells us that the disciples had begun ὁδὸν ποιεῖν (several mss. even have ὁδοποιεῖν τίλλοντες τοὺς στάχυας). It is clearly assumed that the disciples had already begun 'to clear a way' and that they had, therefore, plucked ears of corn in great quantities.[1] We are not, however, told why they were doing this.

Do we also have preserved for us the *answer* which Jesus gave to those who reproached the disciples for breaking the sabbath by plucking the ears of corn? After the foregoing remarks we shall scarcely be able to claim that the quotation from I Sam. 21.1–7 was an integral part of Jesus' reply in justification of the disciples.[2] On the other hand, we may suppose that Jesus' original answer is preserved for us in Mark 2.27, 'The sabbath was made for man, not man for the sabbath.' The introductory formula καὶ ἔλεγεν αὐτοῖς does not present any difficulty for this view, since in Mark the narrative about David had already been interpolated. Moreover, so far as its content is concerned, Mark 2.27 fits this passage well. The saying does not seek in any way to justify the behaviour of the disciples. Their plucking of the ears of the corn was by no means to be excused. There was no obvious necessity which would justify this breach of the sabbath: the disciples were not in danger of their lives, nor were they bringing help to others in urgent need; nor does Matthew's introduction of the motive of hunger in any way mitigate the seriousness of the offence.[3] (According to Luke the

[1] In this way it is easier to explain why the disciples caused such a stir. The translation in the sense of the Latin *iter facere* sounds strongly pleonastic after the verb παραπορεύεσθαι.
[2] The same is true of Matt. 12.5–6; see pp. 73f., 81 below.
[3] Matthew thinks the disciples were guiltless (12.7) because they were hungry. But from this point of view one cannot argue against the binding force of the sabbath commandment. The disciples would have to be reproached for not having prepared their meals on the previous day as everyone else did; and even if they omitted to do this not out of carelessness, but

breach of the sabbath was particularly serious; he tells us that the disciples plucked the ears of corn even before the first sheaf of the harvest had been offered to God.)[1] The sentence, 'The sabbath was made for man, not man for the sabbath,' if it was spoken in this connection, is nothing less than the enunciation of a new principle. In uttering it Jesus was throwing overboard the entire sabbath theology established by post-exilic Judaism (if we may accept Mark 2.27 as a genuine saying of Jesus: this has yet to be demonstrated, see pp. 64ff). The rabbinic parallel to Mark 2.27, 'The sabbath is given to you; it is not you who are given over to the sabbath',[2] may not be compared with Mark 2.27, since it is intended to justify a breach of the sabbath only in the case of danger to life.[3] For Jesus, however, his saying

---

because of the turmoil of their missionary activity, they could have fasted for the whole day. (In Mark 8.2 par. we read that the people had remained with Jesus for as long as three days without having a proper meal.) A breach of the sabbath on account of hunger would have been excusable only if someone were to eat who was in danger of his life through sheer exhaustion, but this is not the case in Mark 2.23–28 par. Matthew, therefore, here marks the beginning of a new Christian casuistry; cf. G. D. Kilpatrick, *The Origins of the Gospel according to St Matthew*, 1946, pp. 116f.; see p. 68, n. 4 below on Matt. 12.12b. R. Bultmann (p. 57, n. 3), p. 16, says that the point of the whole pericope 'is that sabbath-breaking to satisfy hunger is defended on scriptural grounds'; this is not a just evaluation either of the original pericope Mark 2.23–28 or of the pericope as we have it in Matthew. W. G. Kümmel, 'Jesus und der jüdische Traditionsgedanke', *ZNW* 33, 1934, p. 121, also misses the real point when he says, 'Jesus here disputes whether one should obey the letter of a law when in so doing one arrives at the very opposite of the divine meaning of the law, which in this case was meant to illustrate God's love for men in the assuaging of their hunger.'

 [1] In Luke 6.1 about half of the textual evidence reads ἐν σαββάτῳ δευτερο-πρώτῳ, 'on the second sabbath after the first'. It was always clear that this description presupposed a continuous series of sabbatical weeks; since the plucking of ears of corn can take place only in the spring, this event was supposed to have taken place during the seven weeks between Passover and the Festival of Weeks (Deut. 16.9f.; Lev. 23.15f.). E. Vogt, 'Sabbatum "deutero-proton" in Lc. 6.1 et antiquum Kalendarium sacerdotale', *Biblica* 50, 1959, pp. 102–5, has now modified this hypothesis by suggesting that it should be interpreted by reference to the calendar derived from the Book of Jubilees; in this case it would be a question of the first sabbath after the days of unleavened bread, which according to this calendar was also the second sabbath after the Passover. Since in this calendar the seven weeks of harvest did not begin until after the week of unleavened bread, 'the second sabbath after the first' would still have preceded the omer-day. On the calendar in the Book of Jubilees, see in greater detail pp. 183ff. below.
 [2] Mekhilta in Ex. 31.13f. (c. AD 180); SB II.5.
 [3] Even if Jesus had quoted a current proverb, as is held by J. W. Bowman,

seems to have been absolutely unlimited in application, and the plucking of the ears of corn by the disciples was nothing less than a demonstration of this. The Jews' conviction that it was their duty loyally to observe the sabbath, the covenant gift of God, and strictly to keep the sabbath commandment by paying no attention to their own needs would, therefore, have seemed to Jesus utterly perverse, for such an attitude had the effect of placing the sabbath *above* human beings. By instituting the day of rest God had wanted to give human beings a blessing, not hardship. If the day of rest no longer spelt blessing but hardship, it had failed in its divine purpose, and as a consequence rebellion against it or disregard of it was no sin.[1] With such views Jesus was sure to provoke the opposition of all devotees of the law.

It is a misunderstanding to hold that Jesus did not attack the sabbath commandment itself, but only the casuistical refinements of the Pharisees. We have already remarked[2] that the whole Jewish sabbath casuistry had developed from the desire to draw out the significance of the commandment to love one's neighbour—but within the framework marked out by the letter of the law. The discussions in the schools of scribes at that time centred only round the question how many exceptions were allowable in sabbath practice. The intention of the casuists, therefore, was to avoid inhuman severity in the interpretation of the law.[3] If Jesus had the same purpose in mind, he would surely have supported their efforts. He saw, however, that all casuistry has its limits and in this case the limits were those of the commandment to keep holy the sabbath day; and this commandment enslaved human beings. For this reason he was not afraid of calling in question the commandment contained in the priestly tradition of the Old Testament.

Religion of Maturity, 1948, pp. 72f., 116, 184 (which is, however, extremely questionable, since we only have this one late rabbinic piece of evidence), he would, in any case, have used it with a quite novel and radical application.

[1] In some respects, therefore, Jesus has harked back to the original meaning of the sabbath as a day of rest introduced on social grounds for the sake of man. With prophetic zeal he has rejected the inclusion of the command to rest within man's duty to God, as if it were for God's sake that man was to rest. This exactly fits in with Jesus' attitude towards the ritual law; see pp. 76f. below.

[2] See pp. 52f. above.

[3] As an illustration we might quote the wistful comment of the author of the article on the sabbath in the *Jewish Encyclopaedia* X, 597, 'In view of the spirit of philanthropy that . . . underlies the Law, it is difficult to understand the controversies with Jesus attributed to the Pharisees in the New Testament.' (Quoted in H. Riesenfeld, *Jésus transfiguré*, 1947, p. 322, n. 16.)

If we also include Mark 2.28 in our discussion, it becomes clear that we are justified in regarding Mark 2.27 as a word of Jesus and that we have probably interpreted the passage correctly. Mark 2.28 in its present form runs thus, 'so the Son of man is lord even of the sabbath'. We should naturally expect Mark 2.27, 'The sabbath is made for man, not man for the sabbath', to be continued in Mark 2.28, 'So *man* (not the Son of man) is lord even of the sabbath.' Some time ago J. Wellhausen[1] suggested that Mark 2.28 originally read like that. The Aramaic *barnasha* which probably underlies the Greek υἱὸς τοῦ ἀνθρώπου can be equally well rendered 'man' or 'Son of man'. In this case Jesus would have ascribed the lordship over the sabbath simply to man and not to himself as the Son of man. The ὥστε in the Marcan text provides weighty support for this theory. As it now stands, v. 28 cannot possibly be understood as a logical conclusion drawn from v. 27: the sabbath is made for man, and *therefore* the *Son* of man (i.e. Jesus, who bears this title) is lord even of the sabbath. The two clauses do not fit.

For this reason it is difficult to accept the suggestion that the two sayings were originally quite isolated sayings and that Mark first put them together, joining them with ὥστε.[2] It seems much more probable that Mark still preserves the original association of the two sayings, although even here we find that there has already been introduced the familiar interpretation of the second clause with reference to the Son of man. Matthew and Luke were aware of the difference between Mark 2.27 and 2.28, and as a result they simply left out Mark 2.27.[3] Finally the theologumenon, 'The Son of man is lord of the sabbath' was entirely detached from its original setting: Luke 6.10 D and Marcion both place this phrase after the account of the healing of the man with the withered hand. We can thus see the importance

---

[1] *Einleitung in die drei ersten Evangelien*, 1911[2], p. 129; also *Das Evangelium Marci*, 1909[2], p. 20. Many have followed him, including O. Cullmann, *The Christology of the New Testament*, ET 1959, pp. 152ff. G. Dalman, *The Words of Jesus*, ET 1902, pp. 234–67, thought otherwise.

[2] E. Lohse (p. 58, n. 1b), p. 83, and H. E. Tödt, *The Son of Man in the Synoptic Tradition*, ET 1965, pp. 130ff., are, for example, both of this opinion. The ὥστε of Mark 2.28 may then be interpreted as the conclusion which the community drew from the *whole* conflict; cf. E. Lohmeyer, *Das Evangelium des Markus*, 1951, p. 66. But then we should have expected to have found the ὥστε in Matthew and Luke as well.

[3] This is particularly clear in Luke, because he retains the words καὶ ἔλεγεν αὐτοῖς; cf. E. Haenchen, 'Quellenanalyse und Kompositionsanalyse in Act. 15', *Judentum—Urchristentum—Kirche, Festschrift für J. Jeremias* (BZNW 26), 1960, p. 157, n. 19.

given to this phrase in the primitive Church as a key to the interpretation of Jesus' attitude to the sabbath.

Mark 2.28, 'The Son of man is lord even of the sabbath', does clearly represent, therefore, a weakening and a limitation by comparison with Mark 2.27 and with the original v.28 (if we may suppose the existence of such a verse), as E. Käsemann[1] has noticed. The primitive Church obviously found man's fundamental freedom with regard to the sabbath enunciated by Jesus in this passage to be something monstrous. It certainly recognized Jesus' own freedom with regard to the sabbath; the primitive Church interpreted this freedom in a messianic sense and did not claim it for itself.[2] It hardly needs to be pointed out that the weakening of Mark 2.28 which the primitive Church has probably undertaken does in its turn confirm the view that in Mark 2.27 an authentic saying of Jesus has been transmitted to us.[3]

The interpretation of Jesus' attitude towards the sabbath which we have so far provided corresponds with the conclusions which we can draw from the healing stories. Although we cannot claim that these narratives are historically accurate in their detail, it is noticeable that the sabbath healings all have one trait in common: Jesus' actions were never answers to pleas for help which would brook no delay. Help given to a sick person in an emergency would have given rise to no objection from the majority of the scribes.[4] The evidence of the Gospels is, however, that the people who were healed by Jesus on the sabbath were suffering from unmistakably protracted illnesses

---

[1] *Essays on New Testament Themes* (p. 54, n. 5), p. 39. Similarly H. Braun, *Spätjüdischhäretischer und frühchristlicher Radikalismus* II, 1957, p. 70, n. 1. On the other hand, W. G. Kümmel, *Promise and Fulfilment*, 1957, p. 46, n. 93, and E. Lohse (p. 58, n. 1b), p. 82, for example, are of the opinion that Mark 2.28 goes much further than Mark 2.27.

[2] The importance of this fact will be apparent when we discuss the attitude of the early community towards the sabbath; see pp. 86ff. below.

[3] In this connection we should mention the point of view advanced by T. W. Manson, *Conjectanea Neotestamentica in honorem A. Fridrichsen*, 1947, pp. 138ff.; cf. T. Preiss, *Le Fils de l'Homme*, 1951, pp. 28f.; he holds that Mark 2.27 is to be translated as follows, 'The sabbath is made for the sake of the Son of man, not the Son of man for the sake of the sabbath.' The designation 'Son of man' would in this case have a collective meaning; it would refer to the 'people of the saints of the Most High' in Dan. 7. But it is open to question whether this collective meaning may be assumed here, all the more so since the train of thought in this verse is then no longer clear: the sabbath is, in fact, not made for the sake of the people of the saints of the Most High (the local community is to be understood here), but for the whole of Israel, even for the whole world.

[4] See the authorities in SB I, 623ff.

and certainly not from acute ailments or infirmities: the man with the withered hand (Mark 3.1ff. par.),[1] the woman whose back had been bent for eighteen years (Luke 13.10ff.), the dropsical man (Luke 14.1ff.), the man by the pool of Bethesda who had been bedridden for thirty-eight years (John 5.1ff.), the man born blind (John 9.1ff.). If therefore Jesus in accordance with the unanimous testimony of the Gospel tradition purposely healed people on the sabbath who were clearly not in acute distress, his deeds of healing were an offence and a provocation.[2] It is easy to understand the indignant statement made by the ruler of the synagogue, 'There are six days on which work ought to be done; come on those days and be healed, and not on the sabbath day' (Luke 13.14).[3] All these people who were healed could certainly have waited for their cure until the next day (cf. Mark 1.32ff.). Why, then, did Jesus heal them on the sabbath of all days? Surely, not *only* because of his compassionate love, but also with the express intention of showing that for him the sabbath commandment had no binding force.

It is only logical that after the sabbath conflicts the opponents of Jesus should have decided to kill him, as we read in Mark 3.6 par. (cf. John 5.18; 7.25).[4] This would have been the natural

---

[1] The embellished account in the Gospel according to the Hebrews (Jerome, *Comm. in Matt.* 12.13) [called the Gospel of the Nazareans in *NT Apoc.* I, p. 148] is clearly an attempt to make the situation seem more urgent, 'I was a mason who earned my living with my hands; I beseech you, Jesus, give me my health back again so that I need not shamefully beg for food.'

[2] The Fourth Gospel further intensifies the situation not only by making Jesus heal on the sabbath day when there was no urgent need, but also by mentioning one occasion on which he bade the sick man carry his bed (John 5.8; cf. 5.10), and by describing another on which he mixed a paste of spittle and earth (9.6; cf. 9.15f.).

[3] This detail lends support to the view that a memory of an actual event underlies the account in Luke 13.10ff., for even though this phrase refers to the Old Testament commandment, it could hardly have been invented in its present form. Also v. 15 represents an independent tradition from Luke 14.5 par. (see p. 69, n. 1 below). The pericope has, of course, no underlying unity: the plural address ὑποκριταί to the ruler of the synagogue (cf. v. 17a: 'all his adversaries') does not fit. On the other hand, it need not necessarily be an indication of a composite and confused passage, as R. Bultmann (p. 57, n. 3), p. 12, thinks, if the healing takes place before the debate and the humiliation of the opponents comes at the end.

[4] K. Bornhäuser, 'Zur Perikope vom Bruch des Sabbats', *Neue Kirchliche Zeitschrift* 33, 1922, pp. 325–34, sees the connection of Mark 2.23ff. par. and

reaction of every pious Jew to Jesus' attitude towards the sabbath. So far as we know, the accusation that Jesus had broken the sabbath did not play any part in the actual trial of Jesus;[1] this does not, however, justify us in concluding that Jesus subsequently succeeded in clearing himself of the reproach of being a violator of the sabbath.[2] His opponents obviously preferred to concentrate on the messianic claim which was implicit even in his infringements of the sabbath, and they did, therefore, direct their principal accusation against this blasphemous pretension.[3]

In view of the public nature of Jesus' breaches of the sabbath and their provocative character, it would be inappropriate to mention that we frequently hear of Jesus' visits to the synagogue on the sabbath.[4] This behaviour does not necessarily mean that Jesus was a zealous observer of the Jewish law or that he was very strict about the sabbath commandment. It stands to reason that Jesus used the opportunity to deliver his message in the synagogues where people were assembled on the sabbath. On every occasion preaching was the purpose of his visit to the

---

Mark 3.1ff. par. resting on a legal basis: after Jesus' first infringement of the sabbath commandment the Pharisees had purposely tried to bring about a second, similar instance in order that they might be able to take legal proceedings against him.

[1] Naturally we cannot bring in here as evidence the Gospel of Nicodemus, 1–2, where the accusation of Jesus (before Pilate!) really amounts to 'Breach of the sabbath by healing the sick'. Luke 23.2, τοῦτον εὕραμεν διαστρέφοντα τὸ ἔθνος ἡμῶν, may not properly be used here, although Marcion (clearly in polemic against Matt. 5.17) adds, καὶ καταλύοντα τὸν νόμον καὶ τοὺς προφήτας. Even later we find an awareness (though it is toned down) of the gravity of this particular offence of Jesus: according to Tertullian, Spect. 30, Jesus was held to be 'sabbati destructor'. Cf. Acta Philippi 15 (Bonnet, p. 8); the Infancy Narrative of Thomas 2 (NT Apoc. I, p. 393).

[2] Thus T. Zahn, Geschichte des Sonntags, vornehmlich in der alten Kirche, 1878, p. 12. The story of the demoniac (Mark 1.21ff. par.) seems to suggest that not every infringement of the sabbath provoked a conflict. We have no reason to mistrust the tradition that this incident took place on a sabbath (as opposed to R. Bultmann [p. 57, n. 3], pp. 242ff.).

[3] John 5.18 (cf. 5.16), 'This was why the Jews sought all the more to kill him, because he not only (repeatedly) broke the sabbath but also called God his Father, making himself equal with God.' Cf. J. Nedbal, Sabbat und Sonntag im Neuen Testament (diss., Vienna, 1956), p. 75.

[4] Mark 1.21 par.; 1.39 par.; 6.2 par.; John 18.20. Luke 4.16 even reads, 'he went to the synagogue, as his custom was, on the sabbath day'. (Cf. the terminology of Acts.)

synagogue.¹ The fact that Jesus taught in the synagogue sheds no light on his attitude to the sabbath itself. Similarly, we may not deduce that Paul kept the sabbath like a Jew from the fact that he employed the obvious evangelistic method of preaching the gospel to the Jews on the sabbath day.²

Matt. 24.20 is a special case, 'Pray that your flight (i.e. in the last tribulation) may not be in winter or on a sabbath.' This passage is not to be considered in discussing *Jesus'* attitude towards the sabbath. The text of Matt. 24.20 is a secondary, expanded version of Mark 13.18, where there is no mention of the sabbath. (Luke has omitted the whole verse which clearly offended him.) The words μηδὲ σαββάτῳ in Matt. 24.20 have, therefore, been introduced from another tradition, and it is usually said that this expansion derives from Jewish Christian circles strict in their observance of the law.³ But the fear of violating the sanctity of the sabbath by fleeing on that day (even in peril of death!) seems to go far beyond what we know from other sources about the strictness with which the Jewish Christians observed the law. It is more likely that the addition μηδὲ σαββάτῳ in Matt. 24.20 (or even the whole verse?) derives from a late Jewish (Maccabaean?) milieu.

We shall now consider the words which, according to the Synoptic Gospels, Jesus said in connection with the sabbath healings. In so doing we shall become aware of the real basis from which originated the authority and freedom of Jesus with regard to the sabbath. The passages are Mark 3.4 (cf. Luke 6.9), 'Is it lawful on the sabbath to do good or to do harm, to save life or to kill?'⁴ and the three versions (Matt. 12.11f.; Luke

---

¹ In all the passages quoted above it is stated that Jesus taught. This is also the case with regard to Jesus' visits to the temple; cf. A. Jaubert, 'Jésus et le calendrier de Qumran', *NTS* 7, 1960, p. 21.

² Acts 9.20; 13.5, 14, 42–44; 14.1; 17.1f.; 18.4, 19; 19.8.

³ P. Cotton, *From Sabbath to Sunday*, 1933, pp. 6off.; H. Braun (p. 65, n. 1), p. 69, n. 4; E. Lohse (p. 58, n. 1a), p. 30, etc.

⁴ The shortened form in Matt. 12.12b, 'So it is lawful to do good on the sabbath', eliminates the scandal of Jesus' double question. Matt. 12.12b marks the beginning of the moralistic misunderstanding of Jesus' attitude towards the sabbath (that the obligation to love one's neighbour displaces in certain circumstances the command to keep a day of rest); and this misunderstanding agreed with good Pharisaic tradition; cf. G. D. Kilpatrick (pp. 61f,n. 3), pp.129f. This misunderstanding has found adherents both in the early Church and also right up to our own time. As early as the time of the *Epistle to Diognetus* (4.3) we find an anti-Jewish polemic being developed on this foundation, which was too slender to bear such a construction, 'And what can it be but impious falsely to accuse God (as do the Jews) of forbidding that a good deed should be done on the sabbath day?' Put more spiritually, the same thought is to be found in Clement Alex., *Strom.* IV.6.29.3,

14.5; 13.15) of the parabolic saying that everyone goes to the assistance of an animal which has got into trouble on a sabbath day, or has fallen into a well or has to be led out to water. Not only is the underlying thought contained in this parabolic saying the same in all three versions,[1] but the saying itself can properly be understood as an illustration of the question of principle asked in Mark 3.4 par., 'Is it lawful on the sabbath to save life or to kill?' At least in the case of the animal which had fallen into the well, the question really was, 'Is it permitted to save an animal on the sabbath, or must it be left to itself and so left to perish?' In the case both of the question of principle in Mark 3.4 par. and also of the question illustrated by the concrete example, the answer is understood: it is permitted to save life on the sabbath.[2] The connection between the four sayings has, however, a yet deeper foundation. No single one of them is, in fact, able really to justify the sabbath healings of Jesus. Mark 3.4 par. cannot be understood to refer directly to the man with the withered hand, for neither is his life saved if his hand is then healed, nor is his life lost if his hand is not then healed.[3] Similarly, from an animal which is in urgent need and so must be helped on a sabbath one cannot legitimately draw

---

'It is by beneficence that the love which, according to the gnostic ascending scale, is lord of the sabbath, proclaims itself.'

[1] Even the form of the question is the same, 'Which of you would not...?' By contrast, the differences in detail count for little, even the fact that different animals are mentioned (υἱός surely only found its way into the text because of a punning addition to the Aramaic original; cf. M. Black, *An Aramaic Approach to the Gospels and Acts*, 1954², p. 126). The choice of different examples (fetching out of a cistern; setting free and leading out to water) has clearly developed from the altered setting of the healing; in one case the comparison revolves around the word ἐγείρειν, in the other around λύειν; it is difficult to decide which example should be preferred.

[2] In the Damascus Document (XI.13f.) the answer is in the negative, but the question is a subject of dispute even in rabbinic discussion. Cf. E. Lohse (p. 58, n. 1a), p. 25, n. 198. Lohse holds ([p. 58, n. 1b], p. 87) that the sayings of Jesus, which clearly presuppose an affirmative answer to this question, point to conditions in Galilee, where it seems that the law was less strictly observed.

[3] E. Lohmeyer, *Das Evangelium des Markus*, 1951, pp. 68f., therefore proposes another interpretation. He understands the 'killing' as an allusion to the hostile lying in wait of the opponents which might lead later (v. 6) to a decision to kill. For him Jesus' question contains 'intense sarcasm' (*Das Evangelium des Matthäus*, 1956, p. 186). But in this case he would be talking about 'killing' in an allusive sense, and this does not explain why the healing should be a 'saving of life'.

inferences which are valid also for a sick human being who does not absolutely need immediate assistance (on a sabbath). The common characteristic of these four sayings is, in fact, this inadmissible and altogether faulty manner of deduction. The repeated assertion that a human being is worth more than an animal (Matt. 12.12a; cf. Luke 13.16) cannot remove this impression. We can solve the difficulty only by assuming either that these words of Jesus originally had no connection whatsoever with the sabbath healings or that for Jesus this sort of 'proof' was, after all, conclusive. The former alternative is purely hypothetical; we cannot imagine in what other context these words may have originally stood.[1] We, therefore, have to decide in favour of the second alternative. For Jesus, at each healing, it was clearly a question of life or death for the person face to face with him. His assistance for both body and soul ('Your sins are forgiven') would brook no delay. If he let a sick person be brought to him (Mark 3.3 par.; Luke 13.2), this meant that God's moment had dawned for that sick person. It also meant that this particular human being at that particular moment was the most miserable of all men who had to be helped then—at that very moment.[2] In the face of this inner compulsion of his divine commission Jesus saw that every outward restraint, even that of the sabbath commandment, became irrelevant. The sabbath commandment was not merely pushed into the background by the healing activity of Jesus: it was simply annulled. The Fourth Gospel has in its own way penetrated to the heart of the matter: in John 9.4 we read, 'We must (δεῖ) work the works of him who sent me, while it is day' (cf. the δεῖ of Luke 13.15) and in John 5.17, 'My father is working still, and I am working.' The sabbath commandment must yield before the ceaseless activity of Jesus.[3] The same insistent messianic claim is also to be heard in the synoptic passages. The

[1] Almost certainly these are not community constructions; see pp. 73f. below.

[2] E. Klostermann's explanation, *Das Markusevangelium* (HNT 3), 1936[7], p. 37, that the omission of a deed is itself also a deed, but a bad deed (cf. W. G. Kümmel, *ZNW* 33, 1934, p. 121) is, therefore, both right and wrong at the same time, for it is not a question here of a general moral truth; the rightness of the proposition depends entirely on the person of Jesus.

[3] Both passages (John 5.17 and 9.4) are direct in their Christology and so are probably to be regarded as constructions by the community; see p. 100 below.

veiled manner in which this claim is made in the Synoptic Gospels seems itself to indicate that we are really standing face to face with Jesus' own self-proclamation.[1] If this was the real core of Jesus' attitude towards the sabbath, we can now see more clearly, as we look back, why he adopted such a provocative attitude when the disciples plucked the ears of corn. It resulted from his messianic consciousness which knew no bounds—in other words, because Jesus knew himself to be lord of the sabbath day.[2] Jesus' infringements of the sabbath recorded in the Gospels were therefore each and all—and this we can see in the subsequent disputes—*in their outward appearance* inexcusable provocations, but in their inner significance veiled proclamations of Jesus' messiahship.[3]

The primitive Church has shown that it rightly understood Jesus' attitude to the sabbath by interpreting it in a messianic sense: the lord of the sabbath (Mark 2.28 par.) had come, and he was one who was greater than the temple (Matt. 12.6) and greater than David (Mark 2.25f. par.). Further: the primitive Church also understood that Jesus' healing activity was, in fact, in the truest possible sense of the word a 'sabbath' activity:

[1] H. Greeven, 'Wer unter euch . . . ?' *Jahrbuch der Theologischen Schule Bethel*, NF 3, 1952, pp. 86–101; cf. E. Lohse (p.58, n. 1b), p. 87, both draw attention to the fact that there are no rabbinic parallels to this sort of question.

[2] The plucking of the ears of corn by the disciples naturally did not come directly within the scope of the divine δεῖ, as did Jesus' healings of the sick. In Mark 2.23–28 par. Jesus, therefore, comes closer to a *general* abrogation of the sabbath commandment. This becomes apparent in the work of interpretation by the early community in Mark 2.23–28 par. (citation of three proofs from scripture; christological emphasis in Mark 2.28 par.).

[3] Cf. B. Reicke, 'Jesus och judarna enligt Markusevangeliet', *Svensk Exegetisk Aarsbok* 17, 1952, p. 77. L. Goppelt, *Christentum und Judentum im ersten und zweiten Jahrhundert*, 1954, p. 46, goes to the heart of the matter when he states (on Mark 3.4 par.), 'The Pharisees make no reply to this question (whether it is lawful to do good or to do evil on the sabbath day). They could only have answered, "You may not ask that! It is good to hallow the sabbath by rest." Jesus' double question marks the end of the sabbath commandment: it is no longer a statutory ordinance and it no longer has absolute validity if this all-embracing, overlapping alternative is valid—namely to save life. That is God's very own work and it is good: to destroy life is the work of Satan (John 8.44) and it is evil. But where is there an activity which truly and continually carries on God's work of preserving life? It is this question which exposes as shallow moralism any way of interpreting Jesus' attitude to the legalism of the Pharisees which is not christologically based and fails to take account of the person of Jesus.'

in him, in his love, in his mercy and his help had dawned the messianic sabbath, the time of God's own saving activity. But we shall have more to say on this subject.[1]

On the basis of these conclusions we can now attempt to evaluate the assessment which Bultmann made about the *Sitz im Leben* of the accounts of the sabbath conflicts contained in the Gospels. We have to inquire whether debates like those transmitted to us in the Gospels could have been held in the primitive Church. In making this inquiry we do not want in any way to prejudge the question concerning the sabbath practice itself of the primitive Church: we shall be concerned only with the analysis of the accounts in the Gospels.[2] It cannot be denied that there is a formal similarity to rabbinical disputes, and this similarity is especially evident in the manner of adducing scriptural proof. It is equally apparent, however, that the synoptic disputes, because of their content, cannot be contained within the framework of this formal analogy. To what rabbi would it ever have occurred to assert that man is lord of the sabbath and may therefore break the sabbath even when there is no imminent danger to life or no other moral obligation to be fulfilled which takes priority over the sabbath? Or what rabbi would have associated the question whether one might in a case of necessity help cattle on a sabbath with the quite different question (which would be answered in the negative) whether on a sabbath one might heal a human being who was not in danger of his life? If the early Christians had defended their sabbath practice against the Jews in such a way, they could not have expected any quarter whatsoever: not only would they have provoked their neighbours by their attitude,

---

[1] See pp. 108ff. below.

[2] In the opposite conclusions of H. Riesenfeld and L. Goppelt we can see the equivocal nature of such a criticism which has its own preconceptions about the sabbath practice of the early community. They are both of the opinion (as opposed to Bultmann) that the pericope Mark 2.23–28 par. goes back to an incident in the life of Jesus, but they give different reasons for this opinion. H. Riesenfeld, *Jésus transfiguré*, 1947, p. 319, says that the story had no place in the life of the primitive community, 'which had quite simply replaced the Jewish sabbath and all its regulations by the Christian Sunday'. L. Goppelt, *TWNT* VI, p. 19, n. 53, asks, 'How could it have been that this situation came to be invented by the Palestinian church which was so zealous for the law (Acts 21.20f.)?'

but by a debate conducted on such lines they would certainly have become guilty of the infringement of the sabbath. Of this there is no doubt: they would have been in danger of being stoned. Apart from the case of Stephen and his companions,[1] we do not know anything about trials of this sort in the earliest decades of the Church's history. It is, therefore, improbable that the first Christians carried on such debates with the Jews about the sabbath and its validity.[2]

The controversies about the sabbath which we read in the Gospels are explicable only if we think of them in connection with actual infringements of the sabbath. In these controversies we also hear the messianic claim of one who was aware of his own mission and knew his divine commission as lord of the sabbath; with incredible boldness he did, therefore, sweep away the barriers of Judaism which were standing in the path of his ceaseless activity. It is *in the life of Jesus*, then, that the form of these controversies has its *Sitz im Leben*.[3] In these controversies we read of the scribes as the opponents of Jesus—and in the case of most of Jesus' words about the sabbath we must suppose there actually were opponents! In his life there were public debates, and an atmosphere of tension pervaded these debates which were so rabbinic in form, but so unrabbinic in content.

Later the primitive Church certainly played its part in the conscious modification and expansion of the tradition: that much we can assert. In some instances it transformed the veiled messianic claim of Jesus into direct christological pronouncements: Mark 2.28 par.; Matt. 12.6; John 5.17. It discovered scriptural proofs which (not always, indeed, in the happiest fashion) were supposed to justify Jesus' attitude: Mark 2.25f. par.; Matt. 12.5ff.; John 7.22f. The Church clearly found it necessary to transform the content of the tradition about Jesus' attitude to the sabbath, and it did not always find

---

[1] He did, in fact, declare open war on the cultic institutions of Judaism, and like many people of the same opinion he had to atone for it with his death. See pp. 126f. below.

[2] Only in the time of Justin Martyr (cf. his *Dialogue with Trypho*, esp. 16.4) could Christians openly express their views on Jewish usages and customs without risking their life. In Palestine this would not have been possible even after AD 70, for Judaism there was still unbroken and powerful.

[3] So E. Fascher, *Die formgeschichtliche Methode*, 1924, p. 221.

it easy to justify this attitude in its own eyes.[1] It is, however, precisely this work of interpretation which indicates that both the sabbath breaches (the healings and the plucking of the ears of corn by the disciples) and also the core of the sabbath debates (the phrase about saving life or killing and the parabolic saying preserved in three versions) go back to the lifetime of Jesus.[2]

The lack of interest in the historical Jesus and the concentration on the form criticism of the Gospels are not justified so far as Jesus' attitude to the sabbath is concerned. Today we cannot possibly think in old-fashioned terms of dividing the material into sources and of reconstructing a history of Jesus' sabbath conflicts[3] as if the evangelists themselves merely had this biographical and chronological interest in their material. We are, however, able to discern inner inconsistencies within the Gospel tradition, and these enable us to distinguish the testimony of Jesus himself from that of the primitive Church. One of the most important inconsistencies is that in the one case the words and actions of Jesus are veiled testimony to himself, whereas in the other they are open messianic proclamation. As a rule we shall not go wrong if we assume that in the former instance we have before us genuine tradition about Jesus, but that in the latter we encounter the influence of the Church's Easter message which has been projected back into Jesus' lifetime: there is, nevertheless, an inner continuity between these two types of tradition. The insertion of explanatory material does, in fact, show that the Church's faith and experience have not moulded the entire tradition in form and content. We could well have expected this to have been the case if we were dealing with nothing but Church tradition. These insertions show that the Church has taken over traditions, revised, expanded, deepened

[1] This work of interpretation is most clearly to be seen with regard to the disciples' questions to Jesus about his sabbath practice; we regret the absence of these questions from the Gospels.

[2] Attention should once again be drawn to the fact that E. Lohse (p. 58, n. 1b) comes to essentially the same conclusion. The point of view developed here differs from his only by taking a more sharply delineated interpretation of the position of Jesus.

[3] The question which healings of Jesus actually took place on a sabbath and how many of Jesus' words can in detail be linked historically with this or that event is less important.

and toned them down, without, however, abandoning them. The historical tradition always remained as the foundation.[1]

By way of a postscript we shall touch on Jesus' attitude to the law in general, although this is hardly directly relevant to the appraisal of his attitude to the sabbath. We do, in fact, come to an overall understanding of Jesus' attitude to the law by studying subsidiary problems such as, for example, Jesus and the sabbath. We may not, therefore, draw conclusions from our overall understanding to help us with the understanding of subsidiary problems, but we can place any additional points alongside those which we have already learnt.

The thorough and careful study by H. Braun[2] rightly regards the general intensification of the Torah as the characteristic mark of Jesus' attitude towards the law. This intensification does not take place on the lines of any clearly recognizable principle, and it is for this reason difficult to summarize. Nevertheless, with all possible caution, we may perhaps suggest two principles which seem to have substantially affected Jesus' attitude to the Torah.[3]

In the first place, Jesus traces the individual prescriptions of the law right back to the intention which lay behind them (Matt. 5.21ff.; also Mark 10.1ff. par.).[4] This tallies with the fact that the commandment to love God and one's neighbour turns out to be a hermeneutic principle for the interpretation of the law (Mark 12.28ff. par.; cf. 10.17f. par.; Matt. 7.12). It also fits in with the attack on the Pharisees, on their hypocrisy,

---

[1] If we compare the Synoptics and John with the gnostic gospels of Jewish-Christian or Gentile-Christian origin, we shall fully realize to what a high degree the canonical Gospels still have about them the feeling of a history which has been actually experienced, although the power of the tradition to mould history has already been at work even here.

[2] *Spätjüdischer-häretischer und frühchristlicher Radikalismus* I and II, 1957. The especial merit of Braun's work is that he draws attention to the links and at the same time he points out the differences. Cf. Braun's more recent work, *Qumran und das Neue Testament II*, 1966, esp. pp. 85ff.

[3] H. Braun, *Spätjüdischer . . . Radikalismus* I, p. 10, n. 2, is against the drawing-up of any principles.

[4] L. Goppelt (p. 71, n. 3), p. 48, 'Jesus removes from the Old Testament commandment its character of a statutory regulation which man can master in order to hide behind it from the claim of God; Jesus makes the total and absolute demand of God, who establishes his dominion by means of this claim, shine through the commandment.'

their disobedience, their man-made commandments (Matt. 23 and frequently elsewhere).

On the other hand—and this is equally important—Jesus opposes any merely external observance of the ceremonial law.[1] His attitude to the sabbath which we have already studied does not stand alone in this respect. We can think of his criticism of the regulations for cleanliness.[2] Even the attitude of Jesus towards the temple, the sacrificial system and the priesthood was ambiguous. Jesus certainly proclaimed his loyalty to these institutions,[3] but he could also take such a strong line against them[4] and speak against them so sharply (cf. Matt. 9.13; 12.7) that his allegedly hostile attitude to the temple played an important part at his trial (Mark 14.58 par.).[5] We must, however, still maintain that Jesus' criticism of Israel's cultic institutions was not itself a point of principle: that is to say, he did not formally abolish them. For this reason Jesus' attitude could give rise to different interpretations even in the primitive Church.

[1] On this whole subject see the series of lectures by E. Lohmeyer, *Kultus und Evangelium*, 1942, which are valuable in many respects. A striking sentence is to be found on p. 82, 'It was never formally said and yet it was tacitly accepted that the gospel of Jesus has detached the cultic commandments from the Old Testament law and annulled them' (cf. p. 106). See also, perhaps, A. Jaubert (p. 68, n. 1), pp. 11–22.

[2] Mark 7.14ff. goes substantially further than the material recorded in 7.1–13. The tradition has quite rightly added in v. 19, in accordance with the sense, '. . . thus he declared all foods clean'; Matt. 15.20 purposely tones this down. For the same reasons Jesus did not hesitate to have table-fellowship with the 'unclean'; E. Käsemann (p. 54, n. 5), p. 39, speaks of a removal of the old distinction between the realm of the sacred and the secular.

[3] Matt. 23.16–22; perhaps Mark 13.2 par.; cf. also Mark 1.44 par.; Matt. 5.23f.; 17.17ff.

[4] Mark 11.15ff. par. In this story there is clearly a bias against the sacrificial system in general; 'prayer' and 'sacrifice' are contrasted. Cf. Braun, *Spätjüdischer . . . Radikalismus* II, p. 63, n. 4.

[5] The primitive community has, then, in its christological interpretation, played off Jesus and the temple against one another; cf. Mark 15.38 par. (also Mark 12.10 par.). Certain Jewish-Christian groups (the Hellenists around Stephen, the Pseudo-Clementine literature, the Gospel of the Ebionites; cf. Pap. Oxy. 840) have launched out into sharp criticism of the temple and of the sacrificial system. There is no question here of any influence from Qumran, where the estrangement from the temple clearly had its origin in the conviction that the temple was profaned only because of the actual practices in use there; cf. H. Braun, *op. cit.*, II, p. 63, n. 2. This attitude of the primitive community with regard to the temple must, therefore, in some way or other have had its basis in the attitude of Jesus.

From this angle the genuineness of certain words of Jesus (e.g. Matt. 5.17ff.; 23.3) does, nevertheless, seem open to suspicion. Sayings which bear traces of an exaggerated loyalty to the law and affirm in principle the law's validity do not seem to fit into the picture which we can discern from other sources about Jesus' attitude to the law.[1] In the μὴ νομίσητε of Matt. 5.17 we get a faint indication that Jesus may really have given the appearance of abolishing the law, but the church which stands behind Matthew's Gospel guards against that.[2] Matt. 5.18 certainly stood in Q. But Luke 16.17 (with 16.16) shows that this saying could be understood as a recognition (almost in resignation) of the power of the law which it was pointless to resist. If one wishes to maintain the genuineness of Matt. 5.17ff.,[3] one has great difficulty in explaining why the law (right down to its last jot and tittle!) should no longer be binding so far as Gentile Christians are concerned.[4]

Jesus' Yes to the law and his simultaneous No in particular instances have always caused surprise.[5] The claim to messianic sovereignty was to be seen above all in the annulling of the law by acts of divine authority,[6] rather than in the intensification of the law. We have already met this claim in our examination of the sabbath conflicts.[7] We should, however, probably be wrong to say that Jesus in his person introduced a new, messianic

---

[1] Against their genuineness are H. Braun, op. cit., II, p. 11; R. Bultmann (p. 57, n. 3), p. 138; W. G. Kümmel (pp. 61f., n. 3), p. 127; and naturally also E. Stauffer, Die Botschaft Jesu damals und heute, 1959, pp. 33ff., etc.

[2] Elsewhere this community is at pains to illustrate how Jesus' words and deeds happened in accordance with the scriptures which they 'fulfilled'.

[3] E.g. T. Zahn, Das Evangelium des Matthäus, 1922⁵, pp. 208ff.; J. Schniewind, Das Evangelium nach Matthäus (NTD 2), 1950⁵, pp. 53ff.; L. Goppelt (p. 71, n. 3), p. 47, etc.

[4] The opinion of T. Zahn (n. 3) that Matt. 5.18 ('until all is accomplished') refers to a continuing 'fulfilment' (=annulment) of the law in the course of the Church's history is unsatisfactory. Equally unsatisfactory is the view of K. Bornhäuser, Die Bergpredigt, 1923, pp. 50ff.; he wants to regard the command to love one's neighbour as the essence of the law which is now valid not merely for Israelites but for all men. H. Ljungmann, 'Das Gesetz erfüllen. Matt. 5.17ff. und 3.15 untersucht', Lunds Universitets Aarsskrift NF Avd 1, 50/6, 1954, provides a strong christocentric foundation for his exegesis, but his theory that Jesus 'fulfils' the entire law cannot easily be substantiated in detail.

[5] Gutbrod, TWNT IV, pp. 1051–7, strongly emphasized this; cf. W. G. Kümmel (pp. 61f., n. 3), pp. 121, 130.

[6] Cf. the criticism by H. Braun op. cit. II, pp. 5–6, n. 2, of E. Käsemann's interpretation of Matt. 5.21ff.

[7] We can also see this claim in the fact that the command to love one's parents must yield place to the imperative to be Jesus' disciple which constitutes a new, eschatological situation; Matt. 8. 21f.; 10.37.

Torah in conscious contrast to the Mosaic law.[1] The very fact that he intensified the Old Testament commandments presupposes that he acknowledged them. In the cases where Jesus' criticism was to some degree directed against them, this happened without a new Torah being put in their place. Even the 'new' commandment of love had its basis in the Old Testament. We must, therefore, abide by our paradoxical conclusion: on the one hand, Jesus recognized the Torah and even intensified it, whilst on the other hand, by virtue of his divine authority, he did not hesitate to make great breaches in it, particularly in its ceremonial regulations.

If we inquire about the real roots of Jesus' attitude towards the law, the answer which seems to suggest itself is that Jesus (and before him John the Baptist) took up again the prophetic message. The prophets in pre-exilic times had tried to bring about a deeper relationship with God, and on ethical grounds they had warned against an overemphasis on the ceremonial and priestly elements in public worship.[2] In post-exilic Judaism these ceremonial and priestly elements had undeniably gained the upper hand. The sabbath theology and sabbath practice of post-exilic Judaism are in themselves eloquent evidence for this structural change. This answer to our question about the roots of Jesus' attitude would not, however, touch the real point, for the message of Jesus is marked by one trait which is absent from the prophets' teaching: all his pronouncements refer to himself. Whenever Jesus intensifies the Torah or makes breaches in its regulations, we encounter again and again his 'I' which stands behind all his teaching and activity as their ultimate justification. We can explain Jesus' unique consciousness of his authority only by assuming that Jesus was convinced that with his coming there had dawned the eschatological kingdom of God which the prophets had foretold. For this reason he called people to be his disciples, healed the sick, forgave sins, went on to establish a new covenant in his blood. In his view the time had come for the promises to be fulfilled. For this reason the important part of

---

[1] This has been emphasized recently by J. J. Vincent, *Disciple and Lord. The Historical and Theological Significance of Discipleship in the Synoptic Gospels,* unpublished dissertation, Basel, 1960.

[2] Cf. Amos 5.21ff.; Isa. 1.11ff.; Micah 6.6ff.; Hos. 6.6; Jer. 6.20; Ps. 40.7; 50.8–13; 51.18.

Jesus' attitude to the law is not the authority which he attributed to the law; the important point is the indication that the time had come for the promises to be fulfilled, that he was offering this fulfilment in his own person. When Paul contrasted the time of the law with the time of salvation he was, therefore, correctly interpreting the attitude of Jesus. It was not that the law was bad, but the law had been fulfilled, superseded, abolished by the new saving reality in the person of Jesus, a reality unknown to the old covenant. The matter of real importance was no longer merely the observance of the law, but the acceptance of the salvation present in Jesus.[1]

This leads us to understand better why the Christians came to introduce a new cult in the name of Jesus, although, as we have already said, Jesus himself had been reserved in his attitude towards ceremonial observances. We can see here particularly clearly the interrelation between the old and new covenants. With his coming Jesus was destined to abolish the ceremonial observances of the old covenant and by means of his death and resurrection to replace them with the new worship 'in spirit and in truth' (John 4.23f.). This worship became the characteristic mark of the new covenant of the end-time. It is no accident that the inner reality of the new covenant was set forth in new worship. In this worship there could clearly be seen the fulfilment and supersession of Judaism by Christianity, for which in his earthly life Jesus had prepared the way and which in his ascension he had completed. In this worship Jesus was seen to be Lord of the Church and of the world. He was the Shekinah, the glory of God, which had previously dwelt in the temple and was now present in the new temple, the Christian Church. Furthermore, in baptism and eucharist Christ brought to those who believed in him the fruit of his sacrificial death on the cross; these rites took the place of the sacrificial system of the Old Testament. We shall see that the Jewish sabbath also found its fulfilment for Christians in the reality of the saving work of Christ. We shall see, too, that the Christian observance of Sunday originated in very close connection with the person of Christ and with the new worship which was based on him and his work.

[1] P. G. Verweijs, *Evangelium und neues Gesetz in der ältesten Christenheit bis auf Marcion*, 1960, pp. 7–39, has attempted to establish these connections.

3. THE SABBATH IN THE EARLY CHURCH

Although the wealth of material on the subject of the sabbath in the early Church would suggest that it be divided into several periods, we are going to attempt in a single chapter to deal with the whole period from the primitive Church right down to the time of Constantine the Great and even perhaps beyond. It is only in this way that we can demonstrate the inner continuity which leads from the primitive Church to the Church of the fathers. We shall see how in the primitive Church deep and solid foundations were laid on which the whole of the later period built. This compactness and continuity are naturally to be seen more clearly in the sabbath theology of the early Church than in its sabbath practice. Its theology comprises a complex of thought which can, to a certain extent, be seen at a glance and systematically unfolded. In default of extant sources its practice, on the other hand, cannot be unambiguously assessed, and we have to reconstruct the development of sabbath practice from occasional hints. It is, therefore, advisable to divide the material in this way and to deal first with the sabbath theology and then with the sabbath practice of the early Church. In order that the outlines should not be unnecessarily blurred, undue stress will not be laid, in the first part, on the geographical and chronological differences between the sources. The second part will then fill in what the first part has omitted in this respect.

A. SABBATH THEOLOGY

The primitive Church would have had no cause to bother itself with the sabbath question if it had not been for its tradition that Jesus had broken the sabbath repeatedly and in a provocative manner. On its own account the primitive Church would never have considered as a problem either the institution of the sabbath or the loyal observance of the sabbath rest. It was Jesus by his attitude to the sabbath who had presented them with this problem. It was a problem still awaiting solution so far as the matter of principle was concerned. Jesus had certainly infringed the sabbath commandment, but in the last analysis he had left unanswered the question about the underlying reason for his action. Moreover, the polemical style of Jesus' explanations of his sabbath healings and of his justification of the plucking of the ears of corn by the disciples had the effect of concealing rather than disclosing this underlying reason. The primitive Church was, therefore, thrown back on its own resources in its attempt to account for Jesus' sabbath conflicts. Once that had happened, the primitive Church could think of asking itself whether the attitude of Jesus towards the sabbath might or should or would have to involve an alteration of some kind in its own attitude towards the sabbath.

The primitive Church was probably right (we have already discussed this point) in detecting a hidden messianic claim being made by Jesus in the liberty which he took with regard to the sabbath. They were, therefore, also right in linking the tradition about Jesus' sabbath conflicts with their acknowledgement of his messiahship. The scriptural proofs which the Church adduced to justify Jesus' infringements of the sabbath all show us their conviction that these authoritative acts of Jesus were evidence of his unique mission.[1] The passage I Sam. 21.1-7 which was quoted in defence of the plucking of the ears of corn by the disciples (Mark 2.25f. par.) was not intended merely as

[1] We may conclude that these scriptural proofs are one and all secondary accretions to the tradition about Jesus, because (among other reasons) they fit so ill in their context. So far as I Sam. 21.1-7 is concerned, we have already proved this; see pp. 59ff. above. This is true in even greater measure in the example provided in Matt. 12.5ff. The illustration that the priests had to sacrifice on the sabbath is added only because of the cue provided by the word ἱερεύς, and it has nothing whatsoever to do with the plucking of ears of corn. Hos. 6.6, 'I desire mercy, and not sacrifice', is even less appropriate in this passage; it is a phrase from scripture which in itself tallied with the mind of Jesus (see pp. 75f. above), but its use here is unhappy. We can, therefore, hardly agree with E. Lohmeyer, *Das Evangelium des Matthäus*, 1956, pp. 183f., who holds that in the material peculiar to Matthew a homogeneous tradition may be discerned; he suggests that this tradition culminates in 12.8, 'For the Son of man is lord of the sabbath' (here by contrast with Mark, Lohmeyer holds, in its right place), and that its origin is to be found in the anti-cultic circles of Galilee (well known to be one of Lohmeyer's favourite theories). Even in the Fourth Gospel the link between 5.1-18 and the subsequent scriptural proof in 7.22ff. is very loose. This proof from scripture hardly applies at all to the situation described in 5.8, 10; there the sabbath was broken by the sick man carrying his bed about and not by the healing in itself, as is presupposed in 7.22ff. This can also make one suspicious concerning the popular assumption that pages have been misplaced, as a result of which—put crudely—John 6 was slipped in between chs. 5 and 7; cf., e.g., E. Schweizer, *Ego Eimi* (FRLANT 56), 1939, pp. 108-11. If the two chapters 5 and 7 originally ran consecutively, it would be a matter for surprise that they are not better connected.

an excuse (even David had once done something forbidden). There was another thought tacitly understood: what was allowable for David was all the more allowable for great David's greater son, the second David, the Messiah. Matt. 12.5f. adds another quotation from scripture which has exactly the same significance, 'Or have you not read in the law how on the sabbath the priests in the temple profane the sabbath' (by offering sacrifices, an obligation taking precedence over the sabbath: Num. 28.9f.) 'and (yet) are guiltless?' Once again this is not just an instance of sabbath-breaking permitted or even prescribed in the Old Testament and serving as an excuse for Jesus' action; in the following verse we can see that much more is involved, 'I tell you, something greater than the temple is here.' We find once again the same thought: what was allowable or even obligatory for the priests is certainly allowable for the heavenly high priest who stands over them all.[1] The Fourth Gospel provides (John 7.19–24) yet another scriptural proof of the same kind: in accordance with the regulations in the law the priests have to circumcise a newborn child on the eighth day of his life even if this day falls on a sabbath. Jesus asks (v. 23b), 'Are you angry with *me* because on the sabbath I made a man's whole body well?' Probably the inference to be drawn here is not primarily from the less to the greater (that Jesus did not merely do something to *one* part of this man's body, but healed his *whole* body).[2] The stress in this sentence lies much more on the 'I' of Jesus: if for the sake of circumcision the priests are allowed and obliged to break the sabbath, how much more may Jesus, whom the Father has sent, break the sabbath for the sake of his work of redemption.[3] The messianic claim also comes

---

[1] On this theme see pp. 113ff. below.

[2] Thus R. Bultmann, *Das Evangelium des Johannes* (Meyer), 1964[10], p. 208; cf. E. Lohse, *TWNT* VII, p. 28. In this case a rabbinic parallel could be adduced. R. Eleazar b. Azariah (about 100) said, 'If circumcision, which affects only one of the 248 parts of the human body, takes precedence over the sabbath, how much more does the whole body (if it is in mortal danger) take precedence over the sabbath'; SB II, p. 488. R. Bultmann (*loc. cit.*) considers the possibility whether the (many) infringements of the sabbath necessitated by the commandment to circumcise were originally contrasted with the *one* work of Jesus.

[3] H. Ljungmann, (p. 77, n. 4), pp. 71ff., provides a similar interpretation. He holds that Jesus was *obliged* to act in this way if he were not to abrogate the law.

unmistakably to the surface in another passage in the Fourth Gospel (John 5.17), 'My father is working still, and I am working.'[1]

In these passages the 'must' of Jesus' divine mission is placed on the same level as the necessity which caused David to eat the shewbread and as the obligation of the priests to sacrifice on the sabbath and to circumcise the newborn on the sabbath. Here we encounter the same kind of 'proof' which characterized the answers of Jesus himself.[2] The comparisons are not conclusive, and they even smack of effrontery unless Jesus' unique position in the divine plan is presupposed: sometimes this position is even expressly stated. He *had* to act as he did, even on the sabbath, if he were not to break his own 'law', that is to say his obedience to the Father.

The patristic writers later took up these scriptural proofs and added to them: in their eyes, however, they were certainly already regarded as conclusive in themselves. Every limitation on the force of the sabbath commandment which could be discovered in the Old Testament would help to prove that the sabbath had no absolute significance. In these writers we do not find the scriptural proofs based on the person and authority of Jesus. From the second century onwards in the Church at large it is apparent that the sabbath is officially finished with and written off as a specifically Jewish institution. It was now only a question of providing further support for this position by means of scriptural exegesis. The discussion was being carried on after a considerable lapse of time. In the following paragraphs we shall draw attention to the most important ideas and illustrate each with some patristic references. These references are not by any means intended to be exhaustive; an enumeration of all the authorities would be too large a task, since the same arguments are used by the fathers again and again.

(i) The uninterrupted work of God (see John 5.17) is emphasized. Justin, *Dial.* 29.3, 'God directs the government of the universe on this day equally as on all others' (cf. 23.3). Clement Alex., *Strom.* VI. 16.141.7, 'God's resting is not, then, as some conceive, that God ceased from doing. For, being good, if he should ever cease from doing good, then would he cease from being God, which it is sacrilege even to say.'[3] We find the sharpest polemic in the Syriac *Didascalia* 26 (Connolly, p. 236), 'If God willed that

---

[1] This passage is discussed at length on pp. 98ff. below.
[2] See pp. 69ff. above.
[3] Passages like the following occur very close to others dealing with the idea of a *creatio continua*, Clement Alex., *Strom.* VI.16.142.1, and Origen, *Hom.* 23.4 *in Num.* Cf. also the *Gospel of Philip* 8; H. M. Schenke, 'Das Evangelium nach Philippus', *TLZ* 84, 1959, col. 6.

we should be idle one day for six . . . God himself would also have remained idle with all his creatures. But now the governance of the world is carried on ever continually, and the spheres do not cease even for a moment from their course, but at God's command (their universal and perpetual motion proceeds). For if he would say, "Thou shalt be idle, and thy son, and thy servant, and thy maidservant, and thine ass," how does he (continue to) work, causing to generate, and making the winds blow, and fostering and nourishing us his creatures? On the sabbath day he causes (the winds) to blow, and (the waters) to flow, and (thus) works. . . .'[1] We are already familiar with the discussion about the 'rest of God' from Jewish sources.[2] There, however, it was purely a question of the interpretation of Gen. 2.2f.; it would never have occurred to a Jew to call in question the validity of the sabbath commandment on account of these considerations.

(ii) The list of the breaches of the sabbath which were tolerated or even prescribed under the old covenant is completed by the fathers. In addition to the priests who offer sacrifice (Matt. 12.5)[3] and circumcise children (John 7.23),[4] Joshua broke the sabbath at God's command on the occasion of the conquest of Jericho[5] and the Maccabees fought on the sabbath.[6]— But even this line of argument which is here directed against the sabbath as such would not have been conclusive for a Jew, for whom the exceptions would only confirm the binding nature of the sabbath commandment.

(iii) A further indication that the sabbath was intended only for the Jews and not for the universal religion of Christianity seemed to be provided by the fact that the patriarchs did not keep any sabbath: similarly, before the time of Abraham men had not been circumcised and yet had been reckoned righteous before God. Justin frequently mentions these righteous men of remote antiquity.[7] Once again, however, we refer to the

---

[1] Reference may perhaps be made to later authors, Epiphanius, *Haer.* 66.23.7; Ambrose, *In Luc.* VII.173; Chrysostom, *De Christi divinitate* 4 (PG 48.810f.).

[2] See pp. 47f. above.

[3] Justin, *Dial.* 27.5; 29.3; Aphrahates, *Hom.* 13.7; Eusebius, *Comm. in Ps.* 91 (EVV 92, PG 23.1169B); Epiphanius, *Haer.* 30.32.10; Ps.-Athanasius, *Hom. de semente* 13, etc.

[4] Justin, *Dial.* 27.5; Irenaeus, *Adv. haer.* IV.8.2; Epiphanius, *Haer.* 30.32.11–12, etc.

[5] Tertullian, *Adv. Jud.* 4 (ch. 1–9 of this treatise probably come from Tertullian); cf. also *Adv. Marc.* IV.12 and II.21; Victorinus, *De fabrica mundi* 6.

[6] Tertullian (n. 5); Victorinus (n. 5); Aphrahates (n. 3). Among later texts we might also mention, Gregory of Nyssa, *Testimonia adv. Jud.* 13 (PG 46.221); Cyril Alex., *Adorat. in spirit. et ver.* 7; Ps.-Athanasius, *Hom. de sabbat. et circ.* 3.

[7] *Dial.* 19.6; 23.3; 29.3; 27.5; 46.2–3. But see also Irenaeus, *Adv. haer.* IV.16.2; Tertullian, *Adv. Jud.* 2; Aphrahates, *Hom.* 13.8; Eusebius, *HE* I.4.8; *Comm. in Ps.* 91 (EVV 92, PG 23.1168A); *Dem. evang.* I.6 (PG 22.57).

evidence of the Syriac *Didascalia* 26 (Connolly, p. 236), 'If God willed that we should be idle one day for six, first of all the patriarchs and righteous men and all they that were before Moses would have remained idle (upon it).' From the fact that the patriarchs did not yet have any sabbath observance, it was deduced (especially by Justin)[1] that the sabbath had been given to the Jews by Moses solely because of the hardness of their heart[2] and in order to remind them of God on at least every seventh day; it was, therefore, given to them only for a time, that is to say until the appearing of Christ. Justin, *Dial.* 23.1–2, then continues the argument, 'But if we do not admit this, we shall be liable to fall into foolish opinions, as if it were not the same God who existed in the times of Enoch and all the rest, who neither were circumcised after the flesh, nor observed sabbaths, nor any other (rites), seeing that Moses enjoined such observances; or that God has not wished each race of mankind continually to perform the same righteous actions: to admit which seems to be ridiculous and absurd. Therefore we must confess that he, who is ever the same, has commanded these and such like institutions on account of sinful men.' The view of Aphrahates in *Hom.* 13 is rather different. Like Justin he holds that the sabbath is not an ordinance dating from the time of creation, but was first introduced in connection with the fall; unlike Justin, however, Aphrahates holds that it was not a punishment for the Jews' hardness of heart, but a regulation about the time of rest for man and beast which became necessary as a result of the fall.[3]—The opinion that the sabbath and the Mosaic law had become necessary in the course of the saving history as a result of sin seems to correspond with the view of St Paul in Gal. 3.19, 'Why then the law? It was added ($\pi\rho\sigma\epsilon\tau\epsilon\theta\eta$) because of transgressions, till the offspring should come to whom the promise had been made (i.e. Abraham's offspring); and it was ordained by angels through an intermediary.' We should, however, note the differences. Paul teaches that the law was the *cause* of the transgressions; and secondly, Paul would never have relativized the law (and with it the place of Israel in the saving history) by suggesting that it derived 'only' from Moses. If Christians no longer stood under the law, this was only because Christ had redeemed them from it. Paul's understanding of the abiding significance and importance of the law for *all* men was, therefore, quite different.[4] Even the

---

[1] *Dial.* 18.2; 19.6; 23.2; 43.1; 92.4.

[2] This expression already occurs in the New Testament; Mark 10.5 par., in connection with the question of divorce; Mark 3.5, in connection with the sabbath conflicts; cf. also Rom. 11.25. In the LXX we find it in Deut. 10.16; Jer. 4.4; Ezek. 3.7.

[3] Yet another interpretation is to be found in the Syriac *Didascalia* 21 (Connolly pp. 190f.), that the sabbath has been imposed on the Jews as a time of mourning, before the event, for the passion of Christ which would one day happen.

[4] It seems that Luke in the two parts of his historical work has adopted a position in contrast with the Pauline view and has especially emphasized

patristic writers were, of course, not able to operate merely with such a simplified point of view. We shall see that the same authors did, to some extent, tread quite different paths in order to demonstrate that the sabbath commandment is no longer binding on Christians. Just because they did full justice to the importance of the sabbath commandment, these other arguments were important.[1]

We have seen that the primitive Church saw the justification of Jesus' breaches of the sabbath to lie wholly in the authority of his eschatological mission. The first Christians would not have dared to have been so critical of the sabbath if it had not been for the person of Jesus and his specific acts of sabbath infringement. The saying in Mark 2.27f. that the sabbath is made for man and not the other way round and that man is lord even of the sabbath was couched in too general terms. The primitive Church applied the truth contained in this saying exclusively to Jesus: he, the lord of the sabbath, the Son of man, was free even in this respect.[2] We seem to find similar teaching in the remarkable saying which Codex D adds on to Luke 6.4 and which occupies there the place of Mark 2.27, 'On the same day he (Jesus) saw a man working on the sabbath and he said to him, "Man, if you know what you are doing, you are blessed; but if you do not know, then you are accursed and a transgressor of the law." ' It is not accidental that this saying comes immediately after the story of the plucking of the ears of corn by the disciples, in which Jesus seemed to set aside the sabbath commandment in very general terms. It is then related how Jesus on the very same sabbath himself met a man who was working and said to him with asperity, 'If you transgress the sabbath commandment without good cause, you are accursed. Only if you know what you are doing (which may be amplified, "I, Jesus, knew what I was doing when I broke the sabbath"), is this permissible for you.' In this way any misunderstanding is removed which could have resulted from Jesus' own attitude

---

the promise to the patriarchs as opposed to the Mosaic covenant; by this means he has intended to underline the universality of the Christian religion, and in so doing he has prepared the way for early Catholicism. Cf. L. Goppelt, *Christentum und Judentum im ersten und zweiten Jahrhundert*, 1954, pp. 229ff.; P. Vielhauer, 'Zum "Paulinismus" der Apostelgeschichte', *EvTh* 10, 1950–1, pp. 1–15.

[1] See pp. 88ff., 100ff., 108ff. below.
[2] See pp. 64ff. above.

in the case of the plucking of the ears of corn by the disciples. In all probability, therefore, we have to regard Luke 6.5 D as an apology for the attitude of Jesus towards the sabbath. In making this apology the Church wanted to qualify sweeping generalizations about the sabbath commandment being no longer binding (Mark 2.23f., 27f.): not everyone was permitted to break the sabbath, only the lord of the sabbath.

The principal stress should without doubt be put on the second half of the logion: a sharp warning is given against frivolous transgression of the sabbath commandment. J. Jeremias[1] also draws attention to this point. It does, however, remain questionable whether this is a genuine saying of Jesus, as Jeremias and others[2] assume. In the first place, Jesus would hardly have made such an apology for his action if our conclusions about his freedom with regard to the sabbath are correct. Secondly, Jeremias[3] himself encounters difficulties when he tries to explain the situation of the occurrence: one has to suppose that Jesus met one of his followers without recognizing him (for no other Jew would have worked on the sabbath). Everything seems to lead us to the conclusion that we are dealing with a construction intended to serve an apologetic purpose. The designation as blessed of the man who knew what he was doing would not, therefore, be of general application to the Christian or even to the gnostic: it would apply in the first instance and above all to Jesus who knew what he was doing and was no frivolous sabbath breaker. We have, therefore, to regard Luke 6.5 D as a church construction of Jewish Christian provenance,[4] since the Gentile Christian church would not have criticized the transgression of the sabbath commandment so severely. This saying belongs to the same area as Matt. 5.17ff., a passage which has a strongly apologetic character.[5]— M.-J. Lagrange[6] holds that Rom. 14.14, 20–23 may be adduced as a parallel to Luke 6.5 D; there it is a question of weak brethren who act against their conscience and who therefore sin if they partake of unclean meats. In the case of Luke 6.5 D we should accordingly be faced with a weak brother and with the question whether work on the sabbath was permissible or not. The sharp tone of the address in Luke 6.5 D does, however, hardly allow this interpretation. It is not usual to make life more difficult for weak

[1] *Unknown Sayings of Jesus*, ET 1957, pp. 49ff.
[2] T. Zahn, *Einleitung in das NT* II, 1899, p. 355; J. Bauer, 'Vom Sabbat zum Sonntag', *Der christliche Sonntag*, 1956, p. 172.
[3] (N. 1), p. 52.
[4] A. Loisy, *Les évangiles synoptiques* I, 1907, p. 513, n. 1, even holds that Luke 6.5 D comes from a pre-Markan source.
[5] See p. 77 above.
[6] *L'évangile selon Saint Luc* (Études bibliques), 1948, pp. 176f., n. 5; J. H. Holtzmann, *Hand-Commentar zum NT* I, 1889, p. 94.

brethren by posing them a question of conscience such as, 'Are you quite certain whether you may do that? If not, you are cursed.'[1]

After this discussion it must seem as if the primitive Church had occupied itself exclusively with the problem how the sabbath infringements of Jesus were to be justified. But did not the attitude of Jesus have some consequences for the life of the Church? Was not the Church as the company of the master's followers authorized to walk in his footsteps? We could easily receive the impression that the Church answered these questions with a decisive No. Instead of deriving from Jesus' liberty towards the sabbath its own freedom in this respect, the Church emphasized by contrast the exclusiveness of Jesus' position (Mark 2.27 compared with 2.28; Luke 6.5 D) and avoided a general critique of sabbath observance. But this impression is deceptive: such a picture would be one-sided. The Church certainly gave great prominence to Jesus' exceptional position; it did, nevertheless, succeed in recognizing that for it, too, the significance of the sabbath had altered since the coming of Christ. The path which led Christians to this recognition did not come directly from the earthly Jesus; as we shall see, it did in a decisive respect, however, derive from him. For the sake of a convenient arrangement of the material we shall distinguish in the following pages between three expressions of sabbath theology; in the last analysis, however, they are all connected and even overlap one another, at least in respect of chronology. It should, therefore, not be supposed that this division of the material aims at establishing development in thought. Nevertheless it can be said that while the first theologumenon simply follows on Jewish tradition and takes it over, the christocentric element in the dispute assumes increasing importance.

(a) The eschatological sabbath and its blessing

In the Church there remained alive the late Jewish belief, according to which the weekly day of rest would find its proper fulfilment in the last days. There was widespread in late Judaism the hope of a new world, which with its rest from toil

---

[1] We need not consider here an alleged rabbinic parallel, which is not a parallel at all, b. Shabbath VII.1f.; cf. C. K. Barrett, *The New Testament Background*, 1956, pp. 153f.

would be like a great sabbath.[1] In a certain sense, therefore, the
Jewish notion was merely incorporated into Christian thought
and hope. Certainly there is not yet any question of a fundamental Christian critique of the Jewish sabbath, precisely
because Jewish thought had never played off the eschatological
promise of a never-ending sabbath against the weekly sabbath
which was its image and model.

The classical text in the New Testament is Heb. 3.7–4.11.
The train of thought is as follows: in the beginning God rested
after his work of creation (according to Gen. 2.2). This rest of
God, which is as it were the concluding work of creation, is
meant to benefit human beings—that is to say, they should
participate in it. This may be seen, albeit in negative fashion,
in Ps. 95.11, where God swears that the Israelites should not
enter his rest because they had been disobedient. God, therefore,
clearly has a rest prepared for his people.[2] In the psalm it is
the Israelites of the desert wanderings who are declared to have
forfeited the promised rest. They did not, indeed, reach the
land of promise, where God wished to bring his people to rest.
The author of Hebrews does, however, take a further step. He
wants to guard against the mistaken view that the Israelites
under Joshua had, in fact, entered God's rest. Had this been so,
David would not say in the same psalm (Ps. 95.7f.), 'Today
harden not your hearts as you did then.' God is, therefore,
giving his people another chance of entering his rest. This is the
vital point for the author of Hebrews: this 'today' has dawned;
David had prophesied the time of Christ in which the promise
of participation in God's rest is renewed. For the people of God
(and they are now those who believe in Christ) there still
remains a sabbath rest.[3]

Here it is clearly said that the future blessing of salvation has
been proclaimed anew in the eschatological 'Today' ushered
in by Jesus; this blessing will consist of rest from toil near God
and with God. This rest does, in fact, exist, and those who believe

---

[1] See pp. 48ff. above.

[2] H. Windisch, *Der Hebräerbrief* (HNT 14), 1931[2], p. 33, comes to the
conclusion that in accordance with this view God has been resting since the
creation of the world. But this does not necessarily follow; it may also refer
to the rest which God has prepared (as a promise).

[3] σαββατισμός; only here in the NT. Cf. Plutarch, *De superstitione* 3. Later
Origen, *Cels.* V.59.

in Christ shall participate in it, provided that they persevere. By contrast with the late Jewish expectation it is apparent that the Christians have a living hope in this eschatological rest. This rest has already become for them a present reality as a result of its renewed proclamation by Jesus. Later we shall have to return to this point.[1]

E. Käsemann entitled his commentary on the Epistle to the Hebrews, 'The wandering people of God'.[2] He derived this title from the comparison drawn in Heb. 3.7ff. between the company of Christians and that of the Israelites on their journey in the wilderness. This description is certainly to the point. The Christians are also on a journey towards a goal which the future will make plain to them; they do not yet live by sight, but by faith. Nevertheless we shall have to ask whether this interpretation of the promises and especially of the sabbath rest as blessings to be enjoyed merely in the future does full justice to the message of the Epistle to the Hebrews.[3]

Almost without exception patristic exegesis understood the eschatological rest to be the sabbath and, *vice versa*, the true sabbath to be the eschatological rest. It is significant that we find once again in this Christian exegesis the same variations of outlook which had appeared in late Judaism and in rabbinic teaching. On the one hand, for instance, there are passages which refer to the future sabbath as the time of fulfilment when God will be all in all. (This is certainly also the opinion of the Epistle to the Hebrews.) On the other hand, however, perhaps even more often we find a chiliastic idea of a preliminary golden age; this age would not be the end, but would last one thousand years and lead to the dawn of the new aeon. The millennium (now naturally understood as the reign of Jesus the Messiah) in this case corresponded to the seventh period of

---

[1] See pp. 111f. below.

[2] *Das wandernde Gottesvolk*, 1939.

[3] There is yet another question to be raised. E. Käsemann is certainly right in bringing late Jewish speculations about the sabbath into the discussion in order to illuminate the background of Heb. 3–4. He holds that the rest presupposed in Heb. 3–4 denotes a heavenly place and that it, therefore, has a purely local significance (*op. cit.*, p. 41); but this conclusion is hardly correct. The spatial speculation about the τόπος of the rest occurs only in later Gnosticism; the references quoted by E. Käsemann (*op. cit.*, p. 44) make this clear; see also pp. 95ff. below. But in the Epistle to the Hebrews we cannot yet reckon with this interpretation. Moreover, in the Epistle to the Hebrews (as opposed to gnostic teaching) the eternal sabbath is not always accessible, but only in the 'Today'; this 'Today' is associated with the saving history and points into the future.

a thousand years, that is to say to the cosmic sabbath; after that would follow the final golden age which came to be called by Christians the 'eighth day'.

It is not possible to quote in detail all the passages which refer to the sabbath of the final age. We shall restrict ourselves to the older and more important evidence,[1] and here we shall distinguish between chiliastic and non-chiliastic texts. It is, of course, difficult to make this distinction, and we shall find ourselves on sure ground only in the cases where the sources themselves suppose that *after* the expected sabbath another epoch will follow, that is to say the eternal eighth day: in these cases we are clearly dealing with a chiliastic viewpoint. On the other hand, the idea of a millennium may well also be present where there is no express mention of one thousand years. The hope of an eschatological sabbath was in any case (even in late Judaism) only possible on the basis of a combination of Gen. 2.2f. (God rested on the seventh day) and Ps. 90.4 (one day in God's sight is as one thousand years). There still remains the question about the nature of this sabbath which was to last one thousand years: was it the preliminary golden age of the millennium or was it the final fulfilment?

(i) *Non-chiliastic passages* (i.e. those which do not *oblige* us to suppose a chiliastic background; in addition we know from the works of Origen, Eusebius of Caesarea and Jerome, for example, that they were opponents of chiliasm).[2] In the Fifth Book of Ezra, a Christian work of the second century directed against the Jews, we find (2.24), 'Rest and be at peace, my people, for your repose will come'; and again (2.34f.), 'Wait for your shepherd! He will give you everlasting rest, for he is near who shall come at the end of the world. Be ready for the rewards of the kingdom.'[3] In Origen (*Cels.* VI. 61) we find that Celsus took offence because in Gen. 2.2f. God is said to have 'rested'. Origen says, 'He does not even know the meaning . . . of the day of the sabbath and the cessation of God, in which those who have done all their works in the six days will feast together with God; and because they have not neglected any of the responsibilities they will ascend to the contemplation of God and the assembly of the righteous and the blessed who are engaged in this.'[4] Again in Origen's *Hom.* 23.4 *in Num.* we find, 'The true sabbath on which God rests from all his works will be the future age,

---

[1] Cf. also the admirable work by A. Luneau which covers a wider field, *L'histoire du salut chez les Pères de l'Eglise. La doctrine des âges du monde* (Théologie historique 2), 1964.
[2] Cf. Origen, *Comm. in Joann.* X.1.10 (8); Eusebius, *HE* III.39.11f.; Jerome, *Comm. in Isa.* X (on 35 *ad fin.*).
[3] *NT Apoc.* II, p. 695. Cf. the Life of Adam and Eve 51.
[4] This thought is typical of Origen; cf. *Hom.* 7.5 *in Ex.*, 'The sixth day is the life in which we now find ourselves; in six days God created this world. Therefore we must lay aside and keep in store on this day as much as we shall need on the following day as well.'

when pain and grief flee away and God will be all in all. On that sabbath God will graciously allow us also to celebrate with him . . .'[1] Eusebius in *Comm. in Ps.* 91(92) writes, 'The perfect sabbath and the perfect and most blessed rest are to be found in the kingdom of God, above the work of creation which was accomplished in six days and beyond all that is visible, in incorporeal and heavenly (circumstances); where pain, sadness and sighing flee away, where we spend a blessed time of leisure pleasing to God once we have been rescued from this mortal life which had fallen a prey to corruption; where, after our liberation from bodily work and from servitude to the flesh, we live and keep the sabbath rest with God and close to God. For this reason the apostle says, "Let us strive to enter that rest." '[2]

(ii) *Chiliastic views* appear more frequently.[3] The Revelation of John (20.1ff.) opens a long list of passages. Here we need not attempt the detailed exegesis of this passage nor inquire whether similar thoughts were not already to be found in Paul's writings (I Cor. 15.23f.; cf. I Thess. 4.16f.).[4] We next find this tradition in, for example, Papias,[5] who received it from oral tradition (from the elder?); from him the tradition reached Irenaeus. In *Adv. haer.* V. 28.3 we read, 'For in as many days as this world was made, in so many thousand years shall it be concluded. And for this reason the scripture says: [Gen. 2.1f. follows]. This is an account of the things formerly created, as also it is a prophecy of what is to come. For the day of the Lord is as a thousand years; and in six days created things were completed: it is evident, therefore, that they will come to an end at the sixth thousand year',[6] and in *Adv. haer.* V. 30.4, 'For the righteous he will bring in the times of the

---

[1] For further references in Clement and Origen see C. Schneider, 'Anapausis', *RAC* I, pp. 414f.

[2] PG 23.1168CD. See also Ambrose, *Or. de obitu Theod.* 29 (PL 16.1457f.); *In Luc.* VIII. 23; Jerome, *Comm. in Ezek.* VI (on 20.10); Chrysostom, *Hom.* 6.1 *in Heb.* (on ch. 4). There are numerous passages in Augustine; see, e.g., *Ep.* 55 (ad Jan.) 11.20; *Civ. dei* 22.30; *Adim.* 16; *Serm.* 9.3. For further references see H. Dumaine, 'Dimanche', *DACL* IV, col. 921f.

[3] Cf. also J. Daniélou, *The Theology of Jewish Christianity*, 1964, pp. 396ff.

[4] Cf. H. Bietenhard, *Das tausendjährige Reich*, 1955.

[5] Eusebius, *HE* III.39.11ff. Teaching about the kingdom which lasts a thousand years is described by Eusebius as myth; according to Irenaeus, *Adv. haer.* V.33.3f., Papias has painted in purely fantastic colours the paradisal circumstances of the thousand-year kingdom (cf. Syriac Baruch 39).

[6] A Greek manuscript (Paris 2215 B.N.) continues as follows, 'On the seventh day he (God) will judge the world; and on the eighth day, which is the age to come, he will lead some to eternal punishment, others to life. That is the reason why some psalms have the superscription "ad ogdoaden".' J. Daniélou, 'La typologie millénariste de la semaine dans le christianisme primitif', *Vigiliae Christianae* 2, 1948, p. 10, comments, 'This final point probably comes from Irenaeus. We should not forget that Eusebius tells us that Irenaeus wrote a treatise *On the Ogdoad*.' (*HE* V. 20.1; Irenaeus wrote the treatise against Florinus, who had fallen under the influence of the Valentinian heresy.)

kingdom, that is, the rest, the hallowed seventh day; and he will restore to Abraham the promised inheritance.'[1] The famous fifteenth chapter of the *Epistle of Barnabas* also seems to be rooted in the chiliastic tradition.[2] We shall give some extracts from this passage. In vv. 4–5 we find, 'Notice, children, what he means by the words, "He completed them in six days." He means this: in six thousand years the Lord will make an end of all things; for, in his reckoning, the day means a thousand years. He is himself my witness when he says, "Behold a day of the Lord is as a thousand years." Therefore, children, in six days—in the course of six thousand years—all things will be brought to an end. "And he rested on the seventh day." This is the meaning: when his Son returns, he will put an end to the era of the Lawless One, judge the wicked, and change the sun, the moon, and the stars. Then, on the seventh day, he will properly rest.' Again in vv. 7–8b we read, 'We shall, as it appears, properly rest and sanctify it (i.e. the seventh day) only when we are able to do so after being ourselves justified and having received the promised blessing; when there is no more iniquity, and all things have been made new by the Lord, then at last shall we be able to sanctify it, because we have first been sanctified ourselves. He further says to them, "Your new moons and sabbaths I disdain." Consider what he means: Not the sabbaths of the present era are acceptable to me, but that which I have appointed to mark the end of the world and to usher in the eighth day, that is, the dawn of another world.'[3] It is fairly plain that chiliastic ideas underlie this passage. The hints which occur in v. 5b concerning the judgement of the world and the new creation at the end point to no other conclusion. In v. 8 the seventh millennium is unambiguously followed by the eighth day, the new aeon. We should otherwise have to assume that in *Barn.* 15 two eschatological ideas have been forcibly yoked together, one which sees the seventh day as the new aeon and another which

---

[1] The following two passages are probably also to be understood in a chiliastic sense: *Adv. haer.* IV. 16, 'the sabbath of God, that is the kingdom ... in which the man who shall have persevered in serving God shall, in a state of rest, partake of God's table', and V.33.2, 'For what are the hundredfold (rewards) in this world, the entertainments given to the poor, and the suppers for which a return is made?' (Irenaeus refers to Luke 14.12–13; Matt. 19.29.) 'These are [to take place] in the times of the kingdom, that is, upon the seventh day, which has been sanctified, in which God rested from all the works which he created, which is the true sabbath of the righteous, in which they shall not be engaged in any earthly occupation; but shall have a table at hand prepared for them by God, supplying them with all sorts of dishes.'

[2] So also J. Böhmer, *Der christliche Sonntag nach Ursprung und Geschichte*, 1931, p. 12, and J. Daniélou in conversation.

[3] The second part of the quotation and also the sentence, 'for a day with him means a thousand years', are not to be found in the OT; they clearly come from an early Christian testimony source. See P. Prigent, *Les Testimonia dans le christianisme primitif*, 1961.

regards the eighth day as the new aeon.[1] This, however, would only make
the understanding of the passage more difficult. We should do better to
regard this chapter as a unity. The transition from the seventh to the eighth
fits perfectly into the framework of chiliastic ideas; the expectation of the
new aeon (i.e. of the eighth day) belongs to the ideas about the time which
will follow the thousand-year kingdom, and the millennium by definition
will not be the final stage. Moreover, *Barn.* 15.8 seems to have strong connections with Slavonic Enoch 33.1f. (This passage is probably a Christian
interpolation in a work which is otherwise Jewish in origin.)[2] The passage
is, in fact, very obscure; it will be reproduced here together with the comments of P. Billerbeck,[3] 'I (God) appoint the eighth day (i.e. the first day
after the week of creation) that the same eighth day may be the first created
over my works and that they (the works of the week of creation) may be
devised after the image of the seventh thousand (i.e. of the seven thousand
years of the week of the world), and that the eighth thousand may be the
beginning of the time of numberlessness and may be unending: neither years,
nor months, nor weeks, nor days, nor hours. (The eighth millennium shall
be the beginning of the *olam ha-ba* of the end time, just as the seven thousand years of the week of the world correspond to the seven days of the week
of creation.)'

Justin Martyr is also a representative of the chiliastic point of view (*Dial.*
80–81),[4] as is possibly also the *Ascension of Isaiah* (4.15). Tertullian joined
the same tradition, *Adv. Marc.* III.24.[5] (We need not be surprised that the
Montanist Tertullian was a chiliast!) In addition, we may refer to the
Commentary on Daniel by Hippolytus (IV. 23.4–6), 'And six thousand years
must needs be accomplished, in order that the sabbath may come, the rest,
the holy day, on which "God rested from all his works". The sabbath is both
type and image of the future reign of the saints when they will reign with
Christ, when he will descend from heaven, as John describes in his Revelation. The day of the Lord is indeed "as a thousand years". Since the Lord
made the universe in six days, six thousand years must be fulfilled. They are

---

[1] So H. Windisch, *Ergänzungsband zum HNT*, 1920, p. 384; cf. H.
Riesenfeld, 'Sabbat et jour du Seigneur', *New Testament Essays, Studies in
Memory of T. W. Manson*, 1959, pp. 215f.

[2] E.g. J. Daniélou (p. 92, n. 6), p. 3.

[3] SB IV.2.990f. See, however, the edition of the longer version by G. N.
Bonwetsch (TU III.14.2), 1922, p. 31. The passage 33.2 reads there (in
terminology which has a stronger Christian colouring), 'As with the first
day of the week, so shall the eighth day of the week perpetually recur.'

[4] The conversion of Israel which was promised for that time plays an
important part in Justin's thought. This idea is, in fact, very important in
Christian chiliasm; cf. H. Bietenhard (p. 92, n. 4), pp. 90ff.

[5] This passage is directed against Marcion's opinion that the idea of a
thousand-year kingdom is a purely Jewish matter. (Marcion interprets it as
the kingdom of the messiah of the demiurge.)

not yet fulfilled, as John (Rev. 17.10) says.'[1] Both the Syriac *Didascalia* 26
(Connolly, p. 234) and also Cyprian, *Ad Fortunatum* 2, transmit a chiliastic
tradition. Even Augustine, *Serm.* 259.2, began by being a chiliast until
following Tyconius he came to think of the millennium as taking place in
the history of the Christian Church (*Civ. dei* 20.7.1f.).[2] Typical chiliasts
were Victorinus, *De fabrica mundi* 6ff., and Lactantius, *Div. inst.* VII.[3]
We must refrain from indicating what actual, detailed events were expected
to be fulfilled in the thousand-year kingdom; there was very great variety,
and they may not always be precisely determined.[4]

(iii) Yet a third point of view took root in Christian gnosticism: the
seventh (or eighth) day was here regarded not as the time, but as the *place
of the consummation*; the true gnostic can always and at any time reach this
place by means of knowledge.[5] Here, of course, it is much more difficult to
decide whether or not a text is thinking like this in gnostic terms. We can-

[1] Cf. also Fragment VII (GCS Hipp. I, 246f.) from Hippolytus's work
Against Gaius, who asserted that according to Matt. 12.29 Satan was already
bound. (Gaius was, therefore, among those who interpreted Rev. 20 as a
reference to the Church; see p. 117 below.) Moreover, Hippolytus became
the father of calculations about the end of the world because in his *Commentary on Dan.* IV.24 (on the basis of a speculation about the ark of the
covenant the length of which came to 5½ yards) he placed the coming of
Christ in the year 5500. (The same reckoning is to be found in the Gospel
of Nicodemus 19 [*NT Apoc.* I, p. 472]. Cf. also Hilary of Poitiers, *Comm. in
Matt.* 20.6.) Attempts to fix the date of the end of the world have repeatedly
caused confusion in the Western Church: without doubt this kind of
apocalyptic runs contrary to the intention both of Jesus (Mark 13.32) and
also of chiliasm itself, which originally (cf. Rev. 20) was interested only in
the symbolism of the seventh day and not in the days or half-days which
precede it.

[2] See p. 117 below.

[3] Further material in A. Wikenhauser, 'Weltwoche und tausendjähriges
Reich', *TQS* 127, 1947, pp. 399ff.; cf. also Hilary, *Tract. Myst.* I.41. The
Ebionites also thought in chiliastic terms, according to Jerome, *Comm. in
Isa.* XVIII (on 66.20). (See also the teaching of Cerinthus, Eusebius *HE*
III.28.2.4–5.) We can, however, hardly agree with H. J. Schoeps, *Theologie
und Geschichte des Judenchristentums*, 1949, p. 82, who holds that the expectation
of the Son of man is to be found in these circles would have actually promoted
the spread of chiliasm. This assumption would only be justified if in the
Church at large the expectation of the thousand-year kingdom went by
default—and this was not the case.

[4] See H. Bietenhard (p. 92, n. 4), and esp. pp. 126ff. The OT basis is, above
all, Trito-Isaiah. In the chapter about the names of Sunday we shall have to
discuss in greater detail the eighth day, which has nothing to do with the
sabbath rest; see pp. 275ff. below.

[5] The gnostic teaching developed from the idea of the seven heavens
which was connected with the astronomical-astrological science of the seven
planetary spheres; this idea became the basis of the gnostic hope of redemption (descent of the redeemer and ascent of the soul to heaven). See p. 30,
n. 2, above.

not simply say that we have an example of gnostic speculation wherever the rest is represented as being attainable in the present. In connection with the saving history there is a perfectly legitimate way of talking about the eschatological sabbath rest dawning now in the present time.[1]

The evidence of the *Epistola Apost.* 12 (cf. 19 and 28) should probably be included here, since this epistle from the second century presupposes knowledge of teaching about the descent and ascent of the redeemer through the seven heavens, 'Rise up (says the risen Lord) and I will reveal to you what is above heaven and what is in heaven and your rest that is in the heavenly kingdom. For my Father has given me the power to take up you and those who believe in me.'[2] The logion from the Gospel of the Hebrews which is preserved for us in Clement Alex., *Strom.* V. 14.96.3, is also well known;[3] 'He who seeks will not stop till he find; and having found, he will wonder; and wondering, he will reign; and reigning, he will rest.' P. Vielhauer[4] adduces several passages from the Pseudo-Clementines, and M. Dibelius[5] some parallels from Hermetic gnosis which refer to the 'rest' in similar terms. We might perhaps even consider Cod. I of the Nag Hamâdi find, p. 120.2–9 (*NT Apoc.* I, p. 249): 'The Saviour said to his disciples: Already the moment has come, my brothers, for us to leave our troubles behind and to abide in the Rest. Verily, he who abides in the Rest shall rest eternally.'—It is only another way of expressing the same idea when the gnostics picture the 'rest' being incarnate in Jesus. We read, for instance, in the Gospel of the Hebrews (*NT Apoc.* I, pp. 163f., cited from Jerome, *Comm. in Isa.* IV, on Isa. 11.2) about the baptism of Christ, 'And it came to pass when the Lord was come up out of the water, the whole fount of the Holy Spirit descended upon him and rested upon him and said to him: My Son, in all the prophets was I waiting for thee that thou shouldest come and I might rest in thee. For thou art my rest; thou art my first-begotten Son that reignest for ever.' (Cf. Ecclus. 24.7; Wisdom 7.27.) The rest of the redeemer spirit also benefits believers who share in it. It is, however, instructive to note that in connection with these ideas we find increasingly the idea of the number 8. In the Acts of Thomas 27 (cf. 50) the Holy Ghost is, for instance, implored by the believers in these words, 'Come, mother of the seven houses, that you may find rest in the eighth house',[6] and in *Epist.*

---

[1] See pp. 108ff. below.

[2] Cf. Clement Alex., *Quis dives salvetur* 23.3, 'For I shall lead you up into the rest (and into the enjoyment) of ineffable and indescribable blessings.' See also II *Clement* 5.5; 6.7.

[3] Cf. *Strom.* II.9.45.5; similarly Pap. Oxy. 654=Logion 2 of the Gospel of Thomas (*NT Apoc.* I, pp. 164, 297).

[4] 'Judenchristliche Evangelien', *NT Apoc.* I, pp. 161f.

[5] *From Tradition to Gospel*, 1934, pp. 279ff. (on Matt. 11.28–30, a passage which he regards as an intrusion into the synoptic tradition; see p. 109, n. 3 below).

[6] The passage is, admittedly, not easy to interpret. The Spirit is probably

Apost. 18 the risen Lord says, 'I have come into being on the eigh(th) (day), which is the day of the Lord.'[1] There is, therefore, connected with the gnostic speculations about the seventh (or eighth) heaven a quite different tradition, that of Sunday, the Lord's day of the Christian Church. We shall see that this designation of Sunday as the eighth day played a great part in the symbolism of baptism: the number 8 represented the Holy Ghost.[2]

(iv) There is also a tradition which comes midway between that which views the rest purely as eschatological hope and that which thinks of it in terms of gnostic speculation: this tradition regards the rest as the place of departed souls. We do, in fact, come across the same idea in rabbinical teaching,[3] where the dead generally still await the rest;[4] Christian authors, on the other hand, emphasize that their rest is already realized.[5] Rev. 14.13 should be mentioned here, ' "Blessed are the dead who die in the Lord henceforth." "Blessed indeed, says the Spirit, that they may rest from their labours, for their deeds follow them!" ' The newly discovered Gospel of Thomas contains the following logion (51, *NT Apoc.* I, p. 516): 'His disciples said to him, "On what day will the rest of the dead come into being? And on what day will the new world come?" He said to them, "That which ye await has come, but ye know it not." '—Also Augustine, *Ep.* 55 (ad Jan.) 13.23 allegorically refers to the sabbath as the rest of the blessed.

As we survey the whole complex of thought which derives more or less directly from Heb. 3–4 and from its eschatological interpretation of the sabbath rest, we must conclude that in no essential respect has any progress been made beyond the Jewish outlook. Both the interpretation of Gen. 2.2f. in terms of a sabbath at the end of time and also the chiliastic speculation about the week of seven thousand years were known in late Judaism. A possible exception is the gnostic teaching about

the Pleroma from which the seven heavenly spheres have emanated; the community, however, is the new reality, the eighth house which corresponds to the Pleroma.

[1] C. Schmidt, in the explanatory notes to his edition of the *Epist. Apost.* (TU 43, p. 281), would like to supplement κυριακή not with ἡμέρα but with μονή. 'In this case Christ will be saying that he has originated through the agency of the Father and that as an independent being he has had his abode in the eighth heaven.' We can see from these difficulties of interpretation that even in the text the ideas are extremely confused.

[2] See pp. 275ff. below.

[3] See p. 50, n. 2, above.

[4] The rabbinic exegesis of Ps. 95 is, for instance, of interest: God will yet take back his oath that he will not let the Israelites enter into his rest; the departed would, nevertheless, still enter this rest. SB III.687.

[5] Perhaps in connection with teaching about the descent of Christ into the realm of the dead; see pp. 286ff. below.

redemption, according to which this rest is available in the present age. There is no evidence that this teaching was derived directly from Judaism, but it did develop no doubt in pre-Christian gnosticism and in gnostic circles close to the Christian Church. Wherever the association with the number 8 occurs, the scheme has usually been amplified and recast already by ideas derived from the Christian use of the eighth day.

We must now consider John 5.17, 'My Father is working still, and I am working', a passage which must be taken together with Heb. 3–4. In this passage account is taken of the concern shown by the theologians of Alexandrian Judaism to avoid an anthropomorphic view of God's rest, which (in connection with Gen. 2.2f.) would picture it in terms of inactivity. These theologians had thus partly cleared the way for the hope of a fulfilment of Gen. 2.2f. at the end of time when the blessed should rest with God.[1] John 5.17 also contains the statement that God works uninterruptedly;[2] moreover, it places an unmistakable emphasis on the ἕως ἄρτι. A time will, therefore, come when God's activity will be ended: a time will come—clearly at the end of the ages—when God will rest.

The ἕως ἄρτι, can hardly be construed in any other way.[3] If it is translated by 'always',[4] an important shade of meaning has been lost from the text. John 5.17 intends to interpret Gen. 2.2f. in the sense that God has never rested from the beginning of creation, that he does not yet rest, but that he will rest at the end. If we glance at the parallel passage in 9.4, 'We must do the works of him who sent me, while it is day; night comes, when no one can work' (cf. 11.9f.), there hardly remains for us any other possibility than to suppose that in our passage as well there is a reference to the conclusion of God's activity.—This parallel passage in 9.4 does, of course, raise another question. There the cessation of the activity of both God and Jesus is described as 'night'. Naturally it can be held that this expression should not be pressed and that it merely emphasizes the importance of the activity in the day. In fact, it would certainly be too drastic if we were to understand the future rest of God at the end of time as 'night' in the qualitative sense. In

[1] See p. 47 above.
[2] We have already shown (pp. 83f. above) that this argument was taken from the Christian fathers.
[3] Cf. R. Bultmann, *Das Evangelium des Johannes*, 1964[10], p. 183; and esp. O. Cullmann, 'Sabbath und Sonntag nach dem Johannesevangelium. ʿEως ἄρτι (John 5.17)', *In memoriam E. Lohmeyer*, 1953, pp. 127ff.
[4] So Chr. Maurer, 'Steckt hinter Joh. 5.17 ein Übersetzungsfehler?' *Wort und Dienst, Jahrbuch der theologischen Schule Bethel* NF 5, 1957, pp. 130–40.

that case we should have to assume that the Fourth Gospel was thinking in terms of the chaotic sabbath of the world before the beginning of the new aeon (see, for instance, II (4) Esd. 7.27–31).[1] Another conjecture may be nearer the point: the 'night', the cessation of the divine activity, could refer to the death of Jesus.[2] The evangelist describes that very time as 'night' (13.30b).

If this were the case, he sees the eschatological world epochs sweep by; the sixth day would be the time of the earthly activity of Jesus, the seventh would signify his rest in the grave and the eighth the new aeon which, in principle, had already begun with the resurrection of Jesus from the dead.[3] In this case, the promised sabbath rest of God would have been brought about by the guilt of men and would have found its fulfilment in the rest of Jesus in the grave:[4] this fulfilment would indeed have to be understood in a purely negative sense. This conjectural interpretation is, of course, purely hypothetical in character, for we do not find any further hint of this point of view in the Fourth Gospel.

In one respect John 5.17 does, however, go further than Heb. 3–4 in that Jesus bases his right to break the sabbath on the fact that God does not yet rest. The fact that the christological interest is concentrated on the person of Jesus shows that in John 5.17 we do not yet have to deal with a fundamental critique of the sabbath commandment. The 'son of the Father' can claim for himself the privilege of not keeping the sabbath.

[1] So G. Stählin, ZNW 33, 1934, pp. 244f. See p. 49 above.
[2] Cf. H. Strathmann, *Das Evangelium nach Johannes* (NTD 4), 1951, pp. 157, 175.
[3] This would mean that the era of the Church could not be identified with the beginning of the millennium.
[4] A passage from the Syriac *Didascalia* 21 (Connolly, p. 190) is more easily comprehensible if we consider it in this connection, 'Fast then . . . on the sabbath also, because it is the sleep of our Lord; for it is a day which ought especially to be kept with fasting; even as blessed Moses also, the prophet of all (things touching) this matter, commanded. For because he knew by the Holy Spirit and it was commanded him by Almighty God, who knew what the people were to do to his Son and his beloved Jesus Christ . . . therefore he bound them beforehand with mourning perpetually, in that he set apart and appointed the sabbath for them. For they deserved to mourn, because they denied their life, and laid hands upon their saviour and delivered him to death. Wherefore, already from that time there was laid upon them a mourning for their destruction.' Christians have, in fact, fasted on Holy Saturday; see p. 143, n. 4, below. Augustine also refers to Gen. 2.2f. (*Gen. ad litt.* 4.11), 'The Lord Jesus Christ, who has endured a freely chosen death, vouchsafed the secret of this rest by his burial. He did indeed rest in the grave on the sabbath, he had this whole day as a holy time of rest, after he had accomplished his work on the sixth day, the preparation, which is the name they give to the sixth day after the sabbath.' (Cf. *Ep.* 55 [ad Jan.]. 9.16.)

For *him* the sabbath commandment is of no importance, for he is God himself. The new point which we find here by comparison with Heb. 3–4 is, therefore, only this: Jesus derives *for himself* the abrogation of the commandment to rest on the weekly sabbath from the eschatological interpretation of Gen. 2.2f.

We may inquire whether John 5.17 is a genuine word of Jesus. Its content entirely fits in with Jesus' consciousness of his mission which we have seen to be particularly prominent in the conflict stories about the sabbath. The form of words which we have here can, however, hardly be ascribed to Jesus. The designation of God as 'my Father' is, of course, not at all strange in the mouth of Jesus; it does, in fact, indicate the very heart of his relationship with God.[1] Nowhere else in Jesus' sayings, however, do we find one like this which speaks of the future sabbath of God. It would seem that the *evangelist* wanted to give a christological basis to the tradition (in itself a Jewish tradition) about God's activity until the end of the world; after that the promised sabbath, the blessed rest, was supposed to begin. The evangelist carried out this intention by supposing that Jesus used this tradition as a means of encroaching on the basis of the sabbath commandment, at least in so far as his own person was concerned.[2]

(b) *The new interpretation of the sabbath commandment*

Jesus himself had posed the sabbath question for the Church by his own attitude towards the sabbath. We have already become familiar with two of the positions adopted by the Church on this problem. On the one hand, it tried to solve it by justifying Jesus' freedom in messianic terms, as he himself also had done. On the other hand, it had taken over from Jewish thought the hope of the eschatological sabbath; this was in two principal versions (sabbath as the end-time or as a thousand-year kingdom). John 5.17 represents the intersection of these two traditions: with messianic authority Jesus applies to himself the idea of God's activity and rest, and so he places himself above the sabbath commandment.

We must now consider another form of the sabbath theology of the primitive Church: its origin is in a novel interpretation of the sabbath *commandment*. This interpretation is properly to be

[1] Cf. G. Schrenk, *TWNT* V, pp. 981ff.
[2] E. Hoskyns, in *Mysterium Christi*, 1930, pp. 74ff., maintains that Jesus was the first to invent the equation sabbath rest = eternal rest and that the Jews only later adopted it from him; this is, of course, out of the question.

45082

regarded as an intensification of the Torah, such as we see in the Sermon on the Mount. This principle is now applied to the sabbath commandment, but Jesus himself was not responsible for its extension in this way. This application did not derive directly from Jesus' own attitude towards the sabbath. Instead it derived from a type of exegesis of the law which may seem to leave what it finds undisturbed, but does, in fact, fill it with new content. This manner of interpreting the sabbath commandment unquestionably went far beyond the Jewish understanding of the law, for this new interpretation led to the literal sense of the law being regarded as open to question and, in the end, to its abandonment in favour of a spiritual reality of a different sort.[1]

Col. 2.16f. may almost be regarded as the key to this new understanding. 'Therefore let no one pass judgement on you in questions of food or drink or with regard to a festival (ἐν μέρει ἑορτῆς) or a new moon or a sabbath.[2] These are only a shadow (σκιά; cf. Heb. 8.5) of what is to come; but (their) substance belongs to Christ (τὸ δὲ σῶμα τοῦ Χριστοῦ).'[3] Here it is asserted that together with all the other festivals and food laws the Jewish sabbath also was fulfilled in Christ, and in such a way that the real meaning of the Old Testament ordinances was for the first time made plain in Christ. It is a bold picture: the sabbath and the other festivals of Israelite and Jewish origin were like silhouettes cast by that which was to come: now, however, the reality has come, the 'substance' which cast these shadows. For this reason no one now looks any more at the silhouettes, for that is now present of which they were but the shadowy image.[4] This picture requires no explanation; it is plain and speaks for itself. It might well indeed stand as a picture of the fact that the law was altogether fulfilled in Christ; not only the ceremonial laws, but the whole law of Moses was, in essence, completely fulfilled in Christ in this way.

Taking their cue from Col. 2.17 the Christian fathers use the word τύπος

[1] In the OT prophets an approach to such an interpretation of the law can be seen in, for example, Isa. 58.6–7.
[2] Here as elsewhere (Mark 1.21; 2.24; 3.2, 4; Matt. 28.1; Acts 13.14 etc.) the plural stands for the singular.
[3] M. Dibelius, *An die Kolosser* (HNT 12), 1953³, p. 34; the body of that which is to come has appeared with Christ.
[4] One is reminded of Plato's simile of the cave.

or εἰκών from time to time when they are referring to the sabbath of the
Old Testament.[1] The word 'fulfilment' generally has for them two con-
notations: first, the eschatological sabbath rest,[2] but then also the new
interpretation which the sabbath commandment received among Christians.[3] Similarly reference is made to circumcision[4] and the passover[5] as
types which are already superseded.

We may now draw the following conclusions from Col. 2.16f.:
Christians did not feel themselves authorized simply to set aside
the sabbath commandment as if it were not for them at all. In
this respect they were no greater than their master. On the
other hand, the fulfilment of the commandment by means of its
intensification (the method of the Sermon on the Mount)
naturally had the effect of abolishing the literal sense and of
replacing it by a new commandment dependent upon the reality
which was present in Christ. This new interpretation of the
sabbath commandment by the Church could almost be con-
densed into an antithesis in the style of the Sermon on the
Mount: this would demonstrate its inner affinity with Jesus'
own exposition of the law. Its sense would require the antithesis
to run like this: 'You have heard that it was said to them of old
time, "Keep holy the sabbath day"; but I say unto you: only
he keeps the sabbath who, in the sight of God, keeps holy all
the days of his life.' The interpretation offered by Christian
writers does at any rate come within this framework of ideas.
The sabbath commandment does not mean, they say, that we
should abstain from work on one day out of seven, but that we
should abstain *at all times* from any sinful act: the Christian
should, therefore, observe a perpetual sabbath and consecrate
every day to God. It is easy to see that this principle covered not

[1] Tertullian, *Adv. Jud.* 4, refers to the 'temporal' and the 'eternal'
sabbath.
[2] So Hippolytus, *Comm. in Dan.* IV.23.5; Syriac *Didascalia* 26 (Connolly,
p. 238); Ambrose, *In Luc.* VII.173; Chrysostom, *Hom.* 6.1 *in Heb.* (on ch. 4).
[3] Justin, *Dial.* 42.4; Irenaeus, *Adv. haer.* IV.16.1–2; Eusebius, *Comm. in
Ps.* 91(92, PG 23.1168D f.); Epiphanius, *Haer.* 30.32.9; Jerome, *In Ezek.*
VI (on 20.10), etc. See also p. 152, n. 2, below.
[4] Council of Carthage III.4 (PL 3.1017); Ps.-Athanasius, *De sabbato et
circonc.* 5.
[5] Hippolytus, *Trad. Apost.* 33 (ed. B. Botte, *La Tradition Apostolique le
saint Hippolyte* (Liturgiewissen-schaftliche Quellen und Forschungen 39),
1963, p. 80). [29.4 in the ETs of B. S. Easton, *The Apostolic Tradition*, 1934,
p. 53, and of G. Dix, *The Treatise on the Apostolic Tradition*, 1937, pp. 56f.]

only the sabbath, but the entire Old Testament festival legislation as well. The Israelite distinguished particular days and
seasons by special pious practices: the Christian marked every
day in this way.[1] Put positively, the new interpretation ran:
you should always worship God in heart and thought and
deed.

Justin provides the first example of this new and more penetrating
interpretation of the commandment to rest. In *Dial.* 12.3 he writes, 'The
new law requires you to keep perpetual sabbath, and you (i.e. Jews) because
you are idle for one day, suppose you are pious . . . The Lord our God
does not take pleasure in such observances; if there is any perjured person
or a thief among you, let him cease to be so (παυσάσθω): if any adulterer,
let him repent; then he has kept the sweet and true sabbath of God.' In
Irenaeus, *Epideixis* 96, we find the passage, 'Nor will he be commanded to
leave idle one day of rest, who is constantly keeping sabbath, that is, giving
homage to God in the temple of God, which is man's body, and at all times
doing the works of justice.' Again in *Adv. haer.* IV. 8.2, 'For the law commanded them (the Jews) to abstain from every servile work (on the festival),
that is, from all grasping after wealth which is procured by trading and by
other worldly business.'[2] Tertullian, *Adv. Jud.* 4 (chapters 1–9 of this
treatise certainly come from Tertullian; cf. also *Adv. Marc.* IV. 12 and II.21),
is the first to transfer to the sabbath as well the prohibition of 'servile works',
on a festival:[3] 'Be mindful of the sabbath, sanctify it: on the sabbath you
may do no servile work except that of service to your soul.[4] Hereby we have
come to know that it is more important that we should always abstain from
every servile work (*sabbatizare*), not only on the sabbath day, but on every

---

[1] It is important to notice that the prohibition of *opera servilia* which was
interpreted by Christians in the spiritual sense as a prohibition of servitude
to sin (cf. John 8.34) is not derived directly from the legislation in the Old
Testament concerning the sabbath, but from that concerning festivals, Lev.
23.7, 8, 21, 25, 35, 36; Num. 28.18, 25, 26; 29.1, 12, 35. Cf. F. Pettirsch, 'Das
Verbot der opera servilia in der Heiligen Schrift und in der altkirchlichen
Exegese', *ZKT* 69, 1947, pp. 258ff. (It is not entirely impossible that
mᵉleʾket ʿabōda and *tāʿabōd* in Ex. 20.9 are in some way connected.) See also
p. 172 below.

[2] Cf. *Adv. haer.* IV.16.1.

[3] H. Huber, *Geist und Buchstabe der Sonntagsruhe*, 1958, p. 55, says that at
the same time the links were made for the transference to Sunday of the
prohibition of servile works. That is not quite correct. We shall (see pp. 169ff.
below) how the way was prepared for Sunday to be considered as the
equivalent of the sabbath.

[4] Tertullian is here using Ex. 12.16 in the LXX: the Massoretic text
reads, 'But what everyone must eat, that only may be prepared by you.' Cf.
Adv. Marc. IV.12.

day.' With this we should consider the testimony of Origen;[1] in *Hom.* 23.4 *in Num.* he writes, 'We want to enquire of what kind should be the sabbath observance of a Christian. On the sabbath day one may carry on no secular occupation whatsoever . . . Whoever, therefore, desists from the works of this world is free for spiritual works; he it is who offers the sacrifice of the sabbath and observes the festival day of the sabbath. He carries no burden in the street. The burden is, in fact, every sin, as the prophet says, "They lay on me a heavy burden" . . . On the sabbath everyone remains seated in his own place and does not leave it.[2] What is the spiritual place of the soul? Righteousness is its abode, truth, wisdom, holiness and everything which Christ is: that is the place of the soul. The soul should not remove away from this place in order to keep the true sabbath . . .: "Whoever abides in me, in him I also abide." ' (Cf. *Selecta in Exod.*, PG 12.289.) In Origen's *Contra Celsum*, VIII.23, we find the following exegesis of Col. 2.16, 'I think that this is what Paul had in mind when he called the feast that is held on days set apart from the others μέρος ἑορτῆς; he hinted by this phrase that the life which is continually being lived according to the divine word is not ἐν μέρει ἑορτῆς but in an entire and continual feast.' In Ptolemy's *Letter to Flora*, 5.12 (SC 24.60), we read, 'And (with regard to) sabbath observance: I desire indeed that you abstain (ἀργεῖν) from all evil works.' We shall also quote from the Syriac *Didascalia* 26 (Connolly, p. 236): 'Wherefore, brethren, every day is the Lord's, for the scripture has said, "The earth is the Lord's with the fullness thereof, the circle of the world that is under heaven, and all that dwell therein." '[3]

It is not surprising that this new way of interpreting the

---

[1] Mention should also be made here of Clement Alex., *Strom.*VI.16.138.1. In all probability Pap. Oxy. I verso lines 4–11, *NT Apoc.* I, p. 106 (cf. Logion 27 of the recently discovered Gospel of Thomas) should also be considered in this connection, 'If you do not fast (with regard to) the world, you shall not find the kingdom of God; if you do not observe the sabbath as befits the sabbath, you shall not see the Father.' The spiritualized interpretation is suggested by the first part; cf. J. Jeremias, *Unknown Sayings of Jesus*, ET 1957, pp. 13f.

[2] Cf. Ex. 16.29. This strict interpretation of the passage which we do not even find among the Essenes is told us by Origen, *Princ.* IV.3.2, concerning the Samaritan Dositheus, the forerunner of Simon Magus.

[3] In Augustine we frequently find this spiritual interpretation of the sabbath commandment, *Joann.* 3.19; *Serm.* 8.3; 33.3; *Enarr. in Ps.* 32.6; *Joann.* 20.2; 44.9; *Spirit. et lit.* I.15.27; *Ep.* 55 (ad Jan.) 12.22. Cf. Epiphanius, *Haer.* 30.32; Jerome, *Comm. in Isa.* XV (on 56.2); XVI (on 58.13); *Comm. in Ezek.* VI (on 20.10); *Const. Apost.* VI.23.3; Cyril Alex., *Ador. et cult. in spir.* 16; *Comm. in Amos* 58 (on 6.3); *Alterc. Simon. Jud. et Theoph. Christ.* 7.28 (TU 1.3, p. 41); Gregory the Great, *Hom.* I.6.18 *in Ezek.* (PL 76. 838); *Ep.* 13.1; Chrysostom, *Hom.* 39.3f. *in Matt.*; *Hom.* 6.3 *in Heb.* Further references in J. Böhmer, *Der christliche Sonntag nach Ursprung und Geschichte*, 1931, pp. 19f.

sabbath commandment developed into a critique of the weekly sabbath itself.[1] What use should a person have for the weekly day of rest who was required in a spiritual manner perpetually to keep the sabbath? Clearly this attitude presupposes Col. 2.16. Moreover, there came to the aid of Christian authors passages from the Old Testament like Isa. 1.13f., 'Bring no more vain offerings—it is an abomination to me. New moon and sabbath and the calling of assemblies—I cannot endure iniquity and solemn assembly. Your new moons and your appointed feasts my soul hates; they have become a burden to me, I am weary of bearing them. . . .' (v. 16). 'Wash yourselves; make yourselves clean; remove the evil of your doings from before my eyes; cease to do evil.'[2] Nor was it difficult to criticize Jewish sabbath observance in its external manifestations.[3]

The new Christian interpretation of the sabbath commandment is not apparent until the second century. (Col. 2.16f. does not yet provide a new interpretation of the commandment.) We should very much like to know how the Christians dealt with the sabbath commandment before the second century and also to know the significance for them of the decalogue which contained the sabbath commandment. Regrettably, the

---

[1] Later this same point of view led to a diminution in the importance of the weekly Sunday. Cf. Tertullian, *Bapt.* 19, 'After all every day is a Lord's day . . .' Origen, *Cels.* VIII.22, 'The perfect (Christian) who is always engaged in the words, works and thought of the divine Logos who is by nature his Lord, is always living in His days and is continually observing the Lord's Day.' This point of view did not, however, fundamentally call in question the importance of worship on Sunday (cf. Origen, *Hom.* 10.3 *in Gen.*).

[2] Cf. Justin, I *Apol.* 37.5ff.; *Dial.* 18.2; *Barn.* 15.8; Victorinus, *De fabrica mundi* 5; Ps.-Athanasius, *Hom. de semente* 1; *Alterc. Simon. Jud. et Theoph. Christ.* 7.28. In this way Christians followed a prophetic tradition which may have been important even for Jesus; see pp. 77ff. above.

[3] Justin, *Dial.* 12.3; Eusebius, *Comm. in Ps.* 91 (92, PG 23.1169); Ps.-Ignatius, *Magn.* 9.2; Chrysostom, *De Lazaro* 1.7 (PG 48.972). Further information in H. Dumaine, *DACL* IV, 1921, col. 919f. As a particularly impressive example we may quote here Augustine, *Serm.* 9.3, 'You are told to keep the sabbath in a spiritual fashion and not by bodily inactivity, as is the custom of the Jews. They only wish to devote themselves to their pleasure and revelries. The Jew would do better by working usefully on the land than by sitting discontentedly in the theatre, and their wives would do better to spin wool on the sabbath day than to spend the whole day shamelessly dancing at home'; cf. *Enarr. in Ps.* 91.2, *'melius est enim arare quam saltare'*; and many other passages. Plutarch, *Quaestionum convivalium* 4.6.672, gives us similar information about the Jews' behaviour.

information which we have on these topics is very meagre. The decalogue which Judaism already regarded as the epitome of the Mosaic Torah probably preserved an undiminished reputation among Christians.[1] Precisely for this reason it is surprising to notice that whenever we come across the use of the decalogue within the Christian Church, the sabbath commandment is always missing: furthermore, those commandments on the first table which do not refer to one's neighbours are generally omitted.[2]

This also applies to the first Christian exposition of the decalogue, Jesus' Sermon on the Mount. Similarly, with the exception of the commandment to honour one's parents (cf. Eph. 6.1–3), the commandments enumerated to the rich young man (Mark 10.19 par.) include only those on the second

---

[1] Cf., in addition to the passages which we shall quote later, those assembled by C. W. Dugmore, *The Influence of the Synagogue upon the Divine Office*, 1944, p. 30; Irenaeus, *Adv. haer.* IV.15.1; *Acts of Pilate* 15.6 (*NT Apoc.* I, p. 466); Tertullian, *De anima* 37; Clement Alex., *Strom.* VI.16.138. We should have striking proof of the high esteem in which the decalogue was held among Christians, if they really were responsible for its elimination from the liturgy of the synagogue; according to the Talmud (cf. SB IV.1.19), this occurred because of the *minim* who said that only the decalogue had been given to Moses on Mount Sinai; cf. C. W. Dugmore, *op. cit.*, p. 105. (In the Syriac *Didascalia* the decalogue was regarded as the law pure and simple, which was to be distinguished from the other commandments given after the transgression with the golden calf; these counted only as 'repetition of the law'. We may well find similar ideas as early as *Barn.* 4.7f. and Irenaeus, *Adv. haer.* IV. 9.1; 15.1f.). Nevertheless this assumption seems to go too far. H. Schneider, 'Der Dekalog in den Phylakterien von Qumran', *BZ* NF 3, 1959, pp. 18–31, has established that even at Qumran the decalogue probably no longer had a place in the liturgy; this conclusion is suggested by the fact that the phylacteries in use at Qumran probably no longer contained the decalogue (as they perhaps did at the time of the Nash papyrus), but contained only four pieces, Ex. 13.1–10, 11–16; Deut. 6.4–9; 11.13–21. Schneider thinks, therefore, that the *minim* mentioned in the Talmud are not Christians, but heretical Jewish groups. On the attitude of the post-apostolic Church to the OT law in general, see (in addition to L. Goppelt, *Christentum und Judentum im ersten und zweiten Jahrhundert*, 1954) now P. G. Verweijs, *Evangelium und neues Gesetz in der ältesten Christenheit bis auf Marcion*, 1960, as well as my discussion in *TZ* 18, 1962, pp. 66.

[2] The double command to love is often thought to sum up the decalogue (Mark 12.29ff. par.; 7.12; Rom. 13.8–10; Gal. 5.14; cf. I Tim. 1.5; James 2.1–13; *Did.* 1.2; Justin, *Dial.* 93.2). Later the double command is thought of as the 'natural law' (Irenaeus, *Adv. haer.* IV.15.1; Tertullian, *Adv. Jud.* 2; Origen, *Comm. in Rom.* II.8–9 (PG 14.890ff.); *Cels.* V.37). But the command to love *God* does not seem to have been understood as summing up the commandments in the *first* table; cf. *Did.* 1.3ff., where various commandments about loving one's neighbour are instanced in the interpretation of the commandment to love God.

table. The same is true of Rom. 13.9 and James 2.8ff. And the exposition of the decalogue to be found in the *Didache* (the observance of these commandments is here the 'way of life') also begins with the second table (2.1ff.).[1] The situation is no different in the letter sent by the governor Pliny to the Emperor Trajan (X.96[97]): Pliny is reporting the result of the interrogations of Christians in Asia Minor:[2] the Christians had assembled early in the morning *stato die* (i.e. probably on Sunday),[3] they had sung a *carmen* to Christ and bound themselves by a *sacramentum*, not that they should commit a crime of some sort (so, it clearly seems, ran the accusation), but that they should not steal, rob or commit adultery, not break their pledged word and not refuse to give up any property entrusted to their keeping, if its return should be demanded. This list of crimes has clear echoes of the decalogue,[4] but once again the first table is missing; the same is true of Aristides, *Apol.* 14.5. Once again we find that Theophilus of Antioch, *Autolyc.* 3.9, in his discussion of the decalogue more or less skips over the first table (he mentions only the two halves of the first commandment and also the fifth commandment); similarly Ps. Clem., *Hom.* XIII.4.2.

One can ask how this abbreviation of the decalogue in Christian circles is to be explained. Was it simply that certain commandments in the decalogue (for instance, perhaps, the sabbath commandment) had no more significance for Christians? Hardly, for otherwise they would not later have gone to such trouble to provide a new interpretation of the sabbath commandment. More probably we should see reflected in this silence a certain amount of uncertainty how the sabbath commandment was to be interpreted in Christian terms. At the same time we may, however, conclude from this silence that it was also demonstrably plain to Christians that the sabbath commandment could no longer be binding on them in the old Jewish manner: otherwise they would certainly have unhesitatingly reproduced it.[5]

---

[1] We are not here discussing the question how much this part of the *Didache* goes back to Jewish tradition.

[2] For detailed discussion of Pliny's letter see pp. 202ff.; 251f.; 253ff. below.

[3] See p. 202, n. 5, below.

[4] Cf. Justin, *Dial.* 12.3; theft, perjury, adultery are mentioned there. We shall later (see pp. 255f. below) have to discuss the question whether the decalogue had any part in the Sunday worship of Christians; cf. O. Cullmann, *Early Christian Worship*, ET (SBT 10) 1953, p. 22.

[5] The decalogue in its entirety is first expounded by Christians relatively late: perhaps first of all by Origen (but we have his sermon on only the first three commandments, *Hom. in Ex.* 8), then by Augustine; see *Serm.* 8; 9; 33; 248–51. (We have, however, already seen that Augustine interprets the

So far we have not yet found any direct answer to the question about the *roots* of the new Christian interpretation of the sabbath commandment. We have indeed said that in its way it has associations with Jesus' Sermon on the Mount. It is, however, surprising that this connection was established so late. Perhaps we shall find that this unsolved question is answered to our satisfaction by the consideration of another strand of sabbath theology. From this we shall particularly notice that, chronologically speaking, it finds a place in the gap between Jesus and the second-century fathers: this gap has hitherto remained unfilled.

(c) The sabbath's fulfilment begun in Christ

The entire Christian ethic, the outlines of which we find in the New Testament, rests on the principle that we live in an interim period. There is a tension between the fulfilment which has already taken place and the consummation which has yet to come. This tension is expressed in the alternation between indicative and imperative which interact on one another.[1] This same tension is to be found, indeed must be found, in the Christian understanding of the sabbath commandment. We find, therefore, among Christians an intensification of the sabbath commandment: Keep the true sabbath, that is to say the spiritual sabbath. We also find that this demand had to be balanced on the other side by a realization of the indicative: Christ has made possible such a 'sabbatical' manner of life for all who believe in him. Similarly, we find that Christians hope in an eschatological sabbath; this hope did, however, have to be balanced by knowledge that the fulfilment of this promise had already begun in the present age and that Christ had already

---

sabbath commandment spiritually, not literally; cf. p. 104, n. 3.) Further passages in Augustine, *C. Faust.* 19.18; *Ep.* 55 (ad Jan.) 12.22; *Spir. et litt.* I.14. 23; 15.27. On this subject and on the wider use of the exposition of the decalogue in Christian catechesis see the recent study by H. Röthlisberger, *Kirche am Sinai. Die Zehn Gebote in der christlichen Unterweisung* (Studien zur Dogmengeschichte und systematische Theologie 19), 1965. This work is not always entirely reliable so far as the early Church is concerned.

[1] Cf. O. Cullmann, *Christ and Time*, ET 1951. It seems that R. Bultmann, *Theology of the New Testament*, ET 1952, is also of the same opinion on this point, but Bultmann's approach means that the time scheme has, in effect, been dissolved, for everything is taking place in that 'Now' where past, present and future all come together.

brought an anticipation of this sabbath. There are, in fact, many hints which lead us to conclude that the Church knew this. Even before the Church took steps to reinterpret the sabbath commandment, it was emphasizing the present reality of the true sabbath in Christ.

The sabbath conflicts recorded in St Matthew's Gospel are prefaced by the saviour's summons (Matt. 11.28–30), 'Come to me, all who labour and are heavy-laden, and I will give you rest (ἀναπαύσω ἡμᾶς). Take my yoke upon you and learn from me; for I am gentle and lowly in heart, and you will find rest (ἀνάπαυσιν) for your souls. For my yoke is easy, and my burden is light.'[1] The similarity with Ecclus. 51.13ff. has often been noticed.[2] Jesus does, therefore, appear here as a teacher of wisdom, but he boldly puts himself in the place of wisdom. It used to be said, 'Take on you the yoke of wisdom' (Ecclus. 51.26, 17). Now it says, 'Take *my* yoke upon you' (Matt. 11.29).[3] Twice it is emphasized that Jesus will give rest to those who learn from him and, according to Matthew, he does indeed say this on a sabbath, or at least in connection with a sabbath.[4] It is easy for us to come to the conclusion that, according to the evangelist, Jesus is promising the rest of the true sabbath.[5]

---

[1] The saviour's summons is also to be found (although in abbreviated form) in the Gospel of Thomas, Logion 90; J. B. Bauer, 'Das milde Joch und die Ruhe, Matth. 11.28–30', *TZ* 17, 1961, pp. 103–6, holds that the version in the Gospel of Thomas should be preferred to that in Matt. 11. Cf. also p. 110, n. 1 below. We must not here concern ourselves with the structure of the whole passage Matt. 11.25–30, which E. Norden has discussed in *Agnostos Theos*, 1913, pp. 277ff.

[2] Cf. also Ecclus. 6.24–28; J. B. Bauer (n. 1), p. 99.

[3] We must not, therefore, necessarily assume with R. Bultmann, *The History of the Synoptic Tradition*, ET 1963, pp. 159f., that in Matt. 11.28–30 we are dealing with 'a quotation from Jewish Wisdom literature put into the mouth of Jesus'. In any case this quotation would have undergone much modification. (M. Dibelius, *From Tradition to Gospel*, ET 1934, pp. 279ff., even associates Matt. 11.28–30 with hermetic gnosis.)

[4] Matt. 12.1ff. (the story of the plucking of the ears of corn on the sabbath) begins with ἐν ἐκείνῳ τῷ καιρῷ.

[5] J. Daniélou, *The Bible and the Liturgy*, ET 1960, p. 226, interprets the passage in this sense; cf. E. Jenni, *Die theologische Begründung des Sabbatgebotes im Alten Testament* (TS 46), 1956, p. 39; but also Jerome, *Comm. in Is.* XVI (on 58.13); Augustine, *Ep.* 55 (ad Jan.) 12.22; *Faust.* 19.9; *Adim.* 2; Ps.-Macarius of Egypt, *Hom.* 35 (PG 34.748). H. Riesenfeld, 'Sabbat et jour du Seigneur', *New Testament Essays, Studies in Memory of T. W. Manson*, 1959, p. 216, n. 4, understands Matt. 11.28–30 against the background of Gen. 3.17ff.; the curse of toil which lay on the first creation is now lifted.

The usual interpretation of the passage understands by 'those who labour' and 'the heavy-laden' all those who are exhausted and oppressed by the cares of life, but this interpretation is probably not quite right. The people who are toiling away and to whom reference is made here are probably those who are trying to procure rest for themselves by fulfilling their legal obligations which weigh heavily on them like a yoke. Jesus takes their burden from them, and fulfils their unsatisfied yearning for rest by his new law, which not only commands but also offers both righteousness and life.[1]

We can mention yet another example. The fourth chapter of Luke's Gospel (Jesus' inaugural sermon on the sabbath day in the synagogue at Nazareth) seems like an anticipation of the course of events recorded in that Gospel.[2] In his sermon Jesus refers to Isa. 61.1–2 (cf. 58.6), where it says, 'The Spirit of the Lord (is) upon me, because he has anointed me to preach good news to the poor; to proclaim release to the captives, and recovering of sight to the blind', 'to set at liberty those who are oppressed', 'to proclaim the acceptable year of the Lord (ἐνιαυτὸν κυρίου δεκτόν)'.[3] This last verse (Luke 4.19) is the one which matters. The context (liberation from every oppression) makes it quite plain that the reference is to the sabbath year or year of jubilee.[4] In Luke 4.21 Jesus is then made to say, 'Today this scripture has been fulfilled.' By means of this quotation from the prophet, Luke's Gospel does therefore describe the effect of Jesus' coming as the inauguration of the sabbath year. This means restitution and restoration for everyone, and especially for the poor.[5]

---

[1] Thus A. Schlatter, *Der Evangelist Matthäus*, 1929, pp. 385f.; O. Bauernfeind, *TWNT* I, p. 353.

[2] Cf. L. Goppelt, *Christentum und Judentum im ersten und zweiten Jahrhundert*, 1954, p. 229; he compares the importance of Luke 4 with that of Acts 2, each in the economy of its particular work.

[3] In Matt. 12.28ff. a similar passage from the Servant Songs is placed at the end of Jesus' conflicts about the sabbath. Cf. also the message to John the Baptist, Luke 7.22.

[4] For the OT ordinance see p. 16 above. A. Szabó, 'Sabbat und Sonntag', *Judaica* 15, 1959, p. 165, interprets the passage as a reference to the eighth sabbath year, that is the jubilee year. Moreover, he emphasizes that according to the synoptics Jesus' activity lasted one year. It is, however, better not to understand the reference to 'an acceptable year of the Lord' as a literal reference to a period of time; cf. U. Holzmeister, 'Das "angenehme Jahr des Herrn" (Isa. 61.2=Luke 4.19) und die Einjahrtheorie', *ZKT* 53, 1929, pp. 272–82.

[5] In contrast to *Barn.* 14.9, Luke omits the conclusion of the quotation from Isaiah, in which we read that the anointed one has come to announce

J. Daniélou[1] holds that an oblique reference to the beginning of the final sabbath is to be found in the genealogy of Christ in Matt. 1. Before the appearance of the redeemer there is a sequence of six generations each with seven names: the seventh generation would, therefore, begin with Jesus. E. Jenni[2] writes about the pericope of Mary and Martha (Luke 10.38–42), 'It is a question here not simply of contemplation and concern for spiritual matters suffering at the expense of domestic activity, but rather of the uniqueness of the person of Jesus. Whenever he is there with his word, daily work not only may but must take second place. The Lord and redeemer to whom the sabbath yields place is himself now present so that we may be mindful of him and seek his company.'[3] Origen, *Comm. in Matt.* XII 36, interprets the six days of Matt. 17.1 (the story of the transfiguration) as follows: 'When he (Jesus) had spent the six (days), he kept a new sabbath.' (Cf. Hilary of Poitiers, *Comm. in Matt.* 17.2; Ambrose, *In Luc.* VII. 6–7.) We shall refrain from mentioning yet more passages of this sort, since the further we stray from the positive content of thought about the sabbath and look for mere external correspondence, the more we find ourselves in the realm of allegory.

At this stage Heb. 3.7–4.11 must once again be mentioned. We have placed this passage among those which look for the fulfilment of the sabbath in terms of Jewish expectation for the future. This passage from the Epistle to the Hebrews and indeed the whole epistle would, however, be misinterpreted, if we were to suppose that the author thought the fulfilment of the promises to be exclusively in the future.[4]

---

a day of revenge and retribution. This announcement refers to the universal judgement; Luke, however, clearly wishes to represent the present time as the time of fulfilment (cf. also the quotation from Joel in Acts 2). Conversely, it would be incorrect to understand the Lucan 'Today' as a reference on the part of the evangelist to a past epoch (i.e. the time of Jesus' ministry) which is now to be differentiated from the time of the Church, as does H. Conzelmann, *The Theology of Saint Luke*, ET 1960, pp. 186f. A reading of the Acts of the Apostles does not give one the impression that Luke regards the history of the Church as of secondary importance; it is for him, rather more, the time when the present lordship of Jesus is proclaimed among heathen peoples through the power of the Spirit.

[1] (P. 109, n. 5), p. 228. Cf. H. Milton, *JBL* 81, 1962, pp. 175–81.

[2] (P. 109, n. 5), p. 38.

[3] We find another interpretation in B. Reicke, *Glaube und Leben der Urgemeinde* (AThANT 32), 1957, p. 120; he holds that the pericope expresses the separation of serving tables from the service of the liturgy (cf. Acts 6.1–6).

[4] This is essentially the position adopted in the commentaries by E. Käsemann, O. Michel, H. Windisch, W. Manson; cf. W. Dolling, *TWNT* II, p. 956, n. 59; G. von Rad, 'There Remains Still a Rest for the People of God', *The Problem of the Hexateuch and Other Essays*, ET 1966, pp. 101f.;

We shall make 11.1 our starting point. Here we find one of the principal themes of the epistle: 'Faith is a ὑπόστασις of things hoped for, an ἔλεγχος of things not seen.' The stress should certainly fall not on the 'hoped for' and 'not seen', but on ὑπόστασις and ἔλεγχος. Faith is concerned with things which are not visible and do not belong to this age, and yet in faith these things turn out to be real: faith is the 'assurance' and 'proof' of their existence.[1] We find exactly the same sense in 3.7–4.11, the passage with which we are concerned. We shall misunderstand the burden of the passage if we do not hear in it the decisive significance of the 'Today'.[2] The new day of the 'Today' has dawned in Christ (v. 7). On this new day it is possible to enter into the rest, and yet more: on this new day this rest has become a reality for those who believe.[3] Despite this, the passage then goes on to say (v. 11) that we should make efforts to enter that rest. This orientation towards the future does, however, correspond to and may even be caused by the anticipation of the future which is made possible in faith. Thus in its own way the Epistle to the Hebrews gives expression to that which is the core of the Christian life—namely the tension of living in a situation between the times: this situation is marked by knowledge of the fulfilment which has already taken place and also by a longing for the visible consummation which has yet to take place. The fact that the recipients of this epistle are clearly in danger of falling away from a real faith acts as an incentive for the author to emphasize that fulfilment is already at work in the present: this fulfilment is, however, for the time being in faith and not in sight. This fulfilment had already been offered in the Old Testament, but no one had participated in it. The distinction between the present time and the time of the generation in the wilderness is clearly marked by the fact that it is now possible to enter into the rest.[4]

The situation is no different with regard to Col. 2.16f. On the one hand, this passage clearly demonstrates that in Christ

---

A. Prešeren, 'Die Beziehungen der Sonntagsfeier zum 3. Gebot des Dekalogs', *ZKT* 37, 1913, p. 576.

[1] 'Confidence' and 'conviction' are too colourless as translations of ὑπόστασις and ἔλεγχος, because they give too subjective a sense; nor does A. Schlatter's interpretation in *Der Glaube im Neuen Testament*, 1905³, pp. 615–18, really go any further. The point, however, is that the fact of faith is itself an objective piece of evidence for the unseen, if it is not too paradoxical to put it this way; it is the making present of the future, and the demonstration that it has real existence. (It is no accident that the term 'hypostasis' becomes of central importance in dogmatic theology, especially in Christology.) On the exposition of Heb. 11.1, see now E. Grässer, *Der Glaube im Hebräerbrief* (Marburger Theol. Studien 2), 1965, pp. 99ff.; 126ff.

[2] One cannot fail to notice the similarity of Luke 4.19 and John 9.4.

[3] Thus J. Nedbal, *Sabbat und Sonntag im Neuen Testament* (diss.), 1956, pp. 113f.

[4] Cf. L. Goppelt (p. 110, n. 2), p. 236.

the Old Testament festivals had received a fresh meaning, which had the result of making them superfluous in their old form. On the other hand, however, it is unmistakable that the passage also intends to convey that in Christ this reality is present; in him the fulfilment had not merely become discernible, but really present (cf. the contrast of σκιά and σῶμα).[1]

Even in the very early Church we can see developing the distinctive features of the view that with the coming of Jesus the true sabbath had dawned.[2] But in what did this sabbath consist which Christ had brought? There had to be a quite special side to the saving work of Christ whereby the Old Testament idea of the sabbath had been brought to its eschatological fulfilment. In order to answer this question, we must look back once again to Jesus' sabbath conflicts. The cause of these conflicts had generally been a healing. The bodily healings effected by Jesus soon came to be regarded by the Church as symbolical of the spiritual healing of a person by Jesus' redeeming activity, symbolical, in other words, of the forgiveness of sins. Jesus' healings as reported in the gospels already contain hints of this deeper meaning.[3] The wording of the parabolic saying in

---

[1] We shall quote here three later authorities. Syriac *Didascalia* 26 (Connolly, p. 238) in reference to Col. 2.16f. says, 'But the Lord our Saviour, when he was come, fulfilled the types and explained the parables, and he showed these things that are life-giving, and those that cannot help he did away, and those that cannot give life he abolished.' Epiphanius, *Haer.* 8.6.8; cf. 30.32.7–9; 66.23, 'Therefore that sabbath prescribed by the law has retained its validity until his arrival; but after it has been abolished, he (God) has given (us) the great sabbath, which is the Lord himself; he is our rest and our sabbath observance.' Gregory the Great, *Ep.* 13.1, 'We spiritually understand and we construe in a spiritual sense what we find written about the sabbath, for sabbath means rest. But as our true sabbath we have our redeemer and Lord Jesus Christ.'

[2] In Christian gnosticism, as we have already partly seen (see pp. 95ff. above), this thought remained alive, although often in a way which did not let its Christian origin be apparent.

[3] Mark 2.1ff. is explicit, and also whenever it is emphasized that your faith has saved you. H. Riesenfeld, *Jésus transfiguré*, 1947, p. 320, particularly draws attention to this; see also his (p. 109, n. 5), p. 211. Stress was perhaps placed on the length of the illness in the case of healings on the sabbath in order to illustrate the fact that the sabbath of the end-time had already dawned. It must, however, remain an open question whether John 5.5 (the man had been ill for thirty-eight years) is, in fact, a reference to Israel's forty-year wandering in the wilderness, as is held by H. Strathmann, *Das Evangelium nach Johannes* (NTD 4), 1951, pp. 103f. In this case Jesus would be offering, as it were, to lead Israel (represented in this man) into the promised land.

Matt. 12.11 clearly seems, for example, to point in this direction.[1] The way in which reference is made here to the *single* sheep which had fallen into the pit reflects the extent to which this parable had already come to be regarded as a parable of Jesus' saving work in general (cf. the relationship with the parable of the lost sheep).[2] The reception of the sinner is a *priestly* work. The priest acts as an intermediary between God and man, and he procures expiation of man's guilt by sacrifice. Subsequent reflection leads us to notice that all the scriptural passages which the Church adduced in order to justify Jesus' infringements of the sabbath refer to priestly functions which have precedence over the sabbath. In the story of David eating the shewbread (in I Sam. 21.1–7) it is, in fact, the priest who, above all, does something forbidden when, in answer to David's request, he gives him the shewbread to eat.

This story which had formerly been well known in the Church seems to have acquired an entirely new meaning: it became a type of the Lord's Supper.[3] A feeling of repletion belonged to the picture of the eschatological sabbath in just the same way as a cheerful family meal was part of the weekly sabbath.[4] The Church's new David, who was at the same time priest after the order of Melchizedek (Ps. 110),[5] now receives from God the eucharistic bread and gives it to his own people; similarly, the Johannine Christ (on a sabbath day, be it noted—John 6.59) proclaims that manna, which he gives and which he is, to be the new bread from heaven. All miracles of

---

[1] This has been noticed by E. Lohmeyer, *Das Evangelium des Matthäus*, 1956, p. 185.

[2] The Gospel of Truth, *NT Apoc.* I, p. 238, makes this point yet plainer when it says after the parable of the lost sheep, 'He laboured even on the Sabbath for the sheep, which he had found fallen into the well. He saved the life of this sheep, because he drew it out of the well, that you may know in (your) hearts—you, the children of the knowledge of the heart—what is the Sabbath on which the work of redemption may not cease, that you may say —of this day above, which has no night, and of the light, which does not pass away because it is perfect. Say therefore in your hearts, that you are this perfect day, and that it dwells in you, this light which does not grow dim . . .'. Cf. Irenaeus, *Adv. haer.* 1.8.4.

[3] H. Riesenfeld, *Jésus transfiguré*, 1947, p. 321, holds that the wording of the passage betrays the influence of the eucharistic liturgy (esp. Luke 6.4: he took . . . ate . . . and gave to his companions).

[4] B. Reicke, *Diakonie, Festfreude und Zelos in Verbindung mit der altchristlichen Agapenfeier*, 1951, p. 113, establishes the same point with reference to Christian works of charity.

[5] Psalm 110 is the passage in the Old Testament which is most frequently quoted in the New Testament; cf. O. Cullmann, *The Earliest Christian Confessions*, ET 1949.

feeding and the Lord's Supper itself are anticipations of the repletion of the eschatological meal on the never-ending sabbath.

There is clear reference to priestly activity in the other scriptural quotations adduced in the gospels in connection with Jesus' sabbath conflicts: even on the sabbath the priests must make proper provision for the offering of sacrifice. Here, too, is 'something greater than the temple' (Matt. 12.5f.). We may now attempt an interpretation of this passage: in Christ the true high priest is at work who supersedes the service of the temple.[1] On the sabbath and even by preference on the sabbath, he, too, must make his 'sacrificial offering', that is to say his work of forgiveness, and what he does his followers must do.[2] Moreover, John 7.22ff. clearly states also that the priests must circumcise on the sabbath. The sabbath work of Jesus is, by means of his forgiveness, to circumcise the entire human being in the heart. In the Church's language this is called baptism, which does, in fact, take the place of circumcision.[3]

All along the line, therefore, Jesus' own attitude was interpreted in the light of Easter and in a way which underlined the priestly side of his Messiahship. The whole cultus of the Old Testament was now fulfilled and replaced by the new 'cultus' of the gospel, in Jesus Christ himself.[4] We cannot fail to notice how the sabbath theology of the Christian Church runs parallel to its temple theology.[5] There is the same spiritualization in both cases. The contrite heart of the penitent and the expiating work of Jesus, the new high priest, have taken the place of the offering of sacrifice. Similarly, he in whom God dwells (John 1.14; cf. Acts 7.49) and the company of those who 'worship in spirit and truth' (John 4.21, 23) have taken the place of the temple.[6] As the spatial limitation on the worship of

[1] See the theological significance of the high priest in the Epistle to the Hebrews; O. Cullmann, *The Christology of the New Testament*, ET 1959, pp. 89ff.
[2] In the last analysis this is probably also the meaning of Hos. 6.6 (Matt. 12.7), that sacrifices are abolished once Jesus has mercy on sinful men.
[3] See pp. 277 ff. below.
[4] See p. 79 above.
[5] Cf. Y. Congar, *Le mystère du Temple*, 1958.
[6] It is no accident that this criticism of the temple is so prominent in the Fourth Gospel (cf. John 2.12–22); it points to the association of this gospel with the group of Hellenists; cf. O. Cullmann, 'L'opposition contre le temple de Jérusalem, motif commun de la théologie johannique et du monde ambiant', *NTS* 5, 1959, pp. 157–73.

God disappeared with the temple, so its temporal limitation went with sabbath. Sabbath came to mean the entire present age and every place where the power of the forgiveness of sins brought by Jesus was effective.[1]

Jesus' priestly work of salvation, therefore, fulfilled and replaced the sabbath for those who believe: this salvation brought them release from sin, joy, liberty and true rest. This was the origin of the imperative addressed to Christians. They were bidden to keep the sabbath spiritually after the pattern suggested by its fulfilment in Christ, that is to say, not to sin, to worship without ceasing, in just the way that the interpretation of the sabbath commandment was formulated in the second century. This interpretation was, in the last analysis, only a result of deeper insight into the meaning of Jesus' saving work. The indicative led to the imperative.[2] It was precisely this imperative which once again made Christians aware that, while they were here below in this world and this life, they were not able properly and completely to fulfil the demand for true sabbath observance. It is, therefore, easily understandable that as a result of this realization there arose once again a strong hope in a future eschatological fulfilment of the sabbath. The late Jewish expectation of the sabbath at the end-time revived, therefore, in Christian circles as a result of an event in the 'middle of time'.

Two examples may be cited. In *Barn.* 15.6f. we read, 'Furthermore he says, "You shall sanctify it, clean of hand and heart."'[3] Consequently, if anyone is able at present to sanctify, clean of heart, the day which God has sanctified, then we are the victims of deception. Consider: we shall, as it appears, properly rest and sanctify it only when we are able to do so after being ourselves justified and having received the promised blessing.' Augustine, *Enarr. in Ps.* 91.2, reads 'Our sabbath is in the heart, within us;[4]

---

[1] So H. J. Holtzmann, *Hand-Commentar zum NT* 4, 1908³, p. 106; W. Bauer, *Das Johannesevangelium* (HNT 6), 1933³, p. 83.

[2] This line of interpretation may be seen in the later view which understood the priests who were allowed to break the sabbath (cf. Matt. 12.5) to be not only Jesus but the apostles and indeed all the faithful (the 'general priesthood' of I Peter 2.9): the privilege of the high priest had passed on to his followers. Cf. Irenaeus, *Adv. haer.* IV.8.2; Tertullian, *Adv. Marc.* IV.12; Ps.-Athanasius, *Hom. de semente* 13.

[3] Barnabas is wrong in ascribing this commandment to the decalogue; it seems to be derived from Jer. 17.22; Ps. 24.4. Cf. P. Prigent (p, 93, n. 3).

[4] One of Augustine's favourite thoughts; cf. *Serm.* 8.4; 270.5; *Joann.* 20.2; *Gen. ad litt.* IV.16.

for many are idle with their limbs, while they are disturbed in conscience. No bad man can have a sabbath: for his conscience is never at rest, he must needs live in turmoil; but he who has a good conscience is tranquil; and that very tranquillity is the sabbath of the heart'; also *Joann.* 20.2, 'And although in this present time we strive for that perfect rest, we shall come to it only when we have departed from this life.'

The circle of ideas is narrowing. The sabbath theology of the early Church has shown itself in all its versions to be christo-centric to the core. With messianic authority Jesus had broken the sabbath without, however, formally annulling the sabbath commandment. The Church took over this tradition. Beside it there stood the Jewish expectation of the eschatological sabbath. The Church took this expectation and adapted it, and this is the novel element in the Christian interpretation: in Christ this promised sabbath had already begun, but only in a preliminary fashion, for the consummation had yet to come. The typically Christian tension between 'already and not yet fulfilled' was applied to the Jewish sabbath hope. The belief that in Jesus Christ the new age had already begun marked the real dividing line between Judaism and Christianity.

We must, of course, concede that chiliasm opposed this idea of anticipated fulfilment, for by definition chiliasm was orientated towards the future. There can be no thousand-year kingdom already present, for such a kingdom essentially belongs to events at the consummation. Augustine in the *City of God* followed Tyconius' famous interpretation of the millennium in terms of the history of the Christian Church. This interpretation has occupied the predominant place both in Catholic and also in some Protestant exegesis of Rev. 20. In making this interpretation he has necessarily rejected chiliasm, for if the thousand-year kingdom is already present, it will not come a second time. A time of salvation which is only temporary cannot occur twice. Conversely, if in opposition to Augustine we were to maintain belief in the future millennium, we should not hold that the thousand-year king-dom is already proleptically realized: the very same reason would lead us to this conclusion. This shows, moreover, that some of its Jewish background still clings to chiliasm. Unlike the other Jewish eschatological conceptions, chiliasm cannot be 'Christianized', i.e. involved in the tension of 'already—not yet'. The sole difference between Christian and Jewish chiliasm is that the Church knows that the Messiah of the seventh millennium will be Jesus.

A further advance made by the theology of the primitive Church was the penetrating, new interpretation of the sabbath commandment, which went far beyond anything which we find in Judaism. It harked back to Jesus' manner of interpreting the law in the Sermon on the Mount. Equally firm was its basic conviction that Jesus had already proleptically brought the true sabbath. At the same time the demand for the 'complete' sabbath, which was to go far beyond anything that was possible on earth, opened up a new way of thinking of the sabbath at the consummation. These three ideas which are present in the early Christian sabbath 'theology are all interconnected: in the last analysis they all revolve round the person of Christ. One could not talk about the future sabbath without at the same time mentioning its fulfilment in Christ. One could not speak of the new meaning of the sabbath commandment for the Christian without referring back to him who had brought this true sabbath and without, at the same time, looking forward to the consummation of the sabbath at the end.

B. SABBATH PRACTICE

While the sabbath theology of primitive Christianity lends itself to fairly clear presentation, it is much more difficult to grasp the details of sabbath practice in primitive Christianity. This difficulty is caused partly by the lack of evidence over wide areas and partly because the several groups of churches differed from one another in their sabbath practice: also, even within a single church customs on these matters were subject to alteration. Moreover, we cannot simply refer to the sabbath theology in order to fill the gaps for which evidence is missing and to bring a degree of cohesion to the tradition. From the sabbath theology it is not always clear how sabbath practice was carried out at that particular place and time. For example, in the Gentile Christian sabbath theology of the second century there is perceptible a certain undercurrent of criticism of the weekly sabbath: nevertheless, as we shall see, there was developing at precisely that time a fresh interest in the weekly sabbath.

The sabbath practice of the primitive Palestinian church cannot be reconstructed from the sabbath theology provided in the Gospels. The evidence does, in fact, point in several directions. There are instances in which the tradition about Jesus reflects an increased christological limitation: in these cases its significance for the Church is, therefore, reduced, as in Mark

2.28 par. ('The Son of man is lord even of the sabbath') and in the episode recorded in the western text of Luke 6.4.[1] Here we may suppose that the tradition was closely related to a sabbath practice which ran parallel to it and did not dare to undermine the literal understanding of the sabbath commandment. The situation does, however, become complex immediately we realize that we find these christological limitations in Gentile Christian Gospels (Mark and Luke). We shall show in due course that the Gentile Christian churches were not subject to the obligation to keep the sabbath commandment. It is, therefore, surprising that it is they which have preserved this christological limitation without doing anything to remove the limits. On the other hand, it is not immediately clear from the Gospel tradition whether the Jewish-Christian churches in Palestine maintained their sabbath observance. In Matthew's Gospel there are at least traces of the view that in quite general terms the Jewish sabbath was held to have been fulfilled in Jesus (Matt. 11.28–30).

Nevertheless, even if we have no direct proof from the Gospel tradition, there is a certain probability in favour of the view that the primitive Palestinian church, at least outwardly, maintained the sabbath. One of the strongest arguments in favour of this assumption is that we have no evidence, from the time of the infant church, of any persecution taking place because the Christians no longer kept the sabbath commandment. (We shall have to discuss later the persecution of Stephen.) If the primitive Palestinian church had no longer kept the sabbath, we should have almost certainly expected such persecutions from the Jews in much the same way as, in the lifetime of Jesus, one of the principal causes of conflict was the fact that Jesus did not observe the sabbath.[2] Moreover, we know that the Christians (again we must say, outwardly at least) remained in the Jewish community. In all probability, for instance, they continued to pay the temple tax (Matt. 17.24–27)[3] and continued to practise circumcision, although we have no explicit

---

[1] See pp. 64ff. and 86ff. above.

[2] We have already stated that this consideration also tells against Bultmann's opinion that the tradition of Jesus' sabbath conflicts originated within the primitive community and is connected with the primitive community's disputes with the Jews about sabbath observance. See pp. 72f. above.

[3] *Epist. Apost.* 5, then, intentionally modifies the sense of Matt. 17.24–27; the centre of interest has now become the catch of fish.

evidence for this.[1] Also we should not overlook the fact that at first they sought for converts to the new faith only among their Jewish brethren (Matt. 10.5f., 23).[2] In addition we hear that the primitive Church practised fasting (Matt. 6.16ff.; Mark 2.18ff. par.; 9.29; Acts 13.3; 14.23; *Didache* 8.1) and possibly had its own food laws (Acts 10.14).[3] Of particular importance in the investigation of sabbath practice is a passage like Matt. 24.20, 'Pray that your flight (in the last tribulation) may not be in winter or on a sabbath.' There can be seen behind this saying an almost exaggerated dread of infringing the holy day. This may have been derived from late Jewish apocalyptic or from nationalist and zealot circles; for this reason it could not be used as a direct source for the theology of Palestinian Jewish Christianity.[4] The very fact, however, that this saying was preserved among Jewish Christians is sufficient proof of the high regard in which they held the sabbath.[5]

Luke 23.56b, 'On the sabbath they (the women after the burial of Jesus) rested according to the commandment', is also often quoted to prove the loyalty of the early Church to the sabbath commandment. The addition 'according to the commandment' (it is omitted in D) certainly suggests this conclusion. Nevertheless it is open to question whether we may use the passage in this way. The addition clearly comes from the author of Luke's Gospel, for only he includes it in his Gospel. At the time when Luke's Gospel was compiled the Gentile Christian Church no longer kept the sabbath. We must, therefore, ask for what reasons Luke 23.56b could have been written. Did the author want to add a characteristic touch to his picture of the primitive Church which was represented as loyal to the law in all respects? This interpretation cannot be ruled out, but it does seem forced. If this had been the case, he would have been able to express this conviction

---

[1] The discussion at the Apostolic Council in Acts 15 revolved round the question whether *Gentiles* had to be circumcised when they were converted: this implies that there was no dispute about the duty of circumcision for *Jews* who believed in Christ.

[2] Matt. 28.19f.; Luke 24.47 and Acts 1.8 represent developments which we doubtless have to date after the events of Acts 8ff.

[3] The passage could, indeed, simply be an embellishment to the story about the sheet with the unclean beasts which Luke used to illustrate the new situation of the Gentile mission. In any case, it is to be placed beside Mark 7.19 for purposes of comparison.

[4] See p. 68 above.

[5] We have indirect corroboration of this inasmuch as the Gentile Christian Gospels (Mark and Luke) have clearly expunged the prayer that the end may not be on a sabbath as being altogether too Jewish in tone.

elsewhere (e.g. in Acts) and in a more general form. Luke 23.56b can only help to explain the fact (which is surprising in itself) that the women had not already gone on the sabbath to the grave with their ointments. They were Jews, and Jews were forbidden by the sabbath commandment to do anything on the sabbath. We have the impression that it became necessary to include this detail because only in Luke's Gospel are the women made to prepare their ointments on the *Friday* evening, and there thus arose the problem why they did nothing on the sabbath. If we read Mark 16.1, the situation appears quite different: here the women do not purchase their ointments until the *Saturday* evening, for the quite simple reason that after the burial of Jesus it had already become too late on the Friday evening as the sabbath had already begun (Mark 15.42). According to Mark's account the women had no choice but to prepare the spices on the Saturday evening and to take them to the grave on the Sunday morning. The question whether it was loyalty to the law which caused them to be inactive on the sabbath does not arise here at all.[1] It is all the more remarkable that the author of Luke's Gospel can report that the women had prepared the ointments on the Friday evening, for he implies (Luke 23.54) that the sabbath had begun immediately after the burial of Jesus. Therefore we conclude that Luke 23.56b does not rest on an historical reminiscence,[2] nor does it shed for us any light on the attitude of the primitive Church towards the sabbath.

We should not exaggerate the loyalty with which the primitive Palestinian church observed the law—at least in the very earliest days. We do not know, for instance, whether the daily visit to the temple recorded in the Acts of the Apostles (2.46; 5.42; cf. Luke 24.53) really was a participation in the worship of the temple. These visits may indicate that the Christians assembled for their own morning worship[3] and that they may perhaps have also carried on their missionary activity[4] in 'Solomon's porch'. This lay in the temple area and is mentioned on several occasions as a place where members of the new faith

[1] This is confirmed by the fact that in the Gospel of Peter 50 we find quite a different explanation for the delay, 'Early on the Lord's day Mary Magdalene, the disciple of the Lord, took her friends with her and went to the grave: it was fear of the Jews (who were ablaze with wrath) which had caused them not to do at the Lord's grave what women were in the habit of doing to their dear ones at their death.'

[2] It is an entirely different question whether the account of the discovery of the empty tomb on Easter morning (which is reported in all four Gospels) and the three-day schedule associated with it are true to the events of history. On this see pp. 228ff. below.

[3] See p. 270 below.

[4] Thus E. Preuschen, *Die Apostelgeschichte* (HNT 4.1), 1912, p. 17; an opposite view in E. Haenchen, *Die Apostelgeschichte* (Meyer), 1959³, p. 154.

met (3.11; 5.12). Furthermore, a passage like Acts 3.1 ('Peter and John were going up to the temple at the hour of prayer, the ninth hour') must not be construed to mean that it was solely for the sake of pious observance that the Christians participated in the hours of prayer which took place three times daily. They may well have done it because they met there many of their fellow countrymen with whom they could converse about their newly found convictions.[1] Even the mention of the offering of sacrifice in Matt. 5.23f. does not necessarily imply that the Christians continued to sacrifice in the temple. We have, in fact, already suggested[2] that the depreciatory attitude later adopted by Jewish Christians towards the temple cultus and the sacrificial system is to be traced back partly to the primitive Church and partly even to Jesus himself.[3]

In all these instances it is necessary, above all, to make the following caveat: if we think we can discern a certain outward loyalty to the law on the part of the primitive Church in Jerusalem,[4] this tells us nothing about the *inner* motives which led to this outward observance. It could well be that in some matters the Christians conformed only in their outward observance in order not to cause unnecessary offence, which would endanger their whole missionary work; this work was much more important for them than these questions of detail. It could even be that for this reason they did originally observe the religious customs and usages of their own people, although they felt themselves inwardly liberated from them. May not the pericope Matt. 17.24–27 be an example of this? The children of God have, properly speaking, no temple tax to pay; yet they may pay it in order to avoid giving offence. This became almost a rule of thumb for Paul in his missionary activity. He aimed at

---

[1] Acts 10.9 nevertheless seems to indicate that the Christians maintained the hours of prayer.

[2] See pp. 75f. above.

[3] Moreover, we see that in *Did.* 14.1–3 an entirely new interpretation has been put on Matt. 5.23f.; the 'sacrifice' now indicates a part of Christian worship. See pp. 271ff. below.

[4] Unfortunately we can do no more than make conjectures about the conditions in Galilee. It is certain that missionary activity was undertaken there by Christians, and perhaps Christianity, like Judaism also, had there a less strict attitude towards the law. E. Lohmeyer, *Galiläa und Jerusalem* (FRLANT 34), 1936, p. 76, and *passim*, holds that it was Galilean Christianity which was particularly loyal to the law.

being 'all things to all men' so that he might gain some (I Cor. 9.19, 23; 10.33). He circumcises Timothy on account of the Jews (Acts 16.3) and for the same reason he takes on himself a Nazirite's vow (Acts 21.26).

We can hardly imagine that the disciples and the first Christians, who had been together with Jesus and had lived through his death and resurrection, would not find themselves obliged to alter their attitude towards the religion of their fathers. We have always tended to regard the early Palestinian church merely as a Jewish sect which was not distinguished from its environment except by its acknowledgement of Jesus as Messiah. In terms of outward appearance this may be correct: the Christians were a particular community, like many others, within official Judaism. We must, however, realize that there was more to it than that. From the very beginning the acknowledgement of Jesus as Messiah opened a gulf between Christianity and Judaism: the rift was so fundamental that it could never be bridged. Two considerations may serve to illustrate this.

In the first place the supporters of Jesus were severely compromised by his trial and for this reason they hardly dared to show themselves in public.[1] They generally assembled in the 'upper room' (Acts 1.13; cf. 12.12; Luke 24.33) and in private houses (Acts 2.46; 5.42)[2] by themselves and secretly. It was therefore an especial sign of grace, even after Pentecost, for the faithful to appear before the people with παρρησία, outspokenness (Acts 4.29-31; cf. v. 13). Normally disputes arose as soon as the Christians preached in public (Acts 3-4; 5.17ff.),[3] but we hear nothing of the disputes which the Christians may have precipitated by their testimony in the synagogues.[4] This indicates either that they no longer took part in the worship of the

---

[1] C. v. Weizsäcker, *Das apostolische Zeitalter der christlichen Kirche*, 1902, pp. 20–27; E. v. Dobschütz, *Probleme des apostolischen Zeitalters*, 1904, p. 28; J. Weiss, *The History of Primitive Christianity*, ET 1937, I, pp. 7f., can explain the fact that the early Christians suffered relatively little molestation only by supposing that they avoided publicity.

[2] O. Cullmann, *Early Christian Worship*, ET 1953, pp. 9f., asks whether the plural here is to be taken literally or whether it does not really mean 'at home' (cf. 'in the temple').

[3] We may perhaps be dealing here with doublets of a single occurrence; B. Reicke, *Glaube und Leben der Urgemeinde* (AThANT 32), 1957, pp. 56ff., is emphatically of this opinion.

[4] Later Paul regularly caused disputes whenever he preached in a synagogue.

synagogue or at least, if they did take part, that they kept silence and did not publicly acknowledge their allegiance to their new faith (cf. John 9.22; 12.42).[1] They had, indeed, every reason to keep quiet. Nevertheless we do hear that in all probability they were soon tracked down and called to account: this certainly happened in the course of the persecution after Stephen's martyrdom (Matt. 10.16f.; 21.34ff.; Mark 13.9; Luke 12.49ff.; Acts 8.3; 9.2; 22.19; 26.12; John 16.2).[2] We can, therefore, accept only with reserve the statement in the Acts of the Apostles that the Christians stood high in the favour of all the people (2.47). The situation is probably summed up more accurately in Acts 5.13, 'None of the rest dared join them, but the people held them in high honour.' The Christians were certainly popular with the simple people, the *'am-ha'arez*, on account of their acts of healing, but equally certainly they were hated by the rulers of the synagogues and by the ecclesiastical authorities. These very officials who had not rested until the false Messiah Jesus had been eliminated could not be kindly disposed towards his followers, who asserted with even more brazen effrontery that Jesus was risen and would reappear to judge the world. Right from the beginning, long before the Jews included the cursing of Christians in their Eighteen Benedictions,[3] there was tension in the relationship between official Judaism and the sect of those who believed in Jesus.

Secondly, closely associated with this outward isolation of Christians was an inner detachment. Christians could no longer feel at home in the synagogues precisely because there was lack-

---

[1] The fact that the apostle Paul, according to Acts 9.2, was carrying with him letters to the synagogues at Damascus does not mean that he hoped to find Christians in the synagogues. By means of these letters he only wanted to accredit himself with the tribunal which could give him a free hand to search out Christians (cf. Acts 8.3). The remarkable phrase ἡ συναγωγὴ αὐτῶν (Matt. 4.23; 10.17; 12.19) also seems to point to the separation of synagogue and Christian community.

[2] The allusions to persecutions are not always equally pointed (cf., for instance, Matt. 10.17 with John 16.2); for this reason, it is very possible that these allusions do not always refer to the same persecution (e.g. the one which broke on the community after Stephen's martyrdom). This particular persecution, according to Acts 8.1, did not affect all the disciples, as is the case with the persecutions foretold in the gospels.

[3] Cf. C. W. Dugmore, *The Influence of the Synagogue upon the Divine Office*, 1944, pp. 3f., 119. Justin, *Dial. c. Tryph.* 16.4, and Jerome, *Comm. in Isa.* II (on 5.18), all refer to the cursing of Christians in the synagogues.

ing in Jewish worship that which was for them of decisive importance—the reference to Jesus Christ, on whom was centred all the worshipping activity of the new people of God. Christian worship no longer revolved around the readings and prayers of the Jews, but around the Lord's Supper, prayer in the name of Jesus, baptism for the forgiveness of sins.[1] It was, therefore, imperative that the Christian community should form itself as a clearly defined entity distinct from the Jewish community. It had become the Church perhaps even before it had realized that this had happened.[2] We shall have to return to this point when we discuss the Christian observance of Sunday.

We misunderstand the nature of primitive Christianity in an important respect if we fail to realize how both inwardly and outwardly the Christian community and the communities of the Jewish synagogues were fundamentally separated from each other. The novel element evident among Christians by comparison with Jews does not date from the Gentile mission; it was implicit in Jesus himself. Similarly with regard to the sabbath a new situation had already arisen with Jesus himself, but the Church only gradually grasped its significance. We can nevertheless discern even in the Jewish Christian community a groping inquiry into the right way to observe the sabbath. In the last analysis this inquiry ran contrary to the Pharisees' interpretation of the law and it resulted in an alarmingly liberal attitude. Matt. 12.12 is couched in general terms, 'So it is lawful to do good on the sabbath.'[3] The question in the Marcan source has become a positive statement, and this has resulted in the law of love being placed above the sabbath commandment.

We should also inquire whether the bitter experience of the

[1] E. Lohmeyer, *Kultus und Evangelium*, 1942, p. 124, quite rightly remarks that baptism for the remission of sins took the place of the sacrificial cultus which had been practised with a view to obtaining forgiveness of sins; see also E. Lohmeyer, *Das Urchristentum I: Johannes der Täufer*, 1932, p. 148.

[2] Cf. W. G. Kümmel, *Kirchenbegriff und Geschichtsbewusstsein in der Urgemeinde und bei Jesus* (Symbolae Biblicae Upsalienses 1), 1943, who sees the emergence of the Church and with it the separation of the Christian community from Judaism based principally on a new understanding of eschatology. G. Strecker, 'Christentum und Judentum in den ersten beiden Jahrhunderten', *EvTh* 16, 1956, pp. 458–77, draws a similar picture; so does L. Goppelt, *Christentum und Judentum im ersten und zweiten Jahrhundert*, 1954, pp. 74f., a work which is itself criticized by Strecker.

[3] Cf. Matt. 12.7, 'I desire mercy and not sacrifice'. But see also p. 68, n. 4, above.

Saturday before Easter did not influence the attitude of Jesus' disciples with regard to the sabbath. The grief and sadness of this memorable day, when Jesus had been taken from them and had not yet shown himself alive, certainly remained deeply engraved in the disciples' memory.[1] May not their sabbath joy have been shattered for ever and been replaced by their rejoicing at the resurrection on the following day, i.e. on Sunday?

This can, of course, be no more than a matter for conjecture, but it is worth noticing both that from early times the Christians held their worship on the Sunday morning and also that the sabbath before Easter Sunday became a fast day in memory of the disciples' bewilderment and of the Lord's rest in the grave. Mark 2.18ff. is a pericope which aims at justifying the fasting of the disciples after the Lord's resurrection,[2] and it may be the first hint of the practice of fasting on Holy Saturday. Matthew and Luke do not explicitly say that the disciples would fast if the bridegroom were taken away from them; these evangelists clearly have in mind the entire interim period.[3] Mark 2.20, however, states quite plainly, 'When the bridegroom is taken away from them, then they will fast *in that day*.' In all probability this is a reference to the particular day in the calendar year between Good Friday and Easter Day: the disciples fasted on this day because the Lord had gone from them and the Church now fasted year by year on this day in memory of his departure.[4]

So far as the origins of the primitive Palestinian church are concerned, we are not, however, entirely clear about its inner relations with Judaism, in particular with regard to the sabbath. The persecution which broke over Stephen and his followers casts a light which therefore seems all the brighter. It draws

---

[1] It is interesting to note that in the later gospels, e.g. Gospel of Peter 26; 58–60; Gospel according to the Hebrews (in Jerome, *Vir. ill.* 2), also in *Epist. Apost.* 9–11, the paralysing grief, to which the disciples then succumbed, is much more strongly emphasized, clearly in connection with the practice of fasting: see the following discussion.

[2] Cf. E. Klostermann, *Das Markusevangelium* (HNT 3), 1936[7], p. 27; C. F. D. Moule, 'The Intention of the Evangelists', *New Testament Essays, Studies in Memory of T. W. Manson*, 1959, p. 174 = *The Phenomenon of the New Testament*, 1967, p. 111.

[3] K. Th. Schäfer, ' ". . . und dann werden sie fasten an jenem Tage" (Mk. 2.20 und Parellelen)', *Synoptische Studien, A. Wikenhauser zum 70. Geburtstag dargebracht*, 1953, pp. 124–47.

[4] Behm, *TWNT* IV, p. 933, n. 65, holds a different view: he interprets this passage as a reference to fasting on Good Friday. On Good Friday, however, Christians remembered the suffering of Christ, not his removal from them. See also n. p. 143, n. 4 below.

attention to the group of Christian Hellenists, i.e. those Greek-speaking Jews who had come to believe in Christ.[1] Acts 6–7 speaks plainly. Obviously Stephen had not minced his words; in public he had attacked the cultic ordinances of the old covenant, in particular the temple and the sacrificial system (6.14; 7.42–49). Stephen's criticism was, however, directed not only against the temple. In Acts 6.14 we read that Stephen said, 'This Jesus the Nazarene[2] will . . . change the customs which Moses delivered to us.' These customs clearly refer to cultic regulations (cf. Acts 21.21; 28.17).[3] According to Acts 7.51 Stephen does not, in fact, seem to have directed his attack principally against bodily circumcision (he merely calls the Jews uncircumcised in heart and ears, cf. Jer. 9.26). It is no-where expressly stated that he had also included the sabbath among his targets for attack, but it would not be at all surprising if he had done so.[4] The Hellenists were (in contrast to the Hebrews) the first Christians to carry on 'vocal' missionary activity,[5] and it would fit well into the picture which we have of them if they publicly claimed for themselves Jesus' own freedom with regard to the sabbath.

The persecution which broke over those outspoken members of the Church clarified the various attitudes within the primitive Church itself. Whoever reckoned to be among the 'Hebrews'

---

[1] Thus E. Haenchen, *Die Apostelgeschichte*, 1959³, pp. 213f., and the majority of commentaries. The Hellenists could hardly be only proselytes, as B. Reicke (p. 123, n. 3), pp. 116f., supposed.

[2] The origin of the name is disputed. E. Schweizer, 'Er wird Nazoräer heissen (zu Mc. 1.24., Mt. 2.23)', *Judentum—Urchristentum—Kirche, Festschrift für J. Jeremias* (BZNW 26), 1960, pp. 90–93, pleads for its derivation from 'Nazirite'; in this case the name would subsequently have been connected with Nazareth and altered to 'Nazarene'. (Schaeder, *TWNT* IV, pp. 879–84, takes another view.) M. Black, 'The Patristic Accounts of Jewish Sectarianism', *BJRL* 41, 1959, pp. 298ff., makes it probable that the Samaritans were called 'Nazarenes' in Aramaic usage (cf. John 8.48). This designation becomes a common nickname among the Jews for Jesus and, also, their name for Christians. In Acts 24.5 Christians were indeed called 'the sect of the Nazarenes', and this title is often found in the Talmud: Sunday was also called the 'day of the Nazarene', cf. W. Bacher, 'Ein Name des Sonntags im Talmud', *ZNW* 6, 1905, p. 202. Later the name merely served to denote some of the Jewish Christians.

[3] L. Goppelt, *Christentum und Judentum im ersten und zweiten Jahrhundert*, 1954, p. 77, n. 5, suggests that we have here the beginning of the later distinction between the moral and the ceremonial law.

[4] Also M. H. Shepherd, *The Paschal Liturgy and the Apocalypse*, 1960, p. 17.

[5] The expression in E. Haenchen (n. 1), p. 226.

now became emphatically loyal in his observance of the law, especially after James, the Lord's brother, had taken over the leadership of the Church.[1] We may even say that this part of the Jewish Christian Church now developed an increasingly 'Judaizing' tendency inasmuch as they kept as a matter of principle the customs and usages of Moses.[2] There is, for instance, evidence that all the stricter groups of Jewish Christians observed the sabbath from that time onwards.[3] We should probably fit in here passages like Matt. 5.17ff. and Luke 6.5 D, the character of which we have already established.[4] These passages seek to provide an apologetic basis for the continued observance of the law. It is possible that this development may have been encouraged by other factors beside the pressure of outward circumstances: it may also have resulted from the fact that more and more Pharisees and priests had joined the Christians (Acts 6.7; 15.5; 21.20) and were acquiring a decisive influence within this part of the Church.

Conversely the courage which had led those who had been persecuted to confess their faith also enabled them to speak more plainly in other circumstances. We know that the Hellenistic Christians who were scattered into the surrounding territories now began to conduct missionary activity in Samaria and among the Gentiles: in so doing they broke the last ties which linked them to the national religion of Judaism (Acts 8.4ff.; 11.19ff.; cf. John 4.38).[5] It is possible that even Peter took part in this missionary work (Acts 10–11), although he was primarily a missionary to the Jews.[6] Barnabas played the next important part in the foundation of the Antiochene church (Acts 11.22–24),[7] and finally Paul joined in this mission which he had not founded.

The fact that uncircumcised Gentiles had accepted belief in

---

[1] But we should not forget that James 'the Just' also became a martyr, Josephus, *Ant.* XX.9.1; cf. Eusebius, *HE* II.23.11–18.

[2] Cf. also G. Strecker (p. 125, n. 2), p. 464.

[3] Eusebius, *HE* III.27; Epiphanius, *Haer.* 30.2.2; cf. 29.7.5; Irenaeus, *Adv. haer.* I.26.2. See also Justin, *Dial.* 47.2.

[4] See pp. 77f., 86ff. above.

[5] Cf. O. Cullmann, 'Samaria and the Origins of the Christian Mission: Who are the ἄλλοι of John 4.38?' ET in *The Early Church*, ed. A. J. B. Higgins, 1956, pp. 185–92.

[6] See O. Cullmann, *Peter—Disciple, Apostle, Martyr*, 1962[2], pp. 52ff.

[7] Cf. E. Haenchen (p. 127, n. 1), p. 315.

Jesus meant that a decision had to be made whether the law of Moses had to be imposed on Gentile Christians or not. This decision was made at the Apostolic Council.

It would make too great a digression if we were to enter upon a discussion of the problems concerning Acts 15 as compared with Gal. 2.[1] Gal. 2 and Acts 15 are concerned with substantially the same event, even if we have to assume that the Apostolic Decree,[2] which in any case is not so much concerned with the fundamental problem of justifying a mission to the Gentiles which is not bound by the law—it is more concerned with the practical question of regulating the conditions under which Jewish and Gentile Christians could associate with one another[3]—was drawn up at a later occasion, perhaps after the incident at Antioch which Paul reports in Gal. 2.11ff.[4] If this is the case, light is shed on the motivation (which is otherwise obscure) why, in Acts 15.21, there should be nothing imposed on Gentile Christians except the four provisions[5] of the decree, 'For from early generations Moses had had in every city those who preach him, for he is read every sabbath in the synagogues.' This passage does not mean that if the Gentile Christians went to the synagogue on the sabbath, they would acknowledge the other requirements of the Mosaic law; this condition would mean that they were obliged to observe a Jewish manner of life, and this would run clean contrary to the acknowledgement that Gentile Christians were free from the law. Acts 15.21 does, in fact, imply a comparison: as the godfearing Gentiles were permitted by the Jews to attend worship in the synagogue without hindrance if they observed the four fundamental precepts as set out in the decree, so now Jewish Christians would also be able without hesitation to associate with Gentile Christians provided that these same precepts were observed.[6]

At the Apostolic Council it was recognized that for the future the mission to the Gentiles was to be under Paul's

---

[1] See E. Haenchen (p. 127, n. 1), pp. 396ff.; J. Dupont, *Le problème du livre des Actes d'après les travaux récents*, 1950, pp. 51ff.

[2] The Western text in which the decree appears as a moral law (cf. Tertullian, *Pud.* 12) is certainly secondary; cf. J. Schümmer, 'Die altchristliche Fastenpraxis', *LQF* 27, 1933, p. 11. The opposite view was put forward by G. Resch, *Das Aposteldekret* (TU, NF 13), 1905, but was countered by A. Seeberg, *Die beiden Wege und das Aposteldekret*, 1906, pp. 53ff.

[3] So H. Lietzmann, *Kleine Schriften* II, 1958, pp. 292–8, and earlier von Weizsäcker, von Harnack, von Dobschütz, etc.

[4] O. Cullman (p. 128, n. 6), pp. 50f.; L. Goppelt (p. 127, n. 3), p. 96, n. 1.

[5] For these provisions see Lev. 17.10ff.; 18.26; also Gen. 9.4. πορνεία certainly means marriage within the prohibited degrees; see H. Baltensweiler, 'Die Ehebruchklauseln bei Matthäus. Zu Mt. 5, 32; 19, 9', *TZ* 15, 1959, pp. 340–56.

[6] So Gutbrod, *TWNT* IV, p. 1059.

leadership[1] and free from the obligation to observe the law. The observance of the law was still obligatory for the mission to the Jews, and precisely for this reason the two missions were separated (Gal. 2.9). This separation was, indeed, not easy to effect in the churches which were partly mixed. Repeated conflicts, the echo of which we hear in the various letters of Paul, were caused by the practical problems arising in such churches.[2]

It is precisely this situation which we see with regard to the question of the sabbath. The sabbath was not explicitly mentioned in connection with the Apostolic Council, but we may suppose that the Gentiles were granted freedom from the sabbath commandment together with their freedom from the other regulations of the Mosaic law. From several passages in Paul's epistles we may gather that he held that the sabbath had lost its authority for Gentile Christians, and in this respect he will not have been in opposition to the Jerusalem church. Nevertheless Paul clearly had to fight in his Gentile Christian churches against influences which would do their utmost to preserve the obligation on Gentile Christians to keep the sabbath.

In Gal. 4.8–11 we read, 'Formerly, when you did not know God, you were in bondage to beings that by nature (φύσει) are no gods; but now that you have come to know God, how can you turn back again to the weak and beggarly elemental spirits, (στοιχεῖα) whose slaves you want to be once more? You observe[3] days, and months, and seasons (καιρούς), and years! I am afraid that I have laboured over you in vain.'

---

[1] This was a truly amazing step to be taken by James and the Jewish-Christian community which he represented.

[2] In this connection reference should be made to Acts 21.19ff. (see p. 138 below), and also presumably to the Apostolic Decree, whether it had been preserved in writing and was available for Luke as a source or not; on this latter question see the discussion of R. Bultmann, 'Zur Frage nach den Quellen der Apostelgeschichte', *New Testament Essays, Studies in Memory of T. W. Manson*, 1958, pp. 68–80, and E. Haenchen, 'Quellenanalyse und Kompositionsanalyse in Acts 15', *Judentum—Urchristentum—Kirche, Festschrift für J. Jeremias*, 1960, pp. 153–64. Possibly the decree was really in force only in the region of Antioch and in Syria and Cilicia (Acts 15.23), and therefore Paul knew nothing about it (Gal. 2.6; Acts 21.25).

[3] παρατηρεῖσθε. On this expression see A. Strobel, 'Die Passa-Erwartung als urchristliches Problem in Lc 17.20f.', *ZNW* 49, 1958, pp. 163f.

By ἡμέραι in v. 10 a reference is certainly being made to the sabbath days which recur week by week. (The list clearly begins with the festivals which recur at short intervals and it goes on to those which recur at long intervals; moreover, Col. 2.16 in every respect runs parallel with Gal. 4.10, and there the word σάββατα appears.) μῆνες is identical with νεομηνίαι (Col. 2.16), καιροί with ἑορταί (also Col. 2.16); ἐνιαυτοί may possibly indicate New Year's Days.[1]

The whole context of the Epistle to the Galatians gives us to suppose that a succession of Gentile Christians had had themselves circumcised (Gal. 6-12; 5.2) and had begun to introduce Jewish customs, especially the calendar of Jewish festivals. Against this Paul protests: if the Galatians cause themselves to be circumcised, they must then become Jews in every respect and keep the whole law; in so doing, they will forfeit the liberty of the children of God and the promises made to them. They cannot have it both ways. For Gentile Christians the calendar of Jewish festivals is finished: they are not allowed to observe it. In order to illustrate this point, Paul embarked on an interesting new train of thought: he describes the attitude of these Christians as slavery to στοιχεῖα.

στοιχεῖα are the elementary principles of knowledge and, above all, the elements of nature (including the four elements: water, fire, air and earth). In Hellenistic syncretistic thought these elements were supposed to be animated by spiritual forces. The stars were particularly identified with these στοιχεῖα-spirits and were appropriately venerated.[2] We have, therefore, to understand the στοιχεῖα in Gal. 4 also in accordance with their normal significance as demonic forces active on the cosmic scale. Of course, this does not mean that the list of days, months, seasons and years in v. 10 must relate to the practice of divination of days and of worshipping the stars, for if this had been the case the Galatians would not have fallen a prey to Judaizing heresy, but to one of the Hellenistic-gnostic variety.[3] This conclusion seems to be excluded by the context which unambiguously refers to the Old Testament law. We must, therefore, point to Jewish circles in which the observance of days and festivals played an important part. In

[1] H. Lietzmann, *An die Galater* (HNT 10), 1932³, p. 26, holds that these were sabbatical years. H. Schlier, *Der Brief an die Galater*, 1949, p. 145, n. 1, gives a list of the various interpreters and of their views.
[2] References in W. F. Arndt and F. W. Gingrich, *A Greek-English Lexicon of the New Testament* (ET of W. Bauer), 1957, pp. 776f.
[3] This is against the view of H. Schlier (n. 1), pp. 144f., who on this point interprets the Epistle to the Galatians too much in the light of the Epistle to the Colossians.

Jubilees (but cf. also Ethiopic Enoch) questions about the calendar play just such a part. Every misfortune has befallen Israel because it abandoned the right calendar and the proper festivals.[1] It must by now have become apparent that in the relevant passages (Jub. 6.32–38; 23.19) there are lists very similar to those which we have in Gal. 4.10 (cf. Col. 2.16); in Jubilees, too, emphasis is placed on the importance of festivals (or seasons), months (or new moons), sabbaths and years. Their proper and exact observance is, according to the Book of Jubilees, a matter of supreme importance. It is, therefore, not absolutely impossible that we may discern here a direct influence on the Christian churches of Asia Minor from Jewish circles which used the Book of Jubilees (the Essenes, for example): this influence would show itself in the importance which Gentile Christian churches accorded to questions concerning the Jewish calendar. It is, of course, true that we still have to investigate the possible course of such influence, for all other traces of it seem to be missing. A. Strobel, [2] however, believes he is able to prove an Essene influence on the Montanists in Asia Minor.

It is disconcerting that Paul here places the observance of Jewish festivals on the same level as the pagan slavery to the στοιχεῖα. If we consider Gal. 4.3f. at the same time, there will be no room for doubting that Paul has actually described the Jews' obedience to the law as slavery to the στοιχεῖα: in this passage he says that 'we were slaves to the στοιχεῖα τοῦ κόσμου' until, in the fullness of time, those who stood under the law were redeemed by Christ. Here he is referring to the main tradition of Judaism, not to some esoteric version of it such as the Essenes: this becomes apparent by the way in which he brings into the discussion his own past as a good Pharisee (Gal. 1.13; Phil. 3.5f.). How did Paul come to hold this radical point of view which would seem to be quite unjustified from a Jewish standpoint? We shall probably be mistaken if we suppose that this entirely represents Paul's attitude to the law.[3] It is clear that in this text the apostle was making a conscious attempt to depreciate in the eyes of Gentile Christians the value of the loyal obligations of Judaism: he was intending to show Gentile Christians their own senselessness in being attracted by the Jewish law. His object was to warn the Galatians by reference

---

[1] Cf., e.g., A. Jaubert, *La date de la Cène*, 1957, pp. 16ff.

[2] 'Der Termin des Todes Jesu', *ZNW* 51, 1960, p. 84.

[3] Thus also M. Dibelius, *Die Geisterwelt im Glauben des Paulus*, 1909, p. 83, who holds that in this passage we should not look for Paul's considered reflections on the law; for that one should look at passages like Rom. 7.12, 14.

to their own past of the perils of Judaizing. He made this point by boldly claiming that the adoption of Jewish customs did not constitute progress for Gentile Christians, but was tantamount to a relapse into pagan ways. In other words, if Gentile Christians began to observe days and festivals in the Jewish fashion, then in the final analysis, Paul says, they fell a prey to the same delusion as did the pagans who in superstitious awe submitted to elemental spirits and demons.[1]

It is unlikely that Paul invented on the spur of the moment the argument set out in Gal. 4. In this connection we should remember the remarkable passages (Gal. 3.19; Acts 7.53)[2] in which the Jewish law is represented as 'delivered by angels'. One might even suppose that Paul and possibly even the Hellenists before him had made use of a pagan misunderstanding of Judaism for the purposes of their own polemic. It could, for instance, easily seem to pagans that the Jewish observances and festivals were closely associated with slavery to the planets. In the light of their own practice in these matters they could discern in the particular attention paid by Jews to certain days and seasons nothing more than religious veneration paid to stars and natural forces. We have already noticed in the introductory chapter[3] that the pagan world in the midst of which the Jews observed the sabbath and its rest from work was inclined to attribute such practices to dread of the evil influences of the planet Saturn, and it makes no difference that this was a crude misunderstanding of the facts.

Paul's point of view was taken up in later Christian polemic. We read, for example, in the *Epistle to Diognetus* (4.5) these sharp words, 'And their (i.e. the Jews') attention to the stars and moon, for the observance of months and days, and for their arbitrary distinctions between the changing seasons ordained by God (οἰκονομία θεοῦ), making some into feasts, others into occasions of mourning;—who would regard this as a proof of piety, and not much more of foolishness?' The fragment of the *Preaching of Peter* (quoted in Clement Alex., *Strom.* VI.5.41.2) says bluntly, 'Worship (God) not as the Jews; for they, thinking that they only know God, do not know him, adoring as they do angels and archangels, the month and the moon. And if the moon be not visible, they do not hold the sabbath, which is called the first; nor do they hold the new moon, nor the feast of unleavened (bread) nor the feast (of tabernacles), nor the great day (of atonement).'

---

[1] With regard to *Jewish* Christians, who remained loyal to the Mosaic law on conscientious grounds, Paul would never have made such a comment; we shall later discuss his attitude towards them; see pp. 137ff. below.
[2] Acts 7.53 (cf. Heb. 2.2) might lead us to believe that the Christian Hellenists had made use of such arguments in their polemic against the Jewish ritual law.
[3] See pp. 29f. above.

Aristides writes in his *Apology* (14, Syriac text) 'They suppose in their minds that they are serving God, but in the methods of their actions their service is to angels and not to God, in that they observe sabbaths and new moons and the passover and the great fast, and the fast, and circumcision, and cleanness of meats: which things not even thus have they perfectly observed.' (Cf. Origen, *Cels.* I.26.) We are now not far removed from the assertion of Marcion that the law of the Jews was given by the demiurge![1]

In certain cases, of course, this criticism of Judaism by pagans and later by Gentile Christians was not wide of the mark, for in a syncretistic type of Judaism tendencies towards angel worship seem repeatedly to have made themselves felt. We shall very soon have to discuss the Colossians' heretical beliefs on this point.[2] But we repeat our opinion that on the basis of this isolated reference to the στοιχεῖα in Gal. 4 we need not assume that Paul already had in mind a particular group of these syncretistic Jews: if this had been the case, he would certainly have dissociated himself from such beliefs and he would not have described his own earlier obedience to the law as slavery to the στοιχεῖα (Gal. 4.3f.).

We cannot answer with any certainty the question who were the people who had confused the Galatian Christians. The majority of critics think in terms of a Jewish Christian disturbance. This is very possible, but we should probably be mistaken if we were to suppose that the mother church in Jerusalem had played any part in this disturbance, for this would mean that it had come to regret the decision of the Apostolic Council.[3] On the other hand, it would be quite conceivable that some Gentile Christians who were impressed by the example of the Jewish Christians had by themselves hit upon the idea that one became a more perfect Christian if one had oneself circumcised and observed some Jewish customs. Paul himself seems to indicate that we should look in this direction: in Gal. 6.12f. he

[1] It already says in the Mandaean 'Book of the Lord of Greatness', ed. Reitzenstein, 1919, p. 40, that the whole number of the planets produced the Torah; cf. the Book of John, 198, ed. M. Lidzbarski, pp. 192f. See H. Schlier (p. 131, n. 1), pp. 111f., for further references from gnosticism. They are clearly pejorative in tone by comparison with the Jewish sources (in Schlier, pp. 109f.); for instance, the Jewish law is traced back to the demiurge and his angels. On the problem of the law in Christian gnosis see P. G. Verweijs, *Evangelium und neues Gesetz in der ältesten Christenheit bis auf Marcion*, 1960, pp. 292ff.
[2] See pp. 136f. Cf. also, however, what is said on p. 30, n. 2, above.
[3] This point of view was commonly held in the school of F. C. Baur. But K. Holl, 'Der Kirchenbegriff des Paulus in seinem Verhältnis zu dem der Urgemeinde', *Gesammelte Aufsätze zur Kirchengeschichte* II, pp. 44–67, is also very strongly influenced by it.

writes, 'It is those who want to make a good showing in the flesh that would compel you to be circumcised, and only in order that they may not be persecuted for the cross of Christ. For even those who receive circumcision do not themselves keep the law. . . .' Not only the expression περιτεμνόμενος[1] points to Gentile Christians, but also the fear of these people lest they be persecuted. It is clear that they wish either to guard themselves against attacks from the Jews or to take refuge from the pagan population under the protection of the *religio licita*.[2] The thesis that it was a question of Gentile Christians who were Judaizing in that way receives some support from a passage in Ignatius' *Letter to the Magnesians* which we still have to discuss.[3]

Before we turn to this passage we must consider two more passages from St Paul. In many respects Col. 2.8–23[4] stands in a close relationship with Gal. 4.8–11. The church in Colossae was also clearly in danger of adopting various practices which ill accorded with its freedom from the law. 2.16 enumerates restrictions on food and drink, as well as festivals, new moons and sabbath; 2.11 may perhaps refer to circumcision. The polemic develops in exactly the same way as that in the Epistle to the Galatians: to observe all this is slavery to the στοιχεῖα. Christ has, however, triumphed over the principalities and powers: he has become their head. For this reason Gentile Christians should not choose once again to be in bondage to these powers. In another context we have already seen that in Col. 2.17 the 'fulfilment' in Christ is contrasted with the 'shadows' in the ordinances.[5]

[1] P[46], B and other texts do indeed read περιτετμημένοι. On account of the present participle which appears in the other mss., E. Hirsch, *ZNW* 29, 1930, pp. 192–7, W. Michaelis, *ZNW* 30, 1931, pp. 83–89, A. Oepke, *Gal.-komm.*, 1957[2], *ad loc.*, all hold the reference to be to Gentile Christians. It is superfluous to add that J. Munck, *Paul and the Salvation of Mankind*, ET 1959, pp. 87ff., who puts forward the view that Judaizing originated in Gentile Christianity, holds the same view.

[2] Similarly Gutbrod, *TWNT* IV, p. 1060; L. Goppelt (p. 127, n. 3), p. 94. Cf. later Justin, *Dial.* 39.6.

[3] See pp. 139f. below.

[4] We do not here have to go into the question whether the Epistle to the Colossians is of Pauline authorship. The majority of exegetes is in favour of Pauline authorship, despite the attendant difficulties; cf. E. Käsemann, *RGG*[3] III, col. 1727f.

[5] See pp. 101f., 112f., below.

In all probability we are once again dealing with Jewish customs which the church in Colossae wishes to imitate. We can, however, partly reconstruct the teaching of the philosophers who were unsettling the Christians,[1] and it would seem that their Judaizing is of a markedly gnostic-syncretistic colouring. They really did regard their worship of God as angel worship (2.18).[2] We are, in fact, dealing with the possibility of a whole stream of syncretistic tradition in which Jewish Christian material is inextricably intertwined with material of Hellenistic and oriental provenance. It is with regard to the requirement of sabbath observance in these circles that we can see how interest in the Jewish custom intersected with astrological superstition. The Elkesaites, for example, took over from Judaism the sabbath and circumcision (Epiphanius, *Haer.* 29.8.5), but they characteristically justified their observance of the sabbath by reference to their awe of the planets (Hippolytus, *Refut.* IX. 16.3).[3] Similar ideas may perhaps underlie the sabbath observance of Dositheus (Origen, *Princ.* IV.3.2), of Cerinthus (Filastrius, *Haer.* 36.2 [CSEL 38.20]), of the Simonians (Ps.-Clem. *Hom.* 2.35.3)[4] and of the Hypsistarians (Greg. Naz. *Orat.* 18.5 [PG 35.991]).[5]

[1] G. Bornkamm, 'Die Häresie des Kolosserbriefs', *TLZ* 73, 1948, col. 11–20 (now *Das Ende des Gesetzes*, 1952, pp. 139–56). Cf. also Titus 1.10–16.

[2] We also should not exclude the possibility that the juxtaposition of restrictions about food (probably fasting) and of festival days is not accidental; it may indicate that these days were also fast days, and it would be yet another sign of the astrological superstition characteristic of the Colossian heresy; see p. 32, n. 2, above. W. Förster, 'Die Irrlehrer des Kolosserbriefes', *Studia Biblica et Semitica (Festschrift for T.C. Vriezen)*, 1966, pp. 71–80, distinguishes the Colossian heresy from syncretism; he regards the Colossian heresy as an heir of Qumran.

[3] Likewise they recommend that nothing should be done on Tuesday (=Mars' day).

[4] Here it is a matter of a 'sabbath observance' which recurs every eleven days. Is there possibly here a reference to a period which would stretch from Saturn's day to the next Mars' day but one and from this day once again to the next Saturn's day but one?

[5] There was, at any rate, in Asia Minor a religious community called the 'Sabbatarians'; cf. E. Lohse, *TWNT* VII, p. 8, n. 44. Also the Masbothaeans kept the sabbath, according to Ps.-Jerome, *Indiculus de haer.*, PL 81. 636C. The negro Jews of Abyssinia, the Falashas, have some quite unusual ideas. Prof. W. Baumgartner of Basel informs me in a letter dated 4 June 1960 that the sabbath has become for them a female angel, almost a divine hypostasis, and it is called Sanbat (the form of the name is probably derived from *sbt*, which had already become feminine in Aramaic and Middle Hebrew). About 1900 E. Littmann saw on the wall of a church a picture of a female figure floating up to heaven; he was told that it was Sanbat. (Details in W. Leslau, *Falascha Anthology*, 1951.) It seems to be no accident that the Christian Church in Abyssinia has also retained the observance of the sabbath; see p. 153, n. 2 below. The hypostatization of the sabbath does, on the other hand, remind us of the Mandaean hypostatization of Sunday; see pp. 190ff. below.

We have already said that it would be unfair to reproach Paul with having referred in general terms to the observance of the law as slavery to the στοιχεῖα;[1] he had in mind only *Gentile* Christians who were dazzled by the lure of Judaism either of an orthodox or of a heretical complexion. This clearly emerges from the apostle's attitude towards *Jewish* Christians, as for example in Rom. 14.5, 'One man esteems one day as better than another (ὃς μὲν κρίνει ἡμέραν παρ' ἡμέραν), while another man esteems all days alike (ὃς δὲ κρίνει πᾶσαν ἡμέραν). Let every one be fully convinced in his own mind.'

It is not certain what we should understand by 'observance of days'. Since the phrase occurs in the context of abstention from food, we might think of it in terms of some kind of fast day.[2] Yet festival days could also be meant. In any case it can concern only *Jewish* Christians who abstained from certain foods[3] as well as observing fast (and festival) days. The context of chapters 14–15 makes this plain. Moreover, Paul would hardly have accepted the situation with so little complaint if Gentile Christians had continued their pagan practices in this way. He did, however, recognize that Jewish Christians might properly consider themselves bound in conscience to the law of their fathers and that Gentile Christians had to respect this obligation.

In the Epistles to the Galatians and Colossians it was principally a question of the observance of particular days. While, however, in those epistles Paul was sharply critical of people who wished to entice his churches to observe days, his judgement here in the Epistle to the Romans is quite mild: everyone should act in accordance with his own conviction. This contradiction is resolved as soon as we realize that in the one case the apostle has in mind *Gentile* Christians who are

---

[1] The Actus Vercellenses I (Lipsius, pp. 45f.) fall into this misunderstanding when, looking back on Paul's missionary activity, they say 'that Paul had often argued with the Jewish teachers and had convinced them (with words such as these) : Christ, on whom your fathers laid violent hands, abolished their sabbath and their fasting and their festivals and their circumcision and abolished the teaching of men and all the other traditions'. (Similarly the Jewish legend about Peter; cf. J. Ringger, 'Das Felsenwort: Begegnung der Christen', *Festschrift zum 70. Geburtstag von O. Karrer*, 1960², p. 300.) Conversely the *Martyrdom of Peter and Paul*, 1f. (Lipsius, pp. 118ff.), makes Paul take the sabbath under his protection against Peter!

[2] Thus M.-J. Lagrange, *L'Épître aux Romains*, 1950, p. 325.

[3] In order not to be polluted by tasting sacrificial meat; Rom. 14.14; cf. I Cor. 8; 10.23ff. In addition they also abstain from wine (14.21); cf. Dan. 1.8.

being tempted to imitate Jewish customs, but in the other case (in Romans) he wants to protect the *Jewish* Christians, who were still practising their Jewish customs, from the Gentile Christians who took offence at this.

We are now in a position to understand Paul's attitude. With regard to Gentile Christians he absolutely refuses to countenance any longing eyes cast at the Old Testament law: they are free from any observance of the law, and no one should mislead them in this respect. In particular, there is never any question of them observing the Jewish sabbath. On the other hand, he grants complete freedom to the Jewish Christians to continue their observance of the law (including, clearly, the sabbath commandment), if their conscience obliges them to do so.[1] It is, therefore, certainly a calumny when in Acts 21.21 Paul is reproached with having taught all Jewish Christians living among Gentile Christians to forsake Moses and with having said that they should not circumcise their children nor follow the customs of Moses. In order to counter this accusation Paul immediately takes a Nazirite vow on himself (21.26), and he repeatedly emphasizes (at least according to the evidence of the Acts of the Apostles) that he has done nothing against the law of his fathers (Acts 25.8; 28.17).[2] Yet it is impossible to mistake the fact that although Paul was himself a Jewish Christian he no longer felt his conscience bound by the law. To all outward appearances he was a Jew to Jews, and he did not shock them unnecessarily by infringing the law. Nevertheless it is very possible that sooner or later he did make them aware that he regarded them as 'weak brethren' if they maintained their traditional Jewish practices after they had become Christians (Rom. 14–15; I Cor. 8.7ff.). This will have had various con-

---

[1] In certain respects, therefore, Paul may seem to be more conservative than the Hellenists and the people in Stephen's circle: it would perhaps be better to say that he was more cautious than they. By their open attack on the ordinances and customs of the Jews they brought on the primitive Christian community persecution from without and division within; Paul, however, in his missionary activity proceeds more diplomatically on the principle of being all things to all men.

[2] Paul's disputes with the *Jews* which are frequently reported in the Acts of the Apostles belong to a quite different category. Apart from their opposition to the gospel about the crucified Jesus, the fact that Paul was preaching to *Gentiles* was naturally in the eyes of Jews (as opposed to Jewish Christians) an act of apostasy from Moses.

sequences. Many Jewish Christians will have followed his example and completely assimilated themselves to the Gentile Christians' manner of life, particularly if they were in a minority in a Gentile Christian church. There is, therefore, some grain of truth in the charges which were brought against Paul in Jerusalem and later by the Ebionites.[1] They alleged that he did not observe the decrees of the Apostolic Council and that he incited Jewish Christianş to forsake Moses. Even if he did not exert any direct influence on Jewish Christians in this respect and even if he went so far as to exhort the Gentile Christians to be considerate towards them, yet his secret aim was to make them into 'strong' Christians when they lived in churches under his control.[2]

An interesting piece of evidence on this point is to be found in Ignatius' *Letter to the Magnesians*, 9.1–3, 'If then they who walked in ancient customs (πράγμασιν)[3] came to a new hope, no longer living for the sabbath (μηκέτι σαββατίζοντες) . . . how then shall *we* be able to live without him (i.e. Jesus), of whom even the prophets were disciples in the Spirit . . .?' From this we can gather that some people had clearly given up their observance

---

[1] Whenever they called him an 'apostate' from the law, this is the basis of their charge, Eusebius, *HE* III.27.4; Irenaeus, *Adv. haer.* I.26.2. Cf. Peter's invective against the 'hostile Simon' (= Paul) in the *Kerygmata Petrou*, Ps.-Clem. *Hom.* 17.19; H. J. Schoeps, *Theologie und Geschichte des Judenchristentums*, 1949, pp. 424f.

[2] L. Goppelt (p. 127, n. 3), p. 97, believes he has established that after AD 70 in the Greek Church between Ephesus and Rome there is no longer any evidence for the existence of Jewish-Christian minorities which had preserved their Jewish manner of life; it was, he holds, only in Syria and Egypt that the separation from Judaism took effect rather later. This opinion may not be entirely justified. We shall shortly be discussing Ignatius, *Magn.* 9.1. Moreover, it is hardly a purely theoretical consideration entirely lacking practical significance (as is held by Goppelt, *op. cit.*, p. 295) which moves Justin (*Dial.* 47) to discuss in detail the question of relations with Jewish Christians: he comes to the conclusion that if Jewish Christians do not seek to persuade Gentile Christians to be circumcised, to keep the sabbath and other customs, they should be accepted as brethren and full communion should be kept with them. The influence of Jewish Christians within the Church at large does, therefore, seem to have been felt for a rather longer period. Even Eusebius, *HE* III.27, distinguishes (the distinction is clearly his own) two groups of Jewish Christians, one of which was almost certainly associated with the Church at large; cf. H. J. Schoeps (n. 1), p. 139 and pp. 216f. below. It was Jerome, *Ep.* 112.13, who first condemned all Jewish Christians without exception.

[3] The longer recension of the fourth century reads γράμμασιν (PG 5.765).

of the sabbath, and Ignatius holds this up to the Magnesians as a laudable example. But who are those who 'walked in ancient customs'? The context[1] leaves us no doubt that they are (erstwhile) Jews; otherwise Ignatius would not contrast them with 'us', who are the Gentile Christians and include Ignatius. Yet we still do not know for certain whom Ignatius means by 'they who walked in ancient customs'. Perhaps he could even mean the prophets of the old covenant, for in *Magn.* 8.2 he says that they had lived 'according to Jesus Christ', and in 9.3 he refers to them once again as 'Jesus' disciples in the Spirit'. This possibility is not to be dismissed out of hand, but it would nevertheless have been bold of Ignatius to claim that the prophets had ceased to observe the sabbath, even if he were thinking of passages like Isa. 1.13f.[2] It is much more probable that he had in mind *Jewish* Christians who no longer kept the sabbath, but all that we know of Jewish Christianity in Palestine makes it unlikely that Ignatius was referring to Jewish Christians resident there, for they and their Ebionite offshoots always maintained their observance of the sabbath. We must, therefore, conclude that in *Magn.* 9.1 Ignatius is referring to Jewish Christians who a short time previously had fully attached themselves to the main body of the Church, which was composed largely of Gentile Christians, and in so doing they had given up their Jewish customs.[3] We cannot help thinking of the 'weak brethren' in Paul's epistles who in the meantime had become 'strong'.

The real importance of this passage from Ignatius, however, is that it provides contemporary evidence that many Gentile Christians were being tempted to observe the sabbath. If this were not the case, Ignatius would not follow his reference to those who 'walked in ancient customs . . . no longer living for the sabbath' by asking (if *they* do that) how could *we* wish to go

---

[1] Cf. perhaps 8.1, 'Be not led astray by strange doctrines or by old fables which are profitless. For if we are living until now according to Judaism, we confess that we have not received grace.' And 10.1b–3, 'For this cause let us be his disciples, and let us learn to lead Christian lives. . . . Put aside then the evil leaven, which has grown old and sour, and turn to the new leaven, which is Jesus Christ. . . . It is monstrous to talk of Jesus Christ and to practise Judaism. For Christianity did not base its faith on Judaism, but Judaism on Christianity.'

[2] See p. 105 above.

[3] The present form σαββατίζοντες also indicates this.

on living without the new hope in a Jewish manner of life. From the way in which Ignatius so suddenly yet specifically refers here to σαββατίζειν we must gather that the danger of σαββατίζειν was, in fact, very acute in the Gentile Christian Church.[1] This must cause us to pay particularly careful attention. The Christian churches in Asia Minor were clearly faced with the same problem as they were fifty years earlier. Just as Paul had warned them then, so now Ignatius puts them on their guard. He presents them with the same alternative: you are either fully Christians or fully Jews; there is no half measure possible. In all probability Paul's polemic had not penetrated deeply. The observance of days and of the sabbath had never been entirely eradicated in the churches of Asia Minor. It even appears as if Gentile Christians had been advocating this sort of Judaism. At any rate, we read in Ignatius' *Letter to the Philadelphians* 6.1 (this letter is in many respects parallel with that to the Magnesians), 'But if anyone interpret Judaism to you do not listen to him;[2] for it is better to hear Christianity from the circumcised than Judaism from the uncircumcised.' With some fair degree of certainty we should, therefore, place the sabbath observance of the Magnesian church in a line with that of the Galatian churches and of the Colossian church: in every case it was a question of imitating Jewish customs. This imitation may have sprung from an interest in Judaism itself (cf. *Philad.* 8.2–9.2), or it may have been a product of superstitious syncretistic ideas.[3]

---

[1] We should not be misled by the fact that in ch. 11 (as also elsewhere, *Trall.* 8.1; *Philad.* 3.1; *Smyrn.* 4.1) Ignatius continues, 'Now I say this, beloved, not because I know that there are any of you that are thus . . .' Ignatius would certainly not speak so specifically about these things if he had not 'learnt' something, perhaps from Bishop Damas (*Magn.* 2.1).

[2] ἑρμηνεύειν; literally 'to be an interpreter for'.

[3] The latter is more probable, since Colossae was geographically closer to Magnesia. Astrological superstition was, moreover, never entirely eradicated in the Gentile-Christian communities. The Fathers wrote entire books against it, Tertullian (cf. also Tatian, *Orat. ad Graec.* 8–11); Origen (mentioned by Eusebius, *Praep. evang.* VI.11.1); Minucius Felix (according to Jerome, *Vir. ill.* 58); Gregory of Nyssa, *Contra fatum* (PG 45.145ff.); cf. also *Quaestio* 115 (de fato) of Ambrosiaster; Augustine, *Enarr. in ps.* 40.3; *Civ. dei* 5.1ff. For further material see E. Schürer, 'Die siebentägige Woche im Gebrauch der christlichen Kirche der ersten Jahrhunderte', *ZNW* 6, 1905, and W. Gundel, *RAC* I, pp. 817ff. In the sixth century the observance of Jupiter's day (=Donar's day) sprang up in Gaul; cf. Caesarius of Arles, *Serm.* 13.5 (CCSL 103.1, p. 68).

After the time of Ignatius, that is to say after c. AD 110, we do not hear anything more about the observance of the sabbath in Gentile Christian churches until the end of the second century. This may be a matter of pure chance, for it is possible that the practice of sabbath observance continued without interruption and there has simply been no evidence preserved. We shall have to inquire whether this assumption is at all probable or whether a definite break did take place between the beginning and end of the second century.

In the first two centuries the observance of the sabbath had in general been abandoned in Gentile Christian churches[1] and the observance of the weekly Jewish festival had been restricted to the fringe of the Christian Church here and there in Asia Minor. The situation does, however, seem to have altered very much in the third century and particularly in the fourth century. The sabbath now begins to be held in high esteem, and this development was widespread, particularly in the east, but also in the west of the Roman Empire.

We find in the west, in North Africa, the first indications that a new importance is attaching to the sabbath. Tertullian (*De oratione* 23) writes that several Christians refrained from kneeling at prayer on Saturday as well as on Sunday.[2] 'Since this dissension is particularly on its trial before the churches, the Lord will give his grace that the dissentients may either yield, or else indulge their opinion without offence to others. We, just as we have received, only on the day of the Lord's resurrection[3] ought to guard not only against kneeling, but every posture expressing anxious care.' Tertullian is therefore opposed to the practice of standing for prayer on the sabbath. This fact is all the more interesting, for it tells us that in Tertullian's day there were already some Christians who marked the sabbath in this way. If the practice of standing for prayer derives its meaning from Sunday worship,[4] this practice on the sabbath can only point to the fact that this day was specially

---

[1] We should also compare Justin, *Dial.* 10.3; 26.1, and the whole sabbath theology of that time with the passages which we have discussed in Paul's epistles and in Ignatius (*Magn.* 9.1).

[2] This was the general practice; see pp. 267f. below.

[3] On the question of the correct reading see p. 158, n. 4, below.

[4] See pp. 267f. below.

significant. In his later treatise *De jejunio* (14) Tertullian himself already seems to be advocating that very same regard for the sabbath which he had previously condemned. It is true that he does not say that one should stand for prayer on the sabbath, but he comes out decisively against the recently adopted custom of fasting on every Saturday. 'If there is a new creation (*conditio*) in Christ, our solemnities too will be bound to be new: else, if the apostle has erased all devotion absolutely of seasons, and days, and months, and years (cf. Gal. 4.10; Col. 2.16f.), why do we celebrate the passover by an annual rotation in the first month? Why in the ensuing fifty days do we spend our time in all exultation? Why do we devote to stations the fourth and sixth days of the week, and to fasts the preparation day? Anyhow, you sometimes continue your station even over the sabbath, a day never to be kept as a fast except at the passover season, according to a reason elsewhere given.'[1]

In the *Liber Pontificalis* 17 we read that Callistus had decreed a fast on Saturday to be observed three times a year in Rome;[2] perhaps Tertullian is referring to this, although the historical worth of this evidence has been contested.—It is not quite clear where the roots of the new western custom of fasting on Saturday are to be found.[3] At the least the whole of western Christendom by this time fasted on Holy Saturday,[4] and it would have been easy to have hit upon the idea of fasting on every Saturday (just as every Sunday was a little Easter). In the passage which we have quoted Tertullian does, however, point us in yet another direction. At this time (voluntary) fasting on Wednesday and, above all, on Friday was customary,[5] and he knows of people who have been 'adding' Saturday to this Friday fast. In this case Saturday would have been made another fast-day in order that, after two days of abstinence, the festival on the Sunday following could be celebrated all the more joyously. Evidence is, in fact, available for this kind

[1] In *Jejun*. 2 Tertullian says that Holy Saturday should be observed as a fast day (his authority is Mark 2.20).

[2] See J. Schümmer, 'Die altchristliche Fastenpraxis', *LQF* 27, 1933, pp. 153ff.

[3] Cf. on the whole subject K. Holl, 'Die Schriften des Epiphanius gegen die Bilderverehrung', *Ges. Aufsätze zur Kirchengeschichte* II, 1928, p. 374; J. Nielen, *Das Zeichen des Herrn*, 1940, pp. 43ff.

[4] As well as Tertullian cf. the letter of Irenaeus about the Paschal Controversy, in which he draws attention to the variety of practice with regard to fasting (in Eusebius, *HE* V.24.12). F. X. Funk, 'Die Entwicklung des Osterfastens', *TQS*, 1893, pp. 179ff.

[5] Cf. also Clement Alex., *Strom*. VII.12.75. On the history of station days see J. Schümmer (n. 2).

of Saturday fasting. It was called '*superpositio*'.[1] Furthermore we shall see that it was customary to fast with candidates for baptism on the Saturday before they were baptized.[2] Another factor which may perhaps have influenced the Church at large may have been Marcion's habit of fasting on Saturday in order to demonstrate his hatred against the God of the Jews.[3] In addition, we have already remarked on evidence of a certain tendency in pagan circles at this time to mark the sabbath in a particular way (e.g. by fasting) out of dread of the planet Saturn.[4] It is difficult to decide which of all these motives was the most important: perhaps several were important at the same time.—In any case the practice was soon fairly widespread, particularly in the Church of the western empire. Rome, for example, observed the weekly fast on Saturday,[5] as did Spain[6] and North Africa,[7] while Milan[8] and the East did not join in this practice.

It is true that in *De jejunio* 14 the sabbath does not yet seem to have acquired any special dignity: it was merely not to be observed as a fast day. In ch. 15 of this same treatise of Tertullian, however, we read that in the forty days preceding Easter not only Sunday,[9] but also the sabbath was to be excepted from fasting. If it was not permitted to fast on Saturday even in a season of fasting, we have a clear indication of the importance of this day of the week. Tertullian speaks yet more emphatically in *Adv. Marc.* IV.12, with reference, of course, to Marcion's practice of fasting on the sabbath; he says, 'He (Jesus) would have put an end to the sabbath, nay, to the creator himself, if he had commanded his disciples to fast on the sabbath day.'[10] It is plain that in Tertullian's view it was not permissible under any circumstances to fast on Saturday (=the sabbath). At

---

[1] Victorinus, *de fabrica mundi* 5; *Canon* 26 of the Council of Elivra (Mansi II.10), which was, moreover, opposed to this. (K. Holl [p. 143, n. 3] holds th, reverse; he says that Elvira helped to spread the practice of fasting on the sabbath.)

[2] See p. 265, n. 4, below.

[3] According to Epiphanius, *Haer.* 42.3.3; cf. Tertullian, *Adv. Marc.* IV.12.

[4] See p. 32, n. 3, and p. 136, n. 2, above.

[5] Augustine, *Ep.* 36 (ad Cas.); Cassian, *Inst. coenob.* III.10; Innocent I, *Ep.* 25.4.7 (PL 20.555).

[6] Council of Elvira *Can.* 26 (Mansi II.10).

[7] Augustine, *Ep.* 36 (ad Cas.) 14.32.

[8] Augustine (n. 7).

[9] The prohibition of fasting on Sunday was the general practice; see pp. 268f. below.

[10] On the significance of the idea of creation in the new Gentile-Christian valuation of the sabbath, see pp. 147f., 152f., below.

least with regard to the prohibition of fasting the sabbath was thus placed on the same level as Sunday.[1]

How did the Gentile Christians come to esteem the sabbath so highly? In the case of Tertullian one might suppose some Montanist influence. The treatise on fasting and the books against Marcion (in contrast to the treatise on prayer) do, in fact, belong to Tertullian's Montanist period, and it is possible that the Montanists were influenced by Jewish-Essene traditions.[2] Nevertheless it would be a mistake if we were to trace back to Montanism alone the high regard in which the sabbath was held among Gentile Christians, for we find the prohibition against fasting on Saturday (parallel with that against fasting on Sunday) just as sharply expressed in non-Montanist literature.[3]

Hippolytus (*Comm. in Dan.* IV.20.3) says, 'Now, however, some are daring to do something similar by putting credence in vain illusions (ὁράμασι) and diabolical teachings (cf. I Tim. 4.1) and by often ordering a fast on the sabbath and on the Lord's day, and this certainly has not been ordained by Christ.' In the *Apostolic Canons* 66 we read: 'If a cleric is found fasting on Sunday or on the sabbath, with the exception of that one alone (this is a reference to Holy Saturday), he shall be cursed; if a lay person is found, he will be excommunicated.' Ps.-Ignatius (*Philad.* 13) explains, 'If anyone fasts on the Lord's day or on the sabbath, with the one exception of the paschal sabbath, he is a murderer of Christ.'[4]

We can obtain a balanced impression of the new regard for

[1] It is noteworthy that the cleric whom Augustine refutes in his letter to Casulanus (*Ep.* 36) regarded the fact that certain churches on principle did not fast on the sabbath as evidence of Judaism, for it meant that the sabbath was put on the same level as Sunday. Augustine, for his part, was much gentler in his judgement; he regarded the variety of practice concerning fasting as 'the queen's (i.e. the Church's) bright garment' in which he delighted. (Ambrose, whom he quotes, was of the same opinion.)

[2] See pp. 131f. above.

[3] The fact that fasting not only on Saturday but also on Sunday had to be forbidden shows that we are no longer dealing with the same people as those about whom Tertullian complained in *jejun.* 14, but now it must have been a question of real heretics. See also p. 268, n. 5, below.

[4] *Canon* 51 of the Council of Laodicaea (Mansi II.571) fixes memorial days of martyrs on Saturdays and Sundays during the period of fasting. (A further result of the exception of Saturday and Sunday from fasting during the Lenten period was that this period lasted eight weeks [8 times 5 days].) Further references: Athanasius, *Epist. heortast.* 6.13 (PG 26.1389); *Syntagma* 2 (PG 28.840); *Peregrin. Ether.* 27. Cf. T. Zahn, *Die Geschichte des Sonntags*, 1878, p. 71, n. 39.

the sabbath among Gentile Christians by looking not only at its negative side (prohibition of fasting) but also at its positive side. From the third century onwards worship was held on the sabbath. In the Ethiopic version of the so-called *Egyptian Church Order* (22),[1] which is nothing less than the *Apostolic Tradition* of Hippolytus,[2] we read, 'On the sabbath and on the first day of the week the bishop, if it be possible, shall with his own hand deliver to all the people, while the deacons break the bread, but the presbyters shall (otherwise) break the (baked) bread.'[3] Here it is clearly assumed that public worship takes place on Saturday and that it is accompanied by the Eucharist.[4] From the time of Hippolytus onwards, particularly in the fourth century, there is an increasing amount of evidence for the Christians' practice of worshipping on the sabbath. This worship included reading from scripture, sermon and often also a celebration of the Eucharist. Often, but not always, it took place on Saturday evening.[5] In this connection we also learn why the sabbath was treated by Christians in this special way: it was a day which served as a memorial of creation, and it was therefore observed indirectly in honour of Christ, who was regarded as the agent of creation.

[1] Botte, p. 60 [24, Easton (p. 102, n. 5), p. 58; Dix. p. 43].

[2] R. H. Connolly, *The So-Called Egyptian Church Order and Derived Documents*, Cambridge Texts and Studies 8/4, 1916; E. G. Schwartz, *Über die pseudo-apostolischen Kirchenordnungen* (Schriften der wissenschaftl. Gesellschaft in Strassburg 6), 1910. T. Schermann, 'Die allgemeine Kirchenordnung', *Frühchristliche Liturgien und kirchliche Überlieferung*, 1914, wanted to trace the *Egyptian Church Order*, as that which was in general use, back to the beginning of the second century.

[3] G. Dix (cf. now Botte, p. 61, n. 2). p. 43, n. 1, held that the words 'on the sabbath' were an interpolation in the Ethiopic text (p. 102, n. 5), C. W. Dugmore, *The Influence of the Synagogue upon the Divine Office*, 1944, p. 34, has convincingly refuted him on this point.

[4] It is not necessary to think in terms of the celebration of an agape, as does v. der Goltz, 'Unbekannte Fragmente altkirchlicher Gemeindeordnungen', *Sitzungsberichte der Preuss. Akademie der Wissenschaften* 5, 1906, p. 10. According to the Ethiopic text of *Trad. Apost.* 22 (see n. 1), a daily Eucharist was clearly known.

[5] There is no question of our supposing with T. Zahn (p. 145, n. 4), p. 75, n. 39 (similarly H. Dumaine, *DACL* IV, col. 949), that the Christian observance of the sabbath had developed from a service held on Saturday evening which had served as an introduction to *Sunday*. Quite apart from the fact that it would be difficult to imagine such a transformation, our evidence clearly points to these Saturday evening services being particularly associated with the sabbath; they had no connection whatever with Sunday.

Reference will be made here to the most important pieces of evidence. Epiphanius (*De fide* 24.7) knows that worship is held on Saturday in several churches (cf. *Testamentum Domini Jesu Christi* I.22f.). Socrates (*HE* V.22) gives more details, 'For although almost all the churches throughout the world[1] celebrate the sacred mysteries on the sabbath of every week, yet the Christians of Alexandria and at Rome, on account of some ancient tradition, refuse to do this. The Egyptians in the neighbourhood of Alexandria, and the inhabitants of Thebaïs, hold their religious assemblies on the sabbath, but do not participate of the mysteries in the manner usual among Christian in general: for after having eaten and satisfied themselves with food of all kinds, in the evening making their offerings they partake of the mysteries.'[2] 'In Cappadocian Caesarea, and in Cyprus (see the quotation from Epiphanius) the presbyters and bishops expound the scriptures in the evening, after the candles are lighted.'[3] The Council of Laodicea (*Can.* 16) ordered 'that on the sabbath the Gospels and other parts of scripture shall be read aloud.'[4] Cassian (*Inst. coenob.* II.6) says that on the sabbath and on Sunday both lections were taken from the New Testament, while on other days lections from the New Testament and the Old Testament were connected with one another; in III.2 we read that there were celebrations of communion at 3 o'clock in the afternoon on Saturday and Sunday. In the *Apostolic Constitutions* we find the most frequent references to the Christian observance of the sabbath.[5] In II.59.3 we read, 'Especially on the sabbath day and on the day when the Lord is risen hasten to church eager for knowledge in

[1] 'Constantinople and almost everywhere.' Thus Sozomen in the parallel text, *HE* VII.19.8.

[2] Cf. Sozomen, *HE* VII.19.8. 'There are several cities and villages in Egypt where, contrary to the usage established elsewhere, the people meet together on sabbath evenings, and, although they have dined previously, partake of the mysteries.' Is this an allusion to a (general) custom of celebrating at three o'clock without having eaten? Cf. Cassian, *Inst. coenob.* III.2.

[3] T. Zahn (p. 145, n. 4), p. 73, n. 39, says, 'The placing of the sabbath virtually on the same level as Sunday, especially with regard to the celebration of the Eucharist, is attested by abundant evidence so far as the churches of Constantinople, Cappadocia and Pontus, Antioch and Egypt are concerned' (see references there). 'In the West, too, there is at least a sermon on Saturday' (p. 74).

[4] Cf. *Can.* 49 (ed. Mansi II.571), 'In the period of fasting there shall be no celebration of the Eucharist, except on the sabbath and on the Lord's day.'

[5] The *Apostolic Constitutions* are a composite work from the end of the fourth century; and this is of unequal value in its several parts. A Jewish collection of prayers does, for instance, underlie ch. 33–38 of Book VII; cf. W. Bousset, *Nachr. der Göttinger Gesellsch. d. Wissenschaften*, 1915, pp. 449ff.; H. Lietzmann, *Mass and Lord's Supper*, ET 1954ff., pp. 102ff. So far as our passage is concerned, this probably means that VII.36.1 is a Jewish prayer which has been adapted for Christian use.

order to devote (your) praise to God who has made the universe through Jesus . . . and who has awakened him from the dead' (cf. VIII.33.2). In the *Apostolic Constitutions* we also find the thought that the sabbath is a memorial of creation, 'Celebrate the sabbath and the Lord's day as festival days, for the former is a memorial of creation, the latter a memorial of the resurrection' (VII.23.3).[1] 'Acknowledge the excellence of God's creation which has taken its origin through Christ, and thou shalt observe the sabbath on account of him who has indeed ceased to work, but who has not ceased to govern with his providential care: this sabbath consists in the meditation on divine laws, not in freedom from work for the hands' (II.36.2); similarly in VII.36.1, 'Almighty Lord, thou hast created the world through Christ and hast sanctified the sabbath as a memorial of him, because thou hast decreed that on the sabbath man should rest from work so that he may meditate upon thy laws and because thou hast appointed a festival day for the delight of our souls in order that we may come (together?) for the memorial of thy wisdom in creation.' Cf. Ps.-Ignatius (*Magn.* 9.1). 'Therefore let us not celebrate the sabbath any more after the manner of the Jews . . . (but let every one of you) delight in the meditation of the law . . . and in the admiration of God's creation.'

From the end of the second century onwards this new regard for the sabbath among Gentile Christians found expression in the prohibition of fasting on Saturday and, above all, in public worship conducted in honour of the sabbath. If we now wish to inquire once again into the origins of this development, we must be on our guard against two kinds of one-sided judgement. The first is the view that this regard for the sabbath first appeared in the post-Constantinian period.[2] This is simply not true. If it were true, we should have to eliminate the two passages in Hippolytus, of which one is directed against fasting on the sabbath (*Comm. in Dan.* IV.20), and the other gives clear evidence of worship on the sabbath (*Apostolic Tradition* 22):[3] moreover, Tertullian's protest against fasting on the sabbath

---

[1] The passage continues, 'You have to observe only one sabbath in the whole year, namely that on which the Lord lay buried, on which it has seemed fitting to fast and not to celebrate; for so long as the creator tarries under the earth, mourning for him is worth more than rejoicing about creation; for the creator in his own right naturally takes precedence over his creatures' (VII.23.4).

[2] Thus T. Zahn (p. 145, n. 4), pp. 69ff., n. 39. Similarly L. Duchesne, *Christian Worship: its Origin and Evolution*, ET 1923, pp. 230f.

[3] [24, see p. 146, n. 1]. The Ethiopic text of ch. 2 even places the consecration of a bishop on the sabbath. The *Apostolic Tradition* of Hippolytus was, of course, not yet known in 1878, when Zahn delivered his lecture.

(*Jejun.* 14f.) and his pronouncement that on the sabbath many Christians in his day did not kneel for prayer would both become very difficult to understand.[1] It must, of course, be admitted that the evidence for the observance of the sabbath by Gentile Christians before the time of Constantine is meagre; after his time it is much more abundant.[2]

The other conclusion which it would be rash for us to draw is that certain parts of Gentile Christendom never gave up their observance of the sabbath and that in the sabbath observance of the third century we do, therefore, see a tradition which has managed to survive without interruption since the time of the primitive Church.[3] In this chapter we have, however, tried to demonstrate just this fact, that the Gentile Christian churches originally did not observe the sabbath. The decree of the Apostolic Council and the epistles of Paul show this sufficiently

---

[1] The principal argument of T. Zahn (*loc. cit.*) is also invalid. He holds that the passages which mention the sabbath and occur in the first books of the *Apostolic Constitutions* (these books go back to the Syriac *Didascalia*) are interpolations, by contrast with those which occur in the later books. (This may, in fact, be true, but only with regard to *Apost. Const.* II.59.3.) From this Zahn deduces that the compiler of the *Didascalia* (about AD 250) clearly did not know the observance of the sabbath. Yet even if the *Didascalia* does not itself advocate the observance of the sabbath, knowledge of this practice is presupposed in this work, for in ch. 26 (Connolly, p. 233) there is an undisguised polemic against people who treat the sabbath as equal to Sunday, 'And you say that the sabbath is prior to the first day of the week' (i.e. not only in chronology, but in importance).

[2] It is difficult to find a reason why the observance of the sabbath gained so greatly in popularity immediately after Constantine. Constantine, at any rate, distinguished no day other than Sunday (with the occasional exception of Friday), Eusebius, *Vita Const.* IV.18.2; Sozomen, *HE* I.8.12; a variant reading which, in the passage from Eusebius, reads 'Saturday' instead of 'Friday' must be discarded (T. Zahn [p. 145, n. 4], p. 74, n. 39). Is the answer simply that the newly won religious freedom helped this ecclesiastical practice (in common with others) to blossom out and spread widely? Or was it the fact that higher-class pagans were now joining the Church in greater numbers and they were able to manage to devote another day to Christian worship in addition to Sunday?

[3] In its essentials this is the position of C. W. Dugmore (p. 146, n. 3), pp. 32, 37, and more recently R. A. Kraft, *Some Notes on Sabbath Observance in Early Christianity* (Andrews University Seminary Studies 3), 1965, pp. 18–33. Also P. Cotton, *From Sabbath to Sunday*, 1933, p. 68 and *passim*, sees the history of the sabbath in the earliest stages of the Christian Church too much in terms of a gradual disengagement of Christians from the sabbath. For a proper grasp of the problem the first step is to distinguish between Jewish and Gentile Christianity, and then within Gentile Christianity once again to differentiate between the several phases.

clearly. If, therefore, the observance of the sabbath has *subsequently* crept back into the churches in Asia Minor, this is not to be attributed to the conscious intention of the first Christian missionaries, but to all sorts of secondary motives (e.g. Gentile Christian imitation of Jewish customs, astrological superstition).

The limit of justifiable conjecture would, therefore, be that a direct line leads from the sabbath observance of the churches in Asia Minor to those of the Church at large in the third and fourth centuries.[1] We have already seen from the evidence in Tertullian that Montanism in Asia Minor might have ascribed considerable importance to the sabbath.[2] Nevertheless the nature of the sabbath observance is so markedly different in these two cases that we cannot help doubting whether there is any connection between them. First, while superstitious awe and the restrictive influence of the law certainly played a part from time to time in the sabbath observances of the churches in Asia Minor, the joyous celebration of the day in the third and fourth centuries was so obviously free from any kind of anxious preoccupation that we can safely discount any influence of the belief in the στοιχεῖα criticized by Paul. Secondly, while in the earlier period the sabbath was marked only by rest from work (and possibly by fasting), in the third and fourth centuries we find sabbath worship of a distinctively Christian character. Thirdly, while the churches in Asia Minor had consciously sought to be associated with Judaism in their sabbath observance, there is a perceptible tendency in the later period for the emphasis to be placed on dissociation from any kind of 'Judaizing';[3] this

---

[1] M. Simon, *Verus Israel*, 1948, p. 383, formulates the problem thus.

[2] See p. 145 above.

[3] The Christian authors emphasized that there should be no Judaizing by, for example, not working on Saturday. *Canon* 29 of the Council of Laodicaea (Mansi II, 570) ordered 'that Christians should not Judaize and should not be idle on the sabbath, but should work on that day; they should, however, particularly reverence the Lord's day and, if possible, not work on it, because they were Christians. If they should be discovered to be Judaizers, they should be excluded from Christ.' Ps.-Ignatius, *Magn.* 9.1, similarly opposes the Jewish manner of observing the sabbath by inactivity, and he requires a spiritual observance of the sabbath by meditation of the law and contemplation of God's creation. In Ps.-Athanasius, *Hom. de semente* 1, we read, 'We have assembled on the sabbath day not because we suffered from the disease of Judaizing, for we do not have anything to do with the false sabbath, but we have come together on the sabbath in order to venerate Jesus, the Lord of the sabbath.' R. McReavey, 'The Sunday Repose from

tendency may clearly be seen in the development whereby the sabbath became the day on which the *first* creation was commemorated, while Sunday represented the second creation. It is, therefore, obvious that we should look around for a further factor which might have led to the sabbath observance of the third and fourth centuries.[1] There might, for example, be some sort of connection between this sabbath observance and the spiritual interpretation of the sabbath commandment which had developed since the middle of the second century.[2] Spiritual interpretation on the lines of Jesus' Sermon on the Mount had the underlying intention of fundamentally calling in question the weekly sabbath observance of the Jews. It sought to prove that the true sabbath observance of the Christians had to be recognized as of permanent validity: there was an obligation not merely to rest on one day of the week, but to abstain from sin on every single day of one's life. A positive demand was, however, added to the negative interpretation of the prohibition of work: this demand derived from the example of sabbath worship and saw in *worship* the proper fulfilment of the commandment to keep holy the sabbath day. It is striking that we discover this interpretation at the same time that we find the first traces of sabbath worship. In Origen (*Hom.* 23.4 *in Num.*) we read, 'We want to see of what sort should be the Christian's sabbath observance. On the sabbath day no secular business may be carried on . . . If, therefore, you go to church and listen to the divine readings and homilies and reflect on heavenly things . . . that is the way to observe the Christian sabbath.' Origen is, of course, of the opinion that this worship should also be extended to include *every* day.[3] But since there are here two contrasted types of sabbath observance, i.e.

Labour', *Ephemerides theologicae Lovanienses* 12, 1935, pp. 302f., has for this reason supposed that an anti-Jewish intention gave rise to the Christian sabbath observance.

[1] We can hardly admit a Jewish-Christian influence at such a late stage, as is done by J. Nedbal, *Sabbat und Sonntag im Neuen Testament* (diss.), 1956, p. 207. There is no question of any Jewish influence.

[2] See pp. 100ff. above.

[3] This sense emerges from the context of the passage and also from parallel passages such as *Cels.* VIII.22. A different view is taken by C. W. Dugmore (p. 146, n. 3), who on p. 31 says with proper caution that it is not certain whether *Hom.* 23.4 *in Num.* presupposes sabbath worship, but on p. 34 uses this passage as 'evidence' on which to base his argument.

renunciation of bodily activity and the offering of worship, this distinction could lead to the supposition that Christian sabbath worship represented the 'true' sabbath observance as opposed to the false Jewish practice. Pseudo-Ignatius, who in the fourth century made characteristic alterations to the original text of the Ignatian correspondence, clearly presupposes the existence of Christian sabbath worship: he writes (*Magn.* 9.2) 'We do not want to observe the sabbath any more in Jewish fashion and to delight in idleness . . . but let every one of you keep the sabbath in a spiritual manner; let him find delight in the meditation of the law, not in the inactivity of the body; let him admire the creative work of God.'[1] The *Apostolic Constitutions* (II.36; VII.36),[2] too, lay stress on meditation on the law as the proper sabbath observance. It would not be surprising if this meditation on the law was a communal activity consisting of scripture-reading and sermon. This derivation of Christian sabbath worship must, of course, remain hypothetical.

We have already learnt that the meditation on the law which comprised part of sabbath worship was, above all, concerned with *creation*: the sabbath was the memorial day of creation, just as Sunday was that of the resurrection.[3] This memorial of creation and of its completion on the seventh day naturally formed a link with the narrative of Gen. 2.2f. The new Christian sabbath observance was, nevertheless, christocentrically orientated in its development. The memorial of creation was for *Christ's* sake. Through him, the pre-existent Son, the world had been created in the beginning: through him, incarnate and risen, the second creation (that of redemption) had been called into being. Saturday and Sunday were memorials of these divine acts: Saturday was the day on which the first creation was brought to completion, and on Sunday the second creation was inaugurated. Elements of both salvation

---

[1] The sentence is probably to be construed in this way, and not 'Let him delight in the contemplation of the law, and let him not in inactivity admire the creative work of God'.

[2] Further passages are also to be found, esp. in Chrysostom, *De Lazaro* 1 (PG 48.972); *Hom.* 6.3 *in Heb.* (on 4.9); and in Cyril Alex., *Hom. paschal.* 6 (PG 77.528); *Ador. in spir. et ver.* 7; *Comm. in Isa.* V.3 (on 56.6–8); *Comm. in Amos* 58 (on 6.3).

[3] Cf. also Ps.-Athanasius, *Sabb. et circonc.* 4: 'The end of the first creation was the sabbath, the beginning of the second (creation) the Lord's day on which he (God) renewed the old creation.'

history and christological interest did, therefore, play a part in the sabbath observance of Christians at that time.[1]

After the fifth century sabbath worship once again disappeared from the Christian Church.[2] Two valid reasons for this disappearance may be suggested. First, the emphasis on the sabbath at that particular time seems to have led to some Judaizing of such a sort that the pre-eminence of Sunday was threatened.[3] Secondly, in the intervening period Sunday itself had come more and more to be regarded as the Christian sabbath. From the earliest times Christians had marked this day by worship. Since the time of Constantine it had also been the official day of rest in the Roman Empire: in both respects it seemed to 'fulfil' the Jewish sabbath. It is to this process that we must now turn.

[1] One might consider whether, in the age of the five-day week, a fresh justification could be given to a Christian sabbath observance in some form or other. It would certainly be interpreted as a mark of our solidarity with the Jews, and care would have to be taken from the outset to guard against any Judaizing misunderstanding. See also p. 301 below.

[2] The Abyssinian Church does indeed, provide an exception; there worship on the sabbath has been preserved. This has been made possible by reason of this church's isolation from other churches; cf. E. Hammerschmidt, *Stellung und Bedeutung des Sabbaths in Aethiopien*, 1963. Moreover, since the time of Alcuin Saturday has been the day of Mary in Roman Catholicism. This observance is based on the belief that on Holy Saturday Mary was the only person who maintained her faith (cf. the ideas associated with the Pietà). See J. A. Jungmann, 'Der liturgische Wochenzyklus', *ZKT* 9, 1957, pp. 45–68.

[3] Cf. Gregory of Nyssa, *De castigatione* (PG 46.309): 'You do not set your mind on righteousness, nor learn virtue, and you neglect prayer; yesterday is the proof of this. With what kind of eyes do you wish to behold the Lord's day, you who do not hold the sabbath in honour? Do you not know that the two days are sisters and that if you behave disrespectfully towards the one, you (also) hurt the other?' Furthermore, we have in the latest portions of the *Apostolic Constitutions* a piece of evidence which even prescribes rest from work for Saturday also—it is, therefore, the first and also the only evidence of a five-day week in the ancient world. 'I, Paul, and I, Peter, have decreed: slaves should work for five days; on Saturday and on the Lord's day, however, they should not have any work, on account of the religious instruction in the church' (VIII.33.1–2). The same command to rest on both 'sabbaths' is also to be found in the Ethiopic *Apostolic Canons* (can. 66, ed. G. Horner, *The Statutes of the Apostles* 1, 1904, pp. 210ff.), but according to R. H. Connolly (p. 146, n. 2), p. 4, this passage is a later interpolation. Chrysostom even knew of many Christians who kept the Jewish festivals and celebrations and went to the synagogues (*Adv. Jud.* 1.1; 8.8). On this subject and on the background of this Judaizing see M. Simon, *La polémique antijuive de saint Jean Chrysostome et le mouvement judaïsant d'Antioche*, Recherches d'Histoire judéo-chrétienne (Etudes juives VI), 1962, pp. 140–53. Gregory I, *Ep.* 13.1, then strongly opposed these sabbatarian influences.

III

SUNDAY AS DAY OF REST

In accordance with the plan of our work which divided the subject into two sections, 'Day of Rest' and 'Day of Worship', we must now add a chapter about Sunday as day of rest: this will conclude the first part of this study, which has been principally devoted to the history of the sabbath, the Jewish day of rest, in the earliest centuries of the Christian Church. This chapter is merely added for the sake of completeness, for Sunday was primarily the early Christians' day of worship. It was only subsequently and relatively late that Sunday became also the Church's day of rest.

This fact must cause some surprise to us present-day Christians: we are accustomed to regarding Sunday as a day of rest perhaps even more than as the day for Christian worship. It is precisely for this reason that we are unable properly to visualize the circumstances of the early Church, for they were exactly the reverse of our own: Sunday was the day above all for worship and only in the second place for rest also. This point must be made even more sharply: in the very earliest days of the Church, Sunday was the day for worship and nothing more, for the Christians were not aware of any command to rest on Sunday. Therefore, if we as Christians today quite naturally demand and observe Sunday as a day of rest, we must know whether and how this can be justified. In this matter there are still many uncertainties which have yet to be dispelled, and the historical perspective may very well be helpful.

In the early centuries of the Church's history down to the time of the Emperor Constantine it would, in any case, not have been practicable for Christians to observe Sunday as a day of rest, on which they were obliged, for the sake of principle, to abstain from work. The reason for this was simply that no one in the entire Roman Empire, neither Jews,[1] nor Greeks, nor

[1] It could happen that one of the festivals fell on a Sunday, but this did

Romans,[1] stopped work on Sunday. The Christians, who for a long time belonged principally to the lower strata of society and in particular to the slave class, could not observe a day of rest which recurred after every six days, in addition to observing the official days of rest; their economic and social circumstances would never have permitted this.[2] There was the further consideration that, by observing Sunday as a day of rest, they would have publicly acknowledged that they were Christians, and until the time of the Emperor Constantine this would have placed them in peril of their lives first among Jews and then above all among Gentiles. Whenever we study the first three centuries of Christian history, we have constantly to bear in mind that Christianity was a proscribed religion. Merely being a Christian rendered a person liable to delation before the authorities: whoever remained steadfast at his trial and did not deny his faith had to reckon with the prospect of death. In addition we know of numerous persecutions in the course of which the Christians were systematically hunted down and which were intended to extirpate Christianity. In such a situation it would have been suicidal for Christians to have observed Sunday as a day of rest and so to have announced to all and sundry that they were Christians. We must indeed regard it as very remarkable that they ever dared to gather for worship on Sunday, for in so doing they were never certain of their lives.[3] Worship did not, however, take place in mid-morning,

---

not often happen. In certain Jewish groups which had their own calendar only two Sundays in the year seem to have had any particular importance, the days on which the fifty-day paschal season began and ended. No one can, however, assert that these Jewish sects also observed a regular weekly Sunday, which was a day of rest as well. On these questions see pp. 183ff. below.

[1] Indeed, as we have noted above (p. 10), for a long time they had no week (or, at least, no seven-day week), nor any festivals which always fell on particular days in the week. The seven-day planetary week made a relatively late appearance and, so far as we know, it did not regard Sunday as a day of rest; at all events, we have no evidence (not even Mithraic evidence) which would point in this direction.

[2] The pagan master of a Christian slave would hardly have met such a request with understanding.

[3] We shall have to discuss this point in greater detail when we consider the significance of Sunday worship for Christians. It is striking that, despite all the risks, they did not give up their custom of meeting in common on Sunday. Their worship was clearly important for them, more important than their life. See pp. 226f., 244ff., 304 below.

as it does in our churches, but either very early in the morning, while it was still dark, or immediately after supper, while the rest of the population was gathering for social intercourse.[1] During the course of the day Christians worked just like anyone else. If this had not been the case, we would have been able to discover at least some allusion in Christian or pagan literature.

Nevertheless this state of affairs cannot by itself serve as proof for the assertion made at the beginning of this chapter that Christians originally did not show any interest in Sunday as a day of rest. Before the time of Constantine it was clearly not possible for them to have rested for the whole day on Sunday, but perhaps they did try to treat Sunday as a day of rest, even if their outward circumstances did not permit them to give full effect to their intention. In other words, they could perhaps have been aware of an inner obligation not only to meet for worship on Sunday, but also to treat Sunday as a day of rest, even if they could not properly satisfy this inner obligation until the time when Christianity was tolerated by the State. We have to direct our attention to this point whenever we examine the few pre-Constantinian texts which can give us any information on this subject. We shall have to ask whether it is ever anywhere stated that Christians desired to distinguish Sunday in particular from other days by rest from work or whether we simply have to take into consideration the fact that Christians naturally could not work *during the time of their Sunday worship*. If this were the case, we should have to speak of a partial rest from work which was necessitated by the requirement of worship and which was limited to the duration of Sunday worship.

On this matter some criticism must be made of some studies on the problem of the Sunday rest in the primitive Church. While they admirably demonstrate that Christians at first knew only a partial rest from work necessitated by the requirements of worship, there is for them from the outset no doubt that this Sunday rest (which was necessitated by the requirements of worship) spread over the rest of Sunday by its own internal pressure and of its own accord as soon as outward circumstances permitted.[2] All these authors allege as the principal cause of this development the joy which

---

[1] See pp. 237ff., 253ff. below.
[2] Cf. H. Dumaine, *DACL* IV, 1921, col. 917 and *passim*; F. Pettirsch, 'Das Verbot der opera servilia in der heiligen Schrift und in der altkirchlichen Exegese', *ZTK* 69, 1947, p. 418; J. Daniélou, *The Bible and the Liturgy*, 1960, p. 244; H. Huber, *Geist und Buchstabe der Sonntagsruhe*, 1958, pp. 71ff.

derived from the saving act of the resurrection and which was experienced in Christian worship. Nowadays we have a deep-rooted feeling that both worship and also rest from work are essential components of a proper Sunday. These two components have, however, acquired the appearance of having an inner connection only because they have been juxtaposed by one another for so long. Of course, we experience 'joy' at worship as much as in rest from work, but in these two cases the joy is of a radically different sort. Free time and leisure time are always a time for joy, but this joy is not to be put into the same category as the joy experienced in worship. Conversely, the joy derived from worship is not necessarily accompanied either beforehand or afterwards by the natural joy associated with rest from work: evidence for this is to be found in weekday worship which, as worship, is as complete as Sunday worship. The *total* rest from work on Sunday cannot, therefore, be traced back either in theory or in practice to the joy experienced in worship.[1] Also we shall soon see that, historically speaking, the rest from work which was at first limited to the duration of Sunday worship did not gradually spread over the whole day. It would be quite a different matter if, as soon as Sunday became a day of rest, it were *fully occupied* with cultic activities: this would be a necessity if idleness were to be avoided (see below).[2]

Until well into the second century we do not find the slightest indication in our sources that Christians marked Sunday by any kind of abstention from work. *Barnabas* 15.9, 'This is the reason why we joyfully celebrate the eighth day' (διὸ καὶ ἄγομεν τὴν ἡμέραν τὴν ὀγδόην εἰς εὐφροσύνην), cannot be used as evidence for the beginning of the Sunday rest.[3] The Sunday joy, to which reference is made here, naturally had its roots in

[1] See pp. 299f. below.

[2] Total rest from work is not, therefore, 'the logical consequence of the Lord's day being the day for worship, prayer, reading from scripture and spiritual exercises' (as H. Huber [p. 156, n. 2], p. 104, asserts); for these activities it was not necessary to have a day entirely free from work. It was much more that the time spent in worship on that day gradually expanded, since it was a question of spending in some useful way the time which was free of work.

[3] As is asserted by H. Dumaine (p. 156, n. 2) col. 943; F. J. Dölger, *Sol Salutis. Gebet und Gesang im christlichen Altertum*, 1925³, p. 142. Dölger even goes so far as to infer from this passage that they expressed 'their festal joy in their clothing and in a better family meal'. He cites in support the parallel passages from Tertullian, *Apol.* 16.11 and *Nat.* I.13. Cf. F. J. Dölger, 'Die Planetenwoche der griechisch-römischen Antike und der christliche Sonntag', *AuC* 6, 1941, p. 223. In these passages Tertullian is controverting the erroneous opinion of pagans that Christians were sun-worshippers because they prayed towards the rising sun and spent Sunday joyously: this is, however, no argument for maintaining that Christians marked Sunday

the fact that Sunday was the day of the resurrection; also, it may well refer to the inner attitude of Christians and to their worship, which, as we know, took place on Sunday.[1]

At this point we must dispel a misconception on a related topic. The fact that *Barn.* 15.9 (cf. Eusebius, *HE* IV.23.11) stated that Christians would 'celebrate Sunday' in such and such a way does not mean that their observance lasted for the whole day. It could well be that there were on this day only certain hours in which they were especially interested for the purpose of their observance. We shall establish this in a particularly impressive fashion when we come to examine the origin of that peculiarly Christian name for Sunday, 'the Lord's day'. It is very probable that this association with the 'Lord' was derived from the fact that on this day the Lord's *supper* took place.[2] If, therefore, a text refers to the observance of 'Sunday', this certainly does not mean that the day in itself was observed as if it were held to possess some special 'quality': it may have been a special day (even, for example, an especially joyous day) solely on account of the worship which took place on it.

In Tertullian's writings we find a passage which is often adduced as proof of the observance of Sunday as a Christian day of rest in the pre-Constantinian era. We have already considered it in another connection:[3] the passage in question is *De oratione* 23: 'In accordance with the tradition, we must only on the day of the Lord's resurrection[4] guard not only against kneeling, but

---

by 'practices likely to be conspicuous in city life' other than by worship. They were suspected of being sun-worshippers not because they abstained from work on Sunday, ate well and put on their best clothes (as if sun-worshippers would have behaved in this way on Sunday!), but solely because it was well known that they prayed towards the east and that the day of the sun had an especial significance for them.

[1] See pp. 267f. below.
[2] See pp. 220f. below.
[3] See p. 142 above.
[4] There are two readings. One reads '*sole die dominico resurrectionis*' (Muratorius), the other '*solo die dominicae resurrectionis*'. The former clearly presupposes the weekly Sunday, the Latin translation of κυριακὴ ἡμέρα being 'dies dominica' or 'dominicus'. The second reading could be understood as a designation of the annual Easter day, as is held by J. Nedbal, *Sabbat und Sonntag im Neuen Testament* (diss.), 1956, p. 194. But such an interpretation is improbable, because Tertullian immediately goes on expressly to mention the Easter period in which Easter day is also included. Moreover, we also possess a parallel text in *De corona* 3, in which Tertullian plainly speaks of the *weekly* Sunday, 'On Sunday (*die dominico*) we consider it wrong either to fast or to kneel for prayer, and we avail ourselves of the same privilege during the time from Easter day till the festival of Pentecost.'

every posture expressing anxious care, deferring even our business affairs (*differentes etiam negotia*) lest we give any place to the devil (*ne quem diabolo locum demus*). Similarly, too, in the period of Pentecost; which period we distinguish by the same solemnity of exultation.' The words which are of interest to us here are, 'deferring even our business affairs lest we give any place to the devil'. H. Huber[1] rightly points out that the mention of the fifty-day Easter period (which is marked by the same distinctive observance) excludes the possibility that the formula '*differentes negotia*' means a *total* rest from work: a total rest from work for fifty days would, in fact, be unthinkable.[2] We conclude, therefore, that *De oratione* 23 refers to a partial rest from work and that this arrangement was made for the sake of worship, and here again we are in agreement with Huber:[3] the rest from work was observed on account of worship. Now, it is obvious that Christians had to lay aside their work for the duration of their act of worship, but in order to answer the question which we posed at the outset we must investigate whether in *De oratione* 23 there can be discerned a Christian practice of prolonging the period of rest beyond the time of worship and even of making the whole of Sunday into a day of rest. In the last analysis the answer to this question depends on our understanding of the phrase added at the end of the sentence, 'lest we give any place to the devil'. Does the devil perhaps gain advantage by the very fact that Christians do some work on Sunday? That can hardly be Tertullian's meaning, for work had for Christians high ethical value[4] so long as it was not undertaken from motives of covetousness or avarice.[5] Why, then,

---

[1] (P. 156, n. 2), p. 73.

[2] This also applies to *Apostolic Constitutions* VIII.33.1–2 (see p. 153, n. 3, above), 'Slaves should work for five days; on the sabbath and on the Lord's day they should be free from work on account of the religious instruction in the church. . . . During Holy Week and during that week which immediately follows, the slaves should rest'; cf. *Testamentum domini nostri Jesu Christi*, II.12, 'Those who are oppressed with burdensome toil must allow themselves some respite in the Easter period and on every Lord's day.' On this passage see H. Huber (p. 156, n. 2), p. 91. The social interest evident in these passages is particularly striking.

[3] *Loc. cit.*

[4] We shall see that Christians were very well aware that idleness was much more likely than work 'to give occasion to the devil'. See pp. 167f. below.

[5] This was, however, always forbidden, and not just on Sunday; cf. Irenaeus, *Adv. haer.* IV.8.2 (see p. 103 above).

should work on Sunday expose to the devil an area in which Christians were peculiarly vulnerable? Christians knew nothing about a particular 'sanctity' attaching to Sunday and limited in time, after the manner of the sabbath in the Old Testament.[1] The words 'lest we give any place to the devil' must then refer to the need of regular assembly for worship: attachment to work and to earning money could keep Christians from taking part in Sunday worship. That would have been a really diabolical intrusion into the life of a church, if its individual members on account of secular business could no longer find enough time to meet together for common worship. Sunday *worship* was the reason for 'deferring business affairs'.

Some support for this interpretation of the passage from Tertullian is given by some instructions in ch. 13 of the Syriac *Didascalia*, which was written about 250: they, too, suggest that what was required, was not a total rest from work, but a partial rest for the sake of worship. A somewhat longer passage from this chapter is reproduced here,[2] 'Since therefore you are the members of Christ, do not scatter yourselves from the Church by not assembling. Seeing that you have Christ for your head, as he promised—for you are partakers with us—be not then neglectful of yourselves, and deprive not our Saviour of his members, and do not rend and scatter his body. And make not your worldy affairs of more account than the word of God; but on the Lord's day leave everything and run eagerly to your church; for she is your glory. Otherwise, what excuse have they before God who do not assemble on the Lord's day to hear the word of life and be nourished with the divine food which abides for ever? For you are eager to receive temporal things and those that are but for a day and an hour, (but) those that are eternal you neglect.' 'But if there be anyone who takes occasion of worldy business to withdraw himself, let him know this, that the trades of the faithful are called works of superfluity; for their true work is religion. Pursue your trades therefore as a work of superfluity, for your sustenance, but let your true work be

---

[1] Tertullian himself emphasized the sanctity of every single day and of all time: *Adv. Jud.* 4; cf. *Bapt.* 19. See p. 103 above.

[2] Connolly, pp. 124ff. The passage recurs almost word for word in *Const. Apost.* II.59.1–2.

religion. Have a care therefore that you never withdraw your-selves from the assembly of the church.'[1]

Here the same problem is being faced: many Christians were clearly not coming to church on Sunday because of their materialistic attitude. The Syriac *Didascalia* is sharply critical of this evil habit.[2] The reason why the devil managed to gain entry in the churches of Christ lay in the fact that the faithful no longer regularly assembled together. Worship, not rest from work, was therefore their bulwark against the devil. The Syriac *Didascalia* did not require any rest from work on Sunday; ch. 13[3] concludes thus, 'Do you the faithful therefore, all of you, daily and hourly, whenever you are not in the church, devote yourselves to your work.'

The passage from Tertullian's treatise *De oratione* exhausts the pre-Constantinian evidence which might be able to point to a Christian rest on Sunday. We agree with G. Förster's[4] judge-ment, 'Exhortations in the pre-Constantinian Church concern solely the duty of worship.' In other words this means: before the time of Constantine Christians had absolutely no interest in

---

[1] Connolly, p. 127. In all probability we find the same concern as early as Heb. 10.25 ,'(Let us) not neglect to meet together as is the habit of some, but encouraging one another, and all the more as you see the Day drawing near.'

[2] One feels reminded of the parable of the great supper (Matt. 22.1–10; Luke 14.16–24). We also find similar statements elsewhere. *Can.* 11 of the Council of Sardica (Mansi III, p. 20), reads, '. . . if a layman has not taken part for three weeks in the Sunday worship of the community in which he lives, he is to be excluded from the communion of the church'; cf. *Const. Apost.* II.61. Equally interesting is the reply of the monk John (d. 530) to the question whether work on Sunday is a sin (quoted in H. Huber [p. 156, n. 2], p. 85), 'For those who work in accordance with God's purpose it is no sin, for the apostle says, "Work day and night, so that you may be burdensome to no man"; but it is a sin for those who work because of pride, covetousness or avarice. It is also good to abstain from work on the Lord's day, on the festivals of the Lord and of the apostles, and to go to church, for this is apostolic tradition.'

[3] Connolly, pp. 128f.

[4] 'Die christliche Sonntagsfeier bis auf Konstantin den Grossen', *Deutsche Zeitschrift für Kirchenrecht* 16, 1906, p. 109, n. 4. Cf. the pertinent remark of T. Zahn, *Geschichte des Sonntags*, 1878, p. 29, 'It was considered very repre-hensible if anyone used the pressure of his business as his excuse for being absent from Sunday worship. Not Sunday work, but that overestimation of this-wordly activity which results in indifference to God's word and to the worship of the local church, was regarded as a scarcely excusable sin.' 'Originally the community's act of worship was the sole cause for the observance of Sunday.'

complete rest from work on Sunday. They made no demand whatsoever that the rest from work should be extended to the whole day, and they did not even desire this. The indifference which the Church showed towards Constantine's Sunday laws reinforces this point. As we shall see, the Church had to contend with new, serious, practical problems which resulted from the total rest from work on Sunday.[1] From the time of Constantine onwards we have two different sources of information to consider with regard to this theme of the Sunday rest: on the one hand, the decrees of the State, on the other the attitudes of the Church. We must treat them separately, since they cover different ground.

I. IMPERIAL SUNDAY LEGISLATION

It is well known that the first laws concerning Sunday were promulgated by the State under the Emperor Constantine the Great. The first dates from 3 March 321,[2] and it runs as follows, 'The Emperor Constantine to A. Helpidius. All judges, townspeople and all occupations (*artium officia cunctarum*) should rest on the most honourable day of the sun. Farmers indeed should be free and unhindered in their cultivation of the fields, since it frequently occurs that there is no more suitable day for entrusting seeds of corn to the furrows and slips of vine to the holes (prepared for them), lest haply the favourable moment sent by divine providence be lost.' A total public rest from work on Sunday was, therefore, decreed by the emperor, and only farmers were exempted. This exception made for farmers has suggested that Constantine has merely applied to Sunday the Roman ferial legislation, that in place of the other festival days he has given special treatment to Sunday, which regularly recurs after every six days.[3] It must, in any case, be emphasized

---

[1] See pp. 167ff. below.

[2] *Codex Justinianus* III.12 (*de feriis*). 3 (cited from P. Krüger, *Corpus Juris Civilis* II, 1954[11], p. 127). The law was probably sent from the Balkans to the Prefect of Rome; cf. F. J. Dölger, 'Die Planetenwoche der griechisch-römischen Antike und der christliche Sonntag', *AuC* 6, 1941, p. 229.

[3] Thus F. J. Dölger (n. 2), pp. 231, 235 (he quotes Cicero, *Leg.* II.12.29; 22.53, and also the *Commentary* of Servius on Vergil's *Georgics* I.272); similarly J. Gaudemet, 'La législation religieuse de Constantin', *Revue d'histoire de l'Eglise de France* 33, 1947, p. 47. The old arrangements for the *nundinae* seem to have survived too: Constantine permitted the holding of markets and the popular merry-making associated with them; *Corp. Inscript. Lat.* III.4121.

that the Old Testament was in no way responsible for the new Sunday legislation: indeed, in Judaism it was, above all, agricultural work which was forbidden on any festival and especially on the sabbath.[1] The imperial law gives one to understand that by the time of Constantine the seven-day week had already gained a firm foothold in the whole empire. Moreover, we hear no hint to the effect that the emperor had introduced it. We shall probably not be far wrong if we assume that this seven-day week was the planetary week, for Constantine does, in fact, use in his decree the planetary name, 'day of the sun'. Nevertheless this should not lead us to any hasty conclusions about the motives which caused the emperor to mark Sunday in this particular way or about the question whether he had in mind the pagan sun's day or the Christian Lord's Day. We do indeed know that, like the majority both of his contemporaries and also more particularly of his predecessors on the imperial throne, Constantine was warmly disposed towards sun-worship.[2] We have already mentioned that the cult of Mithras was at that time widespread, particularly among the soldiers, and the emperor was their supreme commander.[3] It is, therefore, possible that Constantine promulgated legislation to make Sunday an obligatory day of rest in order to unite the empire under a monotheistic sun-religion.[4] Constantine did, of course, know about the Christian

---

[1] H. Huber, *Geist und Buchstabe der Sonntagsruhe*, 1958, p. 77, comes to the same conclusion. It should also be noted that the Constantinian law (by contrast with the Jewish sabbath commandment) forbade only public, but not private activity.

[2] Cf. F. Staehelin, 'Constantin der Grosse und das Christentum', *Zeitschrift für schweizerische Geschichte* 17, 1927, pp. 385–417; esp. pp. 411f.; F. H. Cramer, *Astrology in Roman Law and Politics*, 1954, pp. 224–31; H. Kraft, *Kaiser Konstantins religiöse Entwicklung* (Beiträge zur hist. Theol. 20), 1955, pp. 7ff.

[3] See pp. 35f. above.

[4] So, e.g. J. Böhmer, *Der christliche Sonntag nach Ursprung und Geschichte*, 1931, p. 16, and Zöckler, *RE*[3] 18, p. 522. In this connection it is worth emphasizing that in the Constantinian era the Christian Christmas was also fixed, on 25 December, the day of the pagan festival of the winter solstice; see O. Cullmann, *Der Ursprung des Weihnachtsfestes*, 1960[2]. We do not propose to embark on the question whether as early as 312 Constantine was already a Christian. For an affirmative answer see H. Lietzmann, *Sitzungsberichte der Berliner Akademie*, 1937, pp. 263ff.; 1938, pp. xxxvllff.; for a negative answer see W. Seston, *Revue d'histoire et de philosophie religieuses* 16, 1936, pp. 250ff.; also *Byzantion* 12, 1937, pp. 482ff.; and *Revue des études anciennes* 39, 1937, pp. 214ff.; 40, 1938, pp. 106f. On the whole question see also H. Kraft (n. 2).

day of worship, and it is possible that by means of this step he wished to win for himself[1] the support of the Christian minority, which had already grown considerably in size and to which he had granted toleration.[2] It is, however, doubtful whether Christian considerations influenced the emperor in initiating his Sunday legislation, as one might suppose was the case from a reading of Eusebius' evaluation of Constantine. Eusebius says that the emperor bestowed especial distinction on the 'day of the Lord and redeemer', and he adds that Constantine's earnest desire was 'gradually to lead all mankind to the worship of God. Accordingly he enjoined on all the subjects of the Roman empire to observe the Lord's day as a day of rest.'[3]

As we also consider Constantine's subsequent Sunday legislation, it becomes all the more probable that when he made Sunday the statutory day of rest he was not necessarily favouring only the Christian day of worship. Three months after the first decree (on 3 July 321) he sent a second injunction to the same prefect of Rome, 'Just as it seemed very inopportune to occupy with legal disputations and injurious strife the day of the sun which has been honoured with the veneration due to it, so (conversely) it is seemly and admirable to fulfil "*votiva*" on this day above all days. Therefore shall everyone have leave on this festival day to emancipate and manumit (slaves), and it shall not be forbidden to take minutes of proceedings in this connec-

[1] It should be borne in mind that Christianity was numerically most strongly represented in the East, that is to say in that half of the empire where reigned Licinius, the last rival of Constantine; cf. F. Staehelin (p. 163, n. 2) p. 399. The new definitive work on the whole subject is by H. Dörries, *Das Selbstzeugnis Kaiser Konstantins*, 1954. He emphasizes the Christian convictions of the emperor, but on this particular point he allows the possibility of a concession to the sun-cult (pp. 343ff.). It must also be remembered that Constantine at first wished to distinguish *Friday* as well as Sunday, according to Eusebius, *Vita Const.* 4.18; cf. Sozomen, *HE* I.8.12; see (p. 149, n. 2), above. (Therefore he promulgated a law for all citizens of the Roman empire . . .) 'to hold in honour the day before the sabbath, in memory of all that the saviour of the world is reported to have accomplished on that day.' Did Constantine originally intend to honour the Christian God in *this* way? (Cf. the significance which the symbol of the cross had for him since the Battle of the Milvian Bridge.) If this were the case, it would be all the more probable to suppose that he made Sunday a day of rest out of respect for the *sun*-god.

[2] In 313 he had renewed the edict of Galerius.

[3] *Vita Const.* 4.18.2. Sozomen, *HE* I.8.12, is here writing without any rhetorical flourishes, 'And he has honoured the Lord's day because on this day Christ rose from the dead.'

tion.'[1] In this passage it is plain that the emperor was concerned with a religious differentiation of Sunday, but it did not have an expressly Christian character: it consisted in the possibility of fulfilling '*votiva*'. These were either vows (that is to say, promises) or prayers. The mention of the manumission of slaves, which could take place on this solemn day,[2] might point to the former. Nevertheless it is certain that the latter are also intended. Sozomen (*HE* I.8.11) writes concerning this law, 'He commanded that God should be served with prayers and supplications.' Alongside this we have also to consider the report which Eusebius gives us in his *Vita Constantini* (4.18, cf. *Laud. Const.* 9.9–10). In this passage he recounts how the bodyguard of the emperor took him as their teacher of piety and no less (than he) honoured the day of the Redeemer and Lord by performing 'on that day the devotion which he loved'. Immediately afterwards we read (4.19) that whereas Constantine allowed Christian soldiers to go to church without hindrance, in another law he had ordered the pagan soldiers to 'appear on each Lord's day on an open plain near the city, and there, at a given signal, offer to God with one accord a prayer which they had previously learnt. He admonished them that their confidence should not rest in their spears, or armour, or bodily strength, but that they should acknowledge the supreme God as the giver of every good, and of victory itself; to whom they were bound to offer their prayers with due regularity, uplifting their hands towards heaven, and raising their mental vision higher still to the king of heaven, on whom they should call as the author of victory, their preserver, guardian and helper.' (In ch. 20 there follows the prayer composed by Constantine himself.) It is curious, to put it mildly, that alongside the worship in church, which was indeed tolerated by Constantine, he is here organizing liturgical prayer of a kind

---

[1] *Codex Theodosianus* II.8.1 (cited from T. Mommsen, *Theodosiani Libri XVI cum constitutionibus Sirmondianis*, I.2, 1905, p. 87).

[2] In this connection we must mention a further order of Constantine which was issued to Bishop Hosius of Cordoba on 18 April 321 (that is to say, a little earlier) and which might be seen as directly connected with the law of 3 July (*Cod. Justin.* I.13.2). In this letter Constantine decides the legal question whether Christians are authorized to manumit slaves without official permission; he says that manumission is valid and legal if it happens in the presence of the whole assembly of the faithful; the clergy are, however, not bound by this rule if they wish to manumit their slaves.

that seems very similar to sun-worship. One cannot avoid the impression that Constantine himself attached more importance to this Sunday worship of his own devising than to the worship of the Church.

We do not have to follow in detail the subsequent history of the State's Sunday legislation. By and large it continued to operate within the framework laid down by Constantine, even if Sunday did come to be clearly labelled as the Christian festival, *dominicus dies*.[1] Particularly noteworthy is the prohibition from 386 onwards of Sunday performances in the circus and the theatre.[2] This regulation had to be repeatedly enacted. It would seem that even then sports fixtures on Sundays were a problem![3] In 409 we first meet a law which granted to prisoners a certain alleviation of their lot on Sundays: better food, a bath, etc.[4]

For the purposes of our study it is important to emphasize that at the start the State's Sunday legislation did not have any predominantly Christian background: it was, rather, the product of political and social considerations. Official regulation of the times of work and leisure was in any case necessary: Constantine met this requirement by skilfully using and combining the respect paid to Sunday by both pagans and Christians. Moreover, he preserved the well-tried Roman ferial arrangement which had forbidden courts to sit and business to be transacted on festivals, but had not forbidden urgent work on the land.

The Christians for their part—and we shall very soon see this more clearly—did not make any special claim to be sanctifying Sunday by abstaining from work. They left to the State the regulation of times for work and leisure, provided that the State conceded them the right of unhindered assembly for worship on Sunday. This, at any rate, was the situation in the early post-Constantinian period, before Christianity had been promoted to being the official religion of the State. How, then, did it happen that the Church suddenly developed a *religious* interest in the rest from work on Sunday and used its influence to ensure that this rest was observed?

---

[1] 3 November 386: *Cod. Theod.* VIII.8.3; cf. II.8.25.
[2] Therefore from the time of Theodosius the Great; *Cod. Theod.* XV.5.2.
[3] *Cod. Theod.* XV.5.5; II.8.20, 23; cf. *Cod. Justin.* III.12.9 (11). One may wonder why this prohibition was enacted; did the sporting events disturb the church services, or did they keep Christians from their worship?
[4] *Cod. Justin.* I.4.9=*Cod. Theod.* IX.3.7.

2. SUNDAY BECOMES 'THE CHRISTIAN SABBATH'

We must first of all examine what attitude the Church adopted towards the Sunday legislation of Constantine and his successors. H. Huber[1] writes, 'It is striking that no council of the Church in this period refers to the imperial legislation about Sunday or thinks of incorporating this law of the State into ecclesiastical legislation.' 'Equally remarkable is the fact that in their writings the fathers of the Church in the post-Constantinian era never treated the State's legislation about Sunday as a basis for their own position. In the Latin fathers of this period we meet absolutely no law about rest from work on Sunday, not even the merest allusion to prohibition of work on Sunday.' 'We think this silence very significant, particularly because we also have evidence which tells against any ecclesiastical legislation for the Sunday rest.' Huber adduces as evidence *Canon* 29 of the Council of Laodicea[2] and also, above all, passages which refer to the monastic life. Jerome (*Ep.* 108.20) reports about convents for women in Palestine, 'They went to church only on the Lord's day . . . and every group followed its own superior. When they had returned, they devoted themselves eagerly to work and made clothes either for themselves or for other people.' Palladius (*Hist. Laus.* 138, PG 34.1236) knows of a virgin called Taor who remained in her cell on the Lord's day and worked without ceasing while the other sisters went to communion. In the *Rule* of Benedict of Nursia (48, PL 66.704) we read, 'On Sundays likewise all shall apply themselves to reading, except those who are assigned to various duties. But if there be anyone so careless and slothful that he will not or cannot study or read, let him be given some work to perform, so that he may not be idle.'

This last quotation points clearly to the problems with which Christians were faced not only in monasteries, but everywhere, since the total rest from work on Sunday had been introduced from the time of Constantine onwards. Suddenly they were

[1] *Geist und Buchstabe der Sonntagsruhe*, 1958, pp. 81f.

[2] Text on p. 150, n. 3, above. It must indeed be added that 'against' in this case does not mean that the Canon is opposed to rest from work on Sunday, which it does, in fact, recommend; the Canon does, however tell against the view that there was an ecclesiastical law regulating the Sunday rest.

condemned to doing nothing on this day, and idleness was and is 'the beginning of all manner of vice'[1]—at least for people who have little intellectual or spiritual endowment. In this social and pastoral problem we may well see one of the most important reasons why the Church now added the weight of the Old Testament sabbath commandment to the State's regulations concerning rest from work on Sunday. The Church was now the state church responsible for the moral life of the whole population: it saw the original meaning and purpose of its Lord's day, its day for worship, threatened by the fact that on this day the great mass of the population indulged in celebrations which were often of a very unchristian sort.[2] In order to guard against this danger (since Christians very easily found themselves affected by this same tendency), the Church was to some extent obliged to give a religious importance and a binding solemnity to the rest from work on Sunday: it did this by demanding that it was kept holy in the Old Testament sense.[3] We must, however, emphasize here that this development shows evidence of two different tendencies. On the one hand, the population was exhorted to increase its religious activity (both public and private) on Sunday: on the other hand, the mere requirement of rest from work was more and more couched in legal terms— especially when the exhortations to worship had little effect. Deep down these two tendencies are interconnected: they are both to be regarded as part of an attempt by the Church to give theological and practical support to the Sunday rest prescribed by the State.[4]

[1] See the Christian polemic against the Jewish sabbath customs, p. 105, n. 3, above.

[2] Cf. the following passage from a sermon of the sixth century, PG 86.1. 417 (it comes from neither Eusebius of Alexandria nor Eusebius of Emesa; cf. H. Huber [p. 167, n. 1], p. 94, n. 66): 'Many wait for Sunday, but not all with the same purpose. Some await it with awe and in order that they may send their prayer up to God and be fortified with the precious body and blood, but the idle and indifferent in order that they may have time for wickedness when they are free from work. The facts bear me out that I am not lying.'

[3] Perhaps the speculations concerning Sunday as the 'eighth day' have contributed towards this development; see pp. 282ff. below.

[4] We have already encountered a similar situation in Judaism (see pp. 47f., 51f. above). There was absolutely no doubt about the strict rest from work for all Jews, but while the Alexandrian tradition of Jewish theology was concerned to interpret the time free from work as a time for worship, the Palestinian Pharisees tended to restrict themselves to developing in detail

A quotation from Ephraem Syrus[1] will show that we are not proposing a purely artificial picture: it is in connection with the Sunday rest that he makes his first reference to the sabbath commandment, 'Honour is due to the Lord's day, the first-born of all days, for in it lie hidden many secrets. Pay your respect to this day, for it has taken away the right of the first-born from the sabbath. . . .[2] Blessed is he who honours it with spotless observance . . . The law ordains that rest be granted to servants and animals, in order that labourers, serving girls and employees may cease from work. While our body rests, it does indeed cease from work, but we sin on the day of rest more than on other days. While we abstain from work on the land[3] and cease work, we run grave danger of being condemned, since we go into trading establishments. The person who is resting commits sins to which work puts an end. Not only for the sake of your body should you honour the day of your salvation. The Lord's day is a holy day. . . .' In this passage Sunday as a work-free day is given a particular dignity which distinguishes it from the other days of the week, and this made sinning on Sunday a particularly grave matter.[4]

In the pre-Constantinian Church we do not find any such direct equation of sabbath and Sunday, for the simple reason that the Sunday rest had not yet been introduced. This development was, however, already in preparation before the time of

---

the regulations about sabbath prohibitions. Both paths were open; they were even complementary, and both started from the same presupposition: on the sabbath day there must be rest.

[1] S. *Ephraem Syri hymni et sermones*, ed. T. J. Lamy, I, 1882, pp. 542–4.

[2] On this thought cf. also Syr. *Didasc.* 26 (Connolly, p. 238).

[3] It is clear that in the fifty years which had elapsed since Constantine's first Sunday law the rest from work on Sunday had already been extended to agricultural work as well. Is this development to be traced back to a tendency to take seriously the Old Testament prohibition of *opera servilia*? (See p. 172 below.) The first official prohibition of agricultural work occurs under Leo the Thracian (457–74), and he justifies this prohibition by comparing it with the Jewish hallowing of the sabbath and with the even greater obligation on Christians to devote at least one day in the week to God. Cf. T. Zahn, *Geschichte des Sonntags*, 1878, p. 77, n. 44.

[4] This same point is made in the sixth century in the sermon just mentioned (p. 168, n. 2): the passage runs, 'There are people who, with charitable intention indeed, say on Sunday, "Come on, let us today help the poor with their work." They do not consider that wherein they would do well, they do in fact commit a sin. Do you wish to help the poor? Then do not rob God of his day. . .' (PG. 86.1.420f.).

Constantine, inasmuch as Sunday had been compared with the sabbath and had been judged superior to it, but at that time this comparison could extend only to worship.

In Origen[1] we find the following comment, 'I ask, therefore, on what day the heavenly manna was first bestowed and (in so doing) I want to compare the Lord's day with the Jewish sabbath. The divine scriptures make it quite clear that manna was for the first time given on earth on the Lord's day. If, as scripture says, it was in fact collected on six consecutive days but was discontinued on the seventh day, which is the sabbath, it must without doubt have begun on the first day (of the week), which is the Lord's day. If, therefore, the divine scriptures state that God caused manna to be rained down from heaven on the Lord's day, but not on the sabbath, then let the Jews acknowledge that even then our Lord's day was superior to the Jewish sabbath, that even then it had been made plain that on their sabbath the grace of God would not come down from heaven to them and the heavenly bread, which is the word of God, would not come to them.[2]

The excellence of Sunday by contrast with the sabbath still had severe limitations, since the sabbath in at least one respect remained more excellent than Sunday: the sabbath, by contrast with Sunday, was a work-free day. Since the time of Constantine that was changing. We find the first traces of this change, as early as Eusebius, although he still places the principal stress on worship. Nevertheless we already find here the phrase that the sabbath was 'transferred' to Sunday. In his commentary on the sabbath Psalm 92[3] he writes that Christians would fulfil on the Lord's day everything which in this psalm was prescribed for the sabbath (worship of God early in the morning, etc.); he then concludes with these words, 'Through the new covenant the word (of God) has, therefore, transferred

---

[1] *Hom.* 7.5 *in Ex.*

[2] Similarly in Ambrosiaster, *Quaest.* 95.3. 'It is certain that the heavenly manna also was given to the Jews on the first day, the Lord's day. . . Manna is the type of the spiritual food which, through the Lord's resurrection, has become reality in the mystery of the Eucharist.' Further passages in H. Huber (p. 167, n. 1), p. 23.

[3] PG. 23.1169C. A. von Harnack, *Geschichte der altchristlichen Literatur*, I, 2 (new impression 1958), p. 575, does, it is true, doubt the authenticity of the *Commentary on the Psalms*.

the sabbath celebration to the light's rising and has given us a type of the true rest in the saving day of the Lord, the first day of light. . . .'

In the *Hom. de semente*[1] we find, 'The Lord has transferred the sabbath day to the Lord's day . . .' Historically speaking, this point of view had, of course, no justification whatsoever, but it soon enjoyed great popularity. In a sermon of the sixth century[2] it is asserted that 'when the Lord came on earth, born of the holy virgin, he made the whole law new, yet he was also creator of the law. . . . Since all now became new, he had to abolish the law of the sabbath and provide for us another day in its stead. For rest and for worship, therefore, he gave us the first day, on which he had begun to create the world, and he called this day the Lord's day.'[3]

However this equation of Sunday with the sabbath may precisely have arisen, at least it is certain that this equation became possible when under Constantine the rest from work enjoined by the State had been imposed upon the Christians' day of worship. This fact compelled the Church to tackle both theologically and pastorally the problem of rest from work, and this soon became all the more necessary when Christian emperors reigned and justified the State's legislation on Christian grounds. It was in the sixth century that the sabbath commandment first became an important part of the justification of rest from work on Sunday. Chrysostom (*Hom.* 10.7 *in Gen.*, PG 53.89), anticipates this development in his exposition of the text 'God blessed the seventh day and hallowed it': he asks 'What do these words mean, "He hallowed it"? . . . (God) is teaching us that among the days of the week one must be singled out, and wholly devoted to the service of spiritual things.' In a later discourse on the Sunday rest by an unknown author[4] we find the following sentences, 'And I command you not to do anything on the holy day of the Lord. . . . Cursed is he who on the holy day of the Lord performs any business,

---

[1] Ps.-Athanasius, *Hom. de semente* 1 (PG.28.144).
[2] See p. 168, n. 2.
[3] Later, in the 'Letter from Heaven' (the legend says that it fell on to the earth at Jerusalem) which was composed in the eighth century, Christ refers to the 'commandment which he had previously given' to hallow Sunday by abstaining from all work; cf. T. Zahn (p. 169, n. 3), p. 8.
[4] TU 20.4b, 1901, p. 5 (ed. C. Schmidt). The speech certainly does not come from Peter of Alexandria, to whom it is attributed; cf. H. Huber (p. 167, n. 1), p. 92, n. 67.

except that which is beneficial to the soul and also the care of cattle.'[1]

The way was thus open for the complete equation of Sunday with the sabbath. It is particularly interesting to notice the significance assumed by the idea of '*opera servilia*' which belonged to the Old Testament legislation for festival days. We have already seen that '*opera servilia*' had played an important part in the spiritual exegesis of the sabbath commandment by the primitive Church.[2] The point of this exegesis was that this commandment was now in force for *every* day: now, however, Christians came to apply it once again to a particular day, and that day was Sunday. F. Pettirsch[3] is right in insisting that through this gate there streamed in all these detailed regulations for the hallowing of Sunday, which referred not to worship but to rest from work: they were all interpretations of the prohibition of '*opera servilia*'. 'They (the Jews) did no servile work on the sabbath: we do none on the Lord's day,' was said as early as Jerome.[4] For him this expression still had a spiritual significance: this significance was, indeed, already confined to Sunday, and it was not long before this expression was expounded in great detail and those forms of work on Sunday were specified which had to be called 'servile'.[5] The Christian casuistry concerning Sunday which then developed (particularly in the Carolingian era) is in no way to be distinguished from Jewish sabbath casuistry. The so-called '*quanto magis* formula' was the favourite, and it was repeated countless times: it consisted in drawing a comparison between the Jewish observance of the sabbath and the Christian observance of Sunday. If the Jews observed their sabbath in honour of God by strict abstention from work, 'how much more' should Christians do likewise on Sunday, for they as the new people of God should surpass the people of the old covenant.

---

[1] The phrase 'things beneficial to the soul' refers to Ex. 12.16 (LXX), a passage which Tertullian (see p. 103, n. 4, above) had already used. The permission to attend to cattle is perhaps derived from Luke 13.15.

[2] See p. 103 above.

[3] 'Das Verbot der *opera servilia* in der heiligen Schrift und in der altkirchlichen Exegese', *ZTK* 69, 1947, p. 439.

[4] *In die dominicae paschae* (Anecdota Maredsolana 3.2, 1895, ed. G. Morin, pp. 414, 17f.

[5] H. Huber (p. 167, n. 1), p. 117, asserts that purely material exegesis of the prohibition is first to be found in the works of Martin of Braga (d. 580).

H. Huber in *Geist und Buchstabe der Sonntagsruhe* (1958) has described this development in detail until the high Middle Ages.[1] A glance into the history of Christian legislation about Sunday shows us that through the centuries the Church has been living on the heritage of the post-Constantinian period. Even today we still live in it: even today we still have the Sunday rest, and even today the sabbath commandment plays an important part in the theoretical and practical justification by Christians of the rest from work on Sunday. In the final chapter of this study we shall have to ask whether we are to be bound for ever in the future to this heritage. We should not forget that this heritage does not derive from pre-Constantinian Christianity, and it was, as we shall see, explicitly disavowed by the reformers. For the moment, however, we must first examine in the second major part of this work the significance which did, in fact, attach to Sunday in primitive Christianity.

[1] Cf. W. Thomas, *Die Anschauungen des frühen Mittelalters vom Sonntag, dargestellt mit Berücksichtigung der Entstehungsgeschichte des christlichen Dekalogs*, dissertation at Marburg, 1929. H. Stockar, *Sonntagsgesetzgebung im alten Zürich*, dissertation at Zürich, 1949, has assembled the material for the Sunday legislation in the canton of Zürich, particularly since the Reformation. For Puritanism see J. Böhmer, *Der christliche Sonntag nach Ursprung und Geschichte*, 1931.

PART TWO

THE DAY OF WORSHIP

In the primitive Church Sunday was the specifically Christian day for worship. It is true (as we have already noticed)[1] that the sabbath was also occasionally marked by worship: in addition, there also developed the custom of weekday worship[2] (especially on Wednesday and Friday), but no other day in the week came near Sunday in importance. The second part of this study will be exclusively devoted to the Christian Sunday and to its observance.

Before we deal in detail with the practice of Christians with regard to their Sunday worship or indicate Sunday's theological significance, we must first inquire into the origin of the Christian observance of Sunday.

---

[1] See pp. 142ff. above; esp. pp. 145ff.

[2] Tertullian, *Orat.* 19, is evidence for the celebration of the Eucharist on station days; cf. J. Schümmer, 'Die altchristliche Fastenpraxis', *LQF* 27, 1933, pp. 81ff. Hints of the daily celebration of the Eucharist occur for the first time in the *Apostolic Tradition* 22 (Ethiopic text [24, see p. 146, n. 1]). cf. Cyprian, *Or. dom.* 18; J. A. Jungmann, *The Mass of the Roman Rite* I, 1951, pp. 218, 246. For the situation in the earliest years of the Church see pp. 225f., 260f. below.

IV

THE ORIGIN OF THE CHRISTIAN
OBSERVANCE OF SUNDAY

UNFORTUNATELY we have at our disposal very few sources which can help us by shedding any light on this problem. Even if an incidental reference in either Christian or pagan literature could lead us to suppose that the Christian observance of Sunday must have already started, this does not enable us to be certain about its origin. Nowhere do we find any evidence which would unambiguously establish where, when and why the Christian observance of Sunday arose. Since this is so, we are in the last analysis obliged to rely on hypotheses.

It is not in itself surprising that we possess so few sources which provide us with information about Christian worship. Whenever one deals with the history of religions, one generally finds that liturgical usages are not recorded in detail while they remain customary practice. They are familiar to all who take part in them; therefore, if they are mentioned somewhere, this is rather more as a matter of chance, and they are dealt with briefly and incompletely as if they were traditional and self-explanatory. It is only if a liturgical tradition is in danger of being lost or if practical differences of opinion have arisen about its performance that it may be laid down in some cultic or liturgical directive what practice is to be followed in the future. Often some form of *disciplina arcani* may play a part in the keeping secret of rites and customs.[1] The origins of a liturgical practice are, therefore, generally elusive.[2] Every liturgical practice must, of course, have originated or have been adopted at some time and at some place, but it is exceptional if we are able to say, 'This is its birth certificate.' Generally we are able to say this only in the case of national festivals which commemorate some historical event.

---

[1] J. Jeremias, *The Eucharistic Words of Jesus*, ET 1964[2], pp. 132ff., sees the *disciplina arcani* at work in the very earliest Christian tradition; see p. 223, n. 3, below.
[2] In the last analysis we cannot discover the origin of the Jewish sabbath; see pp. 18ff. above.

Nevertheless we must now with all due caution make the attempt to trace to its origins the Christian observance of Sunday. At a first glance it could seem as if the Christian observance of Sunday had originated in opposition to the Jewish observance of the sabbath. Have Christians merely shifted sabbath worship on to the day following the sabbath?[1]

This conjecture is generally supported by a reference to *Didache* 8.1 which is said to provide an instance of parallel development. The passage runs, 'Your fasts should not coincide with those of the hypocrites (i.e. the Jews). They fast on Mondays and Thursdays; you should fast on Wednesdays and Fridays.' In this case it is said that an anti-Jewish attitude was clearly the reason why the fast days were shifted.[2] In fact, *Didache* 8.1 does not read like the introduction of a new fasting custom, but rather as the defence of a traditional Christian fasting custom against Judaistic tendencies.[3] In *Didache* 8.1, therefore, we are not dealing with the birth certificate of the Christian practice of fasting. If, nevertheless, one were to wish to interpret this passage as pointing to the origin of primitive Christian fast days as a sort of anti-Jewish protest, one would have to answer the underlying question: why did the Christians in this instance make *Wednesday* and *Friday* in particular and not other days, e.g. Tuesday and Saturday, to be their fast days? Does this fact not indicate that both Wednesday and Friday already had for them some special significance?

There is indeed one weighty argument which can be brought forward in support of the thesis that the Christian observance of Sunday originated in opposition to the sabbath worship of the Jews. In the chapter on sabbath practice[4] we have already indicated that, on the one hand, Christian believers could no longer take part in the sabbath worship in the synagogues because of discrimination against them by the Jews and, on the other hand, they were no longer satisfied by Jewish worship, because it lacked any reference to the risen Lord.[5] It was,

[1] This theory starts from the assumption that the Christian observance of Sunday originated relatively early at a time when Jewish influence was still strong enough to make itself felt. We also shall advocate—on other grounds, of course—an early date for the beginning of the observance of Sunday.

[2] See E. Schwartz, 'Osterbetrachtungen', *ZNW* 7, 1906, pp. 27ff. He quotes the Mohammedan Friday as another example. Similarly also F. J. Dölger, *IXΘΥΣ* II, p. 536; also *AuC* 6, 1950, p. 216.

[3] Cf. A. Jaubert, 'Jésus et le calendrier de Qumran', *NTS* 7, 1960, p. 27.

[4] See pp. 123ff. above.

[5] W. Bousset and (following him) R. Bultmann are certainly mistaken in believing that a distinctively Christian 'cult' was possible first of all in

therefore, an inner necessity for the developing Church to assemble for its own worship, where the new life bestowed on it could develop its own characteristic form.[1] The case for this argument is not, however, strong enough, for the real problem lies in the question which we cannot help asking: why did the Christians select the *first day of the week* as their day for worship? Why did they not, like the Jews, also meet on the sabbath for their own worship either in the morning or in the afternoon or, if some of them still went to the synagogue, towards evening? That would certainly have been the simplest solution, for the sabbath was in any case a work-free day.

H. Riesenfeld[2] has put forward the suggestion that Christians did originally assemble for worship on Saturday evening. On the evidence of extant material, however, it seems much more probable that from the outset Christians assembled on Sunday evening and not on Saturday evening.[3] Riesenfeld is especially anxious to demonstrate that theological reasons led the Christians to meet on the sabbath, inasmuch as for them the sabbath was fulfilled in the coming of Jesus and they celebrated this fulfilment in their worship. Sabbath theology did, in fact, play an important part in primitive Christianity, as we have already seen,[4] but in the first two centuries it never appears to have been associated in any special way with the Christians' weekly worship. Its significance rather lay in the fact that it dissociated from the sabbath *day* the idea of the 'rest' which Jesus had brought and which will come to fulfilment at the end. The Christians did, moreover, emphasize that they would assemble 'on the first day of the week'; does this not

---

Hellenistic circles. Worship related to the living Lord was the source of the life of the Christian community; and its origins are to be found in the earliest time of the first Palestinian community. See O. Cullmann, *The Christology of the New Testament*, ET 1959, pp. 203ff. It is quite another question if we ask whether certain Hellenistic elements found their way into the Christian view of worship as a result of the introduction in Greek-speaking Christendom of the title 'Kyrios', which already had its own cultic associations. On this point see W. Kramer, *Christ, Lord, Son of God*, ET (SBT 50) 1966.

[1] So also M. Goguel, 'Notes d'histoire évangélique, App. 1: Le dimanche et la résurrection au troisième jour', *Rev HR* 74, 1916, p. 33.

[2] 'Sabbat et jour du Seigneur', *New Testament Essays. Studies in Memory of T. W. Manson*, 1958, pp. 210–17. Before him J. Wordsworth, *The Ministry of Grace*, 1903[2], pp. 304f.; M. Villein, *Histoire des commandements de l'Eglise*, 1909[2], p. 23; H. Leclerq, *DACL* 13, col. 1523. Now also C. F. D. Moule, *Worship in the New Testament*, 1961, p. 16. J. Daniélou and Dom Botte tell me that they hold a similar view. Cf. the discussion of my book by J. Daniélou in *Recherches de science religieuse* 52, 1964, pp. 117f.

[3] On this point see the discussion on pp. 200ff. below.

[4] See pp. 8off. above.

unmistakably express their opinion that their worship did *not* take place on the sabbath?[1] Finally, it remains unclear how Riesenfeld would have us think worship had 'shifted' from Saturday evening to Sunday morning. We are not convinced by the argument that they suddenly came to realize that it was on that night that Jesus had risen.

Why did Christians hit upon this extremely inconvenient idea of holding their worship on Sunday? If in opposition to Judaism they were willing to meet on any day but the sabbath, why did they make Sunday their day of worship and not, for instance, Monday or Friday? Their choice of Sunday was certainly not made fortuitously. We have, therefore, to occupy ourselves in the following pages with the problem why Sunday had such significance for Christians that it became their day of worship. There are in principle two possible solutions to this problem: *either* we conclude that the observance of Sunday originated in Christianity, in which case we have to ask what factors contributed to its emergence: *or* we are convinced that the Christian Church adopted its observance of Sunday from elsewhere. We must come to one conclusion or the other in our search for the origin of the Christian observance of Sunday, for it cannot have been both devised and adopted by Christians. So far as the subsequent history of the observance of Sunday is concerned, it is quite possible to imagine some interplay between creativity and dependence. This could happen either if the Christian Church enriched its own creation, the observance of Sunday, with elements borrowed from related phenomena in surrounding cultures or if it gave new Christian content to the observance of Sunday which it had originally adopted from elsewhere.

I. WAS THERE A PRE-CHRISTIAN OBSERVANCE OF SUNDAY?

We begin by investigating the possibility that the observance of Sunday was adopted by Christians from elsewhere. As is the case with regard to the origin of the Jewish sabbath,[2] a great number of suggestions has been made.

---

[1] Thus also J. Hild, *Dimanche et vie paschale*, 1949, p. 29, n. 1.
[2] See pp. 18ff. above.

(*a*) A favourite thesis is the supposition that in pre-Christian times veneration of the sun was in some way associated with Sunday (as the name itself would suggest). If this were so, Christians would have adopted for their purposes not indeed the veneration of the sun but the day associated with it.[1] On this point a clear statement of opinion is essential. We can consider the possibility that the origin of the Christian observance of Sunday was influenced by some sun-cult only if a 'day of the sun' existed before the Christian observance of Sunday, that is to say if we can prove the existence of the seven-day planetary week in pre-Christian times. The mere fact that a sun-cult was in existence does not justify us in concluding that in connection with this cult there was a special significance attaching to a regularly recurring day (that very day being identical with the first day of the Jewish week!). For this reason the possibility of any influence by the sun-cult on the origin of the Christian observance of Sunday may be considered extremely unlikely. We have already established[2] that the Mithraic 'Sunday', which was, in fact, based on the order of the planetary week and which may perhaps have been marked by a special liturgy, certainly did not serve in any way as a model for the Christian observance of Sunday. For the same reason we must exclude all suggestions pointing in general terms to a sun-cult which could have had some influence on the Christian observance of Sunday.[3]

All kinds of sun-worship were, of course, at that time very widespread, even in Palestine.[4] Sun-worship does not seem to have been indigenous among the Hebrews, but it soon found acceptance among them, coming more probably from Tyre than from Babylon.[5] Solomon's temple was probably laid out like a Tyrian sun-temple, because at the solstices the sunlight penetrated through the east doors right into the dark space about the

---

[1] Cf. perhaps H. Gunkel, *Zum religionsgeschichtlichen Verständis des Neuen Testaments*, 1910[2], pp. 74f.; A. Loisy, *Les mystères païens*, 1930, pp. 223ff.; also, *Les évangiles synoptiques* I, 1907, p. 177.

[2] See pp. 35ff. above. Cf. also M. Goguel (p. 179, n. 1), p. 32; C. Clemen, *Religionsgeschichtliche Erklärung des Neuen Testaments*, 1909, p. 150.

[3] P. Cotton, *From Sabbath to Sunday*, 1933, pp. 130ff., is also too uncritical in this connection.

[4] See, above all, W. Baudissin, 'Sonne, bei den Hebräern', *RE*[3] 18, pp. 489ff.

[5] As was held by E. Schrader, *Die Keilinschriften und das Alte Testament*, 1903[3] (revised by H. Zimmern and H. Winckler), pp. 369f.

altar.[1] The Davidic southern kingdom may also have adopted the Syrian sun-calendar, while the northern kingdom returned to the use of the old agricultural calendar.[2] The sun-cult does, in fact, seem to have been fairly widespread among the Israelites before Josiah's reform: we need only refer to II Kings 23.11, '(Josiah) removed the horses that the kings of Judah had dedicated to the sun, at the entrance to the house of the Lord . . . and he burned the chariots of the sun with fire.'[3] After the exile in Babylon, however, we hear hardly anything about sun-worship among the Jews: only the morning prayer to the sun (which was very widespread in the ancient world)[4] seems here and there to have been customary among the Jews.[5] It does, nevertheless, remain clear, and the passages cited in n. 5 below establish the point, that sun-worship does not by itself imply any observance of Sunday, for the sun was paid the same veneration on *every* morning irrespective of the day of the week. It was only later when the seven days of the week had been named after the planets and when the sun had its own particular day that there could develop a special form of sun-worship which was exclusively associated with this day. This was a later development, and it did not occur in the sphere of Judaism.[6]

[1] Cf. F. J. Hollis, 'The sun-cult and the Temple at Jerusalem', *Myth and Ritual*, 1933, pp. 87–110; J. Morgenstern, *VT* 5, 1955, pp. 34–76.

[2] J. Morgenstern (n. 1); S. Talmon, 'Divergences in Calendar-Reckoning in Ephraim and Juda', *VT* 8, 1958, pp. 48–74.

[3] Cf. Isa. 27.9. The cult of the high places was probably associated with the worship of heavenly bodies.

[4] H. Gressmann, *Altorientalische Texte zum Alten Testament*, 1926[2], pp. 15–18, 242–8, has assembled the evidence for Egypt and Babylon. For India, Persia, Syria and also for the area of Greek and Roman culture (esp. of Pythagorean influence) see F. J. Dölger, *Sol Salutis*, 1925[2], pp. 20ff., 38ff., 48ff. See also p. 191, n. 8 below. Also in Tertullian, *Nat.* 1.13 (cf. *Apol.* 16.10), we find, 'Do not you (i.e. pagans) for the most part move your lips at sunrise, endeavouring sometimes also to worship the heavenly bodies?' Leo the Great, *Serm.* 22.6 (*in nativ. dom.*, PL 54.198), condemns Christians who blow a kiss to the sun before they enter St Peter's church; cf. F. J. Dölger, *op. cit.*, p. 2.

[5] Ezek. 8.16 is clearly relevant here: in the forecourt of the temple twenty-five men are worshipping the sun towards the east (therefore in the morning). Possibly also Wisd. 16.28, 'To make it known that we must rise before the sun to give thee thanks and must pray to thee at the dawning of the light.' Philo, *De vita contempl.* 3.27, reports about the Therapeutae; they would pray for a good day as the sun was rising so that their spirit might be filled with heavenly light. Josephus, *Bell. jud.* II.8.5 (128), provides information about the Essenes, that before sunrise they would say nothing profane, but would address certain traditional prayers (πατρίους εὐχάς) to the sun and, in so doing, they would beseech it to rise. Similar practices are to be found among the Mandaeans; cf. M. Lidzbarski, *Mandäische Liturgien*, 1920, p. 179. On the orientation of Christian prayer see pp. 289f. below.

[6] We shall indeed have to ask whether the Jewish and Christian practice of *daily* morning prayer has not some connection with the custom of morning prayer to the sun which, as we have just indicated, was widespread in the ancient world.

(*b*) An entirely separate question is that concerning an ancient Jewish calendar of solar character, the structure of which can be inferred as a result of recent research.[1] We shall not consider all the evidence, since the most important conclusions drawn from it have become quite widely known. This calendar is used, above all, in Jubilees and in Ethiopic Enoch. Traces of it are also to be found in many other writings of priestly origin[2] and at Qumran.[3] In every case it is extolled as the proper, authentic, original calendar from which those Jews who adopted a lunar calendar had deviated and, in so doing, had grievously sinned. This calendar is significant for our purposes not because of its solar construction but because the days of the week received special emphasis: the year in this calendar is composed of exactly 52 weeks (= 364 days): therefore in every year each day always falls on the same day of the week. The most striking point of all is that, if one translates into the appropriate days of the week the information about dates based on this calendar, one finds that preference is almost always given to the same days, namely Wednesday, Friday and Sunday. This fact is noteworthy, and it seems at one stroke to solve many problems which were hitherto obscure—especially the origin of the Christian observance of Sunday. While in official Judaism the first day of the week had no outstanding

---

[1] We refer to the studies by J. Barthélemy, 'Notes en marge des publications récentes sur les manuscrits de Qumrân', *Revue Biblique* 59, 1952, pp. 199–203, and above all by A. Jaubert, *VT* 3, 1953, pp. 250–64; 7, 1957, pp. 35–61; also *RHR* 146, 1954, pp. 140–73, and her book, *La date de la Cène*, 1957. More recently also M. Testuz, *Les idées religieuses du livre des Jubilés*, 1960. A good survey of the literature on this calendar is to be found in J. A. Walther, *JBL* 77, 1958, pp. 116–22. A. Strobel, *ZNW* 51, 1960, pp. 69–101; cf. also *TLZ* 86, 1961, col. 179–84; *Revue de Qumrân* 3, 1961, pp. 395–412, has attempted to prove that this calendar (Strobel calls it the old Zadokite–Essene calendar) was connected with the twenty-eight-year solar cycle and was actually used, although hardly before the middle of the second century BC.

[2] E. Kutsch, 'Der Kalender des Jubiläenbuches und das Alte und das Neue Testament', *VT* 11, 1961, pp. 39–48, does, it is true, criticize this view, particularly in so far as the work of the priestly writers and of the chronicler is concerned.

[3] Fragments of the Book of Jubilees have been discovered in the caves at Qumran, but the use of this solar calendar has also been established quite independently of these fragments. Cf. the report by M. Milik, *VT Supplementum* 4, 1957, pp. 24–26.

significance,[1] in this calendar it indisputably occupies a special position. Do we not have before us the direct precursor of the Christian Sunday?

It is true that this thesis has not yet been advanced in these very words, although A. Jaubert[2] speaks of a 'tendency'. She is interested above all in the pre-eminence of the other two days, Wednesday and Friday. In this calendar not only the beginning of the year but also the day of the passover festival regularly fell on a Wednesday. For this reason A. Jaubert holds that Jesus before his passion ate the passover meal with his disciples on a Tuesday evening (whereas it was then held on the Friday evening according to the official calendar)[3] and that he was arrested in the early hours of Wednesday morning (and not on Thursday night, as the evangelists report). This supposition is supported by patristic evidence (especially the Syriac *Didascalia*), which presents this chronology for Holy Week and so accounts for the fast on Wednesday.[4]

[1] Cf. SB I, p. 1054, 'The first day of the week (Sunday) was not merely the first day of creation, but it was also regarded as the day on which the sacrificial worship of the tabernacle began.' By comparison with the dignity of the sabbath, this was a modest distinction. Both these distinctive marks, beginning of creation and beginning of sacrificial worship, derive from the fact that Sunday was the beginning of the week.

[2] 'Jésus et le calendrier de Qumran', *NTS* 7, 1960, p. 28; the custom of Sunday observance is said to be certainly rooted in the (or an) ancient priestly calendar. E. Hilgert, *Jubilees and the Origin of Sunday* (Andrews University Studies 1), 1963, pp. 44–51, speaks also of a 'psychological disposition'.

[3] E. Vogt, *Biblica* 39, 1958, pp. 72ff., has tried to provide support for this thesis. He began with a fragment of a calendar found at Qumran; he then placed this calendar side by side with the 'official' calendar and calculated that in the seventh year the passover of the Qumran calendar must, in fact, correspond with an official passover celebrated on a Friday. This reconstruction does not, of course, constitute a proof.

[4] Cf. recently A. Jaubert, 'Une discussion patristique sur la chronologie de la passion', *Recherches de science religieuse* 54, 1966, pp. 407–10. This thesis has been attacked by Blinzler, *ZNW* 49, 1958, pp. 238ff., and by A. Strobel, *ZNW* 51, 1960, pp. 76ff. We cannot here follow the details of the discussion. There seems to be one particular difficulty: what was the origin of the fasts on Wednesday and Friday observed by the Christian Church? Was it historical circumstance (in this case the arrest and the death of Jesus) which caused these days to be distinguished in this way, or did the particular prominence of these days in the old solar calendar lead to certain events from the life of Jesus being commemorated on these days? There is a certain incompatibility between these two points of view: it might even be said that one has to choose between alternatives: *either* Wednesday and Friday were significant for Christians because something important for Christians had happened on these days, *or* Wednesday and Friday were accorded special importance by Christians because these days already had some sort of pre-eminence in the old solar calendar; in this case, Christians have only

We must next inquire to what extent Sunday was given prominence in the solar calendar. A. Jaubert[1] calls those days which receive special prominence (Wednesday, Friday and Sunday) 'liturgical' days. This expression is certainly misleading, for there is no evidence that these weekly recurring days received 'liturgical' distinction.[2] All that we know is that

---

subsequently transferred to these days the recollection of certain historical events which did not, in strict historical fact, take place on them. In the thesis of A. Jaubert these two points of view seem to be combined: on the one hand, that Jesus was, in fact, arrested in the early hours of Wednesday morning and was crucified on the Friday; on the other hand, that the preeminence accorded by Christians to Wednesday and Friday reflects nothing else than the influence of the old solar calendar. Which is right? It is impossible to hold both points of view at the same time, unless we are to suppose some extraordinary circumstance, for instance that Christ had so arranged it that the days prominent in the solar calendar should be given historical prominence by their association with his passion. One might attempt a solution of this problem along the following lines: Jesus did, in fact, die on a Friday (in accordance with the mutually corroborating evidence of the evangelists; cf. the further arguments adduced by A. Strobel, *art. cit.*). His death did, therefore, by chance fall on one of the days prominent in the old solar calendar. This coincidence had its consequences: Wednesday, which was also prominent in the old solar calendar and which had not yet been distinguished by any event in Christian history, attracted its own event: hence the conclusion that the arrest of Jesus must have taken place on that day. This supposition is, in any case, more plausible in this form than it would be the other way round; if that had been the case, Jesus would really have been arrested in the early hours of Wednesday morning, and subsequently the memorial of his passion would have been transferred to Friday, the other day prominent in the solar calendar. The historicity of Jesus' death on the Friday is, however, in the last analysis appreciably better attested than that of his arrest on the Wednesday. (We shall later discuss Sunday as the day of the resurrection; see pp. 228ff. below.)

[1] In her studies detailed above, p. 183, n. 1.

[2] It may be that we should take into account the fact that in Qumran the courses of priests may have relieved one another on Sunday and not on Saturday. On this see S. Talmon, *Scripta Hierosolymitana* 4, 1958, p. 175. It is, however, difficult to see how this amounts to 'liturgical prominence'. J. van Goudoever in a letter of 11 March 1961 drew my attention to the possible liturgical prominence of Sunday at least. If the day was reckoned at Qumran not in the normal way from sunset to sunset, but from sunrise to sunrise (see Talmon, *art. cit.*; see also p. 201, n. 1, below), then the celebration at the close of the sabbath, the so-called *habdalah*, must have been observed on Sunday morning. This is ingenious, but we notice, first, that the days were normally reckoned in liturgical usage from evening to evening (even at Qumran), while in secular usage (not only at Qumran) they were reckoned from morning to morning, and, secondly, the *habdalah* ceremony was indissolubly associated with a meal (see pp. 241f. below); it is, therefore, hardly conceivable that the *habdalah* sentences were recited at Qumran in the early morning.

in the calendrical particulars Sunday is given especial prominence as the day on which fresh enterprises may be begun after
the conclusion of the sabbath,[1] just as Friday frequently appears
as the day on which enterprises begun before the sabbath must
be terminated. We do not hear of special worship on Sunday or
of special prayers, of rest from work or of festive celebration.
Even in the circles in which this solar calendar was used the
sabbath remained undisputably the day for solemn celebration
and worship.[2] More than one question does, therefore, remain
unanswered if we want to see in this pseudo-liturgical Sunday
of the solar calendar the precursor of the Christian Sunday.
At the very least, it would have been an entirely novel 'invention' of the Christians to make this day into the day of worship.
Moreover, with equal justification they could have given
liturgical prominence to either Wednesday or Friday (which
were also 'liturgical days' in the solar calendar) if there was
really no historical reason obliging them to choose Sunday in
particular and no other day.[3] If Christians had taken this novel
step of according liturgical prominence to Sunday within the
solar calendar, it is remarkable that this 'liturgical' Sunday does
not appear more frequently in the gospels: why was not the
life of Jesus also 'dated' by the solar calendar, as was Genesis in
the book of Jubilees? It would have been reasonable to expect
this if the first Christians really had shown evidence of holding
in such high regard the liturgical days of the week in the solar
calendar.

There is, of course, a second aspect of this question which
must be considered. In this solar calendar, not only is special
prominence accorded to the particular days in the week,
Wednesday, Friday and Sunday, but also the annual festivals
regularly fall on one of these days. For our purposes it is

---

[1] E.g. as the day of departure. In the Greek astrological catalogues we
also find that Sunday was considered as a favourable day for beginning a
journey by sea; cf. *Chronica minora*, ed. T. Mommsen, 1892, p. 44; *Catalogus
codd. astrol. graec.* VII, 1908, pp. 88ff.

[2] The high estimation of the sabbath indirectly derives from the fact that
this day never appears in calendrical datings as the day of any enterprise.
Moreover, we know that the sabbath was observed with extraordinary
strictness among, for example, the people at Qumran, where this solar
calendar was certainly known; see p. 53, n. 1, above.

[3] The 'historical' solution of the problem, therefore, remains the most
probable, as we shall see; see pp. 215ff. below.

significant that the first and the last day of the fifty-day time of harvest (= Pentecost) were always celebrated on a *Sunday* in this calendar.

It has, indeed, long been known that there was a group of Sadducees (the Boethusians)[1] who interpreted Lev. 23.15 differently from the Pharisees. This passage refers to the time from the omer day to the festival of weeks: it reads, 'Afterwards (i.e. after the passover) you shall count from the morrow after the sabbath . . . seven full weeks shall they be. . . .' While the Pharisees understood the expression 'the morrow after the sabbath' to mean 'the day after the passover festival' (i.e. 16 Nisan), a day which could fall on any day of the week, the Boethusians interpreted the passage literally: they understood it to mean that one should begin to count on the day after the (weekly) sabbath, that is to say on the Sunday after the passover festival. It has now been shown that this custom of beginning the fifty-day time of harvest on a Sunday was more widespread than had hitherto been assumed. Wherever this solar calendar which we are discussing was in use, Sunday was also the first day of the seven harvest weeks. There are further traces of this custom to be found among the Samaritans and Karaites[2] and among the Christians.[3] Nevertheless there are also differences to be noticed between these groups which counted the Easter period from the Sunday onwards and accordingly observed Pentecost, the fiftieth day, on a Sunday as well. Some counted from the first Sunday after the passover falling *within* the week of unleavened bread (Boethusians and Samaritans), others from the first Sunday *after* the week of unleavened bread (those who used the solar calendar). It is possible that this difference may be explained by the fact that in this fifty-day time of harvest between Easter and Pentecost we are still dealing with a relic of the ancient Semitic seasonal year: this year was composed of seven such fifty-day periods, which were associated with the agricultural cycle.[4] When the work of harvest did not begin at the same time in different parts of the country, dislocations of this sort could easily result.[5]

The first day of the fifty-day time of harvest was the so-called omer day, the day on which the first sheaf was presented to God

[1] References in SB II, pp. 598–600. Cf. A. Jaubert, *NTS* 7, 1960, pp. 5f. Y. M. Gintz, 'The Yahed Sectarianism, Essenes, Beth(e)sin', *Sinai* 32, 1954, pp. 11–43, even wanted to establish a connection between the Essenes and the Boethusians (= [B]eth-Esin).

[2] Cf. J. van Goudoever, *Biblical Calendars*, 1961[2], pp. 20ff.

[3] See W. Rordorf, 'Zum Ursprung des Osterfestes am Sonntag', *TZ* 18, 1962, pp. 177ff.

[4] See W. Rordorf, 'Jahr', *Biblisch-Historisches Handwörterbuch* I, 1962, and p. 23 above.

[5] This solution is proposed by J. Morgenstern, 'The Calendar of the Book of Jubilees, its Origin and its Character', *VT* 5, 1955, pp. 34–76.

in the temple (Lev. 23.9–13). The last day was the festival of weeks, or Pentecost: originally this was purely a harvest festival which in the Book of Jubilees and later in rabbinic Judaism became also the festival on which was commemorated the giving of the law at Sinai.[1] The consideration of these festivals and of the customs and ideas associated with them is certainly important if we are inquiring into the origins of the festivals of Easter and Pentecost and particularly into the origin of their observance on Sunday in the Christian Church.[2] Yet this consideration of the Jewish omer day and of the festival of Pentecost (even though here and there these regularly fell on a Sunday) sheds little light on the origin of the weekly Christian observance of Sunday. How did a *weekly* observance develop out of an annual festal celebration? And which circle of ideas would have been decisive for the interpretation of this weekly Sunday festival, that of the omer day or that of the festival of Pentecost? In fact, it is not possible to detect the influence of either of these on the Christian practice of Sunday worship.

It is, of course, possible to advance yet another version of this thesis. It was customary in certain Jewish circles (among the Therapeutae and Samaritans) to observe the night before the first day of Pentecost (among the Therapeutae every fiftieth night) in a special way: there was a communal meal and spiritual conversation, Miriam's dance (Ex. 15) was re-enacted, and this gave to the celebration the stamp of being without qualification a memorial of Israel's passage through the sea at the exodus from Egypt. This is extremely significant for the understanding of the later, Christian, Easter night which came to be the Christians' favourite time for baptism.[3] It must, however, be maintained that even from here no line leads directly to the weekly Christian Sunday, for we still face the problem how the annual observance (or in the case of the Therapeutae an observance recurring every fifty days) could have become a weekly observance.[4] The principal

---

[1] Cf. E. Lohse, *TWNT* VI, pp. 44–53; G. Kretzschmar, 'Himmelfahrt und Pfingsten', *ZKG* 66, 1954, pp. 209–53; J. van Goudoever (p. 187, n. 2), pp. 139ff., 228ff.

[2] See W. Rordorf (p. 187, n. 3).

[3] On these problems see W. Rordorf (p. 187, n. 3).

[4] J. van Goudoever (p. 187, n. 2), p. 174, does indeed point to other examples (e.g. among the Falashas) where a festival which was originally held annually came to be celebrated monthly or even weekly. He draws attention to the sabbath, which according to Deut. 5.15 contained a weekly memorial of the exodus from Egypt. This passage is, however, demonstrably a secondary motivation which was added to justify a long-standing weekly observance of the sabbath (see p. 14 above). In *this* sense the annual Easter

objection which tells against a dependence of the Christian Sunday observance on this celebration of the passage through the sea is the fact that the weekly Sunday worship did not take place on Saturday evening, but on Sunday evening.[1]

J. van Goudoever[2] has now proposed a fresh theory which seems to help towards a solution of this question. He says that the Christian Sunday was, in fact, celebrated weekly from the very beginning, but only during seven consecutive weeks in the year, i.e. during the seven weeks of the time of harvest. He bases this theory on the fact that in the first Christian evidence for a Christian observance of Sunday (I Cor. 16.2; Acts 20.7; Rev. 1.10) it is in every case a question of Sundays which fall within this period of seven weeks. We shall, however, see that this contention can be sustained only with regard to Acts 20.7.[3] In addition, two points would still remain unexplained. First, the five Sundays between the first and last Sundays of the time of harvest had no particular significance in Judaism.[4] If, therefore, Christians specially marked these Sundays by worship, we have no parallels for this in Judaism and the roots of this practice must be sought in Christianity itself. Secondly, even Goudoever does not solve the problem how the transition was made from

---

festival has also naturally influenced the weekly Sunday and its worship, but it is precisely this consideration which forbids us from drawing from this passage retrospective conclusions about the *origin* of the weekly observance. One would, on the contrary, have to inquire (even with regard to the festival of the Therapeutae and to the observances of the Falashas) whether a festival which regularly recurred at short intervals did not originally have its own independent roots and only subsequently became associated with the annual festival.

[1] On this see pp. 200ff. below.
[2] (P. 187, n. 2), pp. 167f.
[3] See p. 196 and n. 3, below; and pp. 205ff.
[4] The last day of the week of unleavened bread could, of course, fall on a Sunday, but this was not regularly the case. On the other hand, it is not possible to hold that at least two consecutive Sundays had a special significance; this has been suggested on the grounds that in the areas where the time of harvest was calculated from a Sunday, it was not always the same Sunday which was the starting-point (it could be either the Sunday within or the Sunday after the week of unleavened bread, see p. 187 above). This view is impossible because in any particular place either the one Sunday or the other, never both Sundays together, counted as the omer-day. It is, therefore, beside the point for P. Carrington, *The Primitive Christian Calendar* I, 1952, p. 38, to give the impression that every Sunday in the pentecostal period may perhaps have been the omer-day (in the same place).

an annual to a weekly custom. He does, indeed, seem to provide a 'bridge' inasmuch as he holds that not just *one* Sunday (Easter Day), but seven consecutive Sundays were regularly observed each year. Nevertheless the question remains urgent and unanswered: how did the Christians come to extend to the whole year the practice of Sunday observance which was originally limited to the weeks from Easter to Pentecost?

Recent researches into calendrical matters evoked both by the study of the Book of Jubilees and related writings and also by the discoveries at Qumran cannot clarify this problem about the origin of Christian Sunday observance. The weekly 'liturgical' Sunday which appears in the calendrical datings was—at least in so far as it has hitherto been possible to ascertain—in no way marked by worship. Moreover, no direct lines lead to the weekly Christian Sunday observance from the annual omer day and day of Pentecost which in this calendar always fell on a Sunday.

(*c*) We have finally to mention the Mandaean Sunday, which might be held responsible for the origin of the Christian Sunday observance.

The Mandaeans are a baptist sect, part of which even today still lives on in the lower half of the Euphrates valley. The greater part of their history remains in darkness, but originally they may well have been resident to the east of Jordan. The origins of the sect certainly lie in early Christian times, if not in pre-Christian times.[1] They call John the Baptist their patron, and moreover they sharply distinguish themselves from both Jews and Christians. Their most prominent feature is their baptismal rites; these may well have their roots in the baptist movement which in late Jewish and early Christian times was widespread in many varieties, particularly in Trans-

[1] In the twenties Mandaism was recognized as a formative influence on Christianity; cf. R. Reitzenstein, *Das mandäische Buch des Herrn der Grösse und die Evangelienüberlieferung*, 1919; M. Lidzbarski, *Mandäische Liturgien*, 1920. The reaction set in with E. Peterson, 'Der gegenwärtige Stand der Mandäerfrage', *Theologische Blätter* 7, 1933, pp. 317–23; H. Lietzmann, 'Ein Beitrag zur Mandäerfrage', *Sitzungsberichte der Preussischen Akademie der Wissenschaften zu Berlin*, 1930, pp. 596–608; H. Schlier, 'Zur Mandäerfrage', *TR NF* 5, 1933, pp. 1–34, 69–92. Now we are approaching an objective appreciation of the Mandaeans which does not fall into the old exaggerations; cf. the works of W. Baumgartner, 'Zur Mandäerfrage', *Hebrew Union College Annual* 23, 1950–1, pp. 41–71; and above all K. Rudolph, *Die Mandäer* I, 1960; II, 1961. C. Colpe, *RGG*³ IV, col. 712, gives further literature. (The following works should also be added: J. Behm, *Die mandäische Religion und das Christentum*, 1927; A. Loisy, *Le mandéisme et les origines du christianisme*, 1934; C. H. Dodd, *The Interpretation of the Fourth Gospel*, 1953, pp. 115–29.)

jordan and Syria.[1] It is difficult to be certain about the detailed origin of these baptismal rites. Early in their history they may have been connected with the sun-cult: the washings in water were supposed to have the effect of washing away the sins which had previously been confessed to the sun.[2] Mandaean baptism is certainly to be distinguished from the baptism of John the Baptist, Jewish proselyte baptism and Christian baptism, since it does not seem possible to understand it as a once-for-all initiatory rite; it could be often[3] repeated, and it therefore had more of the character of a cultic washing.[4] Mandaism later adopted all the elements of gnostic syncretism (release and ascent of the soul, mythology about the primeval man, etc.).

Among the Mandaeans Sunday did, in fact, play some part. All the passages which mention it do, however, belong to the latest sections of the Mandaean literature, which was in any case edited only in the seventh or eighth century.[5] In these passages Sunday frequently appears as the personification of the power of light. Of particular interest is a hymn[6] in which the splendour of Sunday passes by the gate of the prison[7] and those who are worthy of the abode of light are loosed from their chains.[8] Also

---

[1] Cf. K. Rudolph (p. 190, n. 1) II, pp. 378ff. In Qumran we already hear of ritual washings: the disciples of John the Baptist should also be mentioned, also the Elkesaites and the Sampsaeans (whose name has nothing to do with *šmš*, but means 'those who wash themselves'; cf. W. Brandt, *Elchasai. Ein Religionsstifter und sein Werk*, 1912, p. 33).

[2] This was the case among the Elkesaites, who were, moreover, baptized in their clothes. W. Brandt (n. 1) also draws attention to the ancient Peruvians and the washings of the Hindus in the Ganges. See also p. 287, n. 1, below.

[3] K. Rudolph (p. 190, n. 1) II, pp. 379, 322, believes he can demonstrate that a regular weekly baptism took place on Sunday among the Mandaeans.

[4] Principally for this reason H. H. Rowley, 'The baptism of John and the Qumran sect', *New Testament Essays: Studies in Memory of T. W. Manson*, 1958, pp. 218–29, also distinguishes John's baptism from the washings at Qumran. But lines cannot be sharply drawn here. O. Betz, 'Die Proselytentaufe der Qumransekte und die Taufe im Neuen Testament', *Revue de Qumrân* 2, 1958, pp. 213ff., tries to prove that in Qumran also there was a once-for-all baptism on admission to the community. The Ps.-Clem. *Hom.* 2.23.1, in any case, refers to John the Baptist as a ἡμεροβαπτιστής. On this whole discussion see H. Braun, *Qumran und das Neue Testament II*, 1966, pp. 1–29.

[5] This was conceded even by M. Lidzbarski in the introduction to his edition of the *Ginza*, 1920.

[6] *Ginza* (left-hand), pp. 112f., ed. Lidzbarski, pp. 558f.

[7] This probably refers to cells in which the souls on their journey heavenwards are detained by the planetary gods; cf. R. Reitzenstein (p. 190, n. 1), p. 25.

[8] Similar texts: *Qolaste* 14, ed. Lidzbarski, pp. 183f., 'Who has seen what I have seen on Sunday, the chief of days? Who saw *Mandā ḏ Haijē*, who went

Sunday was clearly the day for baptism: *Ginza* (right-hand section) 288[1] complains about those who are unjustly called Mandaeans; these are they who 'on the evening before the day'[2] and on Sunday do not have their sons baptized and do not cause their daughters to receive the sign of life.[3]

In view of the secondary associations of ideas which have been connected with Sunday, it is quite impossible to say anything definite about the age of the Mandaean Sunday observance. It is generally traced back to Nestorian-Syrian and, therefore, to Christian influence.[4] One Mandaean text in particular seems to put us on to this track: it states in a somewhat resigned fashion, 'Mirjai (= symbol for the Mandaean community) has conceived hatred against the Jews and love

---

thither and came into the world? He went thither and came into the world. The earth lies there and trembles. He speaks, his voice is charming, speech was on his lips. Speech was on his lips, he threw the world to the winds and abandoned it—the seven sit there in confusion. They weep and prolong their lamentation, because their secret has become public?' *Qolaste* 15, ed. Lidzbarski, p. 186, 'What is my day among the days? One day. What is my hour among the hours? One hour. What is my day among the days? The day on which the glory of *Mandā d Haijē* has gone up. My day is Sunday, the chief of days. The day on which the glory of *Mandā d Haijē* has gone up. On my day the glory of Sunday went up over us and illuminated us exceedingly.' Cf. also E. S. Drower, *The Thousand and Twelve Questions*, 1960, pp. 171, 253, 262.

    Qolaste 9, ed Lidzbarski, pp. 177f., strongly resembles the 15th Ode of Solomon (cf. also Eph. 5.14 = Clement Alex., *Proptrept.* IX. 84.2), 'I arose early from my sleep, I had seen glorious splendour. Arise, ye sleepers, honour and praise the great life, praise the image which shines and gleams in sublime light.' (We probably have here a reference to the *daily* prayer addressed to the sun; see the texts quoted above, (p. 182, nn. 4–5). In certain respects the nocturnal light rituals of the mystery religions are also related; cf. Aristophanes, *Frogs* 340ff.; Apuleius, *Metam.* 11, 23, also the text of Firmicius Maternus reproduced below, (p. 197, n. 2), and also probably the *Acts of Thomas* 27, 153).

[1] Ed. Lidzbarski, p. 285.

[2] Perhaps this is a reference to Easter night, in the course of which baptism was performed in the Christian Church. K. Rudolph (p. 190, n. 1) II, pp. 328ff., thinks in terms of the weekly Saturday evening.

[3] The text continues, 'whom one cannot enlighten that life is older than death, light older than darkness, good people more excellent than wicked people, sweet more pleasant than bitter, day older than night, Sunday older than the sabbath, Nazarenes older than Jews. . . .'

[4] E.g. J. Behm (p. 190, n. 1), p. 10. Now also (even though with caution) K. Rudolph (p. 190, n. 1), II, p. 327; he also employs the philological argument that Habšabā derived from *had b^ešabbā* (therefore from the Syrian-Christian name for Sunday).

towards the Nasirenes (in all probability, Christians). On the sabbath Mirjai undertakes work, on Sunday her hands are still.'[1] The Mandaean 'precursors', like the other 'precursors', must therefore be discarded in the search for the origins of the Christian Sunday observance.

It remains now to be seen whether from the earliest evidence for the Christian Sunday we can derive any information about the origin of the observance.

2. THE EARLIEST EVIDENCE FOR A CHRISTIAN OBSERVANCE OF SUNDAY

In the following pages we shall principally concentrate on the three well-known New Testament passages which pre-suppose the Christian observance of Sunday or at least seem to allude to it: I Cor. 16.2; Acts 20.7 and Rev. 1.10. From these passages we shall be able to gain a sufficiently broad basis for us to ask, with all circumspection, the further question about the origin of the Christian observance of Sunday.

(a) In I Cor. 16.1ff. we read, 'Now concerning the contribution for the saints (in Jerusalem): as I directed the churches of Galatia, so you also are to do. On the first day of every week, each of you is to put something aside (at home) and store it up, as he may prosper, so that contributions need not be made when I come.[2] And when I arrive, I will send those whom you accredit by letter to carry your gift to Jerusalem.' Here, in the spring of 55 or 56, Paul is giving definite instructions how to make the collection, which he also mentions in other passages in his letters.[3] It is plain that he has already given the same instruction to the Galatian churches: everyone should regularly put some money aside. The collections are, therefore, not yet made in the course of worship and administered by the officers of the church, as they came to be later.[4]

---

[1] *Qolaste* 44, ed. Lidzbarski, p. 211; cf. on this K. Rudolph (p. 190, n. 1), II, p. 326.

[2] On the expression λογεῖαι for the monetary collections see A. Deissmann, *Light from the Ancient East*, 1927, pp. 104ff.

[3] Gal. 2.10; II Cor. 8f.; Rom. 15.31. On the significance of these collections see O. Cullmann, *Catholics and Protestants: a proposal for Realizing Christian Solidarity*, ET 1960.

[4] E.g. Justin, I *Apol.* 67.6; perhaps Acts 5.1ff. is also an allusion to this. See pp. 272f. below.

We cannot avoid rendering παρ' ἑαυτῷ by 'aside at home'[1]. J. Nedbal[2] is of the opinion that the direction 'aside at home' has no sense, since on Paul's arrival the collection of money would have to take place, and this is precisely what Paul wanted to avoid. This objection is, however, artificial: Paul wants to ensure regular saving on the part of everyone, in which case the collection of that which has been put aside is quickly arranged. H. Dumaine[3] also reads much too much into the text: he inquires whether the elders would have remembered Paul's command on every Sunday or whether just the final collection of the money set aside took place on a Sunday. J. Moffatt[4] even holds that the money set aside was brought on that very day to the church when it assembled for worship.

We can ask why Paul enjoins the *individual* collection. This is no doubt associated with the purpose for which this money was being collected. Unlike other money set aside it was not intended for immediate distribution (to the poor and needy), but for long-term uses. In this case it was psychologically better to leave the money with the individual contributor until the time of the definitive payment: on the one hand, everyone would feel ashamed in his own eyes and in the eyes of other people if he did not discharge his obligation to put some money aside and, on the other hand, the realization that the money saved was visibly increasing spurred the individual on to further saving. The possibility is, therefore, not to be excluded that in I Cor. 16.1f. Paul was making a special arrangement: for this particular collection it was better that the church should not meet (as for other collections or as hitherto), but that everyone should save up by himself. In this case particular importance would attach to the interpretation of παρ' ἑαυτῷ.[5]

In connection with our study we must now principally devote our attention to the question why Paul orders the setting aside of money saved for the collection to take place on Sunday: κατὰ μίαν σαββάτου (-των), on every first day of the week it has to happen. For the very reason that the setting aside of money was to be an individual matter, it is extremely surprising that Paul fixed a special day for it. He could well have enjoined the Corinthians to remember the collection at least once a week. Moreover, could he not have left it to the discretion of each individual to decide for himself when he preferred to discharge

---

[1] Cf. H. Lietzmann, *Die Korintherbriefe*, 1949[2], p. 89.
[2] *Sabbat und Sonntag im Neuen Testament* (diss. 1956), pp. 157ff.
[3] *DACL* IV, col. 886.
[4] *The First Epistle to the Corinthians*, 1947, p. 271.
[5] We are certainly not justified in having recourse to the late exegesis of the passage in Chrysostom, *Hom. 43 in I Cor.* (PG 61.367ff.), as is done by J. Kosnetter, 'Der Tag des Herrn im Neuen Testament', *Der Tag des Herrn*, 1958, pp. 38f.

this duty, according to his own financial circumstances? It is easy to understand how A. Deissmann[1] thought that the 'first day of the week' was perhaps generally observed as a payday in the pagan environment and so for quite a number of the members of the Corinthian and Galatian churches. He himself, however, admits that no support can anywhere be found for this conjecture.[2] We must, therefore, assume that the first day of the week had a particular significance for the Gentile Christian churches themselves. This is also suggested by another consideration. The use in this passage of the Jewish designation of Sunday ('first day of the week') presupposes the observance of the seven-day Jewish week in the Gentile Christian churches, but these Gentile Christian churches no longer observed the sabbath with which the Jewish week stood or fell. We did, therefore, earlier[3] ask the question whether Sunday, instead of the sabbath, had not perhaps become the pivotal point of the seven-day chronology. A text like I Cor. 16.1f. could be a pointer in this direction: it is, in any case, possible that Paul ordered the setting aside of money to take place on Sunday of all days in order to guarantee its regularity, because the Christians had already begun to fix their calendar by reference to the weekly Sunday. There is, of course, nothing said in I Cor. 16.1f. about the reason why Sunday had been given this particular significance in the Gentile Christian churches. On this point we must look to other passages for information.[4]

We still have to consider the question about the time of year at which I

---

[1] (P. 193, n. 2), p. 309; also *Enc. Bib.* III, p. 2813.

[2] A. Deissmann, *loc. cit.;* cf. A. Thumb, *ZDWF* 1, 1900, p. 165. Deissmann even wonders whether the Sebaste days in the Hellenistic East had perhaps been especially popular days. These Sebaste days, however, never recur at weekly intervals (see p. 206, n. 6 below), nor do they have anything to do with Sunday. It is, therefore, purely arbitrary to consider them together with I Cor. 16.1f. One might equally well compare them with Tertullian, *Apol.* 39.5f., where Tertullian refers to a fixed monthly day on which members of the community pay something into the chest.

[3] See pp. 41f. above.

[4] We have indeed said that Paul may have given an *exceptional* direction that everyone on this occasion should lay money aside by himself at home. This would presuppose that there was already a regular communal collection on Sunday which was generally observed. It should also be noted that in II Cor. 9.12 the collection is actually called λειτουργία; it is, therefore, given a name associated with worship. Yet we cannot for this reason assert that there was already an act of worship on Sunday.

Corinthians was written, for J. van Goudoever[1] holds that the Sundays mentioned in I Cor. 16.2 fell within the period from Easter to Pentecost. In 16.8 Paul says that he wants to remain at Ephesus ἕως τῆς πεντεκοστῆς. In the first place it is, however, not at all certain that he means by this the day of the festival of Pentecost, i.e. the last day of the Pentecostal period. In the New Testament this day is generally called ἡμέρα τῆς πεντεκοστῆς (Acts 2.1; 20.16), while the word πεντεκοστή used absolutely means the whole fifty-day period of rejoicing from Easter to Whitsun (at any rate in later general linguistic usage among Christians).[2] In this case, however, I. Cor. would have been written *before* Easter: it is possible that there is another reference to this in 5.7f., where Paul alludes to the unleavened bread and to Christ the paschal lamb. These allusions make more sense if Easter were soon to come and were not already past. Above all—and this is the decisive factor—it would be completely incomprehensible that Paul should have thought of the collection of money being restricted to the seven Sundays from Easter to Pentecost. There is no doubt at all that he wanted to know that they would be continued throughout the year; for this reason we can be certain that he made no distinction between the Sundays from Easter to Pentecost and the other Sundays of the year.

(*b*) We learn substantially more from Acts 20.7–12 about the early Christian observance of Sunday. Paul finds himself on his last journey to Jerusalem, where he hopes to arrive in time for Pentecost (20.16). After the days of unleavened bread[3] he sails to Troas where his companions await him. The narrative story here passes over into the first person plural. It is almost universally recognized[4] that the 'we-passages' in Acts (16.10–17; 20.4–15;[5] 21.1–18; 27.1–28.16) are not fiction, but go back to an eyewitness account, a sort of itinerary.[6] We have, therefore, before us in Acts 20.7–12 a particularly reliable tradition,

[1] See p. 189 above.

[2] Cf. E. Lohse, *TWNT* VI, p. 52.

[3] Therefore the Sunday mentioned in Acts 20.7 does, in fact, fall between Easter and Whitsun. That is the only passage to which J. van Goudoever (see p. 189 above) can appeal in support of his thesis. On Rev. 1.10 see pp. 205ff. below. *Acta Pauli* (Pap. Heidelberg p. 3, *NT Apoc.* II, p. 371) does not offer any support to his thesis, since in the second century—and Goudoever admits this—Sunday was in any case the day for worship throughout the year without interruption.

[4] Also by E. Haenchen, *Die Apostelgeschichte*, 1959³, pp. 77f. (with reserve).

[5] The list of names in v. 4 probably also belongs to the 'we-source'; cf. R. Bultmann, 'Zur Frage nach den Quellen der Apostelgeschichte', *New Testament Essays. Studies in Memory of T. W. Manson*, 1958, p. 74.

[6] Cf. A. Jülicher, *Einleitung in das Neue Testament*, 1931³, pp. 439ff. It is quite another question, with which we cannot concern ourselves here, whether the 'we-source' originally extended further and had already been

although it also may not be a unity. The text runs, 'On the first day of the week, when we were gathered together to break bread, Paul talked with them, intending to depart on the morrow; and he prolonged his speech until midnight. There were many lights in the upper chamber where we were gathered. And a young man named Eutychus was sitting in the window. He sank into a deep sleep and Paul talked still longer; and being overcome by sleep,[1] he fell down from the third storey and was taken up dead. But Paul went down and bent over him, and embracing him said, "Do not be alarmed, for his life is in him." And when Paul had gone up and broken bread and eaten, he conversed with them a long while, until daybreak, and so departed. And they took the lad away alive, and were not a little comforted.'

We shall now turn our attention to this Eutychus episode.[2] It is, indeed,

---

used in Acts before chapter 16 (see 11.28 D), and whether in particular it is connected with the so-called 'Antiochene' source (Harnack, Jeremias and now once more Bultmann [p. 196, n. 5]).

[1] This translation is certainly justified. In any case, we must take into consideration the intensification from καταφερόμενος to κατενεχθείς; it also fits the progress of the story. Otherwise, with Owen and the Zürich bible, we should have to excise κατενεχθεὶς ἀπὸ τοῦ ὕπνου as a pleonastic gloss.

[2] The possibility is not to be completely excluded that the Eutychus story was subsequently inserted into the 'we-source'; cf. E. Haenchen (p. 196, n. 4), p. 519; M. Dibelius, *Studies in the Acts of the Apostles*, ET 1956, pp. 17ff.; R. Bultmann (p. 196, n. 5), pp. 75ff.; also, earlier, A. Loisy, *Actes des Apôtres*, 1920, p. 764. In some respects we find a parallel to the Eutychus story in the description of the mysteries given by Firmicius Maternus, *De errore prof. rel.* 23 (PL 12.1032): On a certain night an image (of the god) was laid on its back on a stretcher and was bewailed with great lamentation. When (the devotees) had performed their elaborate lamentation for the dead, a light was brought . . .; and the priest muttered in a slow whisper, 'Be of good courage, ye devotees of the rescued god: good fortune shall spring up for you out of trouble.' Of course, this does not mean that the Eutychus story was originally a mystery myth, but it cannot be denied that there is some sort of relationship in the subject-matter. It is, in fact, difficult to decide where the insertion which comprises the Eutychus story does actually begin (if we have to assume that this passage was inserted). Does it begin in v. 9 where the name of Eutychus is mentioned, or in v. 8 where the lights are mentioned, or as early as v. 7b after the short introduction? Arguments may be suggested in favour of all these possibilities. In v. 8 'we' once again appears; is that a sign that we are dealing with a genuine 'we-source', or is this an inserted 'we'? This latter possiblity might be substantiated by the fact in v. 7b there is a remarkable change from 'we' to 'they': 'we were gathered'—'Paul talked with them'. The difficulty of distinguishing a clear division in the layers of tradition may well be another indication that Acts 20.7ff. may perhaps be a single unit of tradition.

not directly relevant to our investigation of the observance of Sunday. What is said in v. 11 about the breaking of bread ('when Paul had broken bread and eaten') only makes explicit what was already implicit in v. 7a. In v. 8 especial interest attaches to the detail that 'there were many lights in the upper chamber where we were gathered.'[1] We have two questions to ask: First, why does the text mention the many lights in this connection? Secondly, can we infer from the inclusion of this detail that lights played some part in the Christian gatherings? With regard to the first question,[2] the mention of the light is often regarded as a reason for Eutychus' sleepiness: the atmosphere was too hot because of the many lights[3] (or lamps). This is, however, hardly the original meaning, for Eutychus was after all sitting by the window. The length of Paul's sermon seems to have made him sleepy. E. Preuschen[4] sees more behind v. 8: the emphasis on sufficient illumination is directed against the current suspicion on the part of pagans that the Christians' evening worship took place in the dark and that unnatural and indecent practices occurred as a consequence.[5] But was there in this passage any obvious motive for such a piece of apologetic? It is better for us to see Acts 20.8 simply as an historical reminiscence, which has found a place in the narrative more or less by chance. It is decidedly more difficult to answer the second question whether the lighting of many lamps at the Christians' gatherings had any religious significance. Light and rituals associated with light have certainly played an important part in the history of religion, including Judaism and Christianity. Easter night, for instance, as early as the time of Etheria's pilgrimage to Jerusalem, was distinguished by a lavish brilliance of light (a symbol of resurrection joy), and today it is still marked in the same way by the Eastern church.[6] We may conclude from passages like Luke 12.35f., 'Let your lamps be burning, and be like men who are waiting for their master' (cf. the parable of the ten virgins,

---

[1] The western text does, in fact, read ὑπολάμπαδες; this would mean that there were many 'windows' in the upper chamber, but in all probability this is a secondary reading which came about by assimilation with the following words, 'and a young man named Eutychus was sitting on (one of the) window sills'.

[2] E. Haenchen, Die Apostelgeschichte, 1959², p. 518, n. 3, summarizes the interpretations which have been suggested.

[3] E.g. T. Zahn, Die Apostelgeschichte des Lucas II, 1927, p. 706; H. J. Cadbury, The Beginnings of Christianity IV, 1933, p. 256.

[4] Die Apostelgeschichte (HNT 4.1), 1912, p. 121; cf. O. Bauernfeind, Die Apostelgeschichte (Theol. Handkomm.z. NT 5), 1933, p. 236.

[5] Cf. Justin, I Apol. 26.7; 27.5; also Dial. 10.1; Minucius Felix, Octavius 9; Tertullian, Apol. 8.

[6] Cf. K. Schmaltz, 'Das heilige Feuer in der Grabeskirche im Zusammenhang mit der kirchlichen Liturgie und den antiken Lichtriten', Palästinajahrbuch 13, 1917, pp. 53–99. On the bringing-in of lights at the agape meal, cf. Hippolytus, Trad. Apost. 25 (Botte, p. 64 [26.18ff., Easton (p. 102, n. 5), p. 158; Dix, p. 50]).

Matt. 25.1ff., and also *Did.* 16.1) that similar customs were practised in New Testament times. Furthermore we can gather from these passages that the holding of light in readiness was associated with the eschatological hope: the lord, the bridegroom, was expected at this hour of night. The Easter vigil itself had, in fact, a very strong eschatological orientation.[1] Since, however, in Acts 20.7ff. it is not a question of Easter night and since we cannot prove the observance of any vigil before the usual Sunday worship (Acts 20.7ff. turns out to be an exception in this respect, as we shall see), we should prefer not to offer any explanations of this detail in v. 8.[2]

The real interest of Acts 20.7ff. for us lies in v. 7a, for the words συνηγμένων ἡμῶν κλάσαι ἄρτον have the mark of a fixed formula. Not only is the verb συνάγειν or συνάγεσθαι (cf. the parallel συνέρχεσθαι) a technical term for the Christians' assembling for worship, but κλᾶν (τὸ) ἄρτον also repeatedly occurs as a description of their common meal which was clearly of particular significance for them: in fact, these expressions often stand side by side (*Did.* 14.1; Ign. *Eph.* 20.2; cf. I Cor. 11.20).[3] Verse 7a is, therefore, self-explanatory within its own terms: one has the impression that it conveys to every reader and hearer the setting of the assembly for the breaking of bread which was known to each one of them. Within this familiar setting is reported the exceptional event of Paul's departure.[4]

It is, therefore, not satisfactory to interpret the situation the other way round by supposing that the assembly was held on Sunday as an exception because Paul wished to depart on the following day.[5] The exceptional

---

[1] See W. Rordorf, 'Zum Ursprung des Osterfestes am Sonntag', *TZ* 18, 1962, pp. 172ff.

[2] Mention must in any case be made of the fact that later texts also speak of 'many lights' in connection with Christian worship, e.g. *Acts of Thomas* 26; *Gesta apud Zenophilum consulem* (= Optatus, Appendix, CSEL 26, 187). The rites associated with fire on Easter night may also be connected with the interpretation of baptism as 'illumination'. See p. 286 below. P. Cotton, *From Sabbath to Sunday*, 1933, pp. 104ff., makes a very unsatisfactory attempt, on the basis of the mention of lights in Acts 20.8, to establish that the Christians had transferred the Jewish sabbath *kiddush* to the Sunday. It is well known that the kindling of lights at this Jewish ceremony on Friday evening was accompanied by a special prayer. We shall still have to discuss the influence of the sabbath *kiddush* meal on the Christian Sunday meal (see pp. 241f. below); Acts 20.8, however, provides no support for this thesis.

[3] On this see pp. 239f. below.

[4] M. Dibelius (p. 197, n. 2), p. 17, n. 37, also distinguishes v. 7 from v. 8ab; moreover, he sees in v. 7a 'Christian embellishment'.

[5] This position is adopted by A. Steinmann, *Die Apostelgeschichte*, 1934, p. 243. Our opinion is shared by, e.g., H. J. Cadbury, *The Beginnings of*

element was not the assembly on Sunday (that was, in fact, the usual practice), but only the fact that Paul prolonged his address until midnight on account of his impending departure.[1]

The controversy whether Acts 20.7ff. refers to the Eucharist or to a normal evening meal[2] is bound up with the interpretation of κλᾶν (τὸ) ἄρτον. We shall return to this question in another connection.[3]

If in Acts 20.7 the first day of the week is associated with these settled formulae of linguistic usage, this leads to the conclusion that it really did have something to do with assembly for worship and with breaking of bread and that the worship of the Christian community did at that time take place on Sunday. At this stage we do not intend to examine more closely what should be understood by the breaking of bread and at what period Sunday began to be connected with this breaking of bread.[4] For the time being it is sufficient for us to know that at the time of the composition of the 'we-source' (therefore, shortly after the events described) Sunday had already been for some considerable while in some form or other *the Christians' regular day for worship*: the fixed formulae lead us to this conclusion.

There remains one more question to be asked, and the answer cannot be found in Acts 20.7 alone. This is the question of the

---

Christianity IV, 1933, p. 255, and C. Marcona, 'La vigilia nella liturgia', *Arcivio Ambrosiano* 6, 1954, pp. 24–29. It is impossible to understand the passage in any other way. It does not say, 'Because Paul wanted to go away on the next day, we assembled on Sunday in order to break bread (for why in this case should there be any mention of Sunday?)', but 'We had in any case assembled on Sunday for the breaking of bread, and because Paul wanted to depart on the next day, he spoke for longer (than was customarily the case)'.

[1] E. Dekkers (see p. 205, n. 4, below) is of a different opinion; he holds that it may be inferred from Acts 20.7ff. that in early Christian history the Eucharist was always celebrated in the early morning.

[2] The majority of exegetes holds that it is a Eucharist; cf. the commentaries by T. Zahn, II, 1927, pp. 704ff.; O. Bauernfeind, 1939, p. 236; H. W. Beyer, 1955, p. 123; E. Haenchen, 1959[3], p. 520; also J. Behm, *TWNT* III, p. 729. For Catholic research see J. Kosnetter (p. 194, n. 5).

[3] See pp. 221ff. below. It is dangerous to try to reconstruct from Acts 20.7ff. (see E. Haenchen [n. 16], p. 520) the form of the Sunday observance customary in Luke's time: a Eucharist without any character of a communal meal, preceded by a sermon. We shall have to be cautious in drawing such conclusions just because of the unusual situation in Troas. Why should not the church at Troas (naturally by way of an exception) have once deferred the time of their Eucharist until after midnight?

[4] See pp. 215ff., 238ff. below.

time at which the assembly for worship took place, particularly the breaking of bread mentioned here. In Acts 20.7ff. it is clear that the gathering was in the evening, but it is not clear whether it took place on Saturday evening or on Sunday evening. Both days are possible: it depends how one reckons the twenty-four hours of the 'first day of the week'. If we use the Jewish method, the evening of the first day of the week is Saturday evening (for the Jewish day begins on the evening of the preceding day):[1] if, however, we use the Roman method (from midnight to midnight), the evening of the first day of the week must mean Sunday evening. For which date shall we decide? The question is of considerable importance, as we have already noted;[2] H. Riesenfeld, using Acts 20.7ff. as his principal starting-point, asserts that the first Christian 'Sunday observances' took place on Saturday evening, and he draws numerous conclusions from this assumption. In this connection, of course, nothing can be deduced from v. 7a ('On the first day of the week, when we were gathered together to break bread'): the gathering could just as well have taken place on Saturday evening as on Sunday evening.

The interpretation of $\tau\hat{\eta}$ $\epsilon\pi a\acute{\upsilon}\rho\iota o\nu$ in v. 7b has been debated even more. Does this expression mean 'on the next morning' or 'on the following day'? The translation 'on the next morning' would allow the Jewish method of reckoning the day and, as a result, the placing of the assembly for worship on the Saturday evening. If, however, we read 'on the following day', we should have to think in terms of the Roman method; in this case we should have to place the assembly on the Sunday evening, since the following morning on which Paul departs cannot (according to this reckoning) be part of the first day of the week. Both these alternatives are possible translations of the Greek. $\dot{\eta}\mu\acute{\epsilon}\rho\dot{q}$ must, of course, be added to $\tau\hat{\eta}$ $\epsilon\pi a\acute{\upsilon}\rho\iota o\nu$, but this expression cannot be pressed to mean that another day of twenty-four hours will have begun; $\dot{\eta}$ $\epsilon\pi a\acute{\upsilon}\rho\iota o\nu$ can simply denote (as in our own parlance) 'day' by contrast with 'night'.[3] It is, therefore, not surprising that both interpretations have been suggested.[4]

[1] Nevertheless in everyday parlance the day began in the morning, possibly also in Qumran and in related circles; cf. S. Talmon, *Scripta Hierosol.* 4, 1958, pp. 184ff., and p. 185, n. 2 above. M. Philonenko (in a letter of 3 July 1959) believes it is possible to find the same arrangement of the day in the Odes of Solomon.

[2] See pp. 179f. above.

[3] The word $a\check{\upsilon}\rho\iota o\nu$ is indeed derived from $\dot{\eta}\dot{\omega}\varsigma$, Aeolian $a\check{\upsilon}\omega\varsigma$, dawn.

[4] The overwhelming majority of exegetes is in favour of Sunday evening;

In parallel texts from Luke's historical writing there is no evidence which enables us to decide whether the author used the Jewish or the Roman method of reckoning. Luke 23.54 (with the exception of the Western Text) in the passage about the burial of Jesus clearly points to Jewish usage: 'It was the day of Preparation, and the sabbath was beginning.'[1] On the other hand, other passages in Acts could be understood in favour of the Roman method: '. . . they put them in custody until the morrow, for it was already evening' (4.3); 'the soldiers . . . took Paul and brought him by night to Antipatris; and on the morrow . . .' (23.31f.). In any case ἡ ἐπαύριον or ἡ αὔριον is used in both passages, so that we are faced with the same perplexity about the exact interpretation as we are in Acts 20.7.[2]—The same alternation between Jewish and Roman methods of reckoning time seems, moreover, to run through the whole New Testament.[3]

The question of the date is, therefore, not to be definitively settled solely from the account of the gathering in Troas. Nevertheless there can be no doubt that even in Acts 20.7ff. we should understand *Sunday* evening as the time of the gathering, but recourse must be had to other texts to fill out the picture. We shall refer only briefly to them here. Above all we must mention a letter from the governor Pliny to the emperor Trajan in AD 112.[4] There it is stated that the Christians went their several ways after a *Sunday morning* service[5] before they once

---

cf. H. Dumaine, *DACL* IV, col. 887; T. Zahn (p. 198, n. 3), p. 704; also, *Geschichte des Sonntags*, 1878, p. 23; A Deissmann, *Encyclop. Bibl.* III, pp. 2813f.; H. J. Cadbury, *The Beginnings of Christianity* IV, 1933, p. 255; A Steinmann (p. 199, n. 5) p. 243; O. Bauernfeind (p. 198, n. 4), p. 236; J. Nedbal, *Sabbat und Sonntag im Neuen Testament*, dissertation at Vienna, 1956, p. 156. In addition to the authors already listed above, p. 179, n. 2, A. Wikenhauser, *Die Apostelgeschichte*, 1956, p. 231, is also in favour of Saturday evening.

[1] The 'lighting up' could refer either to the kindling of lights before the beginning of the sabbath or to the rising of the first star; E. Lohse, *TWNT* VII, p. 20, n. 159, is in favour of the latter interpretation.

[2] No conclusion can be drawn from Luke 2.37; Acts 20.31; 26.7, where 'night and day' are mentioned in Jewish sequence, for on the other side stand Luke 18.7; Acts 9.24, where the reverse order is given, 'day and night'. (Does this inconsistency derive from the sources which have been used?) In much later times there is evidence of these two ways of reckoning the day: Sozomen, *HE* VII.19, and Cassian, *Inst. coen.* 2.18, report that in Egypt (by contrast with the Church at large) Sunday lasted from Saturday evening to Sunday evening.

[3] Cf. J. Morgenstern, 'The Reckoning of the Day in the Gospels and in Acts', *Crozer Quarterly* 26, 1919, pp. 232–240, and *Some Significant Antecedents of Christianity* (Studia Post-Biblica 10), 1966, pp. 8ff.

[4] X. 96 (97).7. On this letter in detail see pp. 251f., 253ff. below.

[5] '*Stato die*' cannot easily be satisfactorily understood except as a reference

again assembled '*ad capiendum cibum*': *cibus* simply means 'food', and then also 'meal'. This expression by itself gives no indication when the food was consumed. Nevertheless we may assume that it is a question of an evening meal on Sunday.[1] Two reasons in particular give us ground for making this assumption: 1. It would have been quite impossible for Christians to have assembled for a second time in the course of the day on Sunday: they had to work.[2] 2. *Cibus* in this passage certainly does not mean only the Eucharist in the narrowest sense of the word.[3] If that were all that was meant, why did the Christians assemble a second time in order to celebrate the Eucharist instead of taking it at the close of their morning gathering, as was, in fact, their practice later?

Also the context suggests that by *cibus* we are to understand the principal meal of the day, which was generally taken about the time of sunset. The letter immediately goes on to report how the Christians defend their '*cibum*' as '*promiscuum tamen et innoxium*' and how they had immediately given up their custom of meeting for a second time on Sunday after the governor acting in accordance with imperial instructions had forbidden '*hetaeriae*'. The assembly of Christians on Sunday and the activity of the *hetaeriae* were, therefore, clearly connected; the second gathering of Christians (by contrast with their meeting in the morning) came under the prohibition of being a

---

to Sunday; see A. Harnack, *Die Lehre der zwölf Apostel* (TU 2.1), 1884, p. 53; M. Goguel, *L'Eucharistie des origines à Justin Martyr*, 1910, p. 264; O. Casel, *Theol. Revue* 20, 1921, p. 183. The objection, which F. J. Dölger, *Sol salutis*, 1925², p. 110, n. 3, brings against it, is not valid.

[1] So also H. Lietzmann, 'Die liturgischen Angaben des Plinius', *Geschichtliche Studien, A. Hauck zum 70. Geburtstag dargebracht*, 1916, p. 38.

[2] A. A. McArthur, *The Evolution of the Christian Year*, 1953, p. 18, does, indeed, hold that the second assembly was also in the morning. He bases this opinion on the *Peregrinatio Etheriae*, in which we find that two assemblies did, in fact, take place in the morning. It is not, however, permissible to have recourse to a text of the late fourth century in order to elucidate a text of the early second century, especially as in the meantime Christianity had developed from being a *religio illicita* to being the official religion of the empire. We have already emphasized (see pp. 154ff. above) that until the time of Constantine it was possible for Christians to assemble only before daybreak, as Sunday was a day of work. Two assemblies on Sunday morning would, therefore, be quite impossible.

[3] Nor may we draw the opposite conclusion, that *cibus* was only an evening agape *without* Eucharist, as is done by L. C. Mohlberg, 'Carmen Christo quasi deo', *Rivista di Archeologia cristiana* 14, 1937, pp. 114ff. In any case we find no trace of a morning celebration of the Eucharist in Pliny's letter; for discussion on this point see p. 258 below.

hetaeria, although the Christians asserted that their meeting was 'harmless' and 'innocent'.[1] The assemblies of the *hetaeriae* (clubs of friends) were the real centres of political intrigues throughout antiquity and were therefore forbidden.[2] The Christian gatherings could be mistaken for meetings of *hetaeriae* only because they had some obvious resemblance to them. We know that the *hetaeriae* used to assemble for feasts in the evening on appointed days.[3] It is, therefore, clear that the Christians came under the suspicion of holding meetings of *hetaeriae* because they assembled for their communal meal on appointed days in the *evening*.[4]

It is, however, not only the letter of Pliny which provides us with evidence of a gathering of Christians on Sunday evening.

[1] The two adjectives certainly refer to the meeting for the meal rather than to the *cibus* in the narrower sense. In this latter sense the adjectives would be intended as a defence of Christians against the charge of Thyestian banquets and of the crimes against morality committed there. (This charge was, in fact, made against the Christians [see p. 198, n. 5]) Yet where in Pliny's letter the parallel is drawn with the *hetaeriae* there is no mention of this charge which had not yet been made against Christians at this early stage. Moreover, it is evident that Acts 2.46 is phrased very similarly; here, too, we find only the word 'food' (τροφή), although a whole meal is clearly meant, and the innocency (ἀφελότης καρδίας) of the meeting of emphasized; cf. B. Reicke, *Diakonie, Festfreude und Zelos*, 1951, p. 204; E. Haenchen, *Die Apostelgeschichte*, 1959[3], p. 154, n. 8. Did the suspicion of being a *hetaeria* attach to gatherings of Christians even then (at the time of the composition of Acts), or did the author have in mind the fanatical aberrations of certain communities?

[2] See the rest of the correspondence between Pliny and Trajan, esp. X.33 (42) and 34 (43). On the whole question see B. Reicke (n. 1), pp. 320–38.

[3] Cf. Cicero, *De senectute* XIII.44f.; *Inscr. lat. select. amplissima coll.* III, p. 212, 6086. Tertullian, *Apol.* 39.20f., defends against all kinds of insinuation the Christian *agape* meal which was held in the evening; he protests against it being confused with a '*factio*' (in the context it could very easily be a question of a meeting of a *hetaeria*), 'Give the meeting of the Christians its due, and hold it unlawful, if it is like assemblies of the illicit sort: by all means let it be condemned, if any complaint can be validly laid against it, such as lies against secret factions. But who has ever suffered harm from our assemblies? We are in our meetings just what we are when separated from each other; we are as a community what we are as individuals; we injure nobody, we trouble nobody. When the upright, when the virtuous meet together, when the pious, when the pure assemble in congregation, you ought not to call that a faction, but a *curia*—a meeting of the senate.'

[4] So also H. Dumaine, *DACL* IV, col. 889. If it were only a question of showing that Christians actually assembled in the evening, this line of argument would in any case be superfluous, since in every instance where κλᾶν (τὸ) ἄρτον occurs in Christian texts (Acts 2.42, 46; 20.7, 11; *Did.* 14.1; Ignatius, *Eph.* 20.2; cf. I Cor. 11.20ff.; *Did.* 9–10) we naturally think in terms of an evening meal. The important point, however, in Pliny's letter is that this meal took place on *Sunday* evening.

In this connection we must also consider the gospel narratives of the Easter appearance of the risen Lord to the disciples; this took place in connection with a meal in the evening—and in this case certainly a Sunday evening![1] The liturgical significance of these narratives should not be underestimated, particularly as we are convinced that they stand in the closest possible connection with the origin of the Christian observance of Sunday. Of this, however, we shall speak later.[2]

There was, therefore, an act of Christian worship, combined with a meal, which took place on Sunday evening.[3] We may then conclude that Acts 20.7ff., a passage which in itself contains no clue to the problem whether the gathering took place on the Saturday evening or the Sunday evening, certainly happened on a Sunday evening. We are driven to this conconclusion by the fact that in no primitive Christian document is there ever any mention of weekly worship on Saturday evening.

This means, however, that the thesis of E. Dekkers[4] receives a heavy blow. Dekkers sees in Acts 20.7ff. the model, as it were, of the most primitive Christian observance of Sunday: a vigil service in the night between Saturday and Sunday, followed by the celebration of the Eucharist very early on the Sunday morning. This position is untenable because the whole process did, in fact, happen in the night between Sunday and Monday. The celebration of the Eucharist after midnight in Acts 20.7ff. is to be attributed to the exceptional circumstances (Paul's farewell speech). The oldest texts provide no evidence that the Christian Sunday assembly had any sort of vigil service. In this connection we may not uncritically enlist the help of the Easter vigil in the night between Holy Saturday and Easter day, for Easter vigil and Sunday evening worship sprang from quite different roots.[5]

(c) The discussion of the third New Testament passage which deals with Sunday will provide for us some additional insights. It is Rev. 1.10. The seer is on the island of Patmos, and on the Lord's day (ἐν τῇ κυριακῇ ἡμέρᾳ) he receives his revelation,

---

[1] It should be noted that John 20.19 in fact presupposes the *Roman* method of reckoning the day.

[2] See pp. 215ff. below.

[3] So also F. Zimmermann, *Die Abendmesse in Geschichte und Gegenwart*, 1914, p. 11; J. A. Jungmann, *The Mass of the Roman Rite* I, 1951, p. 18.

[4] 'L'église ancienne a-t-elle connu la messe du soir?' *Miscellanea liturgica in honorem L. C. Mohlberg* I, 1948, pp. 233–57; also, 'La messe du soir à la fin de l'antiquité et au moyen âge', *Sacris eruditi* 7, 1955, pp. 99–130.

[5] See pp. 227ff. below, and W. Rordorf (p. 199, n. 1).

which he describes as an 'ecstasy of the spirit'.[1] Here for the first time we come across a new designation of the day and one which we know only from Christian sources: '*the Lord's Day*'. The adjective κυριακός (derived from κύριος) is certainly not a word invented by Christians: we also find it in Roman official documents, where it means 'imperial'.[2] Where the word occurs in Christian linguistic usage (in the New Testament only in Rev. 1.10 and I Cor. 11.20), it naturally refers to the Lord Jesus: ἡ κυριακὴ ἡμέρα is the day belonging to the Lord Jesus, just as τὸ κυριακὸν δεῖπνον (I Cor. 11.20) denotes the meal associated with the Lord Jesus.[3]

If the evidence does not justify us in saying that the title κύριος was transferred to Jesus in reaction to the imperial cult which was then beginning,[4] we should be equally mistaken if we were to interpret the Christian term κυριακὴ ἡμέρα as a reaction against the 'lord's days' of the pagan environment. There were no such Lord's Days which could serve as analogies. Nevertheless the Σεβαστὴ ἡμέρα[5] is frequently adduced as a counterpart to the κυριακὴ ἡμέρα. Like *augustus*, σεβαστός means 'sublime, majestic, venerable'. It is well known that on 17 January 27 BC the senate conferred the honorific title 'Augustus' on the Emperor Octavian. It now seems that the Σεβαστὴ ἡμέρα which is repeatedly attested on inscriptions from the time of the empire in the East and above all in Egypt and Asia Minor was, in fact, an 'Augustus day' which clearly recurred every month.[6] It is, however, by no means

---

[1] ἐγενόμην ἐν πνεύματι must certainly be translated thus.

[2] In the combination λόγος κυριακός (imperial treasury) it is attested on an inscription perhaps for the first time in AD 68; cf. A. Deissmann (p. 193, n. 2), p. 358. Further material in P. Cotton, *From Sabbath to Sunday*, 1933, p. 122, n. 3.

[3] One can ask why κυριακός occurs in the NT only in combination with the words ἡμέρα and δεῖπνον. W. Förster, *TWNT* III, p. 1095, believes that it is connected with the fact that these things are only indirectly associated with the 'Lord', but this explanation is not wholly convincing. In the formation of the phrase κυριακὴ ἡμέρα a contributory factor has been the desire to distinguish this day from the other, related ἡμέρα τοῦ κυρίου (LXX for *yōm Yahweh*). Later we come across the expression τὸ κυριακὸν (οἰκίον) for the church building; see p. 240, n. 5, below.

[4] This title of majesty is intelligible enough against the background of its use for God in the LXX. In course of time, as other κύριοι demanded worship, there was an element of conscious distinction; traces of this may be found in the New Testament (I Cor. 8.5f.; 12.3; Jude 4; Rev. 1.5; 17.14; 19.16).

[5] This suggestion comes from H. Usener, *Bull. dell' Istituto di Corrisp. archeologia*, 1874, pp. 73ff. A. Thumb, *ZDWF* I, 1900, p. 165, and A. Deissmann (p. 193, n. 2), pp. 306ff., have adopted it, and many others have done so after them (see p. 207, n. 1).

[6] Possibly as a monthly remembrance day of the Emperor's birthday; cf. II Macc. 6.7. On the other hand, it has not yet been established that the Σεβαστή was celebrated weekly.

obvious that the designation κυριακὴ ἡμέρα was devised 'in conscious contrast' to the Augustus day.[1] Not only do the two adjectives σεβαστός and κυριακός have no connection with one another, but when the title κυριακὴ ἡμέρα is applied to Sunday (and this still has to be demonstrated), it refers to a day which recurs weekly and which already had a distinctive observance before the new name was devised for it. As a connecting link one would at least have expected that first of all the title σεβαστός, 'by conscious contrast', would also have been applied to Jesus.[2] We come, therefore, to this conclusion: although κυριακός has no equivalent in Hebrew and Aramaic, does not occur in the Septuagint and, therefore, must go back to the Greek-speaking Christian Church, the use of this adjective is satisfactorily explained by the use of the title κύριος for Jesus, and this title has its roots deep in the Old Testament.

The great question which we now face concerns the meaning of κυριακὴ ἡμέρα in Rev. 1.10. It is normally understood as a new designation of the weekly Sunday,[3] but this view is contested on many sides. We need not consider any adventist interpretation which would seek to understand the κυριακὴ ἡμέρα of Rev. 1.10 as a reference to the sabbath,[4] as there is no basis whatsoever for this in the text.[5] Nevertheless it is not infre-

[1] A Deissmann (p. 193, n. 2), pp. 359ff., M. G. Glazebrook, *ERE* 12, 1921, p. 104. Cf. R. H. Charles, *The Revelation of St John* I, 1920, p. 23; P. Cotton (p. 206, n. 2), p. 126; E. Lohmeyer (rev. G. Bornkamm), *Die Offenbarung des Johannes* (HNT 16), 1953², p. 15, etc.

[2] Even less satisfactory is the explanation considered by P. Cotton (p. 206, n. 2), pp. 126ff., that the name the 'Lord's day' arose as a result of the increasingly widespread influence of the planetary week, in which each planet was 'lord' of a particular day, for in Christian circles of the first century we find no trace of an allusion to the planetary week. Moreover, it is improbable that, in order to counter astrological superstition, Christians substituted Jesus of all people for a planetary god.

[3] Mention may be made of R. H. Charles (n. 1); W. Hadorn, *Die Offenbarung des Johannes*, 1928, p. 34; E. B. Allo, *L'Apocalypse*, 1933, p. 11; M. Kiddle and M. K. Ross, *The Revelation of John*, 1940, p. 11; A. Wikenhauser, *Die Offenbarung des Johannes*, 1949, p. 31; E. Lohmeyer, rev. G. Bornkamm (n. 63). More recently also W. Stott, 'A Note on the Word KYRIAKH in Rev. 1.10', *NTS* 12, 1965–6, pp. 70–75 (where there is also a discussion of other topics). H. Dumaine (p. 204, n. 4), col. 859, n. 4, refers to a Syrian, an Ethiopic and an Arabic version of Rev. 1.10 which actually read, 'on the first day of the week'.

[4] J. N. Andrews, *History of the Sabbath and First Day of the Week*, 1876², pp. 187ff.

[5] T. Schermann, *Die allgemeine Kirchenordnung. Frühchristliche Liturgien und kirchliche Überlieferung*, 1914, p. 472, is inclined to see in Philo, *Opif. mundi* 89, an indication that the sabbath was called κυριακὴ ἡμέρα, but this conjecture is too vague for us to be able to use it as a basis for discussion.

quently asserted that in his vision the seer felt himself in some way transported to the 'last day', i.e. to the 'day of the Lord',[1] and that the content of his revelation is eloquent evidence in favour of this assumption.[2] Despite the similarity of the designations κυριακὴ ἡμέρα and ἡμέρα (τοῦ) κυρίου, however, their difference is in this instance more important than their similarity. If this were not the case, why did not Rev. 1.10 use for the 'last day' the name customary in the Septuagint and in the New Testament, namely the 'day of the Lord'?[3] Is not this new phrase much more probably an indication that there was an express intention to avoid confusion with ἡμέρα (τοῦ) κυρίου? This suggestion seems all the more likely as Rev. 1.10 is the only passage in which the phrase κυριακὴ ἡμέρα (which often occurs in later literature) is said to mean the 'last day'.[4]

Much more worthy of consideration is the suggestion that κυριακὴ ἡμέρα in Rev. 1.10 should be understood as a designation for Easter Day: this suggestion has recently been revived. A. Strobel[5] writes that the 'Lord's day' in Rev. 1.10 'certainly does not merely mean any ordinary Sunday . . . but 16 Nisan'.[6]

---

[1] The Greek translation of *yōm Yahweh* is, indeed, ἡμέρα (τοῦ) κυρίου. Here we must not go into the question how the original *yōm Yahweh* developed into the eschatological 'day'; see G. von Rad, *TWNT* II, pp. 946-9; also L. Dürr, *Ursprung und Ausbau der israelitisch-jüdischen Heilandserwartung*, 1925.

[2] Cf. A. Deissmann, *Enc. Bibl.* III, p. 2815; F. J. A. Hort, *The Apocalypse of St John*, 1908, pp. 14-16. On the other side are H. B. Swete, *The Apocalypse of St John*, 1906, p. 13; N. J. A. White, *Dict. of the Bible* III, 139.

[3] Or the other expression for it which also appears in Rev., ἡ μεγάλη ἡμέρα τοῦθ εοῦ (6.17; 16.14).

[4] Moreover, it is hard to imagine how the Revelation as a whole is supposed to take place on the 'last day'. How could we then understand, for example, the letters? J. Kosnetter (p. 194, n. 5), p. 40, also makes this point. On the other hand, it is, of course, undeniable that the similarity of κυριακὴ ἡμέρα with ἡμέρα τοῦ κυρίου could also give rise to association of ideas, so that the κυριακὴ ἡμέρα could, for example, be understood as some sort of anticipation of the ἡμέρα τοῦ κυρίου; but this shift of meaning is nowhere perceptible. Cf. Delling, *TWNT* II, p. 956.

[5] 'Die Passah-Erwartung in Lk. 17.20f.', *ZNW* 49, 1958, p. 185. Cf. also C. W. Dugmore (p. 210, n. 3); and from a different point of view K. A. Strand, *NTS* 13, 1966-7, pp. 174-81.

[6] Why not 15 Nisan (=Quartodeciman κυριακή according to Strobel)? That would be even more likely if the passover *midrash* Wisd. 18 really has influenced the Apocalypse; cf. Strobel (n. 5), pp. 176ff.

J. van Goudoever[1] interprets Rev. 1.10 as a reference to Easter Day and uses the internal evidence of the book of Revelation as support. He refers to 14.14ff., where there is mention of the 'harvest' which is executed with a sharp sickle by the Son of man seated on the clouds, and the harvest in Palestine did, in fact, begin on 16 Nisan. Immediately afterwards the vintage is mentioned, and in exactly parallel terms: it also is an image of the judgement to be pronounced on the world. If this image were taken literally, it would have to be dated in the autumn. Is it then a question of spring or of autumn? It is better not to look for a 'dating' and to let the harvest of the crops and of the fruits remain pure images which, at least in Revelation, no longer have any connection with the actual state of the agricultural process.[2] There is, therefore, not sufficient internal evidence in Revelation to justify the interpretation of the 'Lord's day' as a reference to 'Easter Day'.

A. Strobel is not, however, content with Rev. 1.10. He believes that the oldest linguistic usage of ἡ κυριακὴ ἡμέρα makes a certainty of his contention that Easter Day is to be understood by this phrase.[3] Since Strobel's thesis, if it should prove to be correct, would also lead to fairly important implications for our question, we must now let the sources speak for themselves and examine Strobel's thesis with reference to the oldest linguistic usage. An unbiased study of the texts will establish that almost without exception we have to decide in favour of the meaning 'Sunday' in the passages where the title ἡ κυριακὴ ἡμέρα or ἡ κυριακή[4] appears.

In *Didache* 14.1 we read, 'On the Lord's own day (κατὰ κυρια-κὴν δὲ κυρίου), assemble in common to break bread and offer thanks; but first confess your sins, so that your sacrifice may be pure.' The context points unambiguously to the weekly act of

---

[1] *Biblical Calendars*, 1961[2], p. 169ff.

[2] Nor should the passing reference to the ἀπαρχή in 14.4 and the other 'Easter' elements in Rev. (theology of the lamb, plagues, Song of Moses, three and a half days) be pressed in this sense, as is done by Goudoever, *loc. cit.*

[3] (P. 208, n. 5), p. 185. In n. 104 (p. 185) he even writes, 'κυριακή as a term applied to Sunday represents, as is generally acknowledged [*sic*!], a secondary development.' He then, indeed, continues, 'At the time of the Apocalypse this (secondary development) has in principle already taken place, and the author may very probably have made use of the special meaning of this term.' But if Strobel considers it possible that in Rev. 1.10 κυριακή already means 'Sunday', what is his evidence for a yet older linguistic usage, since Rev. 1.10 is the first passage in which ἡ κυριακή is ever mentioned?

[4] Very frequently in use as a shortened form. Cf. the parallel instances ἡ (ἐπ-) αὔριον, ἡ Σεβαστή, ἡ κρονική, etc.

worship on Sunday, for which the Christians assemble to 'break bread'. If, moreover, a 'confession of sins' is required from them, this does not justify the assumption that we have here a reference to some exceptional act of worship, e.g. the annual Easter service. The Christians knew that this 'purity' had to be restored afresh every week, lest the fellowship at the Lord's Supper be marred as a result.[1] In this injunction it is probably the 'strongly eschatological orientation' of the passage which causes Strobel[2] to think of the Easter celebration as its pattern. Leaving aside the question of the 'pattern', Strobel himself in any case admits that κυριακὴ ἡμέρα does *here* (that is, about the year 100) already mean 'Sunday'.[3]

The only difficulty in this text is the pleonastic expression κυριακὴ κυρίου; κυριακή (ἡμέρα being understood) would be sufficient. Why is κυρίου added? It is not easy to find an explanation. Perhaps the simple word κυριακή (used already here without ἡμέρα) had become by this time a technical term; the *Didache* in this passage wanted to insist that a 'confession of sins' necessarily belonged to the 'breaking of bread', so it added an explanatory κυρίου, thereby emphasizing the character of Sunday as the 'Lord's day' and drawing attention to its solemn sanctity.[4] There is absolutely no justification for holding, on the basis of this addition, that κυριακή was clearly a pagan 'lord's day' by origin and had been Christianized by the addition of the genitive κυρίου, as is held by M. S. V. McCasland.[5] We do not know of any pagan 'lord's day', nor would a 'Christianization' consisting solely of a pleonasm be considered very happy.

Ignatius in the passage quoted above, *Magn.* 9.1,[6] refers to those who walked in ancient customs having come to a new hope; they would no longer keep the sabbath (μηκέτι σαββατίζ-

[1] On this see pp. 243ff. below.
[2] *Loc. cit.*
[3] On the other hand, C. W. Dugmore, 'Lord's Day and Easter', *Neotestamentica et Patristica in honorem sexagenarii O. Cullmann*, 1962, pp. 272–81, is of the opinion that in *Did.* 14.1 it really is a question of Easter day. His reason is the unusual designation κυριακὴ κυρίου: on this see the discussion in the body of the text. The quotation from Mal. 1.11 in *Did.* 14.3 also seems to point to the weekly observance, for in this passage it is strongly emphasized that a pure sacrifice is brought to God in every place and (at every) time. That could hardly fit an observance celebrated but once a year.
[4] Similarly F. Spitta, *Die Offenbarung des Joh.*, 1889, p. 244. J.-P. Audet, *La didaché*, 1958, p. 460, omits κυρίου (with the Georgian version; cf. *Const. Apost.*); in this case the difficulty is, of course, eliminated.
[5] 'The Origin of the Lord's Day', *JBL* 49, 1930, p. 82.
[6] See pp. 139ff. above.

οντες, but live for the Lord's day (ἀλλὰ κατὰ κυριακὴν ζῶντες).[1] We cannot help noticing how κυριακή stands parallel to the preceding σαββατίζειν (= to keep the sabbath): this almost necessitates the translation 'Sunday'. The only objection which could be raised against this translation is that Ignatius appends to κυριακή the qualifying clause: 'on which also our life sprang up through him (sc. Christ) and his death'. That clearly refers to the resurrection on Easter Sunday, but it provides no justification for holding that κυριακή must here mean Easter Sunday! The Christians at their weekly Sunday worship could very easily remember that Christ had risen on a Sunday, on Easter Sunday to be precise.

The same consideration applies to the passage in Justin's *First Apology* (67.7), where he states, 'Sunday is the day on which we all hold our common assembly, because . . . Jesus Christ our saviour on the same day rose from the dead', and to *Barn.* 15.9, 'This is the reason why we joyfully celebrate the eighth day—the same day on which Jesus rose from the dead.' In both cases reference is made to the resurrection of Jesus and so to Easter day. We should have to conclude that in these passages both Justin and the author of the *Epistle of Barnabas* are referring to the annual Christian act of worship on Easter day, but they clearly mean the weekly Christian worship which takes place every Sunday. This is placed beyond all doubt by the expressions which they use, ἡ ἡμέρα τοῦ ἡλίου, ἡ ἡμέρα ἡ ὀγδόη.[2]

[1] The only Greek manuscript (cf. J. B. Lightfoot, *The Apostolic Fathers* II, 1, 1885, p. 129) does, indeed, read κατὰ κυριακὴν ζωὴν ζῶντες, but the Latin text of the thirteenth century (*secundum dominicam*) is to be preferred for two reasons. First, neither the Aramaic translation nor the longer recension of the *Letter to the Magnesians* (from the fourth century) knows the reading κυριακὴν ζωήν. Secondly, the sense of the passage is completely obscured by this reading. What is meant by 'no longer to keep the sabbath, but to live according to the Lord's life'? When Ignatius continues ἐν ᾗ καὶ ἡ ζωὴ ἡμῶν ἀνέτειλεν δἰ αὐτοῦ καὶ τοῦ θανάτου αὐτοῦ he can only mean that on (Easter) Sunday Christ rose. If we were to translate this, 'in the Lord's life our life also is risen through him and through his death', no intelligible sense could be given to the passage. The reading of the Greek ms. will, therefore, probably have been caused by an accidental dittography.

[2] Here we must mention the opinion of H. Schlier, *Religionsgeschichtliche Untersuchungen zu den Ignatiusbriefen*, 1929, pp. 44ff., n. 2. He wants to interpret the κυριακή in *Magn.* 9.1 as the day of baptism, and subsequently he sees two conflicting trends of thought clashing in *Magn.* 9.1; the one sees the baptism and epiphany, the other the death of the redeemer on the cross as the turning-point in the life of their respective adherents; this latter line may be seen expressed in the relative clause ἐν ᾗ καὶ ἡ ζωὴ ἡμῶν κτλ by means of the words καὶ διὰ τοῦ θανάτου αὐτοῦ, which Schlier holds were added later. This distinction is, however, artificial. The whole aim of the passage is to illustrate the *corporate* 'resurrection of life' on Easter day rather than the illumination of

In two passages in the Gospel of Peter[1] ἡ κυριακή does, in fact, denote Easter day, since these passages occur in connection with the report of the Easter events. The narrative in the Gospel of Peter does at this point clearly depend on that of the canonical Gospels. Thus κυριακή appears here as a translation of the expression μία (τῶν) σαββατῶν, which we find in Mark 16.2 par. μία (τῶν) σαββατῶν does, however, merely designate the weekly recurring first day of the week. Thus the evidence of the Gospel of Peter, far from substantiating the meaning of ἡ κυριακή as 'Easter day' represents a further argument in favour of holding that the κυριακή was, in fact, the weekly Sunday!

We should, therefore, no longer be surprised when the designation ἡ κυριακή occurs in the Gospel of Peter. It should strike us as much more strange that the Easter narratives in the Gospels use the designation μία (τῶν) σαββάτων for Easter day. We might conclude from this expression that some quite ordinary Sunday was meant, unless we knew from the context that it was the Sunday after the feast of the Passover. For Christians, clearly, the exact dating (day of month, year) was less important than the fact that the resurrection took place on a Sunday and that Sunday recurred every week. Does this not suggest that we must devote more attention to the significance of the *weekly* Sunday in primitive Christianity?

If we consider together the passages discussed here (Rev. 1.10; *Did.* 14.1; Ign., *Magn.* 9.1; Gospel of Peter 35; 50),[2] we

___

the individual in the act of baptism. 9.2, which refers to several who deny this mystery, is also more easily comprehensible on the assumption that these people were denying the resurrection rather than the efficacy of the sacrament of baptism. The recollection of the objective events of the death and resurrection of Christ does, of course, always have some effect on the life of the faithful; Ignatius gives expression to this when he testifies that Christians had received faith by means of this mystery. But one cannot play the one off against the other and so wrench apart the unity of this text and of its message. One would have more justification for supposing that Clement Alex., *Strom.* VII.12.76.4, understands κυριακή to mean the baptismal day; he writes, 'He (the gnostic), in fulfilment of the precept, according to the Gospel, keeps the Lord's day, when he abandons an evil disposition, and assumes that of the gnostic, glorifying the Lord's resurrection in himself.' Nevertheless it should be plain that Clement is undertaking a conscious reinterpretation of the concept. In the Christian Church Sunday was, of course, also the day for baptism, but the title the 'Lord's day' does not derive from this practice; see pp. 220f., 274f., below.

[1] 35, 50 (*NT Apoc.* I, pp. 185f.).
[2] Eusebius, *HE* IV.26.2, tells us that Melito of Sardis has also written a work περὶ κυριακῆς λόγος, but it is not clear whether this work was about Sunday or Easter day.

cannot fail to notice that they all come from the area of Syria and Asia Minor. There is, therefore, a certain probability that the origin of the title ἡ κυριακή ἡμέρα is to be located geographically in this area.[1]

It is unnecessary to consider all the other passages which provide evidence for the use of κυριακὴ ἡμέρα. Apart from those instances which do not admit of a decision in one sense or the other,[2] the reference in every case is to the weekly Sunday. It would be worth our while, however, to pick out a few typical texts. In the latter half of the second century Bishop Dionysius of Corinth writes to Bishop Soter of Rome (recorded by Eusebius, HE IV.23.11) that the Corinthians had celebrated the holy Lord's day and in so doing they had read out the letter of Soter and also that of Clement, as was their normal custom. Here we clearly have to think in terms of an exercise taking place on every Sunday rather than on merely one Sunday in the year.[3] The same point stares us in the face in Tertullian, where the Latin translation 'dominicus dies' occurs: from this time onwards Sunday always has this name in the official language of the Western church (cf. domenica, dimanche). In these passages from Tertullian which we have already quoted (Cor. 3 and Orat. 23)[4] dominicus dies and Easter-tide stand side by side (in Cor. 3 Easter day is called dies paschae!), and it is impossible to interpret dominicus dies as meaning any day other than the weekly Sunday.[5] Nor can there be any doubt about the meaning in Origen (Cels. VIII.22), since Eastertide and κυριακή stand side by side.[6] Eusebius (Mart. Pal. 7.1) cannot be quoted in the opposing sense as is done by Strobel (see n. 7). It is characteristic that Easter day here is not simply called κυριακή, but a periphrasis is used, (κυριακὴ ἡμέρα) τῆς τοῦ σωτῆρος ἡμῶν ἀναστάσεως.[7]

---

[1] R. H. Charles, The Revelation of St John I, 1920, p. 22, was first of this opinion. H. B. Swete, The Apocalypse of St John, 1906, p. 13; E. Lohmeyer (rev. G. Bornkamm), Die Offenbarung des Johannes (HNT 16), 1953², p. 15, have followed him.

[2] E.g. Epist. Apost. 18 (Coptic text) (see p. 97 above); Clement Alex., Strom. VII.12.76.4 (p. 211, n. 2). See also p. 212, n. 2.

[3] On this see pp. 267, 248f. below.

[4] See pp. 142f., 158ff. above.

[5] Fragment 7 of Irenaeus (Ps.-Justin, PG 7.2.1233), like the passages from Tertullian, is concerned with the prohibition of bending the knee on the κυριακή; it, too, must, therefore, be a reference to the weekly Sunday.

[6] Further texts: Origen, Hom. 7.5 in Ex.; Peter of Alexandria, Can. 15 (PG 18.508); Eusebius, Comm. in Ps. 91 (92, PG 23.1172); etc. (and frequently in the Const. Apost.). For the epigraphy (esp. the inscriptions on graves) see H. Dumaine, DACL IV, col. 864–6, 868ff.

[7] In Eusebius, Sunday has in any case become a weekly Easter festival, HE III.27.5; Solemn. pasch. 7.12 (PG 24.701A, 706C). (But in this text annual 'passover' and weekly κυριακή are once again contrasted.) Cf. also the Paschal Canon of Hippolytus, left side, line 3. Strobel (p. 208, n. 5) is not justified in

There remains room for hardly any doubt that ἡ κυριακὴ ἡμέρα was always and from the very beginning (i.e. as soon as the title occurred in the Greek-speaking churches of Syria) a new Christian designation for the *weekly* Sunday. It was natural that κυριακή could also exceptionally refer to Easter Day, because Easter Day also fell on the first day of the week, but generally this meaning is made explicit by some form of appositional construction.

In the Christian Church Easter was called τὸ πάσχα, in accordance with Jewish usage.[1] Then there soon followed the false etymological derivation from πάσχειν and the allusion to the death of Christ.[2] But the correct meaning of 'passing by' or 'passing over' which Philo[3] had given in Greek-speaking Jewry was also kept alive by Christians.[4]

If Christians created a new name for the first day of the week, this is a sign that this day was particularly important for them. We may assume that it gained this special importance as the *day for worship*, although in Rev. 1.10, where the title appears for the first time, we do not learn anything about this. The point has, however, been established that the seer by referring to the day wishes to emphasize that he received his revelation on

---

drawing on Eusebius. *HE* V.23.2, in support of his thesis. The non-Quartodeciman churches emphasized that Easter could be celebrated only on a κυριακή. If κυριακή in this passage means 'Easter day', we are left with a tautology which could not have given rise to any dispute (and there would have been no room at all for any disagreement if the Quartodecimans also had their κυριακή on 15 Nisan, as Strobel maintains). It is clear that the non-Quartodeciman churches insisted that Easter should always be celebrated on the same day of the week, namely Sunday; for them, therefore, κυριακή meant 'Sunday'.

[1] On the whole problem cf. T. Schermann, *Die allgemeine Kirchenordnung. Frühchristliche Liturgien und kirchliche Überlieferung*, 1914, pp. 494ff. J. Schümmer, 'Die altchristliche Fastenpraxis', *LQF* 27, 1933, pp. 51ff. (in disagreement with Schermann) demonstrates that in Tertullian '*dies paschae*' strictly speaking denotes Holy Saturday, but that *via* the Easter night it could also be transferred to Easter Sunday.

[2] E.g. Tertullian, *Bapt.* 19; (Ps.-)Tertullian, *Adv. Jud.* 10; probably also the Ethiopic text of *Epist. Apost.* 15; Melito, *Hom de pascha* 100 (SC 123, p. 120); Irenaeus, *Adv. haer.* IV.10.1; Justin, *Dial.* 40.1–3. Cf. B. Lohse, *Das Passafest der Quartadecimaner*, 1954, pp. 52f., who shows that this interpretation was already known to the patristic writers.

[3] *Sacrif. Abelis et Caini* 17.63; *Spec. leg.* II.147; but, in a different sense, *Quis rer. div.* 192.

[4] Clement Alex., *Strom.* II.11.51.2; Origen, *Cels.* VIII.22; Ambrose, *Cain. et Abel.* I.8.31 (CSEL 32.1, p. 36); Pap. Oxy. V. No. 840, lines 24–28.

Patmos in exile on the Church's day of worship.[1] This assumption seems all the more justified when we notice that the last things as they are portrayed in the Apocalypse of John contain a striking number of reminiscences of liturgical forms and procedures.[2]

To sum up, we can say: from the oldest (New Testament) texts concerning the Christian observance of Sunday we may conclude that Sunday clearly played an important role even in the Pauline churches. On Sunday money was put aside for the saints in Jerusalem (I Cor. 16.2), and Christians assembled for the breaking of bread on Sunday (Acts 20.7a). Also, in Syria a new Greek name came to be used for the day of the week which was made distinctive by Christians in this way: it was ἡ κυριακὴ ἡμέρα or simply ἡ κυριακή (Rev. 1.10). On the basis of these conclusions can we say anything about the probable origin of the Christian observance of Sunday?

3. THE ROOTS OF THE OBSERVANCE OF SUNDAY IN THE EASTER EVENT

After all that we have learnt in the preceding pages about the oldest evidence for a Christian observance of Sunday, we have discovered that it seems to have been a creation of *Gentile* Christendom. All three New Testament passages which speak more or less plainly of Sunday and of the Christians' predilection for it belong either to the area of the Pauline churches (I Cor. 16.2; Acts 20.7) or to the sphere of Greek-speaking Christianity in Asia Minor or Syria (Rev. 1.10). In the preceding period we lack any direct evidence about a Christian observance of Sunday. If in the following pages we do nevertheless raise the question whether the observance of Sunday did not have older roots in Jewish Christianity and in Palestine, we must realize from the outset that there is no unambiguous evidence available for the solution of this problem: the most that we can achieve is to give our opinion a certain degree of probability.

---

[1] E. Lohmeyer (p. 213, n. 1), p. 15; also earlier W. Hadorn, *Die Offenbarung*, 1928, p. 34.

[2] Cf. O. Cullmann, *Early Christian Worship*, 1953, p. 21.

H. Dumaine,[1] C. Callewaert[2] and others[3] have already been of the opinion that the Christian observance of Sunday originated within the primitive Christian community. Not all the arguments which they marshal in favour of this view are equally useful. For example, the fact that in I Cor. 16.2 and Acts 20.7 Sunday is called 'the first day of the week' and is, therefore, given a Jewish name can no longer be used as support for the thesis that the observance of Sunday was of Jewish-Christian origin. The Gentile Christians, had, in fact, at their disposal no other name which they could use for their day of worship: the planetary week with its 'Sunday' had not yet been introduced.[4] Sunday's title as 'the first day of the week' is, therefore, only one sign of the fact that even in Gentile surroundings Christians continued to use the Jewish week; it must not, however, be used as evidence that Gentile Christians also adopted an observance of the first day of the week which was already practised by Jewish Christians in Palestine.

This situation must cause some surprise. Why did the Gentile Christians continue to use the Jewish week after they had abandoned the sabbath, which was nothing less than its backbone? We must conclude that Sunday had become for them the new backbone of the seven-day week.[5] By itself this fact does not speak for either a Jewish Christian or a Gentile Christian origin of the observance of Sunday: it only provides evidence of the importance for Christians of this observance.

Much more important is the conclusion which can be drawn from Eusebius' evidence about the Ebionites.[6] Eusebius writes that there are (even in his time) two groups of Jewish Christians: both strictly adhered to Jewish customs (including the observance of the sabbath), did not acknowledge the apostle Paul and used only the Gospel according to the Hebrews. One group did, however, represent an even stricter tendency than the

---

[1] 'Dimanche', *DACL* IV, col. 892ff.
[2] 'La synaxe eucharistique à Jérusalem, berceau du dimanche', *Ephemerides theol. Lovanienses* 15, 1938, pp. 34-73.
[3] P. Cotton, *From Sabbath to Sunday*, 1933, p. 71; J. Nedbal, *Sabbat und Sonntag im Neuen Testament* (diss., 1956), pp. 17of.; J. Bauer, 'Vom Sabbat zum Sonntag', *Der christliche Sonntag*, 1956, p. 170; J. Kosnetter, 'Der Tag des Herrn im Neuen Testament', *Der Tag des Herrn*, 1958, pp. 43f.
[4] See pp. 26ff. above.
[5] See pp. 41f. above.
[6] *HE* III.27.5; cf. Theodoret, *Haer. fab. comp.* II.1, (PG 83.389).

other.[1] He say of the more liberal group, 'On Sundays they celebrated rites like ours in commemoration of the Saviour's resurrection.'[2] H. Dumaine,[3] in particular, has indicated that this evidence is very important for our question, since it tells of a *Jewish*-Christian observance of Sunday, thus guaranteeing that the observance of Sunday must go back to very early times. He holds that after their separation from the main body of the Church the Ebionites would certainly not have adopted the Church's Sunday observance. It is, of course, true that the evidence of Eusebius comes from the beginning of the fourth century, and for this reason we cannot without further ado draw conclusions from it about the earliest times. Moreover, Irenaeus in his report about the Ebionites (which is, in fact, almost identical with that of Eusebius) makes no mention of a Sunday observance.[4] We cannot, therefore, entirely exclude the conjecture that several Jewish-Christian groups desired to join the main body of the Church, and to this end they may also have adopted the Church's Sunday observance in addition to their own observance of the sabbath.[5] Nevertheless, it could also have happened the other way round: some Jewish-Christians of more orthodox leanings may originally have known the observance of Sunday and then for some reason or other they may have later given it up.[6] In this case, the group of Jewish-Christians who, according to Eusebius' description, used to practise the observance of Sunday side by side with that of the

---

[1] They rejected, for instance, the virgin birth.

[2] Here also κυριακαὶ ἡμέραι are not Easter days; this is corroborated by the fact that a reference is made to the sabbath immediately before. Eusebius' linguistic usage does, moreover, forbid any other interpretation. See p. 213, n. 7, above.

[3] (P. 216, n. 1), col. 893; cf. C. Callewaert (p. 216, n. 2), p. 51.

[4] *Adv. haer.* I.26.2.

[5] Thus T. Zahn, *Geschichte des Sonntags*, 1878, pp. 68f., n. 38; H.-J. Schoeps, *Die Theologie des Judenchristentums*, 1949, p. 139. Ignatius, *Magn.* 9.1, presupposes something similar: some Jewish Christians no longer observed the sabbath, but they kept Sunday; see pp. 139ff. above.

[6] One might perhaps think of that wing of Jewish Christianity which was emphatically loyal to the law and which had probably become a separate group even before the fall of Jerusalem (see pp. 127f. above). Perhaps this group resumed contact with the Jewish synagogue communities and took part in their worship on the sabbath; in this case, however, the Sunday assemblies of the other Christians (who had perhaps already come into bad odour with them on account of a polemic against the sabbath) must have seemed of dubious authority or, at the very least, superfluous.

sabbath would have retained the original practice of Jewish Christianity. We shall try to prove by means of other arguments that this interpretation of the passage in Eusebius has a good deal of probability.[1]

First of all, we intend to investigate the question whether it is probable that the observance of Sunday originated in the Pauline churches.[2] What motives could have been at work here? From the outset the possibility seems excluded that in these churches Sunday was substituted for the Jewish sabbath as a day of rest, for Paul has been so strong in his polemic against any kind of devotion to particular days among the Gentile Christians.[3] A more probable solution would be that some time had to be found in the Pauline churches for the *worship* of the community and that Sunday was selected for this purpose. The practical necessity of having a regular time for worship in these churches would, in fact, have been the reason for such an innovation. But from all that we have said about the sabbath practice of the primitive Church[4] we know that this necessity already existed in yet earlier times. Even the Church of the very earliest times no longer felt at home in Jewish sabbath worship: therefore it had to assemble in a place by itself and at a special time, even though it may have continued to keep the sabbath in outward appearance. The practical necessity for a regular time of worship in the Christian communities does therefore, point to a *pre*-Pauline origin for the observance of Sunday.

If the observance of Sunday had been invented in the Pauline churches as a substitute for Jewish sabbath worship, we should, moreover, have expected that in his letters Paul would have referred more to the observance of Sunday and, more particularly, that he would have answered the objections of a Judaizing opposition: a recently introduced observance of Sunday would, in fact, have provided an ideal point on which his op-

[1] For the same reason one can ask whether at the Apostolic Council (Acts 15) the observance of the sabbath was not required of Gentile Christians because Sunday had already taken the place of the sabbath among Jewish Christians; cf. H. Dumaine (p. 216, n. 1), col. 892f.

[2] Since we have evidence for the observance of Sunday in the Pauline communities during Paul's lifetime (I Cor. 16.2; Acts 20.7), we might even have to ascribe to Paul himself the radical step of introducing the observance of Sunday.

[3] Gal. 4.10; Col. 2.16f.; see pp. 130ff. above.

[4] See pp. 124f. above.

ponents could have seized. Is not their silence the most eloquent proof that the observance of Sunday had been recognized by the entire apostolic Church and had been adopted by the Pauline churches? In this case, we should have to assume that the 'Judaizers' who disturbed the Gentile-Christian churches[1] wished to introduce the sabbath merely in addition to the observance of Sunday and not in its place.[2]

We cannot, therefore, agree that the observance of Sunday was first introduced in the Pauline churches. We shall now take a further step and ask how Christendom (and presumably pre-Pauline Christendom) came to distinguish *Sunday* in this particular way. The practical necessity of a regular time for worship in the Christian communites certainly played an important part in the origin of the Christian observance of Sunday, but, as we stated at the beginning of the second main section,[3] this does not explain how it was *Sunday* which Christians made their day for worship. The selection of Sunday as the day for worship must in some way be connected with the resurrection of Jesus, which according to the evidence in the Gospels took place on a Sunday.[4] We are driven to this conclusion, since we have not been able to establish any pre-Christian observance of Sunday.[5] In fact, we are convinced that the Christians' observance of Sunday is closely associated with Easter, but we want to introduce some slight modifications into this thesis as it is customarily presented. It is normally assumed that the observance of Sunday first arose in the Pauline churches and the resurrection of Jesus is generally made responsible for the choice of Sunday. This choice would then have been made, as it were, out of respect for the day of Jesus' resurrection and in memory of it. We shall try to show that the observance of Sunday stood in a different kind of relationship to the resurrection of Jesus, and as a result of this it obtained its central place within the life of the community. We hope that in this attempt we shall be able to make its pre-Pauline origin yet more probable.

---

[1] See pp. 134f. above.

[2] Thus G. Dix, *The Shape of the Liturgy*, 1945[2], p. 337; C. Callewaert (p. 216, n. 2), p. 50.

[3] See pp. 177f. above.

[4] Mark 16.2 par., 9; John 20.1, 19. We shall later discuss the question whether this detail is historically credible; see pp. 228ff. below.

[5] See pp. 178ff. above.

It must be a cause of some surprise that the memory of the resurrection did not occupy a more prominent place in Christians' Sunday worship. The Easter narratives were not read out,[1] nor in the earliest times did they assemble on Sunday morning,[2] as would surely be expected if they really did regard the observance of Sunday as a commemoration of the resurrection. Moreover, H. Riesenfeld[3] has rightly noticed that in the earliest texts which bear on the Christian Sunday there is absolutely no mention of Jesus' resurrection, and when the resurrection does appear as a reason for this distinction of Sunday, one has the impression that this motivation may be a secondary addition. For instance, we read, in the first place, in Ignatius' *Letter to the Magnesians* (9.1) that Sunday was observed 'on which also (ἐν ᾗ καί) our life sprang up through him (sc. Jesus) and his death'. Again, we read in the *Epistle of Barnabas*, at the end of ch. 15, that the Christians would celebrate Sunday with an act of worship, 'on which day also (ἐν ᾗ καί) Jesus rose from the dead'. Finally, in Justin's *First Apology* (67.7) the primary motivation for the observance of Sunday is to commemorate the first day of the creation of the world and only secondarily, in addition, the resurrection of Jesus. It is only at the end of a long process that the title ἀναστάσιμος ἡμέρα occurs for Sunday. For a long while previously it had been called 'the first day of the week', 'the Lord's day', 'the eighth day' and 'Sunday'.[4] Nevertheless we are able to show that the Easter event was in reality the constitutive factor in the origin of the observance of Sunday.[5]

We intend to use as our starting-point the new Christian name for Sunday, 'the Lord's day'. Hitherto we have not so much as asked whence this name comes or what it means. It certainly does not mean that Sunday as a day (i.e. as a period of twenty-four hours) belongs in some special way to the 'Lord'

---

[1] This custom seems to have developed in the West at the time of Ambrose; for the tradition of the Eastern Church see *Peregrinatio Etheriae* 24.

[2] See pp. 238ff. below.

[3] 'Sabbat et jour du Seigneur', *New Testament Essays. Studies in Memory of T. W. Manson*, 1958, p. 212.

[4] See p. 275, n. 2, below.

[5] Reference must be made here to a further objection. It has been said (H. Gunkel, *Zum religionsgeschichtlichen Verständnis des Neuen Testaments*, 1910², p. 74; S. V. McCasland, *JBL* 49, 1930, p. 68) that it is incomprehensible why the Christians had celebrated the memorial of the resurrection not merely annually, but *weekly*. This question is, however, not difficult to answer. We have emphasized that not only the memory of the resurrection but equally the necessity of regular worship for Christians led to the observance of Sunday; their worship naturally had to take place more frequently than merely once a year. Moreover, in the following pages we shall try to show that for a quite different reason a weekly act of worship was associated with the fact of the resurrection.

Christ and is for this reason hallowed.[1] There was indeed an early secondary association of the title 'the Lord's day' with the idea of a weekly anticipation of the eschatological ἡμέρα τοῦ κυρίου, but in the last analysis the new name κυριακὴ ἡμέρα was deliberately chosen on account of other associations.[2] It would be better to hold that Sunday was supposed to keep alive in a special way the memory of Jesus' resurrection and that for this reason it was called κυριακὴ ἡμέρα.[3] Yet it does seem as if yet another motive played a quite decisive part in the choice of this name. The only occasion on which κυριακός occurs in the New Testament (apart from Rev. 1.10) is in I Cor. 11.20, and there it is associated with δεῖπνον in the sense of the 'Lord's Supper'.[4] We have, therefore, every reason for assuming that there existed an inner connection between κυριακὴ ἡμέρα and κυριακὸν δεῖπνον. Since the expression κυριακὸν δεῖπνον seems to have been used earlier than the corresponding expression κυριακὴ ἡμέρα, it is probable that the title κυριακὴ ἡμέρα is derived from the designation κυριακὸν δεῖπνον: in other words, it seems probable that the whole day on which this 'Lord's Supper' took place received the title the 'Lord's day'.[5] If this is, in fact, the case (and this conclusion is almost irresistible), we can infer that the Pauline Lord's Supper was celebrated on *Sunday*, since Sunday would not otherwise have received its title the 'Lord's day'. This conjecture is confirmed by Acts 20.7a: we have already noticed that the phraseology of this passage gives evidence of a fixed formula, and this led us to conclude that the community customarily assembled on the first day of the week for the breaking of bread.[6] Surely, by the breaking of bread in Acts 20.7a nothing else but the 'Lord's Supper' is meant.

But what about the primitive Palestinian community? Did they already celebrate a common meal on Sunday? In order to answer this question we must broach the problem of the relationship of the Lord's Supper to the breaking of bread. If we

---

[1] See the discussion on p. 158 above.
[2] On the eschatological side of Sunday observance see pp. 243ff. below.
[3] Cf. H. Dumaine (p. 216, n. 1), col. 869.
[4] This passage is not unique. Later, Tertullian can refer to the *dominicum convivium* (*Ad uxorem* II.4) or to the *dominica solemnia* (*De fuga* 14; cf. Commodian, *Carmina*, CSEL 15.89).
[5] Thus M. Goguel, *RHR* 74, 1916, pp. 30, 34.
[6] See pp 199ff. above.

can show that the Pauline Lord's Supper and the breaking of bread practised by the primitive community were identical, we are justified in supposing that the breaking of bread (just like the Lord's Supper) took place on Sunday.

H. Lietzmann[1] has indeed propounded the theory that in the breaking of bread and the Lord's Supper we are dealing with two different types of Eucharist. The breaking of bread would correspond to the original type: it is connected with the ordinary table-fellowship which Jesus used to enjoy with his disciples in his lifetime, and above all it was emphatically a meal of eschatological joy without any reference to the death of Jesus (Lietzmann finds this type of Eucharist once again in the *Didache* and in the *Liturgy of Serapion*). On the other hand, the Lord's Supper would correspond to another type which was possibly created by Paul (I Cor. 11.20ff.): this type was deliberately based on the tradition of Jesus' last meal before the passion, and it later led to a sacramentalism which may be seen in its developed form in the liturgy of Hippolytus. The theory is, however, untenable in this stark form.[2] In the first place, the type of Eucharist which was associated with the death of Jesus did have a markedly eschatological character,

---

[1] *Mass and Lord's Supper*, ET 1954ff.

[2] There are variations on it by other scholars. E. Lohmeyer, 'Das Abendmahl in der Urgemeinde', *JBL* 56, 1937, pp. 217–52; also 'Vom urchristlichen Abendmahl', *TR* NF 9, 1937, pp. 168–227, 273–312; 10, 1938, pp. 81–90), located the first type in Galilee (its roots lying in the feedings by the lake with their eschatological and agapeistic character), the second in Jerusalem (its roots in the supper before Jesus' passion); Lohmeyer is of the opinion that both types were united at an early stage in *one* celebration, like the two foci of an ellipse. O. Cullmann, 'The Meaning of the Lord's Supper in Primitive Christianity', *Essays on the Lord's Supper*, 1958, pp. 5–16, would like to trace the meals in the primitive community (as opposed to Lietzmann) back to the meals of the disciples with the risen Lord, and he emphasizes (cf. his controversy with F.-J. Leenhardt in *Early Christian Worship*, 1953, p. 17, n. 1) that even in the meal associated with the tradition of the breaking of bread there was *always* present some element of remembrance of Jesus' death. Also B. Reicke, *Diakonie, Festfreude und Zelos*, 1951, has shown the possibility of both emphases being combined, by pointing to the farewell meals of the dying patriarchs which were celebrated joyously (Jub. 22.1–9; 31.22; Test. Naph. 1.1–4; 9.2). E. Schweizer, *RGG*[3] I, col. 15ff., tries to formulate a new version of the problem of the two types of Eucharist: in Luke 22.15–18, 27–30 and John 13.1ff. there is outlined, he maintains, one self-contained tradition about Jesus' last meal; this tradition refers only to Jesus' serving and it also contains an eschatological element. Parallel to it there is the institution narrative which I Cor. 11.23–25 presents in its original form. Schweizer asks whether the institution narrative may not have been evolved out of the former tradition, since the two traditions cannot both be true to events as they happened. Yet even this solution seems to split up the tradition too much. Schweizer has to draw on the 'analogy' of the Qumran meals, in order to make it comprehensible that

particularly with regard to the words over the wine (Mark 14.25 par; I Cor. 11.26). Secondly, we cannot be so sure that in the other type of Eucharist represented in the 'breaking of bread' by the primitive community there was no drinking of wine, despite the evidence which is adduced in support of this contention.[1] Thirdly in I Cor. 11.23, when Paul recollects the words of institution, he believes he is referring to an ancient tradition which even derives from the Lord.[2] It is, therefore, more probable that the 'breaking of bread' in the primitive community[3] was from the outset related to the last meal of Jesus, was celebrated as a rule with bread *and* wine and that the words over the wine also gave it eschatological meaning.[4] There is also the following consideration which tells against the differentiation of two types of Eucharist. The first meal of the disciples with the risen Lord took place shortly after Jesus' last meal with them before the passion and it certainly caused them vividly to remember their last meal, particularly as both meals took place in fundamentally the same setting: the Lord was there (perhaps in the same room), gave thanks, broke the bread and gave it to his followers. The presence of the exalted Lord and the recollection of the words which he had spoken before his death *had* to merge into *one*. We

---

the primitive community did in any case repeat the meal. Also it remains difficult to explain how, out of the tradition of Jesus' last meal, which had a message only of service and of the eschatological future, there could have developed such massive declarations as those contained in the interpretative words over the bread and cup: it is not enough to point to the idea of the covenant as the sole connecting link. It is much more plausible to assume that the narrative of the institution also has its roots in history. We should, therefore, do well to refrain from extracting a special tradition from Luke and John (for ch. 13 stands beside ch. 6) and from playing this tradition off against Paul and Mark.

[1] See pp. 240f., n. 8, below. In any case, wine was always drunk with meals at Corinth. Otherwise the expression $\mu\epsilon\theta\acute{\upsilon}\epsilon\iota\nu$ in I Cor. 11.21 is not intelligible; cf. Acts 10.41: the disciples ate and drank with Jesus after he rose from the dead.

[2] Our interpretation of I Cor. 11.20ff. clearly depends on how we understand the abuses at the celebration of the Lord's Supper at Corinth. They were hardly a direct result of the primitive Christian manner of holding the meal, but were rather a degenerate version of it, perverting its meaning and causing Paul to refer vigorously to the tradition. Cf. B. Reicke, *Diakonie, Festfreude und Zelos*, 1951, pp. 251ff.

[3] The name may in this case be part of the *disciplina arcani;* cf. J. Jeremias, *The Eucharistic Words of Jesus*, ET 1964[2], pp. 132ff. Or the beginning of the meal was simply taken to denote the whole of it, *pars pro toto.*

[4] This means that the character of a passover meal would have been lost. Yet despite the investigation by J. Jeremias (n. 3) and A. Jaubert into new variants on this theme (see p. 184 above), one has to ask whether the paschal features are not secondary accretions. In any case, from the texts before us it cannot be conclusively proved that Jesus' last meal was a passover meal.

do not know whether Jesus did not perhaps once again give the bread and
the wine to the disciples, saying, 'This is my body, this is my blood . . .'[1]

At the outset it is important to remember that the breaking
of bread in the primitive community and the Pauline Lord's
Supper are in complete agreement in their outward setting.[2] In
both cases we are dealing with an observance which had a
liturgical character and took place within an evening meal.[3]
So far as I Cor. 11.20ff. is concerned, this point is clear straight
away, since δεῖπνον was the technical term for a meal in secular
linguistic usage as well (cf. also v. 23); at the same time this
meal in Corinth had a cultic character, as is shown by the
words of institution which this narrative contains and also by
some of Paul's other observations.[4] The situation is no different
when we consider the texts which refer to the primitive community's 'breaking of bread'.[5] Here, too, it is a case of an evening
meal (that is evident in Acts 20.7ff.; but cf. also Luke 24.30, 35)
which occupies a central position within the worshipping life
of the community. In Acts 2.42 we read, 'They [those who
believed] devoted themselves to the apostles' teaching and
fellowship, to the breaking of bread and the prayers.'[6] The fact
that the breaking of bread is mentioned in this context of the
community's life points to its significance. The full extent of this
can be seen in v. 46, 'And day by day, attending the temple

[1] Those who consider the appearances to be merely visions or 'back
projections' cannot, of course, follow us in this point; they can regard the
disciples' meals purely as a continuation of their table-fellowship with
Jesus during his lifetime (especially of the last meal before the passion).
As an example we may perhaps mention A. Schweitzer, *The Mysticism of
Paul the Apostle*, ET 1931, pp. 242ff. We shall deal later with the question of
the 'historicity' of the appearances; see pp. 228ff. below.

[2] On the form of this community meal in detail see pp. 238ff. below.

[3] Observances on Sunday morning occurred later (see pp. 253ff. below);
but it is not permissible to maintain, as does E. Dekkers, that the morning
observances were original and that there were at first no evening ones;
see p. 205 above.

[4] So also F. M. Nielen, *Gebet und Gottesdienst im Neuen Testament*, 1937,
p. 280.

[5] Cf. T. Schermann, *BZ*, NF 8, 1910, pp. 33–52, 162–83; H. J. Cadbury,
The Beginnings of Christianity IV, 1933; E. Lohmeyer, *JBL* 56, 1937, pp. 230f.;
B. Reicke (p. 223, n. 2), p. 11.

[6] We do not have to study here the significance of these several expressions.
It is open to question whether worship is, in fact, meant here; see pp. 247f.
below. κοινωνία in any case denotes community of possessions (cf. v. 45);
B. Reicke, *Glaube und Leben der Urgemeinde* (AThANT 32), 1937, p. 57.

together and breaking bread in their homes, they partook of food with glad and generous hearts, praising God and having favour with all the people.' Side by side with the gathering in the temple there appears here the breaking of bread 'in their houses' as the most important event in the life of the young community. Circumstantial details are given, and its joyous and innocent character is underlined. The eating of the 'meal' is the climax of the whole celebration; this is indicated by the word ἀγαλλίασις, the eschatological gladness with which the meal is consumed.

This 'gladness' is certainly associated with the presence of the exalted Lord at the meal.[1] But since the Lord (at any rate after a certain time) was no longer present physically, the certainty of his presence had to be associated more and more with the elements of bread and wine which were distributed 'in remembrance of him' and with his own words. It is hardly possible to come to any other conclusion than that even in the earliest times of the primitive community there had developed a *sacramental* understanding of the meal which was closely associated with the special 'food' and 'drink' which were consumed at it. It is, indeed, no accident that in Acts 2.46 the gladness attaches particularly to the eating of the 'food'. Therefore the consumption of the eucharistic elements does already occupy a prominent position within the whole process of the breaking of bread.[2] Cf. also I Cor. 10.17.[3]

As the basis of a distinction between the Lord's Supper and the breaking of bread, it is generally pointed out that the latter took place *daily*. Acts 2.46, the passage which we have just quoted, has to serve as proof, but we must not without qualification take the expression καθ' ἡμέραν in Acts 2.46 together

---

[1] The old Christian cry 'Maranatha' is well known, 'Come, Lord', or 'Our Lord comes', I Cor. 16.22; *Did.* 10.6; Rev. 22.20. Even in Greek-speaking areas this word (like Abba and Amen) has retained its Aramaic form; it must, therefore, have been of decisive importance in the primitive community; cf. O. Cullmann, *The Christology of the New Testament*, 1963, pp. 208ff., and pp. 232, 243, n. 4, below. The Old Testament pattern of festal joy at the annual celebrations has certainly had some influence, at least in so far as festal joy played a part in the cultic meal; cf. B. Reicke (p. 223, n. 2), pp. 201ff., esp. pp. 225ff.

[2] R. Bultmann, *TWNT*, I, p. 20, probably demythologizes too much when he regards ἀγαλλίασις as referring only to the fact that at worship the community celebrates and appropriates God's (eschatological) act of salvation.

[3] Even Acts 27.37–38 has a sacramental colouring; cf. B. Reicke, *TZ* 4, 1948, pp. 401–10. Later Ignatius, *Eph.* 20.2.

with κλῶντες ἄρτον.[1] The Western text, in fact, transposes καθ' ἡμέραν to v. 45, and in v. 46 it reads only πάντες δὲ προσκαρτεροῦντες ἐν τῷ ἱερῷ καί κατ' οἴκους ἐπὶ τὸ αὐτὸ κλῶντες δὲ ἄρτον. On the basis of this text we are hardly justified in maintaining that the breaking of bread took place daily in the primitive community. In Acts 6.1ff. we do indeed read of a daily διακονία τραπέζαις. This daily provision for the needy members of the community (in Acts 6.1 widows are mentioned) is, however, certainly not to bé identified with the community's breaking of bread, as E. Lohmeyer supposes.[2] Of course, there was a connection between agape and Eucharist (to use the later expressions), but the difference between them is not to be disregarded.[3] A passage like Acts 6.1–6 is, in fact, an argument for the thesis that the breaking of bread as distinct from the *diakonia* did *not* take place daily.

There is yet another reason which tells against the breaking of bread having taken place daily. The whole community assembled for the breaking of bread ἐπὶ τὸ αὐτό. συνέρχεσθαι or alternatively συνάγεσθαι ἐπὶ τὸ αὐτό was a technical term for the coming together of Christians for their meal of worship. We find this expression in I Cor. 11.20; 14.23 (in this passage it is taken for granted that the *whole* community is assembled); cf. Acts 1.15; 2.1 (again it is emphasized that *all* were gathered together); 2.44 D; 2.46 D; 2.47. The following patristic passages should perhaps also be mentioned: I *Clement* 34.7; *Barn.* 4.10; Ign., *Eph.* 5.3. The same expression is also applied in I Cor. 7.5 to the marital relationship of husband and wife, and it is also used, by contrast, to describe the assembling of foes: Acts 4.26 (= Ps. 2.1f. LXX); 16.35 D; cf. Matt. 22.34 and Rev. 19.17). In Justin's *First Apology* (67.7) it is still emphasized that the *whole* community assembled together. This communal assembly which was connected with the breaking of bread and seems to have been integrally associated with it may also be inferred from another detail mentioned by Justin in the same passage: he refers to the custom of taking the eucharistic elements to the homes of all those who were prevented by urgent circumstances from taking part in the

---

[1] Thus also F. M. Nielen (p. 224, n. 4), p. 275, n. 10. It must, of course, be conceded that, because of the preceding καθ' ἡμέραν and because of the construction with τε . . . τε, the text seems to indicate the daily breaking of bread. It is precisely then that we must treat with caution the evidence of Acts. Its author loves to idealize the circumstances of the primitive community (particularly in his generalizing summaries). We have already had occasion to ask critical questions with regard to his remark that the faithful enjoyed favour with all the people; see p. 124 above.

[2] *JBL* 56, 1937, pp. 231ff.

[3] See B. Reicke (p. 223, n. 2), pp. 9ff., and pp. 242f. below.

meal. The community clearly held that in its table-fellowship it was constituted as the body of Christ by its participation in the common meal of worship (cf. I Cor. 10.16ff.).[1]

It is, however, unlikely that the community assembled in its full numerical strength on *every* evening for the breaking of bread, and we have already been led to suppose that this breaking of bread was very probably not merely an agape-meal, but a fully eucharistic Lord's Supper (cf. also Acts 20.7ff.; Luke 24.30). A daily Lord's Supper in the primitive community is not, on this score, improbable, because the great number of the faithful (three thousand according to Acts 2.41 as early as Pentecost) would not have been able to meet in one place. (We have, in fact, to reckon with the possibility that the Jerusalem church was already divided into several house churches.)[2] We should, however, still have to suppose that the primitive community had at the very first a high degree of enthusiasm which was reflected in its sense of community and in the eschatological expectations which were presumably associated with it. The sources themselves do not provide evidence for this assumption.[3]

We do, therefore, hold that the community's breaking of bread did *not* take place daily. We are much more of the opinion that, because the breaking of bread was presumably identical with the Pauline Lord's Supper, it, too, was celebrated on

[1] The importance of the visible communal gathering in the primitive community is emphasized also by E. Schweizer, *Church Order in the New Testament*, *ET* 1961, §27a, p. 221.

[2] H. Kosmala, *Hebräer-Essener-Christen*, 1959, p. 349, is right in not wanting to understand ἐπὶ τὸ αὐτό in a local sense, but as a translation of the Hebrew *yahad* = communal assembly (cf. Ezra 4.3; Ps. 2.2 LXX). From Acts 12.17 it is, for example, apparent that James and other brothers were not present at that gathering, even though it was the night of the passover vigil. It is extremely probable that they were simply present at the celebration in another house at the same time. In Acts 2.46 D the phrase κατ' οἴκους may not lack foundation. Nevertheless it is noteworthy that, according to Acts 1.15, 120 faithful were assembled in one place. We may see in this fact their desire to assemble in one place in as full numbers as possible.

[3] There is nowadays a tendency to lay great stress on the high state of eschatological tension in the primitive community (A. Schweitzer, *Geschichte der Leben-Jesu-Forschung*, 1951[6], pp. 390ff.; M. Werner, *Die Entstehung des christlichen Dogmas*, 1941; and more recently. E. Grässer, *Das Problem der Parusieverzögerung* (BZNW 22), 1960[2]). As a result of the delay in the parousia, Christianity would, in this view, have undergone a crisis until at last primitive Catholicism was established on a new basis. In primitive Christianity, however, there may well have been a much greater continuity even with regard to eschatological expectations than would be supposed by this point of view. Evidence for this is furnished by the Christians' weekly observance of Sunday which, as we shall try to show, remained constant from the earliest days.

Sunday evening. We hope to be able to provide better support for this thesis by including the Easter events within the scope of this investigation.

It is not possible for us to approach the accounts of the Easter events in the Gospels without first asking the question about their 'historicity'.[1] This question always revolves round two problems. 1. The obvious inconsistency of the narratives in the Gospels. 2. The insufficient evidence for the discovery of the empty tomb.

1. In Mark and Matthew it is presupposed that the first appearance of the risen Lord took place in Galilee, but in Luke and John it took place in Jerusalem on the evening of Easter day. These two points of view seem mutually to exclude one another. If one relies on the Galilee tradition (as normally happens, for it is the 'older'),[2] the first appearance cannot possibly be placed on the evening of Easter day because of the great distance from Jerusalem to Galilee. One is then inclined to prefer the time-schedule of the Gospel of Peter, which breaks off at the point where the disciples return to the lake of Tiberias with Peter after the festival of unleavened bread (i.e. eight days later). There Peter would have first seen the Lord (a recollection of this may perhaps be apparent in John 21.1ff.; cf. Luke 5.1ff.), and afterwards the whole company of the disciples would have seen him. Finally they would all have returned to Jerusalem (e.g. at the festival of Pentecost) in order either to wait for the kingdom or to begin missionary activity there among the brethren. In this way the oldest account of the Easter appearances in I Cor. 15.5–8 can also be fitted in. There only remain the questions whether the mention of the appearance to the 'five hundred' refers to the event at Pentecost[3] or to another appearance in Galilee[4] and, also, where the appearances to James (cf. Gospel of the Hebrews, cited by Jerome, *Vir. ill.* 2) and 'to all the apostles' are to be placed.[5] In this case the narratives in Luke and John would, of course, have no historical value whatsoever.

2. The empty tomb. The principal point which is repeatedly made in this connection is that Paul did not know about an empty tomb[6] or, at

---

[1] On the form-critical problem see C. H. Dodd, 'The Appearances of the Risen Christ. An Essay in Form-Criticism of the Gospels', *Studies in the Gospels. Essays in Memory of R. H. Lightfoot*, 1957, pp. 9–36.

[2] The Fayum fragment, however, does not know Mark 14.28.

[3] E. von Dobschütz, *Ostern und Pfingsten*, 1903; for further authors see W. G. Kümmel, *Kirchenbegriff und Geschichtsbewusstsein in der Urgemeinde und bei Jesus* (Symbolae Biblicae Upsalienses), 1943, p. 46, n. 19. Now S. McLean Gilmour, *JBL* 80, 1961, pp. 248–52; 81, 1962, pp. 62–66.

[4] H. von Campenhausen, *Der Ablauf der Osterereignisse und das leere Grab*, 1958[2], pp. 13ff.

[5] According to H. von Campenhausen (n. 4), pp. 18f., also in Galilee.

[6] Indirect evidence for this has been deduced from the physical nature of his hope of resurrection; e.g. A. Oepke, *Wissenschaftliche Zeitschrift der Karl-Marx-Universität Leipzig* 3, 1953–4, pp. 109–15.

least, that he did not base his belief in it on the report of its discovery by the women. Also, reference has often been made to the unreliability of these narratives themselves. It is on the third day that the women want to anoint the dead Jesus (*pace* John 19.39f.), and as they make their way to the grave they remember that the stone is too heavy for them to roll away. The last clause of Mark's Gospel (16.8), that the women out of fear had not said anything to anyone, seems particularly open to suspicion. This seems to be an indication that the tradition of the empty tomb was not known in the earliest times. Nevertheless, H. von Campenhausen[1] has endeavoured to demonstrate the historicity of the discovery of the empty tomb. He holds[2] the sequence of Easter events to have been as follows: the women really had discovered the empty tomb on Easter morning, and they had related their experience to the disciples, who became very excited on hearing their report.[3] Peter, who of all the disciples was most disposed to believe it, led the disciples in a trek back to Galilee, where the appearances did, in fact, then take place.

In favour of von Campenhausen's reconstruction is the evidence 'risen on the third day' which appears as early as I Cor. 15.4. It is decidedly difficult to imagine the origin of this evidence if it does not derive from an historical reminiscence.[4] But one has to go on and ask the question whether the

---

[1] (P. 228, n. 4.) His solution has been contested by H. Grass, *Ostergeschehen und Osterberichte*, 1956. Of the same opinion as von Campenhausen is W. Nauck, 'Die Bedeutung des leeren Grabes für den Glauben an den Auferstandenen', *ZNW* 47, 1956, pp. 243ff. Cf. also K. H. Rengstorf, *Die Auferstehung Jesu*, 1960[4].

[2] He traces Mark 16.8 (and John 20.15 as well; pp. 31f.) back to an apologetic interest. The disciples had nothing to do with the empty tomb; therefore, they could not be accused of body-snatching (pp. 35ff.).

[3] *Op. cit.*, pp. 49f. The disciples had, therefore, remained in Jerusalem, though hidden.

[4] There have indeed been many attempts to explain this evidence otherwise, but none of these attempts provides a satisfactory answer. See the illuminating survey by J. Dupont, 'Ressuscité "le troisième jour" ', *Biblica* 40, 1959, pp. 742–61. One is naturally tempted to apply κατὰ τὰς γραφάς in I Cor. 15.4 not only to the statement 'risen', but also to the additional phrase 'on the third day'. By 'scripture' is naturally meant the Old Testament, not the New Testament (in this instance, for example, Jesus' predictions of his passion in Matt. 12.40); this is clear from Luke 24.44f. and John 20.9. In the whole of the Old Testament, however, there is only one single passage which can really be adduced as 'scriptural proof' for 'risen "on the third day" ', Hos. 6.2. It is scarcely credible that a passage which, moreover, never explicitly occurs in the New Testament, could have led to the emergence of the phrase 'risen "on the third day" ', as is assumed by H. Grass (n. 1), pp. 127ff., because he believes in the historicity neither of the Jerusalem appearances nor of the empty tomb. (The same may be said about Jonah 2.1; cf. Matt. 12.40, although this theme did play a fairly considerable role in Christian art.) The formula 'according to the scriptures' in I Cor. 15.4 will, therefore, refer only to the fact of the resurrection (cf. John 20.9)

historical reminiscence could not equally well apply to the first appearance which took place on Easter evening and which therefore also took place on the third day.[1] The case has not, in fact, been completely established that the Lucan and Johannine tradition of the Jerusalem appearances must have been invented.[2] The argument that the Galilean appearances have been transposed to Jerusalem for theological reasons may hold good for Luke, but hardly for John, who (in the supplementary chapter) also recounts another Galilean appearance. The principal question which remains unclarified is why the appearances in this case were transposed not only geographically but also temporally from a later point in time to Easter evening. The assumption that the narration of the Easter appearances already reflects the practice of Sunday observance does not explain why the appearances were placed on *Easter* Sunday evening in particular (and not, for example, on a Sunday one or two weeks later, thus being consistent with the Galilean tradition). There still seem good grounds for the assumption that the Lucan-Johannine tradition is an authentic one, not indeed that it

---

and not to the detail 'on the third day' as well. Parallels from comparative religion about dying and rising gods (for instance, J. Morgenstern [see above, p. 202, n. 3] speaks of a Canaanite fertility god!) and also the idea that the soul lingers for three days near a dead person have been adduced as explanations of the phrase. It has also been said that 'three days' simply means 'a short time' (thus J. Bauer, *Biblica* 39, 1958, pp. 354–8). But none of these suggestions can make it intelligible how the detail that Jesus rose 'on the third day' acquired such importance that it was taken into the confession of faith. The supposition that the mention of 'three days' rests on an historical reminiscence is still the most plausible solution. The only objection which can be brought against it is the complexity of the tradition: sometimes we find 'on the third day' (I Cor. 15.4; Matt. 16.21; 17.23; 20.19; Luke 18.33; 24.7; Acts 10.40), sometimes 'after three days' (Mark 8.31; 9.31; 10.34; Matt. 27.63; 17.23 D; Luke 9.22 D; cf. Mark 14.58; 15.29; Matt. 27.40, 63f.) and once even 'after three days and three nights' (Matt. 12.40). Is it credible that an historical reminiscence could be given so imprecisely? This difficulty may be solved relatively easily: 'on the third day' is the reminiscence of the discovery of the tomb on Easter morning (it appears in Paul of all places); 'after three days' is that of the first appearance on Easter evening (possibly the older tradition); the third variant 'after three days and three nights' did not refer directly to the historical events, but it derives from Jonah 2.1 (it is, moreover, only mentioned in connection with the sign of Jonah, Matt. 12.40). Later this variant was, in fact, also historicized, and the calculation was made to begin on Maundy Thursday evening; thus Aphrahates, *Hom.* 12.5; cf. Syr. *Didascalia* 21 (Connolly, p. 189). Of course, it should not be denied that theological, apologetic and other considerations came to be associated with the historical detail of 'three days' and that scriptural proofs for it were also adduced.

[1] F. Hahn, *Christologische Hoheitstitel*, 1963, pp. 205f., is also of this opinion.

[2] It is older than both Luke and John, since it underlies both gospels; cf. A. R. C. Leaney, *NTS* 2, 1955–6, pp. 110–14; B. Lindars, *NTS* 7, 1961, pp. 142–7.

should or may be played off against the Galilean tradition, for that would be equally misguided.[1] But why should not *both* traditions be allowed to have their kernel of truth? Why should not the appearances have taken place partly in Jerusalem, partly in Galilee?[2] Why should not the appearances to Peter and to the Eleven still be located in Jerusalem[3] and the appearance to the 'five hundred' in Galilee, particularly if, as E. Lohmeyer[4] surmises, a greater revelation was expected there than merely a proof of the resurrection?[5] In this case the appearance to Peter on Easter day would have been the cause for the disciples to have assembled again on Easter evening. (Luke 24.34 also seems to presuppose this.) The disciples certainly would not have assembled merely because they were expecting the resurrection on the third day or because the women had brought news of the empty tomb. (Cf. Luke 24.21ff.; also perhaps *Epist. Apost.* 10f.)

We may, therefore, conclude that real historical events are reflected in the narratives both about the appearance on Easter evening and also about the Jerusalem appearances in general.[6]

In the following discussion we shall direct our attention exclusively to the account of the first appearance on Easter evening, because it alone can be of any interest to us with regard to the origin of the observance of Sunday. We should think of the disciples' first encounter with their risen Lord taking place in exactly the same setting as their last meeting with Jesus before his passion: all the disciples (on the second occasion Judas Iscariot was, of course, missing) were assembled

[1] A. Schweitzer, *The Mysticism of Paul the Apostle*, ET 1931, pp. 245f., wants to relegate the accounts of the Galilean appearances to the status of secondary tradition. He understands the προάγειν of Mark 14.28; Matt. 26.32 in the sense that Jesus was to lead the way at the head of the column of disciples (cf. Mark 10.32); the disciples had remained in Jerusalem in expectation of this event. The accounts of the Galilean appearances would then subsequently demonstrate the 'fulfilment' of the prophecy.

[2] Cf. E. Lohmeyer, *Galiläa und Jerusalem*, 1936, who, despite the problems raised in some of his detailed exposition, did nevertheless try to do justice to both traditions.

[3] The message of the *angelos interpres* beside the tomb (Mark 16.7; Matt. 28.10) is not taken seriously by critical scholarship.

[4] (N. 2.)

[5] Cf. Matt. 28.16-20. It is, however, also possible that we have to allot the appearances to two groups of disciples which were quite distinct from one another, one in Galilee, the other in Jerusalem, and that not all the disciples, therefore, travelled from Jerusalem to Galilee and from Galilee back to Jerusalem again.

[6] E. Haenchen, *Die Apostelgeschichte*, 1959[3], p. 109, n. 4, indeed holds that the accounts of the meals are of anti-docetic origin. R. Bultmann, *The History of the Synoptic Tradition*, 1963, p. 305, wants to explain them as being derived from the liturgical tradition of the community.

indoors (perhaps on both occasions at the same house)[1] in the evening, and it is particularly important to notice that they were assembled at a meal. If we disregard John 21.1ff., this setting is associated only with the Jerusalem appearance on Easter evening.[2] The later kerygmatic summary of the gospel material in Acts 10.41 explicitly refers to the disciples having eaten and drunk together with the risen Lord. The συναλιζόμενος of Acts 1.4 is probably also a reference to this meal: the Lord 'took salt' (= shared a meal) with the disciples.[3]

The parallelism stares us in the face if we place the accounts of the first appearance of Jesus on Easter evening beside the breaking of bread as practised in the earliest Christian community. The disciples, just like the later community, were gathered in the 'upper chamber'; importance attaches to the fact that all were present; the focal point of the occasion is a communal cultic meal, without doubt in memory of Jesus' last meal and of the Easter meal. Also the eucharistic cry of the community, Maranatha (= our Lord comes),[4] which derives from the oldest deposit of tradition, is incomprehensible without the picture of the actual table-fellowship with the Lord.[5] Moreover, the whole sequence of the meal—giving of thanks, word of interpretation, distribution of bread and wine at the beginning and end of the meal (I Cor. 11.25)—exactly resembles the meals taken by the disciples with Jesus before and after his death. It would appear, therefore, that the breaking of bread was a continuation of their actual table-fellowship with the risen Lord.[6]

We are now approaching the core of our subject. If it really did happen that Jesus' last meal before his death, together with the Easter meal, the breaking of bread and the Pauline Lord's Supper, all stood in a line of direct continuity with one another,

[1] Cf. A. Schweitzer (p. 231, n. 1), p. 248. He holds that in Mark 14.15; Acts 12.12; 1.13 it is always the same house.

[2] Luke 24.30f.; possibly also John 20.19ff.; cf. Mark 16.14; Gospel of the Hebrews (in Jerome, Vir. ill. 2); the Emmaus story also fits into the same context.

[3] Thus O. Cullmann, 'The Meaning of the Lord's Supper in Primitive Christianity', Essays on the Lord's Supper, 1958, pp. 11f.

[4] See p. 225, n. 1, above; and p. 234, n. 4, below.

[5] See also Rev. 3.20.

[6] This is also emphasized by O. Cullmann, Early Christian Worship, 1953, pp. 16ff.

we cannot avoid the question which is so important for our particular subject, whether the observance of Sunday was not intimately associated with this whole chain of tradition. We have seen that the breaking of bread, which was very probably identical with the Lord's Supper, did at the very latest by the time of the Pauline epistles take place regularly on Sunday evening. Furthermore, we know that this same breaking of bread was also practised in the very earliest community in the same way, although no definite information has been handed down to us about the time of the observance. We have, however, come to see that this breaking of bread had its own roots in the Easter meal, when the risen Lord was present in visible form with his disciples, and we can assign a definite point in time to the Easter meal: it happened on a Sunday evening!

It is a strange fact that no mention is made in the Easter narratives that Jesus appeared to his followers on 'Easter day', i.e. 16 Nisan. We find only the neutral phrase that it happened 'on the first day of the week', on a Sunday just like any other weekly Sunday. The Christians were, therefore, aware that their own Sunday observance stood in a line of continuity stretching back to this 'first Sunday observance.'[1]

It must, moreover, be emphasized that the Easter meal was decidedly more important for the tradition of the primitive community than the memory of Jesus' last meal. The Lord's Supper was celebrated not on Thursday evening[2] but on Sunday evening. From this alteration of the date we conclude that the meeting of the disciples with the risen Lord on Easter evening must have been for them like a second institution of the Lord's Supper. On these grounds alone we must almost believe in the historicity of the Easter meal, since we cannot otherwise satisfactorily explain what caused the meal which was supposed to commemorate the last meeting before Jesus' death to be transposed to the Sunday. Anyone who thinks that the accounts of the Easter meal result from an historicization of a liturgical

[1] When the evangelists prefaced their Easter narratives with this plain 'on Sunday', some contributory part was also played by the custom of Sunday observance which had already been introduced. This does not mean, however, that they invented a connection between Easter appearance and Sunday observance, but only that they give evidence of an already existing relationship.

[2] Or on Tuesday evening, according to the thesis of A. Jaubert; see p. 184 above.

practice[1] will not be able to explain how Sunday managed to acquire such considerable significance within the Christian community, since we cannot establish the existence of any observance of Sunday either before or outside the Christian Church.

Everything, therefore, seems to indicate that the origin of the observance of Sunday is to be traced directly to the Easter event.[2] We also have various hints which can only confirm us in this opinion. It is, in fact, possible that Jesus appeared to his disciples not only on Easter Sunday evening, but also on the following Sunday and perhaps even on other Sundays after that. We have a text which presupposes that the disciples were assembled on the next Sunday after Easter and that they witnessed an appearance. John 20.26 reads, 'Eight days later, his disciples were again in the house. . . .'[3] Even Thomas was present this time; the disciples were, therefore, for the first time together in their full numerical strength. This one text from the latest canonical Gospel must not, of course, be pressed. In this instance, there is more justification for supposing that in his precise statement about the date the evangelist was influenced by the liturgical usage of his day. If, however, the evangelist was clearly of the opinion that the Christian observance of Sunday was rooted in the Easter event itself, he is then only expressing what was common ground for Christians at the end of the first century. In this case we have to ask whence this opinion derives. Was it perhaps based on a tradition which was not invented out of thin air? Other evidence also points to a similar conviction within the community.[4] The phraseology of Acts 10.41, 'We ate and drank with him after he rose from the dead', is so couched that it need not necessarily be interpreted as a reference to a *single* meal with the Lord. With even greater justification the

---

[1] See p. 231, n. 6 above.

[2] Cf. also H. Lietzmann, *The Beginnings of the Christian Church*, 1953, pp. 68f.

[3] There is no doubt that by 'eight days' a week is meant.

[4] Acts 2.1ff., the story of Pentecost, should not be considered here (H. Dumaine, *DACL* IV, col. 896, holds differently); although it is to be dated on a Sunday (at least in accordance with the Johannine chronology), it is probably to be understood in a different connection; it has much more to do with the origin of the Christian festival of Whitsun than with the weekly observance of Sunday. (We also find in this passage that worship is taking place in the morning, not in the evening.)

same may be said of Acts 1.3f., where we read, 'To them he presented himself alive after his passion by many proofs (τεκμήρια), appearing to them during forty days, and speaking of the kingdom of God. And while eating with them . . .' The participle συναλιζόμενος[1] seems in this context to indicate several meals. Moreover, this summarizing account makes it plain that we have to think of the time of the physical presence of the risen Lord (roughly speaking between Easter and Ascencion) as containing more 'proofs' (i.e. appearances) than are recorded in the Gospels.[2] The list of appearances which Paul gives in I Cor. 15.5–8 also points to the same conclusion (cf. Acts 13.31). Are we to think that even then Sunday was already playing a special role? We might almost suppose this to have been so if we were then to read in *Barnabas* 15.9 about the reasons for the observance of Sunday, that on Sunday Jesus had risen, appeared (to the disciples) and ascended into heaven.[3] Not only the appearances, but also the

[1] On the translation of this expression 'to have a meal', see p. 232, n. 3 above.

[2] Cf. Tertullian, *Bapt.* 19: during the fifty days the Lord's resurrection frequently occurred!

[3] The construction καὶ φανερωθεὶς ἀνέβη εἰς οὐρανούς must not be understood to mean that there was but one event and that Jesus (according to the author) also ascended into heaven after the first appearance (on Easter day). It is much more likely that we should think in terms of different Sundays. We have, indeed, other evidence which seems to point to an idea that Jesus also ascended on Easter day. Luke 24.50ff. is well known; cf. also the Gospel of Peter, 35–42; (Ps.-) Tertullian, *Adv. Jud.* 13; Jerome, *In die dom. paschae* (ad Ps. *117*), ed. G. Morin, *Anecdota Maredsolana* III.2, 1895, p. 418. See W. Bauer, *Das Leben Jesu im Zeitalter der neutestamentlichen Apokryphen*, 1909, pp. 277f.; T. Zahn, *Geschichte des neutestamentlichen Kanons* I, pp. 924ff. J. van Goudoever, *Biblical Calendars*, 1961[2], pp. 195f., moreover, draws attention to the reading in Codex Bobbiensis of Mark 16.4, which A. Resch has published among the *Agrapha* (TU 30.3/4), 1906, p. 41. The representations in ancient Christian art should also be studied; cf. *RGG*[3] II, Table 11.1. There is, therefore, evidence of some tension between two traditions. The one tradition treats the resurrection of Jesus and his 'exaltation' as one and the same event; the resurrection on the third day was at the same time the moment of Jesus' enthronement at the right hand of God, i.e. of the 'ascension'. The other tradition is represented by the report in the Gospels that Jesus 'appeared' in a variety of ways; in this tradition the 'ascension' denotes the conclusion of the appearances. It is, however, a mistake to play the two ideas off against one another. This same consideration must also inspire us with caution concerning the 'tradition' of an immediate ascension by Jesus from the cross. G. Bertram, *Festgabe für A. Deissmann*, 1927, pp. 187ff., tried to demonstrate that this was the original tradition. As evidence there may perhaps be cited Matt. 27.51–53; Luke 23.42; the double meaning of the expression 'lifting up' in the Fourth Gospel (lifting up on the

Ascension as well is by this time placed on Sunday. Is this a secondary tradition? Did it simply originate in the later general tendency to date on Sunday the most important events in the salvation history?[1] Or is it possible that yet another old tradition has been preserved here?[2]

We can now summarize the result of our investigation. On the one hand, we maintain that Sunday evening assumed a particularly important role because of the disciples' meals with the risen Lord which took place not only on Easter Sunday evening but also on one or more Sunday evenings after. On the other hand, bread was regularly broken in the Pauline churches on Sunday evening, and we notice that this breaking of bread corresponded with the disciples' meals with their Lord after his resurrection even in detailed arrangements (same setting, same sequence, prayer for the coming of the Lord). We are, therefore, almost compelled to conclude that there was a direct connection between these meals on the one hand and the breaking of bread

---

cross and, at the same time, lifting up at the right hand of God) and the Gospel of Peter 19. But all the Gospels subsequently report the resurrection as well! The interest in the ascension taking place at the crucifixion might well have first occurred in gnostic circles, where it was important to know that the ἄνω Χριστός was separated from the κάτω Ἰησοῦς at the moment of death.

[1] For an example see *Dormitio Mariae* 37, *Apocalypses apocryphae*, ed. C. Tischendorf, 1866, p. 107. But cf. also J. Daniélou, 'La typologie traditionelle dans la liturgie du moyen âge', *Settimane die studio del Centro italiano di studi sull'alto medioevo* 10, 1963, pp. 141–61.

[2] We must note the fact that the festival of the Ascension has strangely migrated. (It is unknown to Paul, although for him, too, the appearances are concluded.) The point of view of Acts which places the Ascension on the fortieth day after Easter (Luke 24.51 has a different tradition) did not at first gain acceptance in the Church's liturgical practice: the festival of the Ascension was celebrated at Whitsun. Cf. G. Kretschmar, *ZKG* 66, 1954, pp. 209–53; and also J. Boeckh, 'Die Entwicklung der altkirchlichen Pentekoste', *Jahrbuch für Liturgik und Hymnologie* 5, 1960, pp. 1–45. But even the 'conclusion' of the appearances with Whitsun, i.e. with the fiftieth day after Easter, may not perhaps correspond with the oldest tradition; it certainly does not represent the only tradition, and it originates in a conscious compartmentalization of the Church's year. There are traces of a quite different view that Jesus showed himself to his disciples for months or even years; reference may be made to E. von Dobschütz, *Ostern und Pfingsten*, 1903, pp. 32f. Above all A. von Harnack, 'Chronologische Berechnung des "Tags von Damaskus" ', *Sitzungsberichte der Preussischen Akademie der Wissensch. zu Berlin* 37, 1912, pp. 67ff., has pointed out the great age of the tradition that Jesus tarried with the disciples for eighteen months (Irenaeus, *Adv. haer.* I. 30.14; 3.2; Asc. Isa. 9.16.)

on the other. There does, then, exist good reason for supposing that in the primitive community the breaking of bread, for which no definite date is mentioned in Acts 2.42, 46, took place weekly on Sunday evening.

Nevertheless, we must finish this chapter with the question open. The present state of our knowledge does not enable us to discover *for certain* the origin of the observance of Sunday. Our discussion of the subject does, however, make it plain that several arguments can be cogently advanced for the opinion that the Christian observance of Sunday is a genuinely Christian creation which reaches back into the oldest period of the primitive community and even to the intention of the risen Lord himself.

V

THE OLDEST FORMS OF THE
OBSERVANCE OF SUNDAY

WE shall see that in the earliest period (which is the period of
our study) the observance of Sunday underwent a development
which can no longer be described as organic evolution. Our
opinion is that at the beginning of the second century a new
form of Sunday observance can be discerned which only to a
limited extent is continuous with the Sunday observance of the
first century: the observance on Sunday evening was superseded
by an observance on Sunday morning. We shall have to inquire
into the reasons for this change and also into the origin of the
observance on Sunday morning. Whilst the observance on
Sunday evening has nowadays almost completely disappeared
from our church life, the observance on Sunday morning, as we
find it taking shape in the second century, can be regarded as
the direct precursor of our present-day Sunday worship.

First we shall deal with the observance on Sunday evening,
then with that on Sunday morning. By this arrangement we
shall be able to comprehend the two most important stages in
the history of the early observance of Sunday in their chronological sequence.

I. THE OBSERVANCE ON SUNDAY EVENING

According to the present state of our information, this was
the original Christian observance of Sunday. For this reason we
have dealt exclusively with it in the chapter on the origin of the
Christian observance of Sunday. We have seen that it was
essentially connected with the breaking of bread in the primitive
community and was even identical with it. The breaking of
bread itself can be traced directly back to the disciples' table-
fellowship with the risen Lord and also to the memory of Jesus'

last meal before his death. If, therefore, we wish to describe the Christians' observance on Sunday evening, we shall have to investigate this breaking of bread in the primitive community.[1] It is clear from I Cor. 11.20ff. and *Did.* 9–10 that the breaking of bread was not what today, in a restricted sense, we call the Lord's Supper or Eucharist, but a complete meal for the satisfaction of hunger. In the accounts of the Last Supper we find exactly the same state of affairs, and in this connection it does not matter whether the last meal of Jesus before his passion was also a passover meal or not.[2] On the other hand, it would be wrong to hold that the breaking of bread was an evening meal without any cultic character, or that in any case the Christians would not have held their proper cultic celebration, the Eucharist, within the framework of this meal. These same passages tell against this supposition.[3]

E. Dekkers[4] has to do violence to the sense of I Cor. 11.20ff. (he does not even refer to *Did.* 9–10!), when he asserts that the 'agape' (as the meal was later called) and the Eucharist were always separate.[5] Dekkers attaches great importance to proving that the Eucharist was from the very beginning celebrated in the morning, but he does not succeed in establishing this point. Acts 20.7ff. is the only text before the time of Justin Martyr which he can adduce in support of his opinion, and he can do this only by assuming that the event at Troas took place on Saturday evening and that the

[1] We are, therefore, filling in the gap which we left above, p. 224.

[2] On this question see, above all, J. Jeremias, *The Eucharistic Words of Jesus*, 1964².

[3] In addition to the arguments set out on pp. 224f. above two further arguments may be quoted which show that the common meal had a specifically Christian, cultic character. The 'Eucharist', the giving of thanks, was part of the breaking of bread; cf. F. M. Nielen, *Gebet und Gottesdienst im Neuen Testament*, 1937, pp. 218ff.; T. Schermann, *BZ*, NF 8, 1910, pp. 33–52, 162–83. It must certainly be a question of more than merely the Jewish grace before meat; for Christians their Eucharist had something specific which was closely associated with Jesus (cf. Luke 24.30f.). If 'Eucharist' could later become merely the name for the 'offering of the Mass' (e.g. Ignatius, *Philad.* 4.1), this must have had its origin in the tradition. Moreover, the phrase 'breaking of bread' did not exist in Judaism; that has been established by G. Beer, *Pesachim*, 1912, p. 96. If Christians called their meal 'breaking of bread', it is clear that they were deliberately intending to distinguish it from an ordinary meal.

[4] 'L'église ancienne a-t-elle connu la messe du soir?' *Miscell. liturgica in honorem L. C. Mohlberg* I, 1948, pp. 233–57; also 'La messe du soir à la fin de l'antiquité et au moyen âge', *Sacris erudiri* 7, 1955, pp. 99–130.

[5] This view is opposed by H. Dumaine, *DACL* IV. col. 889; J. A. Jungmann, *The Mass of the Roman Rite* I, 1951, pp. 14f.

Eucharist was normally celebrated early on Sunday morning. Both these assumptions are highly improbable; indeed, they seem simply impossible.[1] Moreover, in this case no sense could be given to the description (given only by Paul) of the actual setting of the words of institution and so of the Lord's Supper itself, that Jesus in the *night* in which he was betrayed took bread (I Cor. 11.23). Nor can Pliny's letter be of any use in support of Dekkers' position, for in his detailed description of the worship on Sunday morning no word is said about the Eucharist.[2]

The gathering for the community meal took place in a private house. In the earliest times the upper chamber in the house of the mother of Mark seems to have played a role of some importance.[3] Later, however, these gatherings also took place in the houses of members of the community[4] (often in the home of the first converts or of the president of the particular community). From the third century onwards there were also churches.[5] The meal, which consisted of the simplest food like bread, salt, fish seems at first to have begun with a prayer of thanksgiving over the bread and to have been concluded with the passing round of the blessed cup.[6] Later bread and cup were both distributed together at the end of the meal.[7] Frequently, especially in Jewish Christian circles, wine was not used and in its place water was drunk.[8]

[1] See pp. 201ff., 205, above.

[2] F. Zimmermann, *Die Abendmesse in Geschichte und Gegenwart*, 1914, p. 29, is certainly right on this point. See pp. 258f. below.

[3] Acts 12.12; 1.13; Mark 14.15.

[4] 'Upper rooms' are mentioned in Acts 9.37, 39; 20.7f. Also see I Cor. 16.15, 19; Rom. 16.2ff., 23; Philemon 2; Col. 4.15.

[5] On the problems associated with this subject see W. Rordorf, 'Was wissen wir über die christlichen Gottesdiensträume der vorkonstantinischen Zeit?' *ZNW* 55, 1964, pp. 110–28.

[6] I Cor. 11.25; Luke 22.20. (P. Neuenzeit, *Das Herrenmahl. Studien zur paulinischen Eucharistie-auffassung*, 1960, p. 71, puts forward the view that at Corinth the giving of thanks over the bread and over the cup were already conjoined at the end of the meal.) J. A. Jungmann (p. 239, n. 5), p. 15, thinks he can find a reference to this original order in Hippolytus, *Trad. Apost.* 21 (Botte, p. 56 [23.2, Easton (p. 102, n. 5), p. 48; Dix, p. 40]), where between the distribution of eucharistic bread and wine another cup of mixed milk and honey (= children's food) and a cup of water are given to the newly baptized.

[7] As early as in Mark 14.21f. par. the rite with the bread seems to be associated with the blessing of the wine at the end of the meal. *Didache* 9–10 should be considered in this connection, although the prayers of thanksgiving here seem already to have been spoken at the beginning of the meal. In *Epist. Apost.* 15 we have a third type of tradition; the agape is celebrated after the Eucharist; cf. Chrysostom, *Hom.* 11.19 *in I Cor.* (PG 51.257).

[8] See the short account in E. Schweizer, *RGG*[3] I, col. 16; also

This is not the place for a more thorough study of the ways in which the meal of the Christian community was dependent upon Jewish table-customs. Others have made this.[1] In particular, the *haburoth* meals, the sabbath *kiddush* (on Friday evening), *habdalah* (at the close of the sabbath) and more recently also the meals of the Qumran community[2] have all been regarded as models for the meal of the Christian community. There certainly did exist a connection between the Jewish cultic meals, at which special prayers were said over bread and wine, and the meal of the Christian community: the *setting* was the same.[3] It should not, however, be overlooked that the *content* had become completely new:[4] this happened by means of the reference to Jesus' death, resurrection and return. It is pointless to trace the memorial of Jesus' death at the Christian meal back to a Hellenistic influence and the eschatological element of messianic expectation back to the Jewish passover night: to do so would only ruin the unity of the Christian observance. The distinctive mark of this observance was the indissoluble unity of its threefold reference to Jesus Christ, the Lord of the community: it was based on the experience of the resurrection of Jesus, which included the reference both to his death and also to his return at the end. The very fact that the meal of the Christian community took place on *Sunday*, the day of the resurrection, is an impressive piece of internal evidence that this Christian observance was a new creation. In this way it is clearly to be distinguished from all Jewish models and also from Jesus' daily table-fellowship with his disciples during his lifetime.

Although the sabbath *kiddush* and *habdalah* took place weekly, they cannot be adduced as parallels to the Sunday meal of the community,[5] precisely because they had a quite specific reference to the beginning and end of the sabbath. No trace can be found of any influence by them on the Sunday meal of the community. H. Lietzmann[6] is right in seeing in the Jewish ritual meals which did *not* take place weekly a closer parallel to the meal of the Christian community than in the sabbath *kiddush* and *habdalah* in which the general table-customs and prayers were arranged with reference to the solemn greeting and leave-taking of the sabbath. Lietzmann does, of course,

---

O. Cullmann. 'The Meaning of the Lord's Supper in Primitive Christianity', *Essays on the Lord's Supper*, 1958, pp. 10f. One can hardly see here a special type of Lord's Supper; see pp. 222f. above.

[1] See the literature listed in B. Reicke, *Diakonie, Festfreude und Zelos*, 1951, p. 70, n. 6; G. D. Kilpatrick, *ExpT* 64, 1952–3, pp. 4–8, should also be added. Reicke himself dismisses the thesis that the Christians merely adopted Jewish table-customs.

[2] K. G. Kuhn, 'The Lord's Supper and the Communal Meal at Qumran', *The Scrolls and the New Testament*, ed. K. Stendahl, 1958, pp. 65–93.

[3] Cf. also J. A. Jungmann (p. 239, n. 5), p. 15.

[4] Cf. also P. Neuenzeit (p. 240, n. 6), pp. 55f., 58f., 70.

[5] As is done by P. Cotton (p. 216, n. 3), pp. 107ff.

[6] *Mass and Lord's Supper*, ET 1954ff., pp. 170f.

then proceed to assign to the Jewish *haburoth* meals a disproportionate influence on the meal of the Christian community.

B. Reicke[1] has drawn attention to the emphasis on mutual love in the earliest Christian meals and to their roots in the festal joy of the Old Testament. The later 'agape' was, in fact, principally concerned with the feeding of the poor and needy, but it is certain that the emphasis on mutual love was already prominent in the first century when the Eucharist also was still connected with a community meal. Evidence[2] for this can be seen in the feeding miracles,[3] in the narratives in Luke (22.24ff.) and John (13.1ff.) associated with the last meal of Jesus before his death, and in the testimony of Acts.[4]

Nevertheless the Sunday act of worship at the Lord's Supper (in contrast to the daily feeding of the poor) probably did not contain any particular emphasis on the element of mutual love. Acts 6.1ff., the account of the choice of the 'Seven', is particularly informative in this connection. Here we learn that there was in the primitive community 'a daily serving of tables' which the apostles conducted. By this expression we clearly have to understand a meal which was for the benefit of the poor, but the Hellenists grumbled because their widows were passed over in this distribution. Widows and orphans, together with slaves, aliens and Levites, counted in the Old Testament (and some of them all over the ancient East) as the five categories of people who were in need of support because they did not possess any land.[5] As the community went on increasing in size, the apostles delegated this *diakonia* to others.[6] But because this provision for the poor took place daily, while the Eucharist took place only once in the week (if our argument in the preceding chapter is correct), there was a clear distinction even in the earliest times between the mere agape and celebration of the Eucharist: the former was instituted in order to feed the poor; the latter was first and foremost the means whereby the community was constituted as the body of Christ.[7] It is significant that Acts distinguishes

[1] *Diakonie, Festfreude und Zelos in Verbindung mit der altchristlichen Agapenfeier*, 1951.

[2] Further references (including patristic passages) in B. Reicke (n. 1), pp. 31ff.

[3] Mark 6.30ff. par.; 8.1ff. par. E. Lohmeyer, *JBL* 56, 1937, pp. 219ff.; also *TR* NF 9, 1937, p. 276, attached great importance to them.

[4] The model community of possessions among the first Christians is repeatedly described, 2.42, 44f.; 4.32ff.

[5] B. Reicke (n. 1), pp. 161ff.

[6] The narratives about Stephen and Philip do, of course, stress that the 'seven' were not only 'deacons', but also preachers and missionaries.

[7] Cf. I Cor. 10.16ff., and the next pages in our study.

between κλάσις τοῦ ἄρτου and διακονία τραπέζαις (or κοινωνία) as two quite different things. We have, of course, repeatedly maintained that the celebration of the Eucharist originally took place within the setting of a meal. The element of mutual love and the emphasis on the meal being a meal for the satisfaction of hunger to which people brought food from home and which particularly benefited the poor[1] did, however, become less prominent. Yet we can doubtless see a relic of the primitive Christian *diakonia* in a practice which was still maintained much later, that of bringing contributions of money and in kind to the Sunday act of worship.[2] This collection in the course of the Sunday liturgy grew all the more important as the agape proper (i.e the meal for the poor) did, in time, cease to be held.

We have now to direct our attention principally to the Eucharist, the central act in the Sunday meal of the community. Without doubt it was the climax of the whole observance, and it certainly had its own particular eschatological character. This did not consist merely in the expectation of the parousia, which was associated with the celebration of the Jewish passover and, by analogy, with the annual Christian Easter festival.[3] The cry 'Maranatha' may not be interpreted in this one-sided manner.[4] Immediately before this cry in the eucharistic prayer in *Did.* 10.6 we do indeed find, 'May grace come, and this world pass away!' But this clause is not intended only as a prayer for the breaking in of the end of the world. (If this were the case, why in the same prayer should thanks be given for food and drink and supplication made for the Church?) This clause was also meant to be the proclamation that, with the communion which was even then beginning, the sacred was entering the realm of the profane and that everything 'worldly' had, therefore, to disappear from the midst of the community. The passage, therefore, continues, 'If anyone is holy, let him advance; if any-

---

[1] The disorders at Corinth (I Cor. 11.20ff.) show this in a lurid light.

[2] See p. 272f. below.

[3] See W. Rordorf, 'Zum Ursprung des Osterfestes am Sonntag', *TZ* 18, 1962, pp. 172ff., and the literature mentioned there.

[4] K. G. Kuhn, *TWNT* IV, pp. 474f. (cf. G. Bornkamm, *Das Ende des Gesetzes*, 1952, pp. 123ff.), emphasizes (here following E. Peterson, *ΕΙΣ ΘΕΟΣ*, 1926, pp. 130f.) that from the context of I Cor. 16.22 and *Did.* 10.6 the translation 'Our Lord is there' suggests itself. Maranatha would then have to be understood as the threatening word addressed to the 'unholy' (see also C. F. D. Moule, *NTS* 8, 1960, pp. 307–10, for the same opinion). In any case there is evidence for the other emphasis (the coming at the end) in Rev. 22.20.

one is not, let him be converted', and in I Cor. 16.22, 'If anyone
has no love for the Lord, let him be accursed.' We have also to
consider the express warning of *Did.* 9.5 that only the baptized
may take part in the Eucharist: this is clearly based on Matt.
7.6, 'Do not give dogs what is holy.'[1] In the community's act of
worship on Sunday there was a vivid awareness that, as its
members partook of the Eucharist, the community itself was
being constituted as the body of Christ, as a new creature. The
power of God made for himself in the community a holy temple
for his own abode. *That* was the coming of Christ as it was now
accomplished in the Holy Spirit during this time between the
times.[2] There was, of course, inherent in this coming the judicial
solemnity of 'the last days', because the Holy Spirit did not let
himself be mocked: he condemned and blotted out sins and
uncleanness.[3]

Various supplementary considerations confirm that the
eschatological element consisted, above all, in the Lord's
present participation at the meal. We have already drawn
attention[4] to the fact that if possible all members of the church
in a particular place were present at the Lord's Supper every
Sunday, even if in towns like Jerusalem where there were many
Christians the company of the faithful was certainly divided
into several house churches. This gathering in full numerical
strength is not primarily rooted in the expectation of the
parousia, but in the conviction that in the fellowship on Sunday
the mystical body of the Lord living on in time takes visible
shape, and for this reason no member may be missing.[5] Impressive evidence for this is the fact that after the celebration the

---

[1] Perhaps Matt. 22.11–14 also originally belonged to this setting; the
man who appeared at the meal without a wedding garment would, in this
case, be an unbaptized person.

[2] So also O. Cullmann, *Early Christian Worship*, 1953, pp. 33, 35f.

[3] It is unnecessary to emphasize that this understanding of eschatology
is to be differentiated from that which treats the individual as an isolated
unit and which is said to consist in repeated making of decisions and in
realization of personal responsibility. The essential point about the understanding of eschatology which we have just described is that it can be actualized
only when it can operate collectively, in a community and in the building
up of the community in the Spirit. The individual is nothing, in this view,
but a member of a larger group which envelops him in his situation within
a cosmic dimension and the time of salvation-history.

[4] See pp. 226f. above.

[5] Here the 'Sitz im Leben' of I Cor. 12.12ff. is to be found.

consecrated elements were taken by the deacons to the home of every absent person (e.g. to those prevented by sickness from being present), so that, at least in this way, they might have a part in the Lord's body.[1] In this connection reference is often made to the preparation for worthy reception of the Lord's Supper which we find required as early as the time of Paul (in I Cor. 11.27ff.). This preparation is, of course, generally misunderstood by us in an individualistic sense, as if it were only a question whether the individual were going to suffer harm by receiving the consecrated elements. We should, however, be thinking in terms of the *community*, which as the body of Christ would suffer harm if the individual member were to approach the Lord's Supper unworthily. The examination, the 'judgement', was something which the whole community had to do. This becomes apparent from its context. *Didache* 14.1 may serve to explain what it was all about, 'On the Lord's own day, assemble in common to break bread and offer thanks; but first confess your sins, so that your sacrifice may be pure. However, no one quarrelling with his brother may join your meeting until they are reconciled; your sacrifice must not be defiled.' The last clause is to be considered beside Matt. 5.23f., 'If you are offering your gift at the altar, and there remember that your brother has something against you, leave your gift there before the altar and go; first be reconciled to your brother, and then come and offer your gift.'[2] Part of the 'judgement' which preceded the fellowship of the Lord's Supper was a confession of one's sins (this may well have happened in public), and approach to the Lord's table was possible only on condition that every dispute with a brother or sister was settled. This was necessary 'so that the sacrifice[3] might be pure'. The judgement on the individual happened in the interests of the whole

---

[1] This custom is first attested in Justin, I *Apol.* 67.5 (cf. later *Testamentum domini nostri Jesu Christi* II.20), but it is certainly much older; it is to be traced directly back to the κοινωνία of the primitive community.

[2] Cf. *Did.* 10.6; Irenaeus, *Adv. haer.* IV.18.1.

[3] Here we do not have to deal with the change of meaning in the idea of sacrifice. In this passage it already seems to be applied to the Lord's Supper. This later becomes the predominant meaning; cf. H. Grass, *RGG*³ I, col. 22ff., 41, and also pp. 271f. below. Parallel to it runs the other meaning which designates as sacrifice the prayer of the faithful or the offerings brought to the liturgy. See also pp. 269f., 272f., below.

community, since the 'holiness' of the community depended on there being no unworthy participant in the Lord's Supper.

Even in Tertullian's[1] time the judgement of the church was practised with considerable severity. 'There is, furthermore, exhortation in our gatherings, rebuke, divine censure. For judgement is passed, and it carries great weight, as it must among men certain that God sees them; and it is a notable fore-taste of judgement to come, if any man has so sinned as to be banished from all share in our prayer, our assembly, and all holy intercourse.'[2] In this passage we can see once again what was involved in the 'eschatology' of the community meal: it was not an expectation of the end, but rather a proleptic antici-pation of the end. We may refer for comparison to I Cor. 11.31ff., 'If we judged ourselves truly, we should not be judged. But when we are judged by the Lord, we are chastened so that we may not be condemned along with the world.' On every Sunday, therefore, there took place a last judgement in mini-ature, whenever the community was assembled for the meal, prepared itself by penitence for the reception of the elements and then, in holiness and joy as the body of Christ, was certain of the Lord's presence. Closely associated with this was the holy kiss which the faithful gave one another before communion.[3] This was the bond of the peace which gave outward expression to the unity of the faithful in the Sprit (and also to their readi-ness to forgive).[4] Christians knew that this unity was repeatedly endangered by personal and collective guilt, and therefore it had to be repeatedly renewed at weekly intervals. This is one of the most important reasons why the Christians' observance of Sunday was maintained with such tenacity even under the

---

[1] *Apol.* 39 (Tertullian is, in any case, already referring in this passage to the morning act of worship); cf. *Bapt.* 20; *Paenit.* 8f. We may perhaps even be reminded of the 'judgements' in the sect's rule at Qumran (I QS VI.24–VII).

[2] Cf. the dismissal not only of the catechumens, but also of the 'penitents' before the beginning of the anaphora in the later liturgies. Private confession did, of course, increasingly come to take the place of public penance.

[3] I Cor. 16.20; Rom. 16.16; I Thess. 5.26; II Cor. 13.12; I Peter 5.14; Justin, I *Apol.* 65.2; Tertullian, *Orat.* 18, who says that the kiss of peace is a seal belonging to all corporate prayer.

[4] Cyril of Jerusalem, *Cat. mystagog.* V.3, 'This kiss is the sign that our souls are mingled together, and have banished all remembrance of wrongs.'

most difficult conditions (e.g. in times of persecution):[1] they would have 'given place to the devil' if they had not regularly assembled.[2] There was, therefore, no more pressing duty than to come to the worship of the community and to allow nothing to stand in the way.[3]

If in our discussion we have laid considerable emphasis on the fact that the experience of the exalted Lord's *presence* at the meal lay at the heart of the eschatological awareness of the community, this certainly does not imply that we deny the purely eschatological prospect directed towards the future (cf. the formula 'until he comes' in I Cor. 11.26; also the idea of the messianic meal: Mark 14.25 par.; Matt. 8.11 par.). We only wish to stress that this element of future expectation was rooted in the common meal as it was actually celebrated time and time again in the community. It is not that the certainty of the exalted Lord's presence developed as a result of disappointment about the expected end, but just the reverse: the hope of the consummation at the end of the times derived its strength from the experience of the fulfilment which had already been realized.

We still have to enumerate briefly the other liturgical customs associated with the Sunday meal of the community. Here, of course, we have to reconstruct material gathered from a variety of sources, since we have only scattered information in accounts which are, moreover, not directly connected with the Lord's Supper. We do, however, know that the act of worship on Sunday evening was the Christians' principal act of worship in the first century.[4] We have, therefore, grounds for assuming that the information about worship to be found in various passages in the New Testament is connected with this principal

[1] See T. Zahn, *Geschichte des Sonntags*, 1878, p. 39. It was, in fact, on many occasions hardly possible to celebrate the Eucharist; cf. Tertullian, *De fuga* 14; Victor of Vita, *Hist. persec. Afric.* I.18 (CSEL 7, p. 9).

[2] Tertullian, *Orat.* 23. See pp. 158ff. above.

[3] Cf. *Did.* 16.2: 'Meet together frequently in your search for what is good for your souls, since "a lifetime of faith will be of no advantage" to you unless you prove perfect at the very last.' Heb. 10.25 should also be considered in this connection, 'We do not want to neglect to meet together (in the sense of no longer attending the assembly), as is the habit of some, but encouraging one another, and all the more as you see the Day drawing near.'

[4] The daily feeding of the poor was in a certain sense only a simplified form of this act of worship; in so far as there was in early Christian times a daily observance in the morning, this was solely a service of prayer; see pp. 260f., 268f. below.

service.[1] Acts 2.42 must be mentioned, 'They devoted themselves to hearing the apostles' teaching and to fellowship, to the breaking of bread and the prayers.'[2] This text is, of course, not easy to interpret. It has been understood as a summarizing description of Christian worship in its several parts.[3] This thesis is, however, hardly to be sustained. The 'breaking of bread' was indeed a fundamental component of Christian worship: also 'the apostles' teaching', the sermon, may be considered within the setting of the community meal,[4] even if it does not exclusively belong there. But this 'fellowship' which probably refers to possessions, was, of course, not limited to the act of worship,[5] and prayer was even less subject to this restriction.[6]

The picture becomes fuller if we also consider I Cor. 14.26–33: we may do this because we have other evidence which shows that the liturgical customs described by Paul in this passage were connected with the meal of the community. In I Cor. 14.26 we read, 'When you come together, each one has a hymn, a lesson, a revelation, a tongue, or an interpretation.' In the assembly there does, therefore, take place a communal edifica-

---

[1] See the combination of the various elements in O. Cullmann, *Early Christian Worship*, 1953, pp. 12ff.

[2] We have purposely given a different translation of προσκαρτεροῦντες. The rendering 'they persevered in the apostles' teaching' seems to us particularly faulty, since it gives the impression that the community had held on to the catechism or to the theology of the apostles. The reference here must be to the apostles' spoken word, i.e. to their preaching.

[3] O. Bauernfeind, *Die Apostelgeschichte*, 1939, p. 54; J. Jeremias, *The Eucharistic Words of Jesus*, 1964, pp. 118ff.

[4] We may not think in terms of a missionary sermon because of the remark that 'they' (the faithful) listened to it. Moreover, we have the text Acts 20.7ff., where it is reported that in Troas Paul spoke to the assembled community before he broke bread. (The unusual element here is *not* that Paul spoke, but only that he spoke for so *long*.) The custom of listening to the 'teaching of the apostles' was so important and was rooted in the life of the community in such a way that if no apostle was present the written word of the apostles soon came to be a substitute for their physical presence. Thus in the Pauline churches the letters of the apostle were read out at the gathering of the community (I Thess. 5.22; Col. 4.16; cf. I Tim. 4.13); well over a hundred years later Dionysius of Corinth wrote to Bishop Soter in Rome that the community on Sunday had once again read out Soter's letter (as it generally did) and also the letter of Clement (Eusebius, *HE* IV.23.11). In Justin, I *Apol.* 67.3, we learn that the 'memoirs of the apostles' (i.e. the Gospels) were also read out. See pp. 226f. below.

[5] E. Haenchen, *Die Apostelgeschichte*, 1959³, p. 153, may be right on this point.

[6] See pp. 267ff. below.

tion of all (cf. 14.31; I Thess. 5.19). One recites a spiritual song, another consoles and admonishes the brethren with a sermon, yet another who is inspired with the prophetic gift of speech reveals some of the hidden things of God, yet another is transported in spirit and speaks incomprehensible sounds, which another who does understand them is able to interpret.[1] In this connection we also have to consider the passages Col. 3.15–17 and Eph. 5.18–20, which are almost parallel to one another:

Eph. 5.18–20	Col. 3.15c–17
'Do not get drunk with wine, for that is debauchery; but be filled with the Spirit, addressing one another in psalms and hymns and spiritual songs, singing and making melody to the Lord with all your heart, always and for everything giving thanks in the name of our Lord Jesus Christ to God the Father.'	'Be thankful. Let the word of Christ dwell in you richly, as you teach and admonish one another in all wisdom, and as you sing psalms and hymns and spiritual songs with thankfulness in your hearts to God. And whatever you do, do everything in the name of the Lord Jesus, giving thanks to God the Father through him.'

The warning in Eph. 5.18, 'Do not get drunk with wine', seems to suggest that we should also associate with the meal the words which follow.[2] The faithful should converse on spiritual matters: they should instruct one another in reasonable speech, sing to one another psalms and hymns and songs.[3] This activity is characteristically designated a giving of thanks, an εὐχαριστεῖν;[4] it clearly took place out of gratitude for the reception of the 'bread of life' and for the fellowship of the brethren.

In *Did.* 10.7 the prophets are also allowed to give thanks after communion as much as they wish. Later, Tertullian[5] describes the celebration of the agape which certainly can be traced back

---

[1] Paul lays great stress on this point in the whole of I Cor. 14; otherwise the community would not be edified and disorder would result, as the spiritual ecstatic cannot control himself.

[2] Thus also B. Reicke, *Diakonie, Festfreude und Zelos*, 1951, pp. 315f.

[3] 'In the heart' denotes the manner of singing; it does not mean that Christians sang only to themselves in private. On this whole question, especially the difference between Christian and pagan music, see J. Quasten, 'Musik und Gesang in den Kulten der heidnischen Antike und christlichen Frühzeit', *LQF* 25, 1930. Perhaps such a Christian hymn is preserved for us in Phil. 2.6–11; cf. also the hymns in Revelation.

[4] So also Clement Alex., *Paedagog.* II.10.96.2.

[5] *Apol.* 39.10–18.

directly to the primitive Christian community meal held in the evening, 'The participants, before reclining, taste first of prayer to God. As much is eaten as is needed by the hungry; as much is drunk as befits the chaste. They satisfy their hunger as those who remember that even during the night they have to worship God; they talk as those who know that the Lord is one of their auditors. After manual ablution and the bringing in of lights, each is asked to stand forth and sing, as he can, a hymn to God, either one from the holy Scriptures or one of his own composing —a proof of the measure of our drinking. As the feast commenced with prayer, so with prayer it is closed.'[1]

It is worth while emphasizing that the free utterances in the spirit, in which, if possible, all present took part, clearly disappeared from the life of the early Church together with the communal meal. Once the Eucharist was separated from the agape and had been transferred to the morning (we shall very shortly examine the reasons which led to this step), we gather from Tertullian that these utterances did remain for a while associated with the agape, but they hardly appeared at all in the morning act of worship.[2] The 'prophesyings' and above all the 'speaking with tongues' seem to have ceased very soon afterwards. Is this decline of free utterance in the spirit connected with the fact that the organic unity of supper (for the satisfaction of hunger) and Eucharist, as it had been known in the first century AD, was rent asunder?[3]

Why was the Eucharist transferred to the morning in the second century? This drastic measure must have been caused by weighty reasons. The problem is not solved by the argument that in the meanwhile the Christians had so much increased in

[1] In antiquity it was customary to remain together for social intercourse and conversation after the communal evening meal (at the so-called 'symposia'); in religious circles they conversed about spiritual matters (cf. the Therapeutae). Among Christians who had yet more cause to rejoice about the sacral meal in which they had just shared and over the fellowship engendered there, this general custom inevitably developed into a quite specifically Christian occasion for thanksgiving and mutual edification.

[2] In Justin's description, I *Apol.* 67.5, only the president of the community addresses prayers and thanksgivings to heaven, 'according to his ability'.

[3] This division was, without doubt, a serious loss, for the Eucharist by itself could not take the place of the table-fellowship enjoyed at an actual meal. That is one of the problems which need to be thought out afresh today. See pp. 304ff. below.

numbers that a communal meal was no longer practicable as it had been in primitive times.[1] In the first place, Christians in earlier times did not all assemble in one place, but in small house-churches where the meal could be conducted simply,[2] and secondly they would certainly not have abandoned without serious cause the core of their communal life, the corporate eucharistic meal in the evening, which was rooted in a tradition going back to the Lord himself.[3] It must, of course, be conceded that the way was open for the transposition of the Eucharist to the morning by the fact that the two components of the community's meal (the supper for the satisfaction of hunger and the celebration of the Eucharist proper) came to be more clearly distinguished than they had originally been, and the separation of the two parts was thus made more easy.[4] Nevertheless the two parts would never have been entirely separated if there had not been some compelling reason: this separation would have been prevented not only by respect for tradition, but also by fear of destroying the organic unity of the observance.

In the letter of Pliny which we have already mentioned[5] there has been preserved a detail which lends itself to shedding some light on this situation: Christians were *forbidden* to assemble in the evening. It is stated there that the Christians had assembled a second time on Sunday in order to partake of an innocent, harmless meal. 'This (they said) they had given up doing after the issue of my edict, by which in accordance with your (i.e. the emperor's) commands I had forbidden the existence of clubs.'[6] We have already mentioned that the

[1] For this view see H. Lietzmann, *Mass and Lord's Supper*, ET 1954ff., p. 210; J. A. Jungmann, *The Mass of the Roman Rite* I, 1951, pp. 16f.; J. Kosnetter, 'Der Tag des Herrn im Neuen Testament', *Der Tag des Herrn*, 1958, p. 46.

[2] See p. 227 above.

[3] As late as Tertullian, *Cor.* 3, there is still apparent an awareness that the Lord actually instituted the Lord's Supper at the very time at which the Lord's Supper was customarily celebrated; therefore, it was not quite proper to celebrate the Eucharist in the morning as well. Cf. also Augustine, *Ep.* 55 (ad Jan.). 6.8.

[4] It is possible that certain disorders in the communities (I Cor. 11.20 ff.) may also have been a cause of this more distinct differentiation. On the whole subject see B. Reicke, *Diakonie, Festfreude und Zelos*, 1951, p. 233ff.

[5] See pp. 202ff. above.

[6] It is, of course, possible that the people who gave evidence (and who had been Christians three or even twenty years previously) did not know that

Christian assembly on Sunday evening could clearly be mistaken for similar assemblies of clubs and societies.[1] As a result, under pressure from the State, Christians had to give up their observance on Sunday evening, but because at that time they already had an observance on Sunday morning,[2] they could transfer to the morning their eucharistic celebration which they could not have possibly renounced. We find this situation in Justin (see pp. 262ff. below). In this process the supper was naturally dropped, since nobody either wanted or was able to consume a substantial meal early in the morning. Against this thesis it may, of course, be objected that Pliny's letter is valid evidence only for the province of Bithynia in Asia Minor and that we may not conclude on the basis of this evidence alone that the whole of Christendom was compelled at that time to abandon its observance on Sunday evening. Yet it is not altogether impossible that the Emperor decreed a prohibition of all clubs throughout the Eastern Empire (for they were a phenomenon common to the whole of the Greek cultural area)[3] and that all Christians were affected by it. This is, in any case, the most plausible explanation of the fact that Christians abandoned their observance on Sunday evening.[4]

The observance on Sunday evening did not, in fact, totally disappear from the Church's life. We have already noticed that the agape (i.e. a meal

---

the community had recently given up the observance on Sunday evening. Yet Pliny interrogated not only these people but also others (e.g. two deaconesses) who did not deny that they were Christians right up to that time.

[1] See pp. 203f. above.

[2] See p. 261 below.

[3] Cf. Pauly-Wissowa 16, col. 1373f.

[4] In this connection it should be noted that although Pliny was relatively tolerant, he did regard Christianity as superstition and as a kind of insubordination; and for these reasons he hated it. He himself says in his letter that his action (prohibition of clubs and then, especially, the trials of Christians) had had a great deterrent effect. Previously the contagion of Christianity had infected people of every class (even Roman citizens) in every town and village, the temples had been deserted and even sacrifice had been discontinued; now, by contrast, the temples were once again frequented and sacrifice was being offered. We can explain this changed state of affairs only by supposing that many people were afraid of being accused as Christians and wanted for this reason to demonstrate that they were good pagans. So also L. C. Mohlberg, *Rivista di archeologia cristiana* 14, 1937, p. 95. We can better understand the steps taken by convinced Christians to assemble in the future only in the morning (and then also at peril of death) if we see these steps against the background of this campaign against Christianity.

for the satisfaction of hunger with a strong stress on mutual love) continued
to be held; the agape was, however, normally arranged at private instigation
for the feeding of the needy.[1] Clearly it was, therefore (once again?), possible
for the meetings of Christians to be held in the evening. These observances,
however, were not confined to Sunday, nor had they any eucharistic
character.[2] We must regard as exceptions the small groups in North Africa
reported by Cyprian[3] (they celebrated the Eucharist in the evening in
association with a meal) and also the occasional eucharistic celebration on
Saturday evening or on Maundy Thursday evening.[4] The Easter vigil was
also in some sense an exception: after a 'night of watching' and fasting a full
meal was consumed and the Eucharist celebrated early on the Sunday
morning. In this instance the primitive unity of meal and Eucharist was
preserved, but in other respects the Easter observance did not in any way
resemble the observance on Sunday evening. It did, in fact, have some effect
on the origin of the observance on Sunday morning, as we shall see.

2. THE OBSERVANCE ON SUNDAY MORNING

Pliny's letter which we have mentioned several times[5] gives
us information about the observance on Sunday morning
existing *before* the Eucharist was transferred from the evening
to the morning. The observance on Sunday morning does not,
therefore, originate from the time when the Eucharist began to
be celebrated in the morning. From Pliny's letter we also learn
—and this makes its evidence particularly valuable—the content
of this morning observance at a time when the evening observance was still regularly being held. In any inquiry into the

---

[1] We have already quoted Tertullian, *Apol.* 39.16–19. The descriptions
in the *Apostolic Tradition* of Hippolytus are well known (25, Ethiopic version
and 26ff., Botte pp. 64ff. [Easton (p. 102, n. 5), pp. 58f., 50f.; Dix, pp. 50ff.,
45ff.]). On the whole subject see B. Reicke, *Diakonie, Festfreude und Zelos*,
1951. H. Veil in his edition of the *Apologies* of Justin, 1894, p. 108, is right in
regarding I *Apol.* 67.1 as a description of an agape, 'The wealthy among us
help the needy; and we always keep together; and for all things wherewith
we are supplied, we bless the Maker of all through his Son Jesus Christ, and
through the Holy Ghost.' Cf. Acts of Peter 29.
[2] In the agape we can see some sort of continuation of the daily *diakonia*
practised in the primitive community (cf. Acts 6.1ff.); as a result the agape
naturally resembled its Jewish model more strongly than did the eucharistic
celebration on Sunday evening.
[3] *Ep.* 63.16.
[4] For the former see pp. 148ff. above, for the latter see Augustine, *Ep.* 55
(ad Jan.). 7.9. On the further history of the evening Mass see F. Zimmermann, *Die Abendmesse in Geschichte und Gegenwart*, 1914.
[5] See pp. 107, 202ff., 251ff. above.

origin of the observance on Sunday morning we have first to look at what is said about it in Pliny's letter, where it is described for the first time: we can then try to work backwards and make conclusions about its origin. We shall reproduce in translation the relevant passage from Pliny's letter:[1] 'They (i.e. the *lapsi*, the apostate Christians) affirmed, however, the whole of their guilt, or their error, was, that they were in the habit of meeting on a certain fixed day (*stato die*) before it was light, when they sang in alternate verses a hymn to Christ, as to a god (*carmen Christo quasi deo dicere secum invicem*), and bound themselves by a solemn oath (*sacramentum*), not to any wicked deeds, but never to commit any fraud, theft or adultery, never to falsify their word, nor deny a trust when they should be called upon to deliver it up; after which it was their custom to separate . . .' We have no serious grounds for mistrusting on principle this detailed information, for Pliny had occasion at the numerous judicial hearings of Christians to gather precise information. Moreover, he was anxious to learn what exactly the Christians did at their assemblies, as an anonymous accusation had been laid against them: not only had many of them been accused by name; in the accusation the Christian assemblies had probably been specifically defamed. One can observe quite plainly in Pliny's report to the Emperor that in the judicial proceedings the Christians had to defend themselves with regard to these assemblies: they stress that in the morning gathering they had not pledged themselves to any crime (as the accusation obviously asserted) and that their evening gathering had consisted in a harmless, innocent meal and not in a club feast.[2] Nevertheless this information in Pliny's letter is certainly both one-sided and incomplete, for Pliny did not want to be informed about the Christian liturgy in its own proper context: he was much more concerned to gain information about matters which were open to suspicion with regard to the Christian gatherings.[3]

[1] X.96 (97).7.
[2] On this point see pp. 203f. above. Pliny subsequently wanted to ascertain whether the *lapsi* were telling the truth and were not concealing some 'crime' or other: to this end he had two deaconesses tortured, but he did not gain from them any different information.
[3] This is stressed by H. Lietzmann, 'Die liturgischen Angaben des Pliniusbriefes', *Geschichtliche Studien für A. Hauck zum 70. Geburtstage*, 1916, pp. 34–38.

The principal difficulty in the interpretation of this passage is the fact that the details contained in Pliny's letter (in so far as they concern the observance on Sunday morning, not that on Sunday evening) are completely without any parallel. Neither before nor after do we find any evidence which tells us about a morning observance which had precisely this form. This means that the details in Pliny's letter are open to several possible interpretations. No one seriously argues that the designation 'on a fixed day' (*stato die*) does not refer to the weekly Sunday:[1] the Christians did, therefore, gather for their observance before dawn on Sunday morning.[2] The content of the observance as it is described in Pliny's letter has, however, given rise to differences of opinion, particularly with regard to the exact meaning of the two expressions '*sacramentum*' and '*carmen*'.

1. H. Lietzmann[3] has proposed the theory that '*sacramentum*' here means the *baptismal vow*. His interpretation has something attractive about it, for it appears that a vow was in all probability associated with the baptismal service. The evidence of the

[1] Cf. L. C. Mohlberg, 'Carmen Christo quasi deo', *Rivista di archeologia cristiana* 14, 1937, pp. 100f., and pp. 202f., n. 5, above. We can be certain of the frequent repetition of the occasion because of the expressions '*soliti essent*' and '*morem fuisse*'. It can hardly be held that Christians—perhaps out of fear of betraying the brethren—had not called Sunday by its name. In any case, they would not have been able to conceal it before Pliny, who had the means of torture at his disposal. The fact that Pliny does not name the day more precisely is an indication that he was familiar with no special name for this day, in other words that the seven-day planetary week and its 'Sunday' were not yet known. Clearly the observance of the seven-day week was still in Pliny's time customary only in Jewish and Christian circles (see pp. 35ff. above, and p. 285 below). This also is perhaps a reason why Pliny would not have been able to reproduce with complete accuracy the evidence which he heard from Christians; see the discussion in the following pages.

[2] There is nothing in itself surprising in the early hour of this observance; the Jews also held their service of prayer before dawn. We have, moreover, already said that no other time would have been possible for Christians; Sunday was for them, as for everyone else, a working day (see pp. 154ff. above). Besides, it was better for them to assemble under cover of night.

[3] In the article quoted above, p. 254, n. 3. F. Hanslik, 'Beiträge zur Geschichte des Urchristentums', *Jahrbuch der österr. Leogesellschaft*, 1933, pp. 29–70, and A. Kurfess, *ZNW* 35, 1936, pp. 295ff., have also followed him, and originally, too, F. J. Dölger, *Die Sonne der Gerechtigkeit und der Schwarze*, 1918, p. 117. (In *Sol salutis*, 1925², pp. 103ff., Dölger's comments have become so cautious and circumspect that it is impossible to be certain which point of view he holds.)

Didache, which probably dates from the first century,[1] tells us that before the baptism (7.1)[2] the way of life and the way of death (ch. 1–6) were put before the candidate: this was a parenetic collection of illustrations which closely follows the commandments in the second table of the decalogue; the candidate had to promise to live in accordance with these principles.[3] On the other hand, we cannot help noticing the relationship between the details of the vow which are mentioned in Pliny's letter, the decalogue and 'the way of life and the way of death': Christians shall commit no theft, no adultery, no breach of confidence.

It is not beyond the bounds of possibility that in Rom. 13.8–14 (cf. II Cor. 4.6) Paul is alluding to something similar. He mentions that the command to love one's neighbour includes all other separate commandments like 'You shall not commit adultery, You shall not kill, You shall not steal, You shall not covet'. In the passage which immediately follows he employs a strange symbolism: Christians should fulfil all these commandments as people who knew that the time had come to awake from sleep (salvation was nearer than when they believed=were baptized); because the night was far spent, the faithful should put off the works of darkness and put on the armour of light. The notions of night and darkness, baptism and commandments, seem to be compressed here into a single complex of ideas. Is this accidental, or is liturgical practice reflected here?[4]

---

[1] Cf. A. Adam, *ZKG* 68, 1957, pp. 1–47; J.-P. Audet, *La didaché. Instructions des Apôtres*, 1958; P. Nautin, *RHR* 155, 1959, p. 192.

[2] The phrase 'after first explaining all these points' is indeed regarded by J.-P. Audet (n. 1), p. 232, as an interpolation by H (=Constantinopolitan text and Georgian version).

[3] Parallel to Pliny's letter we find Aristides, *Apol.* 15.4. Cf. Justin, I *Apol.* 61.2; Tertullian, *Cor.* 3; *Spect.* 4; II *Clem.* 6. Of course, it is not said whether this promise was said immediately before the baptism or some little time beforehand (in connection with a 'catechetical instruction'). On the assumption that in Pliny's letter we do have a reference to baptismal practice, the evidence of this letter favours the view that the vow immediately preceded the baptism or was, in any case, renewed at the very moment of baptism. In the very earliest times there was no lengthy instruction before baptism. The connection between Christian baptism and Jewish proselyte baptism should also be taken into consideration; in the latter the obligation to keep the law was the most important element. See also what is said on pp. 265f. below. It can even be supposed that the name '*sacramentum*', which originally was applied only to the baptismal vow, later became a name for the whole baptismal action, *pars pro toto*. H. von Soden, *ZNW* 12, 1911, pp. 210ff., convincingly advances this view.

[4] Exactly the same observations may be made with regard to Eph. 4.20–5.14.

There is only one difficulty in Lietzmann's interpretation of the '*sacramentum*'; we should have to assume that baptism was administered weekly on Sunday morning. Lietzmann[1] himself has replied to this objection. He says that in this one instance Pliny did not reproduce with entire accuracy the Christians' statements that they had assembled for baptism on *every* Sunday: it is more probable that they had assembled only when candidates for baptism were available. One certainly cannot dismiss the possibility that at this time baptism was administered in the early hours, particularly on Sundays before dawn, just as it was administered on Easter morning after cockcrow, i.e. early in the morning.[2] Lietzmann's rejoinder must, nevertheless, be modified, for Lietzmann leaves unexplained why the community as a *whole* assembled for the services on Sunday morning (and

[1] (P. 254, n. 3), p. 37; cf. R. Hanslik (p. 255, n. 3), p. 70.

[2] Cf. *Acta Pauli* (Pap. Heidelberg p. 3; *NT Apoc.* II, p. 371): Artemilla is baptized before dawn on Sunday; also Ps.-Clem. *Recogn.* X.72: the community fasts before Peter baptizes Faustinian on Sunday. We shall see on p. 262 that, according to the evidence of Justin, I *Apol.* 61 and 65, the baptismal liturgy took place on Sundays. Another important argument in support of the thesis that Sunday was the day for baptism is the fact that even in early times the designation the 'eighth day' occurred for Sunday and this title stands in the closest possible connection with baptism (see pp. 275 ff. below). This name would not have been given to Sunday if baptism, for preference, had not taken place on the weekly Sunday. It would clearly be simplest if we were able to prove the existence of a pre-Christian baptismal rite associated with Sunday; this would help us to explain how the custom of baptizing on Sunday originated in the Christian Church. In connection with Mandaism (see pp. 190f. above) we have already noticed that about the time of Christian origins there was a fully developed baptismal movement in the area of Transjordan and Syria. In this case, however, ritual washings were either undertaken daily or were, in any case, not restricted to Sunday; the restriction of baptism to Sunday first occurs in post-Christian Mandaean texts. So long as we have no knowledge of a pre-Christian baptismal rite prescribed for Sunday, we must assume that the Christian administration of baptism on Sunday developed as a result of the custom of administering Christian baptism on Easter Sunday morning. We have, therefore, to consider the possibility that the last part of the Easter vigil, which consisted of baptism and prayer, was also celebrated on ordinary Sundays. It is perfectly understandable that there was a tendency in Christendom not to administer baptism on any day or at any time; there was a preference for an appointed day and a desire to approximate in this respect to the most worthy and proper time of all for Christian baptism (Easter Sunday morning). Thus the custom arose of baptizing throughout the year, as often as was necessary, on Sunday morning. The regular community meal had already long been customary on Sunday evening, and this custom may also have had its influence on the time for baptism: apart from the Lord's Supper, baptism was the most important liturgical act, and so its

this is presupposed by Pliny's letter). Normally only the baptizer, the baptizand and a few witnesses would assemble for a baptism.[1] We shall try to resolve this difficulty, particularly by giving a different interpretation to the *'carmen'* from that provided by Lietzmann.

Other interpretations of the expression *sacramentum* do not carry the same conviction. In the first place one might think of the Eucharist,[2] but so far as we know a vow was not associated with the Eucharist.[3] *Did.* 14.1f. (cf. 4.14) can, of course, be cited in support of this view:[4] this is the passage which mentions the confession of sins by the community before the breaking of bread. We have no evidence, however, that in this confession of sin any part was played by an obligation under oath to observe commandments similar to those in the decalogue. Moreover, the internal evidence of Pliny's letter tells against regarding the *sacramentum* as an allusion to the Eucharist. We have already noted that the Christians assembled once again on Sunday evening in order to have a meal, and everything points to the fact that *this* refers to the Eucharist.[5]—With greater justification one might suppose that Christians were in the habit of pledging themselves to observe the commandments of the decalogue at a morning service quite unconnected with the Eucharist. We have already seen that the decalogue played a not unimportant part in their life,[6] but, of course, we hear nothing about liturgical use of the decalogue. C. J. Kraemer[7] argues much too rigidly when he maintains that the decalogue was recited by Christians and from this draws the conclusion that the Christians celebrated nothing else but the Jewish morning liturgy.[8] A *sacramentum* (and that is more than merely a recitation) was not,

---

performance came to take place on Sunday morning. We have endeavoured to make it appear probable that in very early times Easter also was celebrated in the night from Saturday to Sunday; see W. Rordorf, 'Zum Ursprung des Osterfestes am Sonntag', *TZ* 18, 1962, pp. 169–87.

[1] See also pp. 265 f. Later the candidates were always baptized apart in the baptistery, and it was only after the baptism that they were led to the faithful; cf., e.g., *Testamentum domini nostri Jesu Christi* II.10. This usage was probably connected with the fact that the candidates were baptized naked.

[2] Cf. F. J. Dölger, *Sol Salutis*, 1925[2], p. 107; E. B. Allo, *1 Ep. aux Cor.*, 1935, p. 292; L. C. Mohlberg (p. 255, n. 1), pp. 106ff.; J. A. Jungmann, *The Mass of the Roman Rite* I, 1951, p. 18; J. Kosnetter, 'Der Tag des Herrn im Neuen Testament', *Der Tag des Herrn*, 1958, p. 45.

[3] So also H. Lietzmann (p. 254, n. 3), p. 36.

[4] Thus L. C. Mohlberg (p. 255, n. 1), pp. 108ff.; cf. J. A. Jungmann (n. 2), p.18.

[5] See pp. 203f. above.

[6] See pp. 105ff. above.

[7] 'Pliny and the Early Church Service. Fresh Light from an Old Source', *Classical Philology* 20, 1934, pp. 293–300.

[8] The recitation of the decalogue did indeed originally belong to the

in fact, associated with the Jewish morning liturgy. In this case we would not be able to understand why the Christians did not appeal to the fact that they were only observing a Jewish (and, therefore, a permitted) custom. We have to be content with Lietzmann's thesis that before baptism the candidate pledged himself in this way to a Christian manner of life. Pliny's report is, therefore, not entirely accurate, inasmuch as he asserts that the *whole* community took an oath *every* Sunday.[1]

2. What about *'carmen Christo quasi deo dicere secum invicem'*? Here, too, a variety of suggestions has been made. It is possible that psalms[2] were sung antiphonally[3] by the Christians. In this case, however, the statement that the *carmen* was sung to *Christus quasi deus* is difficult to understand.[4] The group of exegetes who interpret the *carmen* as the *Kyrie eleison*[5] seems to be nearer the mark, for the *Kyrie eleison* is directed to Christ as to a

---

Jewish morning liturgy (in the Nash Papyrus the decalogue still stands beside the *Shema*); but it is not established that the *Minim*, on account of whom the recitation of the decalogue in the daily liturgy was abandoned, were the Christians (see p. 106, n. 1, above).

[1] We should otherwise have to assume that the community renewed its baptismal vows Sunday by Sunday. This is, however, improbable, particularly if we remember that the baptismal vow was regarded as the decisive moment in the life of a Christian. Under no circumstances was one allowed to break it; if one were to do so, either one forfeited grace (Heb. 6.4ff.) or one could regain it on one occasion at the most in a 'second repentance' (cf. Hermas; Tertullian, *Paen.* 9). It was for this reason that many of the faithful postponed their baptism for as long as possible.

[2] Thus R. C. Kukula, *Kommentar zu den Pliniusbriefen*, 1916, pp. 111f.; O. Casel, *Theologische Revue* 20, 1921, p. 183, speaks of a hymn.

[3] H. Lietzmann (p. 254, n. 3), p. 35, holds that antiphonal singing of the psalms first occurred in the fourth century; he draws attention to Theodoret, *HE* II.24.8f., where it is regarded with amazement as a novelty. Singing(or singing speech) from side to side was, however, certainly a much older custom. Tertullian, who in *Apol.* 2.6 quotes the passage from Pliny, definitely understands *'carmen dicere'* in the sense of *'canere'*. Nor perhaps is Ignatius, *Eph.* 4.1, meant merely figuratively. On the whole subject see J. Quasten, 'Musik und Gesang in den Kulten der heidnischen Antike und christlichen Frühzeit', *LQF* 25, 1930: J. Kroll, *Die christliche Hymnodik bis zu Klemens von Alexandrien*, 1921; more recently R. P. Martin, *Vox Evangelica* 3, 1964, pp. 51–57.

[4] R. Hanslik (p. 255, n. 3), p. 66.

[5] W. Lockton, *JTS* 16, 1915, p. 550; F. J. Dölger, *Sol Salutis*, 1925², pp. 115 ff. (Dölger associates the formula *Kyrie eleison* with the ancient sun-cult; see the following discussion.) L. C. Mohlberg (p. 255, n. 1), pp. 120ff., elaborates this thesis and holds that there is a reference here to intercessory prayer in which the *Kyrie eleison* was said several times as a refrain. J. A. Jungmann (p. 258, n. 2), p. 18, suggests that behind the *'carmen'* we already have the *Sursum Corda* and *Sanctus*. J. Quasten, *RAC* 2, col. 905ff., summarizes the various views.

god; it could, moreover, be misunderstood by pagans as a *malum carmen*, i.e. as a magical invocation.[1] Yet one would like to understand by the *carmen* a formula with more substantial content than the *Kyrie eleison*, perhaps a confession of faith in Christ.

H. Lietzmann[2] suggested that we should think in terms of the baptismal creed which was couched in the form of question and answer. It is beyond dispute that in connection with the ceremony of baptism there was also an acceptance of the baptismal creed which probably took the form of question and answer.[3] But it is difficult to understand the *carmen* as a reference to the baptismal creed, since it is clearly presupposed that *everyone* (not only baptizer and baptizand) join in saying (or singing) the *carmen* by turns.

The fact that Christians recited a *carmen* may in any case make us think of the influence of the Jewish morning liturgy[4] which was held daily in the synagogue before sunrise. In this liturgy *Shema* and *tephillah* embellished with acts of praise were prayed in the form of versicles and responses.[5] The Christians, of course, took over only the liturgical setting; the content would have been fundamentally altered (*Christo quasi deo*). We could, however, with equal justification think of an influence deriving from the practice of morning prayer addressed to the sun (or to the sun-god): this, we know, was widespread in the ancient world;[6] it was already reinterpreted by Jews[7] and later by

---

[1] The reproach of *mala carmina* (=magical formulae) probably played a not inconsiderable part in the trials of Christians. H. Lietzmann (p. 254, n. 3) emphasized this point. H. von Soden, *ZNW* 12, 1911, pp. 224ff., observes that the oriental cults seemed particularly suspect to the Romans principally because of their (initiatory) sacrament (which seemed like a rival oath of loyalty) and because of their *mala carmina*.

[2] See p. 254, n. 3.

[3] Cf. F. J. Dölger, 'Die Eingliederung des Taufsymbols in den Taufvollzug nach den Schriften Tertullians', *AuC* 4, 1934, pp. 138–46; O. Cullmann, *The Earliest Christian Confessions*, 1949, pp. 19ff.

[4] By this means we should be better able than Lietzmann (p. 254, n. 3) to explain why there were present at the morning service described in Pliny's letter not only the people immediately concerned with the baptism, but also the other members of the community; baptism was, in fact, not the only purpose of the assembly, but, as on every morning, a service of prayer was held.

[5] Cf. J. Elbogen, *Studien zur Geschichte des jüdischen Gottesdienstes*, 1907.

[6] See pp. 181f. above.

[7] We cannot help noticing how strong is the note of praise to the first ray of sunlight in the first benediction of the *Shema* which had to be recited at sunrise (text in Dölger, *Sol Salutis*, 1925², p. 121); it is clear that the custom of morning prayer (which was originally a pagan custom) has influenced the Jewish morning liturgy.

Christians.[1] In favour of this supposition is the time of the recitation of the *carmen* (before daybreak) and especially the Christians' custom of praying towards the east, for which there is very early evidence.[2]

In this case we should have to trace the origin of the abundant symbolism which Christians soon derived from the equation 'Christ=Sun'. This symbolism developed very richly as soon as there was the 'sun's day' in the planetary week. Its origin, must, however, be very old, since the eschatological hope was associated with it: the parousia was expected from the direction of the rising sun (i.e. the East).[3]

In summing up we shall very cautiously attempt to reconstruct the earliest history of the observance on Sunday morning. A Christian service of prayer was originally held daily:[4] we can discover traces of it in the recitation of the *carmen* for which evidence is to be found in Pliny's letter. This daily service was expanded on the day of the resurrection, and there developed the practice of administering baptism at this time on Sunday if candidates were present.

Pliny's letter describes for us the observance on Sunday morning at this stage of its development. The report of the Roman governor is, of course, to this extent misleading in that he seems to suggest that baptism was administered on *every* Sunday and that the *whole* community pledged itself with an oath to lead a pure life in accordance with the commandments. As we have seen, we may correct this erroneous impression in the following way: the *whole* community did, in fact, assemble on *every* Sunday to recite the *carmen*, but the *sacramentum* i.e. the baptismal vow (if Lietzmann's conjecture is correct) was said only on the Sundays on which candidates for baptism were received into the community.

[1] The position of H. Usener is obviously similar; his view is given by H. Lietzmann, *Mass and Lord's Supper*, ET 1954ff., p. 211, n. 2.

[2] There is copious material in F. J. Dolger (p. 259, n. 5), pp. 136ff. On p. 198 he summarizes his conclusions (in spaced type), 'The Gentile Christians with their custom of praying towards the East have simply retained a habit derived from their pagan past; but they have given to this custom a new content and so detached it from its pagan associations.' See also pp. 289f. below.

[3] See p. 290 below. The geographically orientated hope of the Parousia did indeed have another interesting feature in connection with the typology of passover and baptism. The passage through the Red Sea took place from west to east; Egypt (the west), therefore, came to be the embodiment of wickedness, and the promised land in the east (cf. the hope of paradise) became the symbol of everything for which they longed.

[4] On this service of prayer see pp. 267ff. below.

In the course of the second century the celebration of the
Eucharist became associated with this service of prayer and
baptism: we have already discussed the reasons for this development.[1] The Eucharist soon became the most important part of
the act of worship on Sunday morning.

It is just this situation which we find in the middle of the
second century in Justin: in his *First Apology* addressed to the
Emperor Antoninus Pius he gives us the first detailed description
of Christian worship. His description of the act of worship on
Sunday morning,[2] however, is immediately preceded, in ch. 65
(cf. ch. 61),[3] by an account of the Christian baptismal service.

He does not indeed give the time of the baptismal service, but we cannot
help noticing that in 65.1 he says, 'After we have thus washed the one who
has been convinced and has assented to our teaching, we bring him to
those who are called brethren, to the place where they are assembled.' It is
clear that the brethren are assembled before the newly baptized joins them:
the baptism therefore took place at a time when the community was in any
case assembled for worship. This conclusion is confirmed by the passage
which follows: as soon as the newly baptized has joined the assembled
community, prayer is offered; then the faithful greet one another with the
holy kiss and the Lord's Supper begins. At this stage we should now consider
ch. 67, where the liturgy on Sunday morning is discussed. After Justin had
described the reading from scripture and the sermon, he continues (67.5):
'Then we all rise together and offer prayers, and, *as we said before*, when we
have finished praying, bread and wine and water are brought.' We are now
driven to ask whether we are not, in fact, dealing with the same liturgy on
these two occasions and whether, on the occasions when baptism was
administered, it, too, was not administered on Sunday morning. If this were
the case, Justin would have separated baptism from the liturgy on Sunday
morning only on account of the plan of his work[4] and, in so doing, he would
have given the impression that he was dealing with two quite different
observances. He does, in fact, subsequently (in ch. 67) emphasize their unity
by referring back to ch. 65. We are, therefore, justified in using not only
ch. 67, but also ch. 65 of Justin's *First Apology* as a source for information

[1] See pp. 250ff. above.
[2] I *Apol.* 67.3–6.
[3] Ch. 62–64 are insertions in which Justin refers to the 'diabolical
mimicries' of baptism in the mystery religions.
[4] In the first place he wanted to explain to the emperor the two sacraments of baptism and the Lord's Supper (ch. 66). We also find an explanation of these two sacraments in the *Mystagogical Catecheses* of Cyril of
Jerusalem.

about the Sunday morning liturgy.[1] It must, of course, be added that in Justin's time, too, the baptismal liturgy did not take place on every Sunday.[2]

We shall give the whole of ch. 65 and 67.3–6 in translation, and we shall then examine in detail the main points in the description of this observance.

(65.1) 'But after we have thus washed the one who has been convinced and has assented to our teaching, we bring him to those who are called brethren, to the place where they are assembled, in order that we may earnestly offer prayers in common for ourselves and for the baptized (illuminated) person, and for all others in every place, that we may be counted worthy, now that we have learned the truth, by our works also to be found good citizens[3] and keepers of the commandments, so that we may be saved with an everlasting salvation. (2) When we have finished praying, we greet one another with a kiss. (3) There is then brought to the president of the brethren bread and a cup of water and a cup of wine mixed with water; and he, taking them, gives praise and glory to the Father of the universe, through the name of the Son and of the Holy Ghost, and offers thanks at considerable length for our being worthy to receive these (gifts) at his hands. When he has finished the prayers and the thanksgiving, all the people present express their assent by saying "Amen". (4) This word "Amen" means in the Hebrew language "So be it". (5) And when the president has given thanks, and all the people have expressed their assent, those whom we call deacons give to each of those present a share of the bread, wine and water over which the thanksgiving was pronounced, and they take away a portion to those who are absent.

(67.3) 'And on the day called Sunday, all who live in cities or in the country gather together in one place, and the memoirs of the apostles or the writings of the prophets are read, as long as time permits. (4) Then, when the reader has finished, the president delivers a discourse instructing us and exhorting us to the imitation of these noble [words]. (5) Then we all rise together and offer prayers, and, as we said before, when we have finished

---

[1] As is done by H. Veil in his edition of Justin's Apologies, 1894, p. 96.
[2] Such numbers of candidates for baptism were not available; in 65.1 only one candidate is presupposed.
[3] πολιτευταί. Perhaps the word should be understood here as simply denoting the members of the community (cf. Phil. 3.20).

praying, bread and wine and water are brought, and the president in like manner offers prayers and thanksgivings, according to his ability, and the people assent, saying "Amen"; then takes place the distribution of that over which thanks have been given and participation by each one, and to those who are absent a portion is sent by means of the deacons. (6) And those who are well-to-do, and who so wish, give as much as each one chooses to; and what is collected is deposited with the president, who succours the orphans and widows, and those who, through sickness or any other cause, are in want, and those who are in bonds, and the strangers sojourning among us, and in a word takes care of all who are in need.'

First of all, something must be said about the time of this observance. It is normally thought to be self-evident that this morning liturgy took place in broad daylight, perhaps about nine o'clock, like our services: this is extremely improbable for the following reasons: (1) This view is supported by no evidence from the text. (2) We have already emphasized on several occasions that Christians had to work on Sunday and that they could, therefore, only assemble either early in the morning or in the evening.[1] (3) There is in the text itself an unmistakable indication that even in Justin's time Christians still assembled for worship before dawn: we read 'so long as time allows' (they did not have limitless time for their worship, but only until they had to go to work). (4) If baptism also really was administered on Sunday morning, we have to think in terms of the continuing baptismal practice as we find it both before and after Justin: baptism used to take place in the early morning, at cockcrow, that is to say, before dawn. (5) Even Tertullian[2] reports only 'nocturnal' assemblies, i.e. 'gatherings before daybreak'. We have, therefore, every ground for assuming that the whole

---

[1] See pp. 154ff., 255, n. 2, above.

[2] *Ad uxorem* II.4 (with reference to Easter night); *Cor.* 3, 'We take also, in meetings before daybreak . . ., the sacrament of the Eucharist, which the Lord both commanded to be eaten at mealtimes, and enjoined to be taken by all.' Too much stress should not be laid on the '*etiam*' in this passage, as if at the time of Tertullian the evening celebration of the Eucharist still continued to exist side by side with the agape. In fact, we know nothing at all about this and we could not even explain why this celebration of the Eucharist should have disappeared; this is particularly strange if there was still a living awareness that Jesus had instituted the meal in the evening. Cf. J. Schümmer, 'Die altchristliche Fastenpraxis', *LQF* 27, 1933, pp. 109ff.

liturgy, as it is described by Justin, took place in the early hours of Sunday morning *before daybreak*.

We can now consider the several parts of the liturgy described by Justin.

(*a*) *The baptism*.[1] It took place only if candidates were present. There does not seem to have been any special catechumenate: it is, at any rate, not mentioned by Justin.[2] He refers only to the immediate preparation for baptism (ch. 61). This consisted in fasting and prayer (=supplication for the forgiveness of sins), and several members of the community fasted and prayed with the candidates;[3] this preparation will have extended over one or, at the most, two days.[4] After the candidates had kept vigil through the last night (note the exact parallel with Easter night), they were baptized early on the Sunday morning: they were immersed three times in running water (if possible),[5] and at the same time the three holy names were invoked over them.[6] We must conclude that at this ceremony the candidates also pledged themselves to follow the

[1] Cf. A. Benoit, *Le baptême chrétien au second siècle*, 1953, pp. 138ff.

[2] It would seem that the baptismal promise was made some time beforehand; cf. Tertullian, *Cor*. 3. In this passage it consisted of a 'renunciation of the devil' which was then repeated at the baptism. See p. 256, n. 3 above. I am preparing a study on the whole question of the baptismal catechesis. Cf. the last monograph on the subject, A. Turck, *Évangélisation et catéchèse aux deux premiers siècles*, 1962.

[3] We can see here the origins of the institution of godparents; on this subject see M. Dujarier, *Le parrainage des adultes aux trois premiers siècles de l'Église*, 1962.

[4] See *Did*. 7.4. Tertullian, *Bapt*. 20, is not to be interpreted in a different sense. Further passages in J. Schümmer (p. 264, n. 2), pp. 164ff.

[5] *Did*. 7.1; cf. Acts 8.38. Hippolytus, *Trad. Apost*. 21 (Botte, p. 44; Easton [p. 102, n. 5], p. 45; Dix, p. 33), also *Acta Pauli* (*NT Apoc*. II, p. 389: baptism of the lion); *Acta Thom*. 121. Further passages in the Pseudo-Clementine literature: *Contest*. 1; *Hom*. XI.35=*Recogn*. VI.15; XIV.1=*Recogn*. VII.38. On the whole subject see T. Klauser, ' "Taufet in lebendigem Wasser!" Zum religions- und kulturgeschichtlichen Verständnis von Didache 7.1–3', *Pisciculi: Festschrift für F. J. Dölger*, 1939.

[6] According to Tertullian, *Cor*. 3, 'making a somewhat ampler pledge'. We cannot discuss here the baptismal action in detail. See the compendious studies by A. Stenzel, *Die Taufe*, 1958, and G. Kretschmar, *Die Geschichte des Taufgottesdienstes in der alten Kirche* (Leiturgia 5.1ff.), 1964ff. From an early time the creed, of course, also played an important role; see the studies on the creed by H. Lietzmann in *ZNW* (now the third volume of his *Kleine Schriften* in TU 74, 1962), and J. N. D. Kelly, *Early Christian Creeds*, 1960[2]. On chrismation and the laying on of hands see G. W. H. Lampe, *The Seal of the Spirit*, 1967[2]. On the problem of infant baptism see O. Cullmann, *Baptism in the New Testament*, ET 1950; J. Jeremias, *Infant Baptism in the First*

'way of life', to lead their lives after the precept of the Gospel, just as we learnt about it in Pliny's letter. It should prove interesting to compare this custom with that of the 'acceptance of Christ' and of the related 'renunciation of the devil' which is mentioned as early as Tertullian.[1] In this latter ceremony (which developed on Gentile-Christian territory) we may perhaps have something similar to the renunciation of the way of death and the acceptance of the way of life.[2] After the baptism the new members of the community were led to the gathering of the faithful,[3] where the liturgy proceeded.

(b) *The sermon.* It is mentioned by Justin only in ch. 67. The baptismal service which he describes in ch. 65 immediately passes into the anaphora of the liturgy. (See (c) and (d) below.) Does this suggest that this part of the liturgy was shortened on the Sundays on which baptism took place?[4] The service of the word consisted in the reading aloud by a lector of pericopes from the Gospels[5] or from the Old Testament prophets and in an expository sermon which followed these readings and was delivered by the president.[6] The sermon took the place of the preaching of the apostles: the written word had now acquired

---

Four Centuries, ET 1960; K. Aland, *Did the Early Church Baptize Infants?* ET 1961, also J. Jeremias, *The Origins of Infant Baptism,* ET 1963, and A. Strobel, *Säuglings- und Kindertaufe in der ältesten Kirche: Begründung und Gebrauch der heiligen Taufe,* 1963.

[1] *Cor.* 3; *Spect.* 4. But see Justin, I *Apol.* 14.1; 49.5; also Hippolytus, *Trad. Apost.* 121; *Testamentum domini nostri Jesu Christi* II.8; *Const. Apost.* III.18.1; VII.40f.; Jerome, *In Amos* III (on.6.14, PL 25.1068). On the whole subject see F. J. Dölger, *Die Sonne der Gerechtigkeit und der Schwarze,* 1918; H. Kirsten, *Die Taufabsage,* 1960.

[2] C. F. D. Moule, *Worship in the New Testament,* 1961, p. 52, holds that the discarding of the old man (=undressing) was connected with this action.

[3] Cf. Tertullian, *Bapt.* 20. See also p. 258, n. 1 above.

[4] This is the view of H. Veil in his edition of Justin's *Apologies,* 1894, p. 96. Tertullian, *Apol.* 39.3, seems to imply that the sermon did not necessarily belong to the Sunday morning liturgy, 'We come together for the consideration of the divine scriptures, if the circumstances of the present moment provide cause for exhortation or recollection.'

[5] The letters of the apostles will, of course, have come into this category, at least in the churches which possessed these letters. As we have seen (p. 248, n. 4, above), the reading of letters formed part of the oldest evening observances. Moreover, we find elsewhere the division of the whole scripture into 'Prophets' and 'Gospel' (which included the epistles). See Friedrich, *TWNT* II, p. 734.

[6] Such a sermon is preserved for us in the so-called *Second Epistle of Clement,* according to 19.1. Cf. also I Tim. 4.13; Acts of Peter 30.1.

greater importance than the spoken word. Since the sermon probably had a firm place in the evening meal of the community,[1] it could be transferred to the morning, together with the celebration of the Eucharist.

There can be no doubt that the pattern of the synagogue service played an important part in the development of *this* part of the liturgy.[2] The weekly reading from the Old Testament scriptures and their exposition were taken over from the Jews: this may also be seen in the liberal use of the Septuagint by the New Testament writers. The reading and exposition of the New Testament scriptures soon joined that of the Old Testament. Christianity was becoming more and more a religion of the written word, and the Christian prophets became scribes:[3] if a person wanted guidance for the present and the future, he was directed with increasing frequency to the holy scriptures and to their reliable interpretation.

(*c*) *The prayer*. Standing with arms outstretched was the characteristic position for prayer on Sunday.[4] On weekdays (especially on Wednesday and Friday) kneeling was the posture for prayer,[5] but this was forbidden on Sunday. We often come across this rule, even in the decisions of councils.[6] Standing for prayer is doubtless associated with the thought of the resurrection.[7] Sunday was a joyous day, and 'every posture expressive of

[1] See pp. 247f. above.
[2] See H. Lietzmann, *Mass and Lord's Supper*, ET 1954ff., p. 211; A. Baumstark, *Vom geschichtlichen Werden der Liturgie*, 1923, pp. 15ff. Cf. also Acts 13.27; 15.21.
[3] We have to suppose that by the time of Justin the core of the New Testament Canon was already in existence; moreover, the president or office-bearer, who in his capacity as preacher is in some ways the successor of the apostles, seems already to occupy a special position.
[4] Tertullian, *Bapt.* 20; cf. I Tim. 2.8.
[5] Tertullian, *Orat.* 23. Jesus himself had taught (Matt. 6.5f.) that one should not stand in public to pray, but should go into one's chamber and shut the doors. We have to assume that kneeling was the normal position for Christians' private prayer.
[6] Ps.-Justin, *Quaest. et resp. ad orthod.* 115 (PG 7.2.1233), speaks of this as an apostolic custom and refers to the *De pascha* of Irenaeus, a treatise which is unfortunately lost. *Acta Pauli* (Pap. Heidelberg p. 1, *NT Apoc.* II, p. 370) (for Pentecost); Tertullian, *Cor.* 3; *Orat.* 23; Epiphanius, *Expos. fidei*, 22.8f.; Athanasius, *Syntagma* 2; Basil, *Spir. sancto* 27.64; *Const. Apost.* II.59.4; Council of Nicaea, *Can.* 20 (Mansi II, p. 677); *Testamentum domini nostri Jesu Christi* II.12.
[7] Christ 'rose' from the dead at Easter—the congregation 'rises' for prayer on Sunday; in both cases ἀνίστασθαι is used. So *Quaest. et resp. ad orthod.* 115; *Const. Apost.* VII.45.1; Augustine, *Ep.* 55 (ad Jan.). 28. We also find the idea that the standing posture is a sign of the future resurrection of the dead, Isidore of Seville, *Eccl. off.* I.24 (PL 83.760).

anxious care'[1] had to be avoided. Kneeling for prayer in the liturgy, as well as fasting, came under this heading.

Certain attitudes are, to some extent, natural attitudes for different types of prayer: this can be seen throughout the world. A penitent who is praying for forgiveness humbly gets down on to his knees before his God, or he may even in an act of submission throw himself down before him on the ground. On the other hand, the man who in his prayer is thanking God for his help and is praising his mighty rule will do this standing and will boldly look upwards. All three positions for prayer were widespread both throughout the ancient world and also among Jews and Christians in particular.[2] If Christians on Sunday prayed standing, this immediately gives us some information about the content of their prayers: they were thoroughly joyous and triumphant. On Sunday the community as a whole could come face to face with God without fear.[3] If kneeling at prayer on Sunday had later to be systematically forbidden, this could be connected with the fact that many Gentile Christians knew no other posture for prayer. They mostly came from the lower classes and had to meet their earthly lord in this submissive manner: pressure had to be put on them to pray in an upright position.

The prohibition of kneeling for prayer on Sunday is paralleled by that on fasting on Sunday: both bans were generally mentioned in the same breath.[4] Fasting was also 'a posture expressive of anxious care (Tertullian, *Orat.* 23), which was incompatible with the character of Sunday as a day of joy; for this reason it was wrong to fast on Sunday. This prohibition became all the more necessary as some heretics began deliberately to treat Sunday as a fast day.[5] On the other hand, Christians have often fasted on Saturday

---

[1] Tertullian, *Orat.* 23.

[2] Cf. H. Leclerq, *DACL* 12.2, 1936, col. 2291–322; F. Heiler,' Die Körperhaltung beim Gebet', *Orientalische Studien, F. Hommel zum 60. Geburtstag* II, 1918, pp. 168–77. It is striking that standing for prayer was normal in the sun-cult; cf. F. J. Dölger, *Sol Salutis*, 1925[2], p. 5.

[3] Tertullian, *Apol.* 39.2, in a characteristically bold figure of speech, describes how Christians like an army with serried ranks would besiege God with requests at their gatherings for prayer.

[4] Cf. Tertullian, *Orat.* 23; *Cor.* 3; Epiphanius, *Expos. fidei* 22.8f.; *Const. Apost.* V.20.19; Council of Gangra, can. 18 (Mansi II, p. 1104); *Fourth* Council of Carthage, can. 64 (Mansi III, p. 956).

[5] Eustathians, Manichees, Priscillianists; cf. T. Zahn, *Geschichte des Sonntags*, 1878, p. 64, n. 24.

(and right into the early hours of Sunday morning);[1] they would then celebrate Sunday with even greater rejoicing and gratitude.

The common prayer seems to have been devoted above all to the praise of God (and of his Son) and to intercession. The great prayer for the Church in I *Clement* 59–61, which certainly goes back well into the first century, may serve as an example. It was a characteristic of the prayer of intercession that it mentioned not only fellow Christians,[2] but all other people as well, especially rulers, and peace also was included.[3] Occasionally this prayer is also designated a 'spiritual sacrifice',[4] as by Tertullian in *Orat.* 27–28: 'The more conscientious in prayer are accustomed to append to their prayers *Alleluia* and such manner of psalms, so that those who are present may respond with the endings of them. And it is certainly an excellent custom to present, like a rich oblation, a prayer fattened with all that conduces to setting forth the dignity and honour of God. For this is the spiritual oblation which has wiped out the ancient sacrifices. . . . We are the true worshippers and the true priests, who, praying in the Spirit, in the Spirit offer a sacrifice of prayer as an oblation which is God's own and is well pleasing to him, that in fact which he has sought after, which he has provided for himself. This, devoted from the whole heart . . . it is our duty to bring to the altar of God, along with a procession of good works, to the accompaniment of psalms and hymns, as that which will obtain for us from God all that we ask for.' We have quoted this passage in full because it shows at the same time that psalms and hymns were often associated with this part of the liturgy,[5] and this must remind us of the phrase in Pliny's

[1] The whole of Christendom fasted in this way on Holy Saturday, candidates for baptism before their baptism, and finally many Christians on every Saturday. See pp. 143f. above.

[2] Cf. I Thess. 5.25; II Thess. 3.1; Rom. 15.30; Col. 4.3; Heb. 13.18, etc.

[3] Already in I Tim. 2.1f. Especially prominent in Tertullian, *Apol.* 39.2, 'We also pray for Emperors, their servants and governors, for the condition of the world, for general peace and for the postponement of the end.' Cf. also Athenagoras, *Suppl.* 37 (Goodspeed, p. 358).

[4] Cf. Heb. 13.15. Generally, however, the idea of sacrifice is applied to the eucharistic liturgy; see p. 272, n. 3, below; cf. p. 245 above.

[5] The sources do not help us to decide whether prayers of a liturgical stamp like the Lord's Prayer (cf. later *Const. Apost.* III.18.2; VII.45.1) or doxologies or blessings, which are frequently found even in the New Testament epistles, also had a fixed place either here or within the eucharistic celebration itself.

letter, 'carmen Christo quasi deo dicere secum invicem'. We have indeed discovered that the content of that carmen may well be difficult to determine, but it does seem that common prayer in the form of versicles and responses is an inheritance from the Jewish morning liturgy.[1]

It is possible that this part of the service may have been the oldest part of the Sunday morning observance, and it may have developed out of an assembly for prayer which originally met daily.[2] In the Acts of the Apostles several traces of this seem to have been preserved. Is not Acts 4.24ff. the model of Christians' gatherings for prayer? There we already find the two characteristic parts of the prayer of the community: praise (vv. 24–28) and supplication (vv. 29f.). Verse 31, however, is directly related to the event at Pentecost which is recorded in Acts 2.1ff., 'And when they had prayed, the place in which they were gathered together was shaken; and they were all filled with the Holy Spirit and spoke the word of God with boldness.' We can, therefore, suppose that there also stands behind Acts 2.1ff. the idea of an assembly for prayer in the morning, although the author of Acts used it in order to contrast the Christian with the Jewish festival of Pentecost. Moreover, the reference in Acts 1.14 that the Christians had continued in prayer with one accord (ὁμοθυμαδόν)[3] (cf. Rom. 15.6) fits in with a way of understanding prayer as a persistent entreaty to God.[4] Since, however, ὁμοθυμαδόν is mentioned in connection with the daily assembly in the temple (2.46; 4.24; 5.12), we cannot help asking whether this assembly in the temple was not a morning assembly for prayer.[5] We cannot help being struck by the fact that frequently in the New Testament sobriety and fasting are mentioned together with prayer,[6] and this also fits in best in the morning.

We have already said (pp. 26of.) that in this daily service of prayer held by the Christians we can see the continuation of the Jewish tradition of holding a daily service of common prayer in the morning: this Jewish custom,

---

[1] See p. 26of. above.

[2] See p. 261 above.

[3] It is not quite correct to translate this merely with 'in corpore', as does B. Reicke, Glaube und Leben der Urgemeinde (AThANT 32), 1957, pp. 21, 61f. We must, however, concede that the word does not denote a unity of emotions. It could denote a praying community which in serried ranks presses on God.

[4] Cf. the parable of the unjust judge, Luke 18.1ff.; Matt. 18.19f.

[5] Cf. Acts 5.21; Luke 24.53; also the evidence of Hegesippus (Eusebius, HE II.23.6) that James prayed standing in the temple; also Mark 11.17 par.

[6] Mark 9.29; Luke 2.37; Acts 13.2f.; I Peter 4.7; 5.8, etc. Cf. H. Strathmann, Geschichte der frühchristlichen Askese bis zur Entstehung des Mönchtums I, 1914. Because the eucharistic celebration was connected with this morning liturgy, there developed the requirement of fasting communion. (On station days the Eucharist was celebrated in the afternoon.) Cf. E. Dekkers, 'La messe du soir à la fin de l'antiquité', Sacris erudiri 7, 1955, pp. 99–130.

moreover, corresponded with a general custom in the ancient world of praying in the morning (to the sun). The subsequent development took place in the manner which we have described: Christians began to baptize on Sunday morning by analogy with Easter morning: thus the assembly for prayer on Sunday morning acquired a special importance (see Pliny's letter) even before the celebration of the Eucharist was transferred to Sunday morning.

(*d*) *The Eucharist*.[1] We have already repeatedly maintained that the Eucharist was originally celebrated in the evening in connection with a meal and that it was transferred to the morning only in the second century (the evidence makes sense for us in this way): in the course of this process the meal and the spiritual conversation which followed it dropped out.[2] The preparation for the reception of communion (i.e. confession of sins and penitence) was very probably taken over into the morning celebration. The kiss of peace between the brethren at the beginning of the Eucharist proper certainly has no meaning if it had not been preceded by an act of reconciliation.[3]

The liturgy of the eucharistic celebration in Justin exactly resembles the one which we find in *Did.* 9–10: first, bread and wine were brought,[4] the president said prayers of thanksgiving over them, the congregation answered 'Amen'.[5]

It is difficult to reconstruct the content of the prayers. The praise addressed to the Father could have already taken the form of the later *Sursum Corda* and Preface;[6] the prayer of thanksgiving 'for our being counted

[1] Cf. also *Acts of Thomas* 27, 29.

[2] See pp. 250ff. above.

[3] This finds expression even later in, e.g., the liturgy of the *Apostolic Constitutions*, II.54.1. Immediately before the kiss of peace the deacon cries, 'That no one have anything against anyone, that no one (remain) in hypocrisy!'; cf. Cyril of Jerusalem, *Cat. myst.* V.3.

[4] The wine was generally mixed with water. This practice will later be given scriptural justification by reference to John 19.34.

[5] The response 'Amen' (properly a Jewish custom) was very important (Justin also stresses this); it gave expression to the fact that it was the community which was praying; the president was only its mouth. His prayer had, therefore, to be sealed by the community in this way.

[6] J. A. Jungmann, *The Mass of the Roman Rite* I, 1951, p. 19, considers a very early origin possible for *Dominus vobiscum* and for the 'decidedly Semitic' *et cum spiritu tuo*, also (p. 16) for the formulae *sursum corda, gratias agamus* and *vere dignum et justum est*. The trishagion which was already customary in the synagogue is to be found in I *Clem.* 34.6. H. Lietzmann, 'Die Anfänge des Glaubensbekenntnisses', *Festgabe für A. Hauck zum 70. Geburtstag*, 1921, pp. 226–42, includes in the early preface a christological confession which later merged with the trinitarian baptismal creed.

worthy to receive these things at his hands' reminds us of *Did.* 10, but it seems that it has become much longer in the intervening period. No doubt the words of institution were also recited,[1] and we probably have to reckon not only with a belief in transubstantiation,[2] but also with a thorough-going sacrificial interpretation.[3]

The distribution of the elements then followed. It was performed by deacons,[4] and the elements were brought even to people who were absent.[5] An important part of the eucharistic liturgy was the collection:[6] this also was a sacrifice (cf. Phil. 4.18). It was no doubt a reminiscence of the community meal to which everyone brought food not only for himself but also if possible for the poor members of the community.[7] For a long time these gifts which were brought to the liturgy were, in part, gifts in kind,[8] although by Justin's time the collection seems to have consisted principally in gifts of money. The proceeds of the collection were applied for the benefit of widows and

[1] This is apparent from ch. 66; the fact that the words of institution are not mentioned in 65 and 67 is, therefore, no reason for holding that they were not read out, and this applies also to *Did.* 9–10. Cf. also P. Neuenzeit, *Das Herrenmahl. Studien zur paulinischen Eucharistieauffassung*, 1960, pp. 98f.

[2] Ch. 66; cf. the fear of letting any of the consecrated element fall to the ground, which Tertullian reports in *Cor.* 3. When we use the expression 'belief in transubstantiation', we mean that the belief had been present for a long time before there was a fully developed doctrine about it.

[3] Cf., on this point, J. A. Jungmann (p. 271, n. 6), p. 25. He quotes I Clem. 36.1; 40–44; Justin, *Dial.* 41; cf. 117; *Did.* 14.1f.; Ignatius, *Philad.* 4; Heb. 13.10; I Cor. 10.21. Cf. J. de Watteville, *Le sacrifice dans les textes eucharistiques des premiers siècles*, 1966.

[4] Cf. already in Acts 6.1ff.

[5] Or only consecrated bread? We have already (pp. 226f.) indicated the significance of this custom.

[6] Reference should probably be made to Acts 5.1ff. (and John 12.5f.?); also I Cor. 16.1ff., especially if our interpretation is correct that it was an exception for Paul to order the setting aside of money at home (see p. 194 above). For the second century see, apart from Justin, I. *Apol.* 67, also *Acts of Peter* 29, 30. 1 (Lipsius, pp. 78ff.). Tertullian, *Apol.* 39.5, refers to a monthly payment of money into the community's funds.

[7] In the primitive community διακονία was a term used for κοινωνία in general.

[8] Oil, cheese, flowers, etc.; cf. G. Kretschmar, *RGG*[3] I, col. 41. A particular form of the distribution of gifts in kind was the agape, the feeding of the poor; cf. B. Reicke, *Diakonie, Festfreude und Zelos in Verbindung mit der altchristlichen Agapenfeier*, 1951. It still seems presupposed in Peter of Alexandria (ed. C. Schmidt, TU 20.4b, 1901, p. 5), 'that bread should be given to the needy on Sunday'.

orphans, the sick, the poor, prisoners, strangers[1] and also the clergy.[2]

In the works of Justin, at the middle of the second century, the principal features of the mass can already be discerned (with its two parts, synaxis and anaphora). In the course of time and in different countries all parts of the mass underwent further development. We do not intend to pursue further the very complicated history of the mass, especially as distinguished work has already been done on this subject.[3]

---

[1] Tertullian, *Apol.* 39.5, mentions the burial of the poor and the relief of aged servants, shipwrecked persons and outlaws.

[2] On these points see B. Reicke (p. 272, n. 8), esp. pp. 51ff., on the payment of the clergy and the revival of Old Testament tithes.

[3] Mention should be made of the two-volume work of J. A. Jungmann, *The Mass of the Roman Rite* I, 1951; II, 1955, and also, for the oldest period, the important study by H. Lietzmann, *Mass and Lord's Supper* (ET 1954ff.); also A. Baumstark, *Vom geschichtlichen Werden der Liturgie*, 1923. It would be a facinating task to study the various forms of Protestant liturgies in their relationship to the history of the early Church. We cannot fail to recognize that the Reformation simply threw overboard several elements which might perhaps have been capable of reformation. This is a contributory cause of the impoverishment from which our liturgies do, in some sense, suffer.

VI

THE NAMES FOR SUNDAY AND THEIR
SIGNIFICANCE

AT first, Sunday had no name of its own among Christians:
they called it by its Jewish name, the 'first day of the week'.[1]
If we want to learn what Sunday meant for Christians, we have
to restrict ourselves to the designations which Christians themselves gave it. Only these names can give us any real insight into
what was important for Christians in their day of worship.
Christians did, in fact, invent two names for Sunday: the 'Lord's
day' and the 'eighth day'. We can see the first name as early as
Rev. 1.10, the second in the second century, although the ideas
which lie behind it must be much older. We shall see that these
two names do, in fact, emphasize the two principal meanings of
the Christian day of worship. Christians have, of course, also
used the designation 'Sunday', which originated in pagan circles,
and they have adapted for their own purposes the symbolism
associated with this name: in this connection they derived a new
meaning from the Jewish name the 'first day of the week'. We
shall follow the chronological order: first of all, we shall briefly
discuss the 'Lord's day', then the 'eighth day' and, finally,
'Sunday', together with the particular interpretation of the
Jewish name, the 'first day of the week', which became associated with it.[2]

I. THE LORD'S DAY

Since we have already dealt in some detail with the oldest
linguistic usage of this name and with its conjectural derivation,[3]
we can briefly summarize our conclusions here. On Sunday

[1] Acts 20.7; I Cor. 16.2; Mark 16.2 par.; John 20.1, 19.
[2] On this see now also B. Botte, 'Les dénominations du dimanche dans
la tradition chrétienne', *Le dimanche: Lex Orandi* 39, 1965, pp. 7–28.
[3] See pp. 202ff., 220f. above.

evening the Christians held their common meal, which was fundamentally different from Jewish meals (even from those of a religious character). They had, therefore, to give to this meal a new name, and they called it the 'breaking of bread' or the 'Lord's Supper' (I Cor. 11.20.). This latter name was the immediate cause for the title the 'Lord's day' being given to the first day of the week: the day on which the 'Lord's Supper' took place was named after it the 'Lord's day'. Whenever a new name is devised for something, it is meant to epitomize that thing as clearly as possible. The Lord's Supper at which the risen Lord was present in spirit had, in fact, become the centre of the early Christians' act of worship on every Sunday.[1] The name the 'Lord's day' does, therefore, derive less from the once-for-all historical event of the resurrection[2] than from the experience of the weekly presence of the exalted Lord among the community assembled for the Lord's Supper, and this practice originated in the appearance on Easter evening. The Lord's presence occurred afresh whenever and wherever the Eucharist was celebrated in remembrance of Jesus' death, resurrection and return at the end. The title the 'Lord's day' was generally used in Greek and Latin ecclesiastical language, and it is still used today in the romance languages and in several Eastern countries. It has been displaced, it is true, in the Germanic and Anglo-Saxon languages by the later name of 'Sunday', which was of pagan origin.[3]

2. THE 'EIGHTH DAY'

We must spend longer on our discussion of this second Christian name for Sunday. We shall see that the title 'the eighth day' is principally to be explained by the practice of baptism on

[1] In the Mass it still remains the centre of the act of worship (even if only in a reduced form as Eucharist without meal); by contrast it has disappeared from the normal Protestant Sunday services (apart from those of Anglicans), but see also p. 305f., n. 1, below. Among us Protestants, therefore, the title the 'Lord's day' no longer has any real justification, all the more so because we often misunderstand it in an Old Testament sense as the day (of rest) sacred to the Lord.

[2] The name was, in fact, later interpreted in this way; Sunday came to be called the 'day of the resurrection', perhaps for the first time in Tertullian, *Orat.* 23. Further references for the designation ἀναστάσιμος ἡμέρα in H. Dumaine, *DACL* IV, col. 884f.

[3] See the tables in F. H. Colson, *The Week*, 1926, pp. 108ff.

Sunday. Baptism was clearly administered on Sunday morning at least as early as the end of the first century.[1] The two Christian names for Sunday did, therefore, derive from the two most important liturgical actions which took place on this day— baptism and the Lord's Supper. On the basis of these two titles invented by the earliest Christians we can sum up the significance which Sunday had for them: it was the day for their two sacraments.

How did this remarkable name 'the eighth day' come about?[2] We have seen[3] that Jews in apocalyptic-chiliastic circles thought of this age as divided into seven periods, and that the seventh was supposed to represent paradise restored on earth. At the end of this seventh period there would dawn the new aeon which would never end: this was, therefore, in some sense 'the eighth day'. This time-table had the seven-day week as its basis: an epoch of one thousand years corresponded to each day of the week. This schedule was also adopted by Christian circles.[4] It must, in fact, have been particularly welcome to Christians, for it tended to give to Sunday an added importance as the eighth day, the day following the sabbath. When the theory about the generations of the world was applied to the days of the week, Sunday as the 'first day of the week' as the symbol of the creation of the world and so the symbol of the beginning of all things: at the same time, it was the day following the sabbath, the special 'eighth day' and so a symbol of the new aeon without end.

Nevertheless we shall probably not find here the origin of the use of 'the eighth day' as a Christian title for Sunday.[5] The idea of the eighth generation of the world first occurs in

---

[1] See pp. 255ff. above.

[2] One cannot properly talk of an 'eighth day' in the week, since this day naturally remains one of the seven days of the week. Sunday was probably never called the 'eighth day' in colloquial speech. As a name it expressed only what Sunday symbolized.

[3] See pp. 48f. above.

[4] See pp. 92ff. above.

[5] We thus disagree with the view of F. J. Dölger, 'Zur Symbolik des altchristlichen Taufhauses', *AuC* 4, 1934, p. 170, and of J. Daniélou, *The Bible and the Liturgy*, 1960, p. 256; cf. his article, 'Le dimanche comme huitième jour', *Le dimanche: Lex orandi* 39, 1965, pp. 61–89. T. Zahn, *Geschichte des Sonntags*, 1878, pp. 58f., n. 15, makes yet another suggestion, 'The custom of calling Sunday the eighth day when it was the first day of the seven-day week of Jews and Christians can only have originated as a second instance of

Christian literature in the second century (first of all in the *Epistle of Barnabas*)[1] at a time when Sunday was already called 'the eighth day'. Even earlier, in the first century we find in many Christian writings a striking use of symbolism attaching to the number eight in connection with baptism. As a consequence it becomes a distinct possibility that Sunday came to be associated with the number eight because baptism was administered on Sunday, and we know that baptism was early connected with symbolism associated with the number eight. Then speculation about the generations of the world, of course, gave added weight to this development.

What was the nature of the symbolism attaching to the number eight in connection with baptism? We have to distinguish two circles of ideas. In the first place, we must refer to the typological relationship which Christians established between Jewish circumcision and Christian baptism. It is well known that baptism was regarded by Christians as the fulfilment of circumcision.[2] One of the important regulations in the Old Testament commandment about circumcision was that the newly born child should be circumcised *on the eighth day* of his life;[3] in addition, anyone who had become unclean in any way should be cleansed by the priest on the eighth day.[4] We can prove that the memory of the stipulation that children should be circumcised on the eighth day found its way into the typology of baptism. For instance, we find the fathers expressing the opinion that the entire saving event of Easter was, in fact, the new

---

that same irrationality which gave to the first or last day of the eight-day Roman week the name of nundinae (ninth day). While the first day of the following week was regarded also as the last day of the preceding week, every seventh day came to be called the eighth day.' Zahn wishes to explain the name in purely secular terms; we can find support in Tertullian, *De idololatria* 14, where we read that pagans had the same festival only once a year, but Christians on every eighth day.

[1] It is extremely probable that we have to regard Slavonic Enoch 33.1f. as a Christian interpolation; see p. 194 above. If this is so, we should be able to go much further back in time, but this does not invalidate the following remarks.

[2] Cf. perhaps Col. 2.11f.; Rom. 2.25ff.; 4.1ff.; Eph. 2.11ff. On this subject see O. Cullmann, *Baptism in the New Testament*, 1950, pp. 56ff.

[3] Gen. 17.12; 21.4; Lev. 12.3; Luke 2.21; cf. John 7.23f.; Acts 7.8; Phil. 3.5. The Christians also made polemical use of this injunction in their struggle against the sabbath.

[4] Lev. 14.10; 15.14, 29; Num. 6.10; cf. Ex. 22.30; Lev. 22.27.

meaning of 'circumcision on the eighth day': before the time of Christ the whole of mankind had been unclean, but by his victory on Easter Sunday Christ had in some way 'circumcised' or cleansed mankind. This bold stroke of typology can have come about only because the weekly Sunday in memory of Easter was already the Church's day for baptism. Because the newly converted were, in fact, baptized on Sunday, the eighth day, and because they thus received spiritual circumcision, so retrospectively the resurrection of Jesus could also be referred to as a circumcision of mankind on the eighth day. Thus Justin could write, 'The command of circumcision bidding (them) always circumcise the children on the eighth day, was a type of the true circumcision, by which we are circumcised from deceit and iniquity through him who rose from the dead on Sunday (namely through our Lord Jesus Christ). For Sunday, remaining the first of all the days, is called, however, the eighth, according to the number of all the days of the cycle, and (yet) remains the first.'[1]

It is possible that symbolism attaching to the number eight already plays some part in John 7.23, 'If on the sabbath a man receives circumcision, so that the law of Moses may not be broken, are you angry with me because on the sabbath I made a man's whole body well?' We have already said that this passage should be regarded primarily as evidence for the liberty with which Jesus behaved with regard to the sabbath.[2] But perhaps even behind this passage there also lies concealed a positive message. It could have been the evangelist's conviction that 'circumcision on the eighth day' which had priority even over the sabbath was already at work in a new manner in the saving activity of Jesus.[3]

Another variety of baptismal typology made use of the *story of the flood*: the water of the flood was compared with the baptismal water, the days of Noah with the days of Christ: as

---

[1] *Dial.* 41.4. The complicated periphrastic explanation of the name 'the eighth day' makes it apparent that it was regarded as a figurative, symbolical designation. Further passages with a similar meaning: Origen, *Sel. in ps.* 118, 'Before the eighth day of our Lord Jesus Christ came, the whole world was besmirched and uncircumcised. But when the eighth day came, that is the day of Christ's resurrection, we were one and all made clean in the circumcision of Christ.' See also Cyprian, *Ep.* 64.4; Augustine, *Serm.* 169.2; *Bapt. c. Donat.* 5.28; *Faust.* 12.16ff.; *De unitate eccl.* I.9; *Civ. dei* 15.26f.; Methodius, *Symposion* VII.6.162.

[2] See pp. 82ff. above.

[3] See the discussion on p. 115 above.

the first humanity was 'cleansed' in Noah, so was the second in Christ. We cannot help noticing that in this connection the number eight once again appears, and it appears in such a way that we have the impression that Christians particularly emphasized the symbolism of this number. In I Peter 3.18–21a we read, 'For Christ also died for sins once for all, the righteous for the unrighteous, that he might bring us to God, being put to death in the flesh but made alive in the spirit; in which he went and preached to the spirits in prison, who formerly did not obey, when God's patience waited in the days of Noah, during the building of the ark, in which a few, that is, eight persons, were saved through water. Baptism, which corresponds to this, now saves you.'[1] II Peter 2.5 is to be placed alongside this passage, '(God) did not spare the ancient world, but preserved (only) Noah, the eighth person, the herald of righteousness, when he brought a flood upon the world of the ungodly.'

These two texts do not stand alone: in patristic writings the same ideas occur. 'By this was meant that the mystery of saved men appeared in the deluge. For righteous Noah, along with the other mortals at the deluge, i.e. with his own wife, his three sons and their wives, being eight in number, were a symbol of the eighth day, wherein Christ appeared when he rose from the dead' (Justin, *Dial.* 138.1). 'Because the first resurrection of the (human) race after the flood happened to eight people (i.e. those who were in Noah's ark), the Lord has begun the resurrection of the dead on the eighth day' (Asterius of Amasa, *Hom.* 20 [on Ps. 6, PG 40.448]).[2] Even in the Clementine Liturgy (*Const. Apost.* VIII.12.22) we read: 'Thou hast brought the flood upon the world because of the great number of godless people, and thou hast saved out of the flood righteous Noah and eight souls, the residue of that (mankind) which has disappeared and the beginning of that which is to come.'

We therefore come across the number eight in connection with this baptismal typology. It was, of course, already contained

[1] The detailed exegesis of this text is very much disputed: we cannot go into the question here. See B. Reicke, *The Disobedient Spirits and Christian Baptism*, 1946, and W. Bieder, *Die Vorstellung von der Höllenfahrt Jesu Christi* (AThANT 19), 1949.

[2] The ark often appears at the same time as a symbol of the Church: first of all in Tertullian, *Bapt.* 8; Hippolytus, *Antichr.* 59; *Comm. in Dan.* III.17.2–9; *Noet.* 18. See F. J. Dölger, *Sol Salutis*, 1925², pp. 272ff.; J. Daniélou, *The Bible and the Liturgy*, 1960, pp. 83ff.; E. Peterson, 'Das Schiff als Symbol der Kirche', *TZ* 6, 1956, pp. 77ff.; E. Hilgert, *The Ship and related Symbols in the New Testament*, 1962.

within the story of the flood: Noah and his seven companions had survived the deluge (Gen. 7.7; 8.16),[1] but it was the Christians who attached special importance to this number eight. For what reasons was this symbolism so important for them? We can refer to the fact that in antiquity the number eight was thought to be the number of completeness and harmony,[2] and that it preserved traces of this significance among the Jews also;[3] but that does not come anywhere near the heart of the matter. The fact that in baptism there took place circumcision not with hands, but 'in the spirit', that the name Noah by derivation meant 'rest',[4] that according to Christian conviction the reception of the Holy Spirit was associated with the act of baptism—all this leads us to suppose that the number eight stood for the Holy Spirit. Perhaps the Christians harked back to an older, Jewish tradition associated with the Logos and Gnosis.[5] In any case, this symbolism can hardly have evolved from the apocalyptic idea of 'the eighth day', since this Christian symbolism (by contrast with that of the apocalyptic tradition) always emphasized the *presence* of the salvation embodied in the number eight. In apocalyptic thinking the eighth day will come after the seventh generation of the world, but the Christian baptismal symbolism underlined the

[1] This typology would be yet more complete if we could assume that Noah was genealogically the 'eighth' from Adam. The Bible does, in fact, record ten generations down to the time of Noah (cf. Pirke Aboth V.2), but there is also a tradition (Ps.-Clem. *Recogn.* I.29) which presupposes only eight.

[2] There was a proverb πάντα ὀκτω (Theon of Smyrna, *Exp. rer. math.* 105.12). In addition, the number eight had acquired considerable importance, especially among the Pythagoreans in connection with the octave of notes and the eight angles of a cube; it was thought to be the embodiment of harmony and of the cosmos. Cf. Clement Alex., *Strom.*, VI.11.84.6; VI.16.140.2f. It is especially interesting that the ark of Noah was the symbol of the spiritual cosmos, of heaven; cf. Clement Alex., *Strom.* V.6.36.3, and p. 279, n. 2, above.

[3] We have already mentioned the connection of the number eight with the purificatory rites. The festival of tabernacles also lasted for eight days, of which the final one was the most important (II Chron. 7.9; Neh. 8.18; John 7.37; cf. also Philo, *Spec. leg.* II.211f.). In addition, the headings to Ps. 6 and 12; Ezek. 40.31, 37; the eight-verse structure of Ps. 118; Eccles. 11.2; I Sam. 17.12 were all frequently used by Christian exegetes when they mentioned the eighth day; cf., e.g., Hilary, *Init. explan. de pss.* 6 et 7; Jerome, *Dial. c. Luciferianos* 22; Gregory of Nyssa, *In Ps. 6 de octava* (PG 44.608ff.).

[4] See also Epiphanius, *Haer.* 30.32.7–9.

[5] See p. 284 below.

fact that with the resurrection the eighth day had already dawned, that the Holy Spirit in full abundance had already come and that on every eighth day, i.e. on every Sunday, he was truly experienced in the administration of baptism.[1] Perhaps in this connection we may refer to John 7.37ff. There Jesus is speaking on the eighth day of the Feast of Tabernacles, that is to say on its great final day, ' "If any one thirst, let him come to me and drink. He who believes in me, as the scripture has said, Out of his heart shall flow rivers of living water." Now this he said about the Spirit, which those who believed in him were to receive; for the Spirit was not yet, because Jesus was not yet glorified.' In this passage the association of the Holy Spirit with the eighth day is certainly not entirely accidental.[2] We can even refer to the story of Pentecost, which according to Acts 2.1ff. is said to have taken place on the fiftieth day $(=6 \times 7 + 8)$ after Easter and, therefore, on the 'fullness' of days (cf. Luke 9.28).[3] Christians clearly held that the Holy Spirit had some connection with the number eight, the number of the *pleroma* (fullness). On the other hand, the Holy Spirit was also thought to be connected in the closest possible way with baptism, at which he was received for the first time (cf. a passage as early as Mark 1.9–11). This connection helps us to understand how the number eight began to play such an important part within the symbolism of baptism. It even found architechtonic expression: it is well known that Christian fonts, baptisteries and frequently even church-towers were constructed

[1] Many patristic quotations could be cited in support of this idea. We may perhaps refer to Hilary of Poitiers, *Init. explan. de pss.* 6 et 7: 'In the octave we have received the kingdom of heaven'; or Ambrose, *Ep.* 44.6, 'On this day (Ps. 118.24) the glory of the entire and perfect circumcision has been poured into the human heart.' Origen, *Sel. in ps.* 118, had already used this very passage in the same sense. These ideas naturally overlap in part with the notion of the 'fulfilled sabbath'; see pp. 108ff. above.

[2] See the discussion of John 7.23 above on p. 278. The eight days of the festival of tabernacles were later interpreted in an eschatological sense; cf. H. Bietenhard, *Das tausendjährige Reich*, 1955, p. 142.

[3] We later find the symbolism of the fifty days in the notion of the 'sabbath of sabbaths'; cf. Ps.-Hippolytus, *In ps.* 4 (PG 10.713); Hilary, *Init. in ps.* 12; Augustine, *Ep.* 55 (ad Jan.), 16.29. Cf. J. Hild, *Dimanche et vie paschale*, 1949, pp. 51ff. The fathers also noticed the fact that in Matt. 5.3–10 eight beatitudes are transmitted to us. Cf. Ambrose, *In Luc.* V.49; Augustine, *Serm. domini in monte* I.3.10; IV.12 (PL 34.1233ff.); Jerome, *Dial. c. Luciferianos* 22.

in octagonal shape.[1] Moreover, the custom of adding an octave to festivals has evolved out of the Easter octave, that week in which the newly baptized still wore their white baptismal robes.[2] Is it not obvious that because baptism was administered on Sunday this day received the name the 'eighth day', just as it had earlier received the title the 'Lord's day' because the Lord's Supper took place on it?

It may also be mentioned here that according to I Sam. 16.1–13 David was the eighth son of Jesse and that the Spirit of the Lord came upon him when Samuel anointed him king. Christians paid attention to this typology as well.[3] It is a remarkable fact that the number eight appears in almost all the Old Testament covenants which are important for salvation-history (Noah, Abraham, David)!

This was the original baptismal symbolism, and in relatively early times it was joined by another symbolism in which the eighth day, as qualitatively better, was contrasted with the seventh day, the sabbath. Because it spoke of eternity, the eighth day surpassed the seventh day. The sabbath symbolized only the kingdom of one thousand years which by its very nature belonged to this transitory world: Sunday, however, as the 'eighth day', represented the kingdom of God, that is to say, the second, new, eternal creation at the end of the times. We have seen how this contrast already appears in the *Epistle of Barnabas* 15.8.[4] 'He (God) further says to them (the Jews), "Your new moons and sabbaths I disdain." You see what he means: it is not the sabbaths of the present era that are acceptable to me, but the one which I have appointed to mark the end of the world and to usher in the eighth day, that is, the dawn of another world.'[5] The same idea is also presupposed in Slavonic Enoch (33.1f.), but we probably have to regard the passage as a Christian interpolation.[6]

[1] The earliest archaeological evidence is in the baptistery at the Lateran; see the material in F. J. Dölger, 'Zur Symbolik des altchristlichen Tauf-hauses', *AuC* 4, 1934, pp. 153–87, esp. pp. 182ff.; H. Leclerq, *DACL* 12.2, *DACL* 12.2, 1935, col. 1900–2; K. Schneider, *RAC* I, pp. 78ff.

[2] It is possible that the first indication of the Easter octave occurs in John 20.26.

[3] E.g. Hilary, *Init. explan. de pss.* 6 et 7.

[4] See pp. 93f. above.

[5] Cf. Clement Alex., *Strom.* VI.16.138.1, 'The seventh day, therefore, is proclaimed a rest—abstraction from ills—preparing for the Primal Day, our true rest.'

[6] Cf. J. Daniélou, *The Bible and the Liturgy*, 1960, p. 256, and p. 277, n. 1 above.

We find this symbolism very frequently from the third to the fifth century. Liberal use[1] is made of it, particularly by the three great Cappadocians[2] and Augustine.[3] Sunday was, at one and the same time, the eighth day which extended beyond the sabbath and also the very first day of all. It therefore included within itself both the time before and the time after time.[4] Particularly important in this connection is the fact that in Gen. 1.5 it does not say that God created the 'first' day, but 'a' day: this seemed to be an indication of its infinity and eternity.[5] The numbers seven and eight could also denote for the fathers simply the difference between the Old and the New Testament.[6]

From this angle it became possible to demonstrate effectively that the sabbath was only provisional in character. This possibility was afforded by the fact that the full reality of the new dispensation became associated with Sunday, because Sunday was the day for worship: beside Sunday, the sabbath could not help paling. It must, however, be plainly stated once again that the Christian Sunday had not been invented as part of the polemic against Judaism. We have tried to show that the observance of the sabbath had already become superfluous for Christians without the observance of Sunday being played off against it. We have also shown that for a long time Sunday was in no sense a day of rest, and for this reason alone it could not stand on the same footing as the sabbath. If in this particular field of numerical symbolism sabbath and Sunday were often compared with one another, this did not happen as a direct result of conflict. The happy circumstance that the Christian 'eighth day' could in this way be contrasted theologically with the 'seventh day' enabled Christians to state what had been true for them from the very beginning: the sabbath was finished so far as they were concerned, and because the Christian act of worship took place on Sunday, there was contained in this day everything new which had been given to Christians, namely the hope of eternal life which was gained by the resurrection of Christ and made a present experience in baptism and the Lord's Supper.

Sunday as 'the eighth day' did come to be regarded as standing for eternal rest and to be equated with the sabbath. It is not impossible that this high regard served as a bridge whereby the

---

[1] H. Dumaine presents a good deal of material, *DACL* IV, col. 882ff.

[2] Cf. J. Daniélou (p. 282, n. 6), pp. 264ff.; F. J. Dölger, *AuC* 4, 1934, pp. 165ff.

[3] J. Daniélou (p. 282, n. 6), pp. 276ff.

[4] As early as the Syriac *Didascalia* 26 (Connolly, p. 236); see also pp. 290f. below.

[5] Cf., e.g., Basil, *Spir. sancto* 27.64; Ambrose, *Hexaemeron* I.10.37; Jerome, *Dial. c. Lucif.* 22.

[6] Cf. Hilary, *Init in ps.* 16; Ambrose, *Ep.* 44.6; Augustine, *Ep.* 55.13.23.

sabbath commandment of the Old Testament could be transferred to the weekly Sunday.[1]

We find one further interpretation of 'the eighth day': this is
concerned not with the future, but with teaching about the
Ogdoad, and it occurs principally in Christian circles influenced
by gnostic ideas. It speaks in terms of the spiritual world,
especially of the place of rest and eternity above this world of
sevenness: the background of this interpretation was the
Pythagorean notion of seven storeys in the heavens which were
embraced by the eighth, immovable firmament. Thus Sunday
became the symbol of the full life and of the perfection which
are attainable by the gnostic even while he is here below. These
ideas had one advantage over those notions of the eighth day
which were purely concerned with the future: they emphasized
(although in a somewhat complicated way) that Christ *had
already brought* and not merely promised life and immortality. On
the other hand, they did threaten to dissolve the message of the
once-for-all saving activity of Christ and to substitute for it a
timeless redemption myth. These gnostic ideas do, in fact, occur
relatively late in our sources: nevertheless, they may perhaps be
held to be directly related to that stream of tradition which led
to the Holy Spirit and Christian baptism being associated with
the number eight, but we have no more precise information
about this relationship.

A few references may be quoted in this connection. Irenaeus[2] reported
that the gnostics would call the place of wisdom 'mother, ogdoas, wisdom,
earth, Jerusalem, Holy Spirit, Lord'.[3] Cf. Hippolytus, *Refut.* VI.32.9;
Clement Alex., *Exc. ex Theod.* 80.1; also Tertullian, *Anim.* 37. Clement
Alex., *Strom.* IV.25.158.4–159.3 leaves one the choice of interpreting the
number eight (he is discussing Ezek. 44.27) as the new aeon at the end or as
the eighth heaven or as the spiritual cosmos.[4]

However common 'the eighth day' had once been as a
symbolic name for Sunday, it dropped entirely out of use. One

[1] See pp. 167f. above.
[2] *Adv. haer.* I.5.3. According to Eusebius, *HE* V.20.1, Irenaeus did, in
fact, write a book about the Ogdoad.
[3] Clearly Κυριακή; cf. Clement Alex., *Exc. ex Theod.* 63.1.
[4] *Acts of Thomas* 27; *Epist. Apost.* 18 (Coptic text) should probably also be
considered in this connection. On this subject see pp. 95ff. above. Further
information about the teaching on the Ogdoad may be found in W. Bousset,
Die Himmelsreise der Seele (new impression 1960); P. Lundberg, *La typologie
baptismale*, 1942, pp. 79ff.

reason (among others) may have been that in two respects this title was obscure. In the first place, if it was understood as a reference to the coming aeon at the end, then (for Christians who were not accustomed to thinking in chiliastic terms) it came into conflict with the parallel ideas of the sabbath rest at the end of time which were trying to describe the same period. On the other hand, if it was understood as an image of the Ogdoad, of the perfection of the spiritual cosmos, then it could easily come into disrepute because it encouraged all sorts of syncretistic notions.

3. SUNDAY

In the introductory chapter of this study[1] we mentioned that a Sunday regularly recurring every seven days is of relatively late attestation: it presupposes the introduction of the planetary week, and this seems only to have happened in the course of the first century of Christian history. Even Justin in his *Apology* to the Emperor Antoninus Pius about AD 150 refers to the 'so-called' Sunday: this expression seems to suggest that the new nomenclature for the days of the week was even then not in general use.[2]

This does not mean that Christ and Christian belief are not already treated by Christian authors in terms which are very similar to those associated with contemporary sun-worship. We do not, of course, intend to investigate in which New Testament texts such echoes may be found.[3] We propose only to pick out three spheres in which the influence on Christian thinking of symbolism associated with the light or the sun is not to be denied: (i) The mention of baptism as an 'illumination' ($\phi\omega\tau\iota\sigma\mu\acute{o}s$). (ii) The idea that after his death Jesus made

---

[1] See pp. 35ff. above.

[2] See also the discussion of 'stato die' in Pliny's letter, p. 255, n. 1, above.

[3] Wherever we find any trace of light symbolism, we may suppose that this is evidence of the indirect influence of sun-worship, even if the Christian sources do generally use important qualifications, e.g. in John 1.9; 8.12; Matt. 4.14f.; 13.43; 17.2; Luke 1.78f.; Rev. 1.16, 18; 12.1. The credal formula 'risen on the third day' has also been traced back to a sun-myth; H. Gunkel, *Zum religionsgeschichtlichen Verständnis des Neuen Testaments*, 1910[2], pp. 72, 79f. It would be interesting on some occasion to study these observations in detail. On this tradition in the Old Testament and late Judaism, see A. Aalen, *Die Begriffe 'Licht' und 'Finsternis' im Alten Testament, im Spätjudentum und im Rabbinismus*, 1951.

his way into hell, that he there burst the bonds of death and then triumphantly mounted up to heaven. (iii) The custom of Christians to pray facing east.

(i) The use of this very term 'illumination' as a designation for baptism is first found in Justin,[1] and in this passage it could well be regarded as a borrowing from the language of the mystery cults. We do, however, probably find similar ideas present in II Cor. 4.4–6, 'The god of this world has blinded the minds of the unbelievers, to keep them from seeing the light of the gospel of the glory of Christ, who is the likeness of God. For what we preach is not ourselves, but Jesus Christ as Lord, with ourselves as your servants for Jesus' sake. For it is the God who said, "Let light shine out of darkness", who has shone in our hearts to give the light of the knowledge of the glory of God in the face of Christ.'[2] We should also bear in mind that Christians were called 'sons of light'.[3]

(ii) The use of solar symbolism in connection with the idea of Christ's descent to Hades occurs much more frequently. There is clear evidence of it in the New Testament. In this study it is not necessary to examine the weight attaching to the various passages which are generally quoted in this connection.[4] Almost all exegetes do, in any case, agree that Christ's descent into hell is presupposed in I Peter 3.19–20, '(Christ) went and preached to the spirits in prison, who formerly did not obey, when God's patience waited in the days of Noah . . .' (cf. 4.6). Significantly this is the same passage to which we have already referred with regard to the association of baptism with the number eight. Should we suppose that there was, in fact, an

---

[1] I *Apol.* 65.1 (but cf. Heb. 6.4); Clement Alex., *Protr.* IX.84.2; VI.68.4; Syriac *Didascalia* 21 (Connolly, p. 186). Then especially Cyril of Jerusalem in his *Mystagogical Catecheses* 1 and 2.

[2] Cf. Eph. 1.18; Eph. 5.14 is also probably a baptismal hymn; also II Tim. 1.10; Heb. 6.4.

[3] John 12.36; Eph. 5.8; I Thess. 5.5. This expression played quite a considerable part at Qumran also. H. Kosmala, *Hebräer-Essener-Christen*, 1960, pp. 117–36, tries to prove that the term 'illumination' is also of Essene origin. But this cannot be right; see my essay, 'La foi=une illumination', *TZ* 23, 1967.

[4] Acts 2.24, 27, 31; Rom. 10.7; Eph. 4.9–10; Rev. 1.18; Matt. 12.40; 27.52f.; John 5.25; Heb. 12.23 should be especially noted in this connection. Cf. also W. Bieder, *Die Vorstellung von der Höllenfahrt Jesu Christi* (AThANT 19), 1949.

underlying link between these two traditions? Here we can only raise the question[1].

The text of I Peter 3.19f. is not easily interpreted. It does, however, seem (as B. Reicke[2] has already shown) that by the 'preaching' of Jesus in the realm of the dead we should not understand a missionary sermon which had as its purpose the conversion of the erstwhile sinners. It is much more probable that this proclamation was meant to emphasize the power of the Son of God 'in the spirit' even in the world of death and demons:[3] this would inspire the readers of the epistle with courage for their own witness in a hostile world.

Ideas associated with the descent into hell assumed some very dramatic touches: Christ was supposed to have forced open the prison of Hades, liberated just souls from it and led them with him to glory, but the 'enemies' he is said to have bound and given over to judgement.

One group of passages puts more emphasis on the liberation of the just, another on the conquest of Hades. To the former group there belong particularly those texts which use an otherwise unknown apocryphal oracle of Jeremiah, 'The Lord God remembered his dead people of Israel who lay in the graves; and he descended to preach to them his own salvation.'[4] Also Ignatius, *Magn.* 9.3 (the earliest passage after I Peter 3.19f.), 'Also the prophets were his (Christ's) disciples in the Spirit and they looked forward to him as their teacher. And for this reason he whom they waited for in righteousness, when he came raised them from the dead.' Cf. Syriac *Didascalia* 26 (Connolly, p. 258). According to the *Epistula Apostolorum*[5] Christ has even administered baptism in the realm of the dead to the just of the old covenant: similarly also Hermas, *Sim.* IX.16.5–7 (there the apostles

---

[1] The longer I consider this subject, the more I find myself convinced that there must originally have been a connection between the Palestinian baptismal movement and Palestinian sun-worship (both were widespread, particularly in Transjordan and in Syria); cf. the comments on pp. 190f., 260f., and p. 257, n. 2, above. In this case the symbolism associated with the number eight would also have originated there. It is also significant that we regularly find allusions to Jesus' descent into hell woven into early Christian baptismal symbolism; cf. P. Lundberg, *La typologie baptismale dans l'ancienne Eglise*, 1942.

[2] *The Disobedient Spirits and Christian Baptism*, 1946, pp. 95ff.; cf. M. Lauterburg, *RE*[3] 8, pp. 200f.; W. Bieder (p. 286, n. 4), pp. 116f.

[3] II Peter 2.4 and Jude 6 regard the prison of the underworld principally as the abode of the 'fallen angels' of Gen. 6.

[4] Justin, *Dial.* 72.4; Irenaeus, *Adv. haer.* III.20.4; IV.22.1; IV.33.12; V.31.1f.; cf. I.27.3 (here directed against Marcion); *Epideixis* 78; cf. E. Hennecke, *Neutestamentliche Apokryphen*, 1924[2], p. 388.

[5] 27 (*NT Apoc.* I, p. 209).

and teachers baptize).[1]—The following texts belong to the second group which emphasizes the conquest of Hades: Odes of Solomon 42.14ff.; Melito, *Hom. de pascha* 102 (SC 123, p. 122); Hippolytus, *Trad. Apost.* 4; *Acts of Thomas* 10; Aphrahates, *Hom.* 6.12; Maximus of Turin, *Hom.* 61 (for Pentecost); (Ps.-) Epiphanius, *Hom.* III *in die resurr. Christi.* The descent into hell is described in especial detail by the novel-like Gospel of Nicodemus, the direct precursor of the medieval mystery plays.[2]

The symbolism of the sun which sets and then rises in fresh glory is certainly reflected in these ideas about the descent of Christ into hell.[3] This is especially apparent where direct allusion is made to the similarity with the sun. In the passage in which he mentions Christ's descent into hell (*Magn.* 9.1ff.) Ignatius uses the same verb ἀνατέλλειν for the resurrection of Christ as is generally used for the rising sun. In a fragment of the treatise on baptism by Melito of Sardis[4] we even find, 'The king of heaven and lord of creation, the rising sun, which appeared also to the dead in Hades and to the mortals on earth: as the only (true) sun he shone down from heaven.'[5] Christian motifs were, of course, introduced into this framework taken over from solar symbolism: we find particularly frequently the motif of Christ preaching to the dead. This motif was itself closely connected with the problem of a theodicy: it could help answer the question about what happened to the righteous and

[1] See also Gospel of Peter 40f.; Origen, *Cels.* II.43 and elsewhere. (He uses this idea for his teaching about the restoration of all things.)

[2] Cf. K. Gschwind, *Die Niederfahrt Christi in die Unterwelt*, 1911; H. Quilliet, *Dict. de Théol. cath.* IV.1, 1911[2], pp. 565ff.; W. Bauer, *Das Leben Jesu im Zeitalter der neutestamentlichen Apocryphen*, 1909, pp. 243ff.; B. Reicke, *RGG*[3] III, col. 408–10.

[3] Cf. W. Bousset, *Kyrios Christos*, 1913[2], second supplement; also *ZNW* 19, 1919–20, pp. 50–66; H. Rahner, *Griechische Mythen in christlicher Deutung*, 1945, esp. pp. 153ff. On the material from the field of comparative religion see R. Ganschinietz, 'Katabasis', Pauly-Wissowa X.2, col. 2359–449; J. Kroll, *Gott und Hölle*, 1932.

[4] VIII.4 (Goodspeed, p. 311). In VIII.3 the descent of the setting sun into the ocean is used as an illustration for the baptism of Christ.

[5] It is possible that Mark 15.33 par. should be considered in this connection. Cyril of Jer., *Mystag. Cat.* IV.10, interpreted the passage to mean that the natural sun was ashamed to shine when the 'sun of righteousness' was expiring. For later references see Hilary of Poitiers, *Tract. in ps.* 67.6 (CSEL 27.280); Athanasius, *Expos. in ps.* 67.34 (PG 27.303); Ambrose, *Hexaem.* IV.2.7. Maximus of Turin, *Hom.* 61 (for Pentecost, PL 57.371), writes, 'We hold the day of the Lord to be so venerable and solemn, because on it the saviour, like the rising sun, gleamed in the glory of the resurrection, after the conquest of darkness in the underworld.'

to sinners who had lived before Christ's appearance on earth. Despite the antiquity of the ideas associated with the descent into hell, it was very late (the first evidence dates from the fifth century) before a mention of the descent was included in the creed.

(iii) The influence on early Christianity of the sun-worship widespread in the ancient world may be seen most clearly in the Christians' practice of praying towards the rising sun.[1] This practice is indeed attested towards the end of the second century,[2] but it is very probably much older, since at a later date Christians would certainly have hesitated to have adopted so 'pagan' a custom unquestioningly. Moreover, it seems likely that the Christian interpretation of the custom (that the return of Christ was expected from the east) is of more recent origin than the practice itself.[3] Here and there in Judaism prayer

[1] It is also reflected in connection with the baptismal liturgy in which the assent to Christ is made towards the east; see p. 261, n. 3, above. We have also suggested (see pp. 260f. above) that the content of the morning prayer to the sun, which was widespread in the ancient world, has affected the Jewish and Christian practice of morning prayer; cf. also p. 260, n. 7.

[2] For the first time in Tertullian, *Nat.* I.13, 'Others . . . hold the sun to be the Christian God, because it is known that we pray towards the direction of the rising sun'; cf. *Apol.* 16.9–11, and *Mart. Pauli* 5 (Lipsius, p. 115). Then perhaps Clement Alex., *Strom.* VII.7.43.6f., 'Since the dawn is an image of the day of birth, and from that point the light which has shone forth at first from the darkness increases . . . (our) prayers are made looking towards the sunrise in the east. Whence also the most ancient temples looked toward the west, that people might be taught to turn to the east when facing the images.' Also Origen, *Orat.* 32; Syriac *Didasc.* 12 (Connolly, pp. 119f.); *Const. Apost.* VII. 45.2.

[3] Clement (n. 2) knows nothing about its origin. In Origen, *Hom.* IX. 10 *in Lev.*, it seems, in fact, to be associated with the hope of the Parousia; this was expected from the east, and Matt. 24.27 now provides the basis for this hope; similarly Ethiop. *Apoc. Petri* 1 (*NT Apoc.* II, p. 668). Cf. also Cyprian, *Dom. or.* 35; *Acts of Thomas* 32; Basil, *Spir. sancto* 27.64. Perhaps we can also use *Epist. Apost.* 16 in this connection. On the whole subject see F. J. Dölger, *Sol salutis*, 1925², pp. 198ff., and J. Daniélou, *The Bible and the Liturgy*, 1960, pp. 30ff. It may be taken as almost certain that the expectation of the Parousia from the east did not give rise to the Christians' practice of praying towards the east; the expectation of the Parousia was much more an interpretation of the custom, which they had already adopted, of praying towards the sunrise. E. Peterson, 'Die geschichtliche Bedeutung der jüdischen Gebetsrichtung', *TZ* 3, 1947, pp. 1ff., has already pointed out the contrast with the Jewish practice of praying towards Jerusalem. See also p. 261, n. 3, above. On the significance of the symbol of the cross in this connection cf. E. Peterson, 'Das Kreuz und das Gebet nach Osten', *Frühkirche, Judentum und Gnosis*, 1959, pp. 15–35; and E. Dinkler, *Die Apsiskomposition von S. Appolinare in Classe*, 1964.

towards the east seems already to have become customary; without any difficulty, therefore, Christians continued to pray in this direction. It is well known that even today, as a result of a pre-Christian convention, Christian churches are still constructed on an east-west axis, so that the prayer of the faithful may likewise be directed towards the east.[1]

When the Christian day for worship first began to be called the 'day of the sun' in pagan circles, the development of symbolism associated with the sun and the light made great advances among Christians also. This development had a closely related consequence: the old Jewish designation of Sunday as the 'first day of the week', which had already been discontinued for some time in the Gentile Christian Church, came back into use again because of the symbolism which could now be derived from it. It was remembered that in the biblical creation story God had created the light on the first day of the first week of the world's history.[2] Thus we can hear Justin saying, 'Sunday is the day on which we all hold our common assembly, because it is the first day on which God, having wrought a change in the darkness and matter, made the world.'[3] Dionysius of Alexandria goes on to draw the parallel between the first and the second creation, 'God has himself made (Sunday) the first day both of creation and also of resurrection: on the day of creation he separated light and darkness, and on the day of resurrection he divided belief from unbelief.'[4] Indeed, the fathers could go so far as to call Christ himself the 'day'.[5]

In the three names for Sunday, 'first day of the week', 'Lord's

[1] Required for the first time in *Const. Apost.* II.57.3.

[2] The first day of the week naturally had this significance already in Judaism; see p. 184, n. 1, above. But this meaning became a matter of immediate importance for Christians about the middle of the second century, clearly in connection with 'Sunday'.

[3] I *Apol.* 67.7; cf. *Dial.* 138.1.

[4] In *Analecta sacra spicilegio solesmensi* 4, ed. J.-B. Pitra, 1883, p. 421.

[5] Clement Alex., *Eclog. proph.* 53.1; *Strom.* IV.22.141.4; VI.16.145.6; Hippolytus, *Ben. Mos.* (Patrologia Orientalis 17.171); Cyprian, *Dom. or.* 35; Eusebius, *Marc.* I.2.13.23. On the whole subject see J. Daniélou, *The Theology of Jewish Christianity*, 1964, pp. 168ff.; F. A. Regan, *Dies dominica and dies solis. The Beginnings of the Lord's Day in Christian Antiquity*, Dissertation at Washington, 1961, pp. 39f. In the 'Splendor paternae gloriae' which Fulgentius of Ruspe, *Ep.* 14.10 (PL 65.401), attributes to Ambrose (see English Hymnal 52), Christ is addressed as 'Day, all days illumining'. See the comment on p. 283 above concerning the first day of Gen. 1.5.

day' and 'eighth day' we can perceive a trinitarian element in the Christian day of worship. The name 'the first day of the week' reminded Christians of the creative work of God, 'the Lord's day' of the saving work of Christ in the midst of time, and 'the eighth day' represented for them the renewal in the holy Spirit which continued to be effected in baptism and which did, at the same time, contain the future perspective.

It is impossible and also unnecessary to set out here the abundant material from early Christian literature in which Christ and the sun were contrasted with one another and the resurrection of Christ compared with the sunrise (Mal. 4.2).[1] There are also the representations in art in which Jesus is depicted as the *sol invictus*.[2] As early as the time of Justin[3] the name 'sunrise' (cf. Luke 1.78f.) is used with reference to Jesus, and the use of this name soon became widespread.[4] The glory of Christ was compared with the light described in Isa. 30.26; this light was said to shine at the end of the times seven times more brightly than the sun. 'And he spake to us, "Verily. I say unto you, I shall come like the sun which gleams with glory, so shall I come to the earth to judge the living and the dead: I shall gleam with splendour seven times more than the sun while I am borne with glory on the wings of the cloud and my cross goes along before me." '[5] In this context we must also remember the transfer of the festival of Christmas to 25 December, that is to say to the day of the ancient festival of the winter solstice.[6]

We can end this chapter in no better way than by reproducing the hymn to the light which was sung by Christians in eastern Syria in their morning office on Sunday.[7] This beautiful acrostic takes up and combines all the elements which we have already noticed in the symbolism of the sun and the light:

[1] A wide collection of material on these topics is available in the book which has hitherto been the standard work on the subject, F. J. Dölger, *Sol salutis*, 1925[2].

[2] Cf. F. Cumont, *Textes et monuments* I, 1896, p. 123, illustration No. 6. The fine mosaic which was found in the tomb under St Peter's at Rome is also well known: it represents Christ with a nimbus and sun-horses; see E. Kirschbaum, *The Tombs of S. Peter and S. Paul*, 1959, pp. 35ff.

[3] *Dial.* 100.4; 121.2; 126.1.

[4] E.g. Melito, *Bapt.* 4; Origen, *Hom.* IX.10 *in Lev.*

[5] *Epist. Apost.* 16; cf. Rev. 21.23; Matt. 17.2; Acts 26.13; Hippolytus, *frag.* VII. *c. Gaium* (GCS Hipp. I.2, p. 247.4).

[6] See O. Cullmann, *Der Ursprung des Weihnachtsfestes*, 1960[2].

[7] C. Burkitt, *JTS* 22, 1921, pp. 377–9, attributed it to Theodore of Mopsuestia, but A. Baumstark, *Geschichte der syrischen Literatur*, 1922, p. 52, to Ephraim. This translation is taken from *Rituale Armenorum*, ed. F. C. Cony-beare and A. J. Maclean, 1905, pp. 382f.

Christ 'illumines' men, he has appeared as the true sun on earth and in Hades, has ascended to the Father in glory and will be our light in eternity.

A light hath shone forth to the righteous: and gladness to them that are true of heart.

Jesus our Lord the Christ: hath shone forth to us from the bosom of his Father: he hath come and taken us out of darkness: and hath enlightened us with his excellent light.

The day hath shone forth on the sons of men: and the power of darkness hath fled: a light hath shone forth for us from his light: and hath enlightened our eyes which were darkened.

He hath caused his glory to shine forth in the world: and hath enlightened the lowest depths: death is extinguished and darkness hath fled: and the gates of Sheol are broken.

And he hath enlightened all creatures: who of old were in darkness: and the dead who lay in the dust arose: and glorified (him) because salvation had come to them.

He gave salvation and granted us life: and was exalted to his Father on high: and furthermore he cometh in his great glory: and enlighteneth the eyes of all who have waited for him.

Our King cometh in his great glory: let us light our lamps and go forth to meet him: and let us be glad in him as he hath been glad in us: and maketh us glad by his excellent light.

Let us lift up glory to his Majesty: and let us all give thanks to his high Father: whose mercies are many and who sent him to us: and hath given us hope and salvation.

His day suddenly shineth forth: and his saints go forth to meet him: and light their torches: all who have laboured and have been wearied and have made themselves ready.

The Angels and Watchers of heaven are glad: in the glory of the just and righteous: and place crowns on their heads: and with one accord sing praises and Hallelujahs.

My brethren, arise and prepare yourselves: that we may confess our King and our Saviour: who cometh in his glory and maketh us glad: in his excellent light in the kingdom.

The name 'Sunday' made itself at home from the fourth century onwards in general Christian linguistic usage.[1] In ecclesiastical language, however, the title the 'Lord's day' was always preferred, and its retention here until the present time

---

[1] Cf. H. Dumaine, *DACL* IV, col. 872ff., but this is true only with reservations; cf. B. Botte, *Revue d'histoire Ecclésiastique* 58, 1963, p. 560.

(cf. the names for 'Sunday' in the romance languages) has clearly resulted from a proper feeling for the primary and central significance of the Christian day for worship.[1]

[1] The use of solar symbolism by Christians may, in fact, also have had a polemical and apologetic significance in the struggles against the cult of Mithras and Manichaeism. See F. J. Dölger, 'Über die Rolle des Manichäismus für das Hochkommen des Sonnenkults vor Konstantin', *AuC* 2, 1930, pp. 301–15.

RETROSPECT AND PROSPECT

WE have reached the end of our historical investigation. In conclusion, I want to summarize those results of this study which could be important for the pressing questions of today. We emphasized in our introduction that there could be no question of transplanting into our own time and without any further examination the primitive Church's understanding and observance of Sunday. That would be quite impossible, since history cannot be put back. Nevertheless it will be necessary for us to take into account the historical background if we wish to discover the theological terms of reference within which can be solved the pressing problems of the modern observance of Sunday. In the last analysis the problem about Sunday, like other problems, depends upon decisions about belief; according to Christian conviction, however, these decisions cannot be made out of the present situation alone, but only in continuity with the history of belief and in confrontation with the Bible. Certain theological terms of reference have suggested themselves as a result of this study of the earliest history of the Christian day for rest and worship: along these lines, therefore, we hope to be able to make a contribution now towards the solution of the problem about Sunday. We are certainly aware that these terms can, to some extent, be called in question, since they rest upon an independent interpretation of the available evidence. With a good conscience we may, however, be bold enough to draw these conclusions, since this study itself demonstrates that these conclusions are the result of serious grappling with the sources: the precise reason for every single statement can be checked in the preceding pages.

The fact that even in the earliest times Christians abandoned the observance of the sabbath leads us straight into the difficult problem of rightly defining the relationship between the old and the new covenant. There are two dangers which have to be avoided: the Judaistic danger which betrays the Christian cause in favour of its Old Testament heritage, and the Marcionite danger which is scandalized by the heritage of the Old Testament and would throw it overboard. The teaching of the Church maintains against these two extremes that the whole Bible, including the Old Testament, is the word of God; but at the same time it emphasizes that the Old and New Testaments differ from one another. It is not for us to discuss in detail these two statements which stand in mutual tension. The underlying unity of old and new covenant and the continuity between them lie in God's love and in man's need of redemption, and these both remain unaltered. In the irreversible sequence of old and new covenant the meaning of salvation history is revealed for our instruction (cf. Gal. 3.19–4.7): God has prepared mankind for salvation, and in particular he has prepared his chosen people to whom he gave his law, until he sent his Son on earth 'when the time had fully come': 'in him the whole fulness of deity dwells bodily' (Col. 2.9): he was the definitive revelation of God to men, and nothing new or higher will ever follow. On the other hand, however, it once again becomes plain in the light of the revelation of Christ that even before his appearance the abundant love of God and his whole purpose of salvation were already at work.

The attitude of Jesus with regard to the law has been very variously interpreted. Jesus has been regarded as a convinced champion of the Jewish law in all its parts and also, by contrast, as one who argued against any kind of authority in the Old Testament law. He certainly comes into neither category. We have tried to show, with regard to the question of the sabbath, that Jesus was the fulfiller of the promises of the Old Testament: in him the reality of salvation was present, and therefore the law in its old sense as a means to the attaining of life and salvation had become superfluous. The law was good and holy; but by fulfilling its underlying meaning Jesus had robbed the law of its significance. Jesus himself had taken the place of the law: readiness to follow the master had taken the place of obedience to the commandments. This is, in fact, the key to understanding the liberty taken by Jesus and his disciples with regard to the law. Jesus certainly let the commandments of the Old Testament remain in being: if, however, they impeded him as he carried out his work of redemption, he exercised his sovereign power and pushed them aside; there then opened the chasm between his commanding spiritual authority and the Pharisees' unspiritual adherence to the letter of the law. Jesus alone had the right to sit lightly to the law, because he was the Son of the Father, and he had from him the power to free men from slavery to the law and to enable them to share his life.

The sabbath commandment was certainly not rescinded either, but it was surpassed in the reality of Christ, in the liberty of the children of God. What the earliest Christians said on this subject still retains its value as a guide for us today: they worked out their views on the basis of a right understanding of the relationship between the gospel and the law. These Christians said that it would be a misunderstanding of the sabbath commandment if we wanted to rest on a single day and to lull ourselves with the illusion that we were in this way fulfilling God's will: the duty of sabbath observance did, in fact, include the whole span of our life, for to keep the sabbath meant to lead day by day holy, sinless lives devoted to the loving service of our neighbour. These early Christians, of course, realized that they were not capable of this behaviour in this life: they, therefore, looked for the sabbath at the end of the times, the blessed rest where sin would be entirely blotted out and sanctification would be complete. Christian thinking about the sabbath did, however, have its point of origin in the experience of the reality of salvation. Christ had brought to his own the true sabbath rest, namely the forgiveness of sins and peace with God. They could now live in God's sabbath which had already dawned. In the face of this fulfilment, the hard-and-fast commandment to rest on every seventh day was bound to lose its importance. It was surpassed by something new, which the godly man of the Old Testament, who kept the sabbath out of loyalty to God's law, could not conceivably have imagined.

Accordingly, in the early years of the Church Sunday was not thought of as inheriting and continuing the tradition of the Jewish sabbath. Sunday had quite different roots. Its significance lay in the Christian understanding of worship at the centre of which was Jesus, the 'Lord'. Right down to the fourth century the idea of rest played absolutely no part in the Christian Sunday. Christians like everyone else worked on that day: it would not have occurred to them to do otherwise. It was only when the Emperor Constantine the Great elevated Sunday to be the statutory day of rest in the Roman Empire that Christians tried to give a theological basis to the rest from work on Sunday which was now demanded by the State: to this end they fell back on the sabbath commandment.

It was, therefore, relatively late when Christians first accounted for the Sunday rest by referring to the sabbath commandment, and this development was largely brought about by external circumstances. Quite apart from these facts, however, this reason for the Sunday rest raised theological questions which are difficult to answer. How could one assert that the sabbath had no more validity for Christians and yet at the same time sanctify Sunday by appealing to the sabbath commandment? In fact, as soon as Christians began to base the hallowing of Sunday on Jewish sabbath observance, they had to take pains to point out the difference between Jewish sabbath observance and Christian Sunday observance, and through the centuries they have found it necessary to continue to draw attention to this difference. From time to time sabbatarians have appeared in the Church who have placed their finger right on this tender spot; they have found it more honourable and more scriptural to observe the sabbath, since this particular commandment from the decalogue is not said to have been annulled either by Jesus or by the apostles. In face of these attacks the defenders of the observance of Sunday could not be content with the statement that the 'fulfilment' of the sabbath commandment was to be found in the Christians' observance not of Saturday but of Sunday, the day of the resurrection. This change of date was so trifling that it could hardly be used to illustrate the necessity and excellence of the hallowing of Sunday. But had not the sabbath commandment itself received a new, evangelical meaning? Had Jesus not shown that it was not a question of slavish observance of the law, but of love of one's neighbour? But to this the further question was and is asked, Was it then a distortion of the law when the Jews were scrupulous about the performance of their sabbath duties, as they still are to this present day? Did they not bear in mind that one must first and foremost respect the will of God and love God with one's whole heart? And did that not mean that one must love his commandments which say very explicitly, '(On the sabbath) you shall not do any work, you, or your son, or your daughter, your manservant, or your maidservant, or your cattle, or the sojourner who is within your gates' (Ex. 20.10); 'You shall kindle no fire in all your habitations on the sabbath day' (Ex. 35.3); 'Take heed for the sake of your lives, and do not bear a burden on the sabbath day' (Jer. 17.21)? Was it not God who required that the sabbath should be observed in this way?

It would, in fact, be a misunderstanding if we were to suppose that Jesus intended merely to infuse and sublimate the Jewish interpretation of the law with a humanitarian spirit. In any case, he did not simply do away with the law, but with unprecedented freedom he made himself judge over the law. Even the ten commandments did not remain outside his grasp. He expressed his opinion about the sabbath commandment in such a way as to show that it was surpassed by the reality of the sabbath which had dawned in him. The promise of the sabbath was now no longer associated with a day, but with Jesus himself.[1]

Therefore we must ask whether it would not perhaps be better if we were to refrain, so far as possible, from basing the hallowing of Sunday on the sabbath commandment? If we do base it on this commandment, we are returning to a time before Jesus who in his person has freed us from the sabbath commandment. The first Christians, after some hesitation, did, in fact, claim the liberty bestowed on them by Jesus: they no longer observed the sabbath commandment, even though it was one of the ten commandments. They came to understand that this commandment had been fulfilled and *abolished* in Jesus.

It has repeatedly become apparent that a strong Old Testament flavour is invariably perceptible whenever we call on the help of the sabbath

---

[1] The Sermon on the Mount cannot be used as an argument for the recognition by Jesus of the ten commandments as the core of the law. Significantly the sabbath commandment is not mentioned in his exposition. The Sermon on the Mount is only an example of the fact that in the light of its fulfilment in Jesus a Christian meaning can also be derived from the Old Testament law, and we have seen that Christians did manage to derive an appropriate meaning from the sabbath commandment. But we should not overlook the fact that the stress of the New Testament ethic is placed on *positive* assertions ('salvation *is* here, for mankind *now*') and not on negative ordinances like those of the decalogue ('thou shalt not', or 'do this or that, otherwise you will suffer for it'). In view of this we ought perhaps to consider whether we should continue to expound the Christian ethic within the framework of the ten commandments. In this sense I am in full agreement with the thesis of H. Röthlisberger, *Kirche am Sinai* (see p. 107, n. 5 above).

commandment to justify the hallowing of Sunday. Even the most significant modern attempt to devise a theology for holidays and festivals, that of Karl Barth (*Church Dogmatics* III.4, ET 1961, pp. 47–72; cf. A. de Quervain, *Die Heiligung*, 1941, pp. 353–80) is not quite exempt from this, despite the abundance of ingenious and thoroughly evangelical ideas which are developed in it. In Barth's view the most important element in a festival is the interruption of work out of respect for God, who demands this in particular from man. The question, however, is not asked whether Jesus has in any way brought an alteration in this demand: it is regarded as quite self-evident that the 'sign' of sabbath observance retains its validity for the new people of God.

Quite a different question is whether the Sunday rest can be given any theological basis *without* calling on the help of the sabbath commandment. There are, broadly speaking, three possible answers, but they are all of very limited validity.

1. One can try to justify the Sunday rest because of the demands of worship. We have already defined our attitude towards this justification.[1] It would never have occurred to anybody to require rest from work for the *entire* day on which worship takes place; and it certainly did not occur to the earliest Christians. Only after the Christians' day of worship had, under Constantine, become the day of rest did the Church try to fill out with cultic observances the remainder of the time which was not occupied with worship. The moral dangers of the leisure required by the law were the principal motive which led the Church to take this step.

We can even raise the question whether it is, in fact, an ideal solution for the day of rest and the day for worship to coincide. Many people in need of rest and relaxation very properly give, in the first place, the necessary respite to their body on Sunday. They sleep for rather longer, or they take part in some activity and do not want to sit still in church on Sunday just as they do on weekdays in the office. This particular problem has arisen only because the time for worship and the time for rest have coincided.

2. The Sunday rest can also be understood as an anticipation of the eternal rest at the end of time. We have seen that the idea of the eschatological rest played an important part in the sabbath theology of the earliest Christians. We have also shown that, because of its early Christian title 'the eighth day', Sunday was thought to be some sort of image of the new aeon coming at

[1] See pp. 156f. above.

the end of time. The rest from work on Sunday does, in fact, also point to the consummation of rest at the end: in the Sunday rest we have, as it were, a foretaste of that rest without end. The beauty and persuasiveness of this idea are indisputable, but this theologumenon is not, strictly speaking, connected with the Sunday rest. In *every* rest there is some foretaste of eternity, even if the rest lasts only half an hour, even if we do not enjoy it on Sunday, but for example on Monday. Rest (i.e. rest from work) is, theologically speaking, an extremely important idea, but we may not equate it with the Sunday rest.

It may here be noted in passing that it would be worth while for someone to devise a Christian ethic concerning the time for work and leisure and, in so doing, to leave quite out of consideration the question of Sunday observance. The two problems have, hitherto, been considered too much from the same angle. 'Leisure time' really meant nothing else but 'Sunday rest'. It is understandable that the ideal of providing leisure time came to be coloured by the ideal of Sunday observance. Also, we must be more restrained in our moral condemnation of Sunday work: it is often done for pleasure, for relaxation, for a beneficial and necessary change from weekday work which itself is often unsatisfying. This Sunday work is often to be given a higher ethical value than is to be given to enforced idleness.

3. The most cogent arguments for the Sunday rest are those which can be made a humanitarian and social point of view. We certainly should not say that these arguments lack theological interest, for we have seen that it was precisely such considerations which led to the formulation of the sabbath commandment rooted in Yahweh's covenant law. First of all, it is necessary for the man who works, particularly for the man who works in the modern industrialized world, to have a fixed and sufficient time for leisure. Moreover, the arrangement whereby this time for leisure is fixed for an entire day and on the same day for everybody has one important advantage over all proposals for a staggered working week. These proposals mean that leisure time is reckoned in hours and is distributed over the whole week: in this case it is almost impossible for members of a family or for friends and acquaintances to see one another during their leisure time. This is a loss which, in course of time, would certainly have very injurious consequences. It must, of course, be added that we cannot justify the Sunday rest on these grounds: another day in the week could equally well be considered.

In the five-day working week Saturday also has been exalted into a day of rest. This illustrates that we are not tied to the biblical pattern which prescribes that we should work for *six* days. From the biblical standpoint we have exactly the same freedom not to work on Saturday as we have freedom, from the biblical standpoint, not to feel obliged to rest on Sunday; and in neither case do we need to have recourse to the sabbath commandment.

Nevertheless, it does appear to us almost as a dispensation of providence that, because of modern industrial development, the Jewish sabbath of all days has come to the fore as the second day of rest. Is this not an appeal to us Christians that, for our part, we should now on this day think about the Jews rather more frequently than we have done hitherto? We could find our inspiration in the sabbath observance (which bore no trace of Judaism) of the Gentile Christian Church of the third to the fifth centuries. At that time Christians remembered on the sabbath the first creation, the old covenant, just as they celebrated on Sunday the second creation, the new life in the holy Spirit. The weekly progression from Saturday to Sunday was for them a real experience of the 'progress' of the salvation history. The new covenant can, in fact, be understood in its distinctiveness only if it is always seen to stand in contradistinction to the old covenant. The five-day working week would repay theological consideration of this sort.

It is, therefore, difficult to justify the Sunday rest by any other means than by reference to the sabbath commandment, but the support of the sabbath commandment does, on the other hand, bring so many theological problems in its wake that we view it with some scepticism. This should not be construed as meaning that we advocate the abolition of the Sunday rest. Nothing could be further from our mind. We have, indeed, already stated that from the theological point of view the staggered working week should be met with a 'No'. If one is already convinced that an *entire* day should be set aside when everyone can rest from work, it is hard to see why Sunday should not in this case continue to be a day of rest. This point is given added weight by the point which we shall shortly make that the churches must ensure that *Sunday* is maintained everywhere and in all circumstances as the day for common Christian worship.

While we view with some scepticism the theological basis of Sunday as a day of rest (on historical grounds as well), we should wish all the more to emphasize the theological basis for *Sunday* as the *day of worship*. There are, in fact, many Christians who are more or less in agreement with what we have already said, but who would also wish to take one further step. They are of the opinion that Sunday is not so important as the day for worship that one could not, if need be, give it up. They have a distinguished advocate for their point of view in Luther. Luther's interpretation of the sabbath commandment is similar to ours: just as we do, he wants to give up appealing to the Old Testament commandment about rest as the justification for keeping Sunday, but he wants to go even further. He regards the fact that Sunday is the day for worship as a merely adventitious arrangement which is, therefore, no longer binding. These are his words in the Great Catechism, 'Such things (namely the holding of worship) are, therefore, not bound to time as they are among the Jews, so that it has to be this day or that day, for no day in itself is better than another: it should, in fact, happen daily, but because the mass of the people (i.e. those prevented by work) cannot wait (=cannot be present), at least one day in the week has to be set aside for that purpose. Because Sunday has from of old been set aside for that purpose, it should be left as it is, so that everything may happen in harmonious order and no one make a disturbance because of unnecessary innovation.'[1] Luther does, therefore, provide no theological basis for Sunday as the day of worship: by contrast, he regards every time and every hour suitable for hearing God's word, which he (rightly) describes as the principal purpose also of the observance of Sunday. Along these lines, however, the importance of Sunday as the day for worship is not given sufficient weight. We should not wish to say that only the necessity to assemble for worship should be maintained, but that the definite time when this had to happen could be surrendered. We should much prefer to emphasize that worship must necessarily take place on Sunday and on no other day of the week.[2] We derive this requirement from the origins of the Christian observance of Sunday. We have attempted to establish

---

[1] *Die symbolischen Bücher der evangelisch-lutherischen Kirche*, ed. J. T. Müller, 1928[12], pp. 399f. From the time of the early Church I know only one text which says something similar, Origen, *Cels.* VIII.22; see p. 105, n. 1, above.

[2] Of course, this does not mean that there is anything against weekday services provided that they are supplementary to the act of worship of Sunday. Luther is, however, right in saying that 'the mass of people' is usually unable to be free in the middle of the week as well as on Sunday.

the probability that it goes back to the meals of the risen Lord with his disciples after Easter. The first repetition of the Last Supper took place on Easter evening, that is to say on a Sunday evening: the primitive community subsequently celebrated the Lord's Supper regularly on Sunday evening. We can even say that because it is the will of Christ that the Lord's Supper be regularly held in the Christian Church, for this very reason there is also a Christian observance of Sunday. Therefore, this observance depends indirectly on Christ's will. At the same time as instituting the Lord's Supper afresh on Easter evening, Jesus has also 'instituted' the day on which it should henceforth be celebrated: on Sunday. Put more epigrammatically this means: no Lord's Supper without Sunday, no Sunday without the Lord's Supper. (We shall return to the second half of this epigram.) In this case the time for worship, i.e. Sunday, is not something fortuitous or trivial, but a matter of primary importance, of equal importance with the necessity of celebrating the Lord's Supper itself. We have seen that the oldest Christian title for Sunday, the 'Lord's day', is probably derived from the 'Lord's Supper'. In this derivation is apparent how closely the action of worship and the time for worship belong to one another: both were stamped with the Lord's name and derived their meaning from him. We have, moreover, seen how the custom of administering baptism on Sunday morning become widespread. This also did not happen by accident, but as a result of an inner logic: reception into the body of Christ, into the community, should also happen on the Lord's day. We finally saw how strongly the early Church was attached to its Sunday: *all* the faithful (unless anyone was prevented by urgent cause or was sick) assembled for worship on *every* Sunday. They knew that here the decisive element in their Christian life was at stake. They needed this assembly in order to be Christians at all, for how could the community be built up except at the community's worship on Sunday? Sunday worship was, in fact, more important for them than their own lives: even in times of persecution they did not omit to assemble together at the risk of being prosecuted and condemned.[1] Furthermore, it was only because of Sunday that the seven-day week continued to be used within

---

[1] See p. 247, n. 1, above.

the Christian Church after Christians had ceased to observe the sabbath.

In face of all this evidence we cannot take upon ourselves the responsibility of abandoning Sunday as the day for worship by saying that it does not much matter when we assemble for worship. This would irretrievably deprive us of a part of our Christian heritage which has its roots in the very midst of God's saving acts. If there is a problem about Sunday, it can be stated in this question, 'Are we willing to stand up for Sunday as the day for worship?' Sunday as the day for worship is nothing less than one of the central elements in the Christian life.

In recent decades we have fortunately moved away from the misconception that private Christianity is enough and that common worship is something of secondary importance and not absolutely necessary. The reverse order is nearer the truth: the individual Christian can be a complete Christian only as a member of an actual community which carries him along. The community, for its part, does not exist unless it regularly assembles on Sunday and builds itself up as the body of Christ.

As far as the future is concerned, work remains to be done on two scores.

1. Provision must be made that unhindered access to church on Sunday is guaranteed under all circumstances for everyone who desires it. This requirement could be important if civil legislation should consider it necessary to alter the existing laws about Sunday rest, but it should not be difficult to secure in those states which cherish religious freedom.

In this case it is particularly important that the churches should be entirely clear how much time their Sunday services require and at what time of day they should take place: in this matter we should not necessarily adhere to our traditional practice. It might be right, for example, quietly to set aside more time for worship. We could also consider whether we want to return to the primitive Christian custom of using Sunday evening.[1]

2. Our services must regain their central importance for the life of the local church. It is clear that this process must begin from inside and work outwards. One cannot simply require everyone to go to church on Sunday: that would serve no useful

[1] Cf. the recent introduction of the evening mass in the Roman Catholic Church. In Protestant churches Sunday morning *and* Sunday evening services have, in fact, also been regularly held for some little time; cf. H. Stockar, *Sonntagsgesetzgebung im alten Zürich*, Dissertation at Zürich, 1949.

purpose. Our services are no longer what they really should be, namely the occasion where the local church is, under the word of God, constituted as the Church in that place. We are, of course, broaching a subject which is so complex and which has in practice so many different elements that we should never venture within the compass of a few pages to draw up rules of universal applicability. Our contribution is restricted to drawing attention once again to the original form of the observance of Sunday as we have managed to discern it in the earliest years of the Christian Church. Knowledge about this form will perhaps be able to offer some hints towards a solution of the problems associated with worship in our own time.

We must now anticipate the problem which is most important for us Protestants: in the ancient Church it was unthinkable for a Sunday to pass without the local church gathering for a celebration of the Lord's Supper. Sunday was absolutely nothing without the Lord's Supper; the Lord's Supper formed the focal point of the worship around which all the other parts of the service found their place. At other times there were also gatherings for common prayer or for a common meal, but only on Sunday for the Lord's Supper.

In the very earliest time the Lord's Supper was even held within the framework of a real meal; also, after the Lord's Supper had been transferred to the morning, so-called agape-meals were still held in the evening. To these meals those members who had sufficient means invited the poor members of the local church, and at the end the participants relaxed and entertained one another with spiritual conversation, verses and songs. We may ask whether we have not lost something of value in that we have completely abandoned these communal meals in the domestic circle. It is a fact that we meet our neighbour most immediately in actual table-fellowship, where he actually becomes for us a brother or a sister. Moreover, it seems that the free utterances in the Spirit (speaking with tongues, prophesyings, etc.) had originally flourished in the setting of these meals: they did, however, rapidly disappear as soon as the custom of meeting for a common meal was abandoned.

The Lord's Supper properly belongs to a complete Sunday act of worship.[1] If we do not celebrate any Lord's Supper on

---

[1] See also A. de Quervain, *Die Heiligung*, 1942, pp. 376f.; O. Cullmann, *Early Christian Worship*, 1953, pp. 34ff. Nowadays we are making efforts to celebrate the Lord's Supper on at least one Sunday in every month, a

Sunday, we have basically no right to call Sunday the 'Lord's day' (or *dimanche, domenica*), for the very thing which should make it the Lord's day, namely the Lord's Supper, is lacking. The sermon *alone* is not able to build up the community. It provides the basis, the foundation on which the community may be built up. The Lord's Supper is the visible actualization of communion with the Lord and with one another, and only the Lord's Supper can make possible the integration of the body of Christ and the common growth of this body. One of the principal defects in our Sunday worship is this lack of a regular celebration of the Lord's Supper. Sunday worship is often so problematical for us because it stands or falls with the sermon or, to put it more simply, with the preacher. It fails to draw on the riches of the Sunday fellowship at the Lord's Supper, which would improve the quality of the common prayer, of the life of the community and also of the sermon as well.

In this connection we may recall that Christians in the early years of the Church caused the elements of the Lord's Supper to be taken to all absent members by deacons (=churchwardens or elders); in this way, at least, the absent members could have a part in the common worship of the rest of the faithful. And not for the last time the collection must be mentioned: it, too, was an expression of the fellowship of all the faithful. The collection was taken during the course of the service, and the amount collected was placed beside the president of the local church. Details of this kind are too numerous for us to mention every one (e.g. that prayer was always offered standing on Sunday or that before the Lord's Supper the kiss of peace was mutually given), for we do not wish to blur our vision of the principal point: the administration of the Lord's Supper intrinsically belongs to a full and proper act of Sunday worship.

On the other hand, of course, we do not wish to forget that our Sunday services still correspond, by and large, to the form

---

custom which elsewhere has been usual for some time. This same tendency towards more frequent communion can also be seen among the Catholics; although in their mass the original unity of the service of the word and the Lord's Supper was never broken, they are coming to see more clearly that it is not sufficient for only the priest and a handful of the faithful to communicate. More frequent communion on Sunday cannot, of course, be arranged by regulation; congregations themselves have to come to realize that a regular celebration of the Lord's Supper is a necessity.

which they had in the days of the early Church: reading from scripture, sermon, prayer, singing and, if candidates were present, baptism were all parts of worship on Sunday. This continuity is also an indication that Sunday worship has preserved right down to the present day the same inner life which it had in the days of the early Church. Nevertheless, it would be worth while to make this life as lively as possible, for our *worship* is the bastion which will be decisive for the solution of the problem whether the Church will manage to preserve its Sunday through the crisis, evidence of which may now be seen on every side.

BIBLIOGRAPHY

This list comprises only those monographs on the subject of Sunday in the primitive Church which have appeared since 1850, together with works dealing with questions which bear directly on this subject. Further references may be found in the notes and in the index of authors. Works of systematic theology and popular treatments of this subject are not included. The first three works are important for their extensive bibliography; other works follow in chronological order, those which are of greatest importance for scholarly research being indicated by capital letters.

Cox, R., *The Literature of the Sabbath Question*, 2 vols, Edinburgh, 1865

DUMAINE, H., Art. 'Dimanche': *DACL* IV, 1921, col. 970–94

HUBER, H., *Geist und Buchstabe der Sonntagsruhe* (Studia Theologiae moralis et pastoralis IV), Salzburg, 1958, pp. 238–43.

Hengstenberg, E. W., *Über den Tag des Herrn*, Berlin, 1852

Hessey, J. A., *Sunday, its Origin, History and Present Obligation*, London, 1860

Wetzel, E., *Über den Ursprung der christlichen Sonntagsfeier*, Stettin, 1874

Andrews, J. N., *History of the Sabbath and First Day of the Week*, 2 vols, Washington, 1876

Haupt, E., *Der Sonntag und die Bibel*, 1878

ZAHN, TH., *Geschichte des Sonntags, vornehmlich in der alten Kirche*, Hannover, 1878; included in: *Skizzen aus dem Leben der Alten Kirche*, Leipzig, 1894, pp. 196–240

Henke, O., 'Zur Geschichte der Lehre von der Sonntagsfeier', *Theologische Studien und Kritiken* 59, 1886, pp. 597–664

Schick, D., 'Die historischen Voraussetzungen der Sonntagsfeier', *Neue kirchliche Zeitschrift* 5, 1894, pp. 727–60

White, N. J. D., Art. 'Lord's Day', *A Dictionary of the Bible*, ed. J. Hastings, New York, 1898, III, p. 139

Deissmann, A., Art. 'Lord's Day', *Enc. Bibl.* III, pp. 2813–16

Rüscher, H. *Sabbat und Sonntag im Lichte des Neuen Testaments*, Gotha, 1913

SCHÜRER, E., 'Die siebentägige Woche im Gebrauche der christlichen Kirche der ersten Jahrhunderte', *ZNW* 6, 1905, pp. 1–66

Förster, G., 'Die christliche Sonntagsfeier bis auf Konstantin den Grossen', *Deutsche Zeitschrift für Kirchenrecht* 16, 1906, pp. 100–13

Zöckler, O., Art. 'Sonntagsfeier', *RE*[3] 18, pp. 521–9

Glazebrook, M. G., Art. 'Lord's Day', *ERE* 12, p. 104

Schwamborn, G., 'Das älteste patristische Zeugnis über die Sonntagsruhe', *Theologie und Glaube* 1, 1909, p. 381

Hülster, A., Die ältesten patristischen Zeugnisse für die Sonntagsheiligung: *Theologie und Glaube* 1, 1909, pp. 211–12

Meinhold, J., 'Sabbat und Sonntag', *Wissenschaft und Bildung* 9, Leipzig, 1909

Jülicher, A., Art. 'Sonntag im Urchristentum', *RGG* V, col. 735–8

Dublanchy, E., Art. 'Dimanche', *Dictionnaire de théologie catholique* 4.1, Paris, 1911, col. 1308–48

Förster, G., 'Römisch rechtliche Grundlagen der Sonntagsruhe', *Deutsche Zeitschrift für Kirchenrecht* 20, 1910–11, pp. 211–71

Förster, 'G., Alttestamentliche Grundlagen der Sonntagsfeier. Der Sabbat', *Deutsche Zeitschrift für Kirchenrecht* 21, 1911–12, pp. 349–85

Preseren, A., 'Die Beziehungen der Sonntagsfeier zum 3. Gebot des Dekalogs', *ZKT* 37, 1913, pp. 563–603; 709–59

GOGUEL, M., 'Notes d'histoire évangélique. Appendix 1 : Le dimanche et la résurrection au troisième jour', *RHR* 74, 1916, pp. 29ff.

DUMAINE, H., Art. 'Dimanche', *DACL* IV, 1921, pp. 858–994

Dumaine, H., *Le Dimanche chrétien, ses origines, ses principaux caractères*, Brussels, 1922

Haynes, C. B., *From Sabbath to Sunday*, Washington, 1928

Thomas, W., *Der Sonntag im frühen Mittelalter* (Dissertation, Göttingen, 1929)

McCASLAND, S. V., 'The Origin of the Lord's Day', *JBL* 49, 1930, pp. 65–82

Boehmer, J., *Der christliche Sonntag nach Ursprung und Geschichte*, Leipzig, 1931

Jungmann, J. A., 'Beginnt die christliche Woche mit Sonntag?' *ZKT* 55, 1931, pp. 605–21

COTTON, P., *From Sabbath to Sunday. A Study in Early Christianity*, Bethlehem, Pa., 1933

McReavy, L. L., 'The Sunday Repose from Labour', *Ephemerides Theologiae Lovanienses* 12, 1935, pp. 291–323

Vuilleumier, J., *Le jour du repos à travers les âges*, Dammarie-les-Lys, 1936

CALLEWAERT, C., 'La synaxe eucharistique à Jérusalem, berceau du dimanche', *Ephemerides Theologiae Lovanienses* 15, 1938, pp. 34–73

Nielen, J. M., *Das Zeichen des Herrn. Sabbat und Sonntag in biblischer und urchristlicher Bezeugung*, Freiburg im Breisgau, 1940

Straw, W. E., *Origin of Sunday Observance in the Christian Church*, Washington, 1940

DÖLGER, F. J., 'Die Planetenwoche der griechisch-römischen Antike und der christliche Sonntag', *AuC* 6, 1941, pp. 202–38

Steinmetzer, F., Art. 'Arbeitsruhe', *RAC* I, 1942, col. 590–5

Chirat, H., 'Le dimanche dans l'antiquité chrétienne', *Etudes de Pastorale Liturgique*, Paris, 1944, pp. 127–48

Odom, R. L., *Sunday in Roman Paganism*, Washington, 1944

Dugmore, C. W., *The Influence of the Synagogue upon the Divine Office*, Oxford, 1944, pp. 11ff.

310   BIBLIOGRAPHY

Rahner, H., *Griechische Mythen in christlicher Deutung*, Zurich, 1945, pp. 125–89
Schrenk, G., 'Sabbat oder Sonntag?' *Judaica* 2, 1946, pp. 169ff.
Yost, F. H., *The Early Christian Sabbath*, Mountain View, California, 1947
Le huitième jour: Vie Spirituelle 76 (Paris, April 1947). Most important
    contributions: Hild, J.-.P, 'Jour d'espérance et d'attente' (pp. 592–613);
    Froger, J., 'Histoire du dimanche' (pp. 502–22)
Dimanche et célébration chrétienne: La Maison-Dieu 9 (Paris, 1947). Most impor-
    tant contribution: Hild, J.-P., 'La mystique du dimanche' (pp. 7–37)
Le jour du Seigneur (Liturgical Congress in Lyons, Sept. 1947), Paris, 1948.
    Most important contributions: Féret, H.-M., 'Les sources bibliques' (pp.
    39–104); DANIELOU, J., 'La doctrine patristique du dimanche' (pp. 105–
    30); Congar, Y., 'La théologie du dimanche' (pp. 131–80)
PETTIRSCH, FR., 'Das Verbot der opera servilia in der Heiligen Schrift und
    in der altkirchlichen Exegese', *ZKT* 69, 1947, pp. 257–327; 417–44
Stockar, H., *Sonntagsgesetzgebung im alten Zürich* (Dissertation, Zürich, 1949)
Naz, R., Art. 'Dimanche', *Dictionnaire de droit canonique* 4, 1949, col. 1227–31
HILD, J.-P., *Dimanche et vie paschale*, Turnhout, 1949
DANIELOU, J., *Bible et Liturgie*, Paris, 1951, pp. 303–87; ET, London, 1960,
    pp. 222–86
CULLMANN, O., Sabbat und Sonntag nach dem Johannesevangelium.
    Ἕως ἄρτι (Joh. 5, 17): In memoriam E. Lohmeyer (Stuttgart, 1951),
    pp. 127–31
McArthur, A. A., *The Evolution of the Christian Year*, London, 1953, pp. 13–29
Kunze, G., 'Die gottesdienstliche Zeit', *Leiturgia. Handbuch des evangelischen
    Gottesdienstes* I, Kassel, 1954, pp. 438–534
Jenni, E., *Die theologische Begründung des Sabbatgebotes im Alten Testament*
    (Theologische Studien 46), 1956
NEDBAL, J., *Sabbat und Sonntag im Neuen Testament* (unpublished dissertation,
    Vienna, 1956)
Der Christliche Sonntag. Probleme und Aufgaben, ed. K. Rudolf, Vienna, 1956.
    Most important contribution: BAUER, J., 'Vom Sabbat zum Sonntag'
    (pp. 170–5)
Thomas, W., Art. 'Sonntag', *Evangelisches Kirchenlexikon*, Göttingen, 1958,
    col. 996–1000
HUBER, H., *Geist und Buchstabe der Sonntagsruhe. Eine historisch-theologische
    Untersuchung über das Verbot der knechtlichen Arbeit von der Urkirche
    bis auf Thomas von Aquin* (Studia Theologiae moralis et pastoralis IV),
    Salzburg, 1958
Der Tag des Herrn. Die Heiligung des Sonntags im Wandel der Zeit, ed. H. Peichl.
    Vienna, 1958. Most important contributions: KOSNETTER, J., 'Der Tag
    des Herrn im Neuen Testament' (pp. 33–57); Jungmann, J. A., 'Die
    Heiligung des Sonntags im Frühchristentum und im Mittelalter' (pp.
    59–75)

RIESENFELD, H., 'Sabbat et jour du Seigneur', *New Testament Essays. Studies in Memory of T. W. Manson*, Manchester 1959, pp. 210–18

Szabó, A., 'Sabbat und Sonntag', *Judaica* 15, 1959, pp. 161–72

GOUDOEVER, J. VAN, *Biblical Calendars*, Leiden, 1961², pp. 164–73

LOHSE, E., Art. 'σάββατον', *TWNT* VII, pp. 1–30

Verlorener Sonntag?: Kirche im Volk 22, Stuttgart, 1959. Most important contributions: Lohse, E., 'Sabbat und Sonntag im Neuen Testament' (pp. 25–36); Beckmann, J., 'Der Sonntag in der Geschichte der Kirche' (pp. 37–60)

LOHSE, E., 'Jesu Worte über den Sabbat', *Judentum—Urchristentum—Kirche. Festschrift für J. Jeremias zum 60. Geburtstag* (BZNW 26), 1960, pp. 79–89

Porter, H. B., *The Day of Light. The Biblical and Liturgical Meaning of Sunday* (Studies in Ministry and Worship 16), London, 1960

Leupin, P., 'Der Sonntag in der Kirchengeschichte', *Schweizerische Theologische Umschau* 31, 1961, pp. 18–34

REGAN, F. A., *Dies dominica and dies solis. The Beginnings of the Lord's Day in Christian Antiquity* (Dissertation, Washington, 1961). Only Chapter 4 ('The Day of the Sun') is published

Dugmore, C. W., 'The Lord's Day and Easter', *Neotestamentica et Patristica in honorem sexagenarii O. Cullmann*, Leiden, 1962, pp. 272–81

Hertzsch, E., Art. 'Sonntag', *RGG*³ VI, col. 140–2

Hilgert, E., 'Jubilees and the Origin of Sunday', *Andrews University Seminary Studies* 1, 1963, pp. 44–51

Rordorf, W., 'Der Sonntag als Gottesdienst- und Ruhetag im ältesten Christentum', *Zeitschrift für Evangelische Ethik* 7, 1963, pp. 213–24

Kraft, R. A., 'Some Notes on Sabbath Observance in Early Christianity', *Andrews University Seminary Studies* 3, 1965, pp. 18–33

Stott, W., 'A Note on the Word KYRIAKH in Rev. 1.10', *NTS* 12, 1965–6, pp. 70–75

Le dimanche: Lex orandi 39, Paris, 1965. Most important contributions: BOTTE, B., 'Les dénominations du dimanche dans la tradition chrétienne' (pp. 7–18); DANIELOU, J., 'Le dimanche comme huitième jour' (pp. 61–89)

Stott, W., *The Theology of the Christian Sunday in the Early Church* (unpublished thesis, Oxford, 1966)

Strand, K. A., 'Another Look at "Lord's Day" in the Early Church and in Rev. 1.10', *NTS* 13, 1966–7, pp. 174–81

INDEX OF REFERENCES

1. OLD TESTAMENT

2. APOCRYPHA AND PSEUDEPIGRAPHA OF THE OLD TESTAMENT

3. JEWISH AND MANDAEAN SOURCES

4. BABYLONIAN AND GRAECO-ROMAN SOURCES

5. NEW TESTAMENT

6. APOCRYPHA AND PSEUDEPIGRAPHA OF THE NEW TESTAMENT

[1] *In NT Apoc. I.*   [2] *In NT Apoc. II.*

7. APOSTOLIC FATHERS, APOLOGISTS, PATRISTIC AUTHORS

[1] *In NT Apoc. I.*

8. CHURCH ORDERS, COUNCILS, LAWS, COLLECTIONS, INSCRIPTIONS

(For Egyptian Church Order see under Hippolytus, *Trad. Apost.*)

INDEX OF AUTHORS

SELECT INDEX OF SUBJECTS